Monsieur d'Eon
Is a Woman

Monsieur d'Eon Is a Woman

A TALE OF POLITICAL INTRIGUE AND SEXUAL MASQUERADE

GARY KATES

BasicBooks
A Division of HarperCollins*Publishers*

Designed by Joseph Eagle

Library of Congress Cataloging-in-Publication Data
Kates, Gary, 1952–
    Monsieur d'Eon is a woman: a tale of political intrigue and
sexual masquerade / Gary Kates.
        p.   cm.
    Includes bibliographical references and index.
    ISBN 0-465-04761-0
    1. Eon de Beaumont, Charles Geneviève Louis Auguste André
Timothée d', 1728–1810.   2. Female impersonators—France—
Biography.   3. Diplomats—France—Biography.   4. France—
Foreign relations—1715–1774.   5. Gender identity—France—
History—18th century.   I. Title.
DC135.E6K37 1995
944'.034'092—dc20
    [B]   95-7335
                                                                 CIP

95 96 97 98 ♦/HC 9 8 7 6 5 4 3 2 1

In loving memory of

Rachel Kates

(1900–1989)

עז והדר לבושה ותשחק ליום אחרון

I almost forgot to tell you that Monsieur d'Eon is a woman.

—*The Marquise du Deffand to Horace Walpole*

Do you know the nonsense that has just been told to me this very minute? It is the number of letters from England saying that d'Eon, who has been there forever, is a woman, truly a woman.

—*Mme d'Epinay to the Abbé Galiani*

The so-called Sieur d'Eon is a girl and is nothing other than a girl.

—*The Comte de Broglie to Louis XV*

Do you know . . . that d'Eon is a girl?

—*King Louis XV to General Monet*

Contents

PART III: INSIDE D'EON'S LIBRARY

PART IV: THE TRANSFORMATION

PART V: D'EON'S CHRISTIAN FEMINISM

TIME LINE

D'Eon's Life	European Events
	1643–1715 reign of Louis XIV
1723 Louis d'Eon marries Françoise de Charenton	1715–1734 regency for Louis XV
	1734–1774 reign of Louis XV
1728 born 5 October in Tonnerre	1731–1734 War of the Polish Succession
	1740–1748 War of the Austrian Succession
1749 receives law degree, College Mazarin, Paris; father dies	
1753 publishes first periodical article and book	1755 Diplomatic Revolution
	1756–1763 Seven Years' War
1756 joins the King's Secret; makes first trip to Russia	
1757–1760 Secretary to the French ambassador to Russia	
1761 appointed Dragoon captain; fights in Seven Years' War	1762 Rousseau's *Emile* and *Contrat social*
1762 appointed secretary to Nivernais, chief of the team to negotiate the Peace of Paris; moves to London	
1763 appointed Plenipotentiary Minister, then secretary to Ambassador Guerchy, feuds with Guerchy, recalled	
1764 publishes *Lettres, mémoires, et négociations*	1764 Pompadour dies
1770–1774 publishes *Les Loisirs*	
1770 rumors begin concerning his gender	
1772 Drouet visits d'Eon in London, returns convinced d'Eon is female	1774–1792 reign of Louis XVI
	1775 Beaumarchais's *Barbier de Seville*
1775 signs the "Transaction" agreement with Beaumarchais, co-signed by Vergennes and Louis XVI, recognizing d'Eon as a woman	
1777 British court recognizes d'Eon as a woman	
1777 returns to France in August	
1777 first dresses as a woman in October	
1777 meets with Louis XVI and Marie-Antoinette in November	
1778 requests to join army as a woman soldier	1778 France enters American War of Independence
	1778 deaths of Rousseau and Voltaire
1779 arrested; thrown into a Dijon prison	
1779–1785 lives with mother in Tonnerre	
1785–1810 returns to London, retires, writes memoirs	1789 French Revolution begins
	1792 France declares war on Austria
1792 petitions the French National Assembly to lead a division of women soldiers against Austria; mother dies	
	1793 Louis XVI is executed
	1804 Napoleon becomes Emperor of France
1810 dies 21 May	

Prologue: The Discovery

MRS. COLE WAS THE FIRST to discover the truth. In 1810 the Chevalière d'Eon and Mrs. Cole had been sharing a London apartment for about fourteen years. They were the same age, eighty-one, and both were quite frail. Like so many elderly spinsters and widows back then, and unfortunately today, they had little money, and lived just above poverty. They ate simple foods and guarded their pocketbooks carefully. Often they had to do without heat, so the two women often spent cold winter days in their separate beds, where they could stay warm beneath their quilts.[1]

During these difficult years, the Chevalière d'Eon and Mrs. Cole had become close friends, taking care of each other as their health declined. And yet they were very different. D'Eon had been an intellectual, the author of more than fifteen published volumes, and countless unpublished manuscripts. D'Eon had once owned a substantial private library and still loved to read and write the day away. Mrs. Cole, on the other hand, was illiterate, and if she was wise, it was the result not of any formal education, but rather of an instinctive deep religious faith. It was the Christian religion that cemented their friendship and formed the material of their more serious conversations.

Years earlier neither Mrs. Cole nor the Chevalière d'Eon had lived in such modest circumstances. Unlike d'Eon, who had never married, nor as far as anyone knew had ever even been romantically involved with anyone, Mrs. Cole had been for most of her adult life the wife of an important British naval officer, who had provided her with a comfortable life. Like the Chevalière d'Eon, Mrs. Cole had presided over a household filled with servants, and had done little difficult housework herself. Perhaps she had lived too long, for these years in the little apartment had been especially hard. The long British struggle against Napoleon had caused food prices to rise dramatically, affecting the elderly even more than the rest of the population. But at least Mrs. Cole could take some solace in her friendship with her housemate.

Now, however, that too was taken away from her. For weeks the Chevalière had been very ill and death was expected at any time. On 4 March 1810, d'Eon had stumbled in the middle of the night and lay on the floor "as if dead" until found by Mrs. Cole the next morning.[2] Father Elizie, a French Catholic priest living in London, was sent to administer last rites. D'Eon managed to cling to life until 21 May 1810, when Mrs. Cole found her housemate's dead body.

Alone in her apartment, Mrs. Cole began to prepare the corpse for presentation to visitors. She naturally wanted her late friend to look presentable. After all, the Chevalière had once been a famous personage, not only in England and France, but throughout Europe. Mrs. Cole, of course, knew by heart the famous details of d'Eon's life: that the Chevalière had been born female but raised male by a father who had desperately wanted a son; that d'Eon had adjusted quite well to the new gender role and became a military officer who served with distinction for France in the Seven Years' War (1756–1763); that d'Eon had become a diplomat and spy for King Louis XV; that during the 1770s, with the accession of Louis XVI, the Chevalière's true sex was unfortunately discovered, and the now-famous d'Eon was forced to assume the appearance of womanhood. Since then, for the last thirty-two years, the Chevalière had been living relatively quietly in retirement, at first in France, then in England after 1785.

As Mrs. Cole started to change the Chevalière's clothes and clean the body, she saw with her own eyes a sight that nearly startled the poor woman out of her wits: the Chevalière d'Eon, her dear friend and housemate for well over a decade, had genitals that were unquestionably male.

At first Mrs. Cole could not move. For several minutes she simply stood alone, stunned, unable to think clearly. After a while, she found the strength to leave the room and tell the news to some close mutual friends. They too were shocked, and advised her to return to her apartment with experts who could verify "so singular an occurrence."

Mrs. Cole did just that. She brought together a diverse group of gentlemen, perhaps ten or twelve in all, including a professor of anatomy, two surgeons, a lawyer, and a journalist. Together, they performed "a complete inspection and dissection of the sexual parts" of d'Eon's body. Each of the physicians signed a detailed medical affidavit concluding that d'Eon had a male body, ordinary in every way from a scientific point of view. They went to great lengths to dispel any myths that d'Eon was a hermaphrodite. True, his facial hair was quite light, and his Adam's apple did not protrude. But the hips were narrow, the shoulders square. And far from having femalelike breasts, he exhibited a strong sternum. In every way, the experts concluded, d'Eon had the body of a man.

A few days later, the following newspaper obituary appeared:

> On Tuesday died in the 69th [actually the 82nd] year of his age, the Chevalier d'Eon; memorable as a political character, and chargé des affaires in this country, from the Court of France, but more so on account of the questionable gender to which this extraordinary character naturally appertained. It will be in the recollection of many, that about 36 years ago policies were opened [bets were placed] to ascertain the sex of this extraordinary non-descript, to the amount of £200,000; which were eventually decided, and paid upon a surgical certificate, after personal examination, that the reputed chevalier was a female. The French physician Perigles, however, who attended the chevalier in his last moments, and examined the body on its dissolution, now positively declares that it in reality proved to be the body of a male.[3]

Introduction

WHY DID THE CHEVALIER D'EON live the second half of his life as a woman? And why should we, two hundred years later, bother ourselves with such a question? The purpose of this book is to address both issues, though the second one is easier to answer than the first.

The Chevalier d'Eon did something that apparently no other public figure in history has done: For over thirty-two years, from age forty-nine until his death at eighty-one, d'Eon succeeded in living every day as a woman among the same public that previously had known him as a male diplomat and military hero. Others, such as the Abbé Choissy, had dressed episodically in women's clothes, but no one else had taken on a female gender identity consistently and permanently for the rest of his life.[1]

Perhaps there have been others who have done so privately. One can imagine a fifty-year-old man moving to a new place where no one knows him, and passing himself off as a middle-aged woman. Still, if such a thing happened, or is happening today, no records exist from which to write its history. The Chevalier d'Eon, on the other hand, managed to switch genders when he was a public personality, and thus had to confront the many stories about him produced by the vitriolic eighteenth-century press.

European folklore and history contain countless examples of women disguising themselves as men.[2] For centuries, women have assumed male identities to empower themselves, becoming soldiers, businessmen, professionals, religious leaders, even politicians. But the idea of a man becoming a woman, and therefore losing status in a patriarchal culture, begs for an explanation. After all, d'Eon obviously enjoyed far more power and material wealth as a man: the scion of a noble family from Burgundy (eastern France), he rose to the top of French society during the aristocracy's heyday before the French Revolution. Why would such a man want to give up this position in order to become a woman?

When I first latched on to this story, I would ask this question of my students and friends. They often responded with another question: What was his sex life like? When I replied that I did not know, many suggested that if I started with that question, I would be able to solve the mystery of his gender switch. At first this seemed like a logical enough track, so I went searching for details of d'Eon's sexual life.

But there isn't much to report on that topic. In the enormous correspondence by and about d'Eon that remains in various archives, there is nothing to suggest that d'Eon ever had a sexual relationship with any man or woman. In an era before Victorian prudery, when such matters were often discussed openly, it is remarkable that no contemporary ever claimed that d'Eon had been involved with someone or other. While it is impossible for the historian to prove, the most likely conclusion, based on the documentation available, is that d'Eon remained a virgin throughout his life.

More surprising, no one during d'Eon's lifetime ever addressed such questions. In the hundreds of newspaper articles, broadsides, engravings, songs, and poems about d'Eon, no one raised the issue of his sexual practices. Even Casanova ignored any consideration of d'Eon's sex life when he discussed the famous case in his memoirs.[3] Thus the question that may have seemed central in understanding d'Eon's motivation—what was his sexual orientation?—turns out to be irrelevant: It's a twentieth-century question applied to an eighteenth-century life. Ironically, however, in this very silence lies the key to understanding the place that the d'Eon story occupies in the historical development of ideas regarding the boundaries between manhood and womanhood.

For better or worse, our own culture assumes a remarkably close correspondence between gender and sexuality. Many of us, in fact, would claim that people's gender roles are largely determined by their sexual identity. Perhaps because of the enormous popular impact of modern psychology, we believe that our sexuality is so fundamental that it largely determines other facets of our personality. So, for example, when we meet a woman who behaves in a thoroughly "masculine" manner, we might think she is a lesbian; correspondingly, we might tend to believe that "effeminate" men are more likely to be gay.[4]

There are at least two problems with applying this sort of thinking to the past. First, images that we identify as masculine or feminine have changed dramatically from those of the past. Such is the case, for example, in Hyancinthe Rigaud's famous portrait of King Louis XIV (below). This greatest of French kings is presented here to his contemporaries as the epitome of manhood: his flowing curly hair, his extravagant shoe buckles, and especially his slender, graceful legs were viewed as symbols of virility by contemporaries. Today, of course, it almost seems to us that Louis is posing in drag. In an age when handsome men were noted for their pretty legs, and in which at least one specialist could claim that a

King Louis XIV (1643–1715). The great Sun King stands majestically on his throne in a pose that was seen as virile by contemporaries, but looks effeminate today. *(From G. F. Bradby,* The Great Days of Versailles: Studies from Court Life in the Later Years of Louis XIV *[London, 1906])*

woman's "most beautiful feature" was her neck, we need to be cautious about applying our own notions of masculinity and femininity to the past.[5]

The second problem has to do with the very mingling of sex and gender. Before the nineteenth century, educated people had not yet decided that sexual identity was necessarily a key component of human personality. While there may have been homosexual subcultures, for example, few people thought in terms of "straight" or "gay" personalities. To be sure, eighteenth-century aristocrats understood as well as we do that certain people might be drawn to particular sexual behaviors; after all, the eighteenth century was the era of the Marquis de Sade. But such proclivities were regarded as matters of taste and interest, the hobby of libertines, not as profound representations of some fundamental feature of the human personality.[6]

Eighteenth-century elites recognized that men's bodies were different from women's. But unlike us, they tended to focus their attention more on the moral and cultural differences between the sexes. The age-long Querelle des Femmes (Argument About Women), the great French literary debate over gender differences that ran from the fourteenth through the eighteenth centuries, concentrated on masculine vs. feminine character, and rarely made biological distinctions paramount. Not until the nineteenth century do we find European thinkers, such as the French physician Cabanis, reasserting Aristotelian notions that the ovaries and uterus determine a woman's "weak and coquettish" character.[7]

Consequently, gender roles among eighteenth-century elites were closer to each other than would be the case for their counterparts in the nineteenth and early twentieth centuries. When Victorians rather suddenly made sex and sexual difference a new cultural paradigm, it had the effect of polarizing the sexes, establishing rigid boundaries between them, and significantly narrowing gender roles for both men and women.[8] To be sure, European culture has always been patriarchal. Women have had to endure exploitation and oppression that still linger today. But often in Europe's long history, and especially during the early modern period, elite women were able to find loopholes in patriarchal institutions and make good lives for themselves. After the French Revolution, many such loopholes closed.[9]

Ironically, the history of European women shows that upper-class women fared better in a hierarchically structured society like the Old Regime than in the more democratic systems that followed in the nineteenth century. Eighteenth-century societies were all characterized to one degree or another by privilege rather than by public laws. Until the French

Revolution and Napoleonic Empire, there was rarely a law that pertained equally to every member of the society. Laws, like privileges, expressed the relationship between sovereign and subject, between king and nobleman, and were therefore constantly negotiated. Put differently, winning exceptions to the law was what being an aristocrat was all about. During the eighteenth century, anyone with enough power, status, or wealth tried to raise himself above the law. In this context where legal and social institutions were unusually flexible, aristocratic women often benefited.[10]

Female power and status were especially prevalent in d'Eon's lifetime. First, strong women were sovereigns in two (Austria and Russia) of Europe's five great states (men ruled in France, Prussia, and in England after 1714). Second, by making themselves governors of that crucial cultural institution the salon, elite women had become important intermediaries in the cosmopolitan movement associated with the Enlightenment. Finally, the foreign policy of Europe's most powerful state, France, was virtually directed by a woman, King Louis XV's mistress Mme de Pompadour, during the years when d'Eon was involved in political life.

Female power and status became so fused with Europe's Old Regime that critiques of eighteenth-century society inevitably focused on women. More than anyone else, Enlightenment philosopher Jean-Jacques Rousseau was responsible for establishing the relationship between women and absolute monarchy. Rousseau imaginatively blended a misogynist social critique of women with a democratic attack on absolutism. He argued that men had become feminized by women, unable to perform the virile tasks characteristic of good politics; because men had become women and women had become rulers, political life had collapsed into decadence. Rousseau's radical vision called for a new age of female domesticity, in which women would remain in the home caring for their husbands and children, leaving the public sphere exclusively to men.[11]

Rousseau is a complicated thinker, and his ideas were picked up by many kinds of readers, who interpreted his writings in various ways. Many of the upper-class female readers whom Rousseau was attacking endorsed his work. They found in his theories the basis for a new kind of female solidarity and could not see how this new ideal of domesticity might be used against them.[12] Likewise, d'Eon himself was attracted to Rousseau's theories, and while d'Eon came to a view about the relationship of women and politics which was radically different from that of the great philosopher, d'Eon's thinking was nonetheless influenced significantly by Rousseau.

Rousseau's ideas were given their most important validation during the French Revolution by the Jacobins, who systematically tried to exclude women from participating in the new regime. The Declaration of the Rights of Man became just that—universal rights and freedoms were never extended to women. Although the French Revolutionaries emancipated black slaves and gave Jews their full civic rights, half the population remained outside the new liberal constitution. Increasingly during the Revolution, women were prevented from joining political clubs, petitioning the National Assembly, or participating in military life. The French nation may have included "everyone," in the words of the revolutionary leader, Abbé Sieyès, but "everyone" did not seem to include women.[13]

In their new misogyny, the Jacobins drank deeply from Rousseau's glass. The French Revolutionaries framed citizenship in terms that were explicitly virile, and directed a potent form of obscene literature against activist women such as Marie-Antoinette, Olympe de Gouges, and Mme Roland who played a public role in the Revolution.[14]

Domesticity became the new, modern ideology for guiding female behavior. "Women must not become legislators, as is the case among some peoples, nor should they become slaves, as is the case among Orientals," wrote one woman author late in the Revolution. "Their goal must be the domestic happiness of men"; likewise, "the first duty of a wife, that which guides everything else, is to make her husband happy."[15]

The continuity between the Jacobins and the Victorians with regard to a narrowing of acceptable gender roles has been one of the major themes of recent feminist historiography. We don't know nearly as much about gender relations during the period just preceding the Revolution, when women had far more public visibility. Elite women could not have achieved so much status before the French Revolution unless there were men who had admired them and championed their cause.

We find examples of pro-women attitudes among aristocrats nearly everywhere before the French Revolution. There was a common belief, expressed best by the French philosopher Montesquieu and the Scottish historian John Millar, that the true test of a civilization was how well it treated its women. Primitive societies, these Enlightenment spokesmen argued, valued physical prowess and dealt with women like chattel, basically using them as sex and work machines; civilized societies, on the other hand, treated women with respect and honor, making sure to include them in every important social occasion. Correspondingly, masculinity had changed dramatically from ancient to modern times. Adam Smith saw modern masculinity as having softened, until in his own epoch virility was defined not by physical strength but by sophisticated conversation and manners.[16]

Of course, I do not mean to imply that women—even upper-class women—had reached equality or parity with men in Old Regime Europe, only that a broad sector of the European intelligentsia believed history was moving in that direction. This was an age when many upper-class men found powerful women fascinating rather than threatening. Indeed, they admired feminine qualities to such an extent that often they tried to imitate them. "In the moral system there seems at present to be going on a kind of Country-Dance between the Male and Female Follies and Vices," British author George Colman observed, "in which they have severally crossed over, and taken each other's places. The Men are growing delicate and refined, and the Women free and easy." Similarly, Montesquieu noted that "there is only one sex left; we are all women in spirit." Like it or not (and Montesquieu was not so sure), Europe was heading down the road toward an androgynous ruling elite, or so many aristocrats believed.[17]

Unless one appreciates how widespread was the perception that traditional gender roles were topsy-turvy, it is impossible to understand either d'Eon himself or the literate public's interpretation of his story. D'Eon's case was not (as biographers have claimed) something "strange" and "alien" in the sense of standing removed from history; d'Eon was not a "man ahead of his time"; rather, everything he did and everything he thought can be traced to themes and ideas that belong to the last decades of Europe's Old Regime. D'Eon understood contemporary perceptions of gender and fashioned his life accordingly.[18]

D'Eon's biographers have tended to minimize historical factors, attributing his behavior to a psychosexual illness. During the years surrounding the First World War, the pioneering British psychologist Havelock Ellis developed an original interpretation of d'Eon's behavior that helped to conceptualize an entirely new way of thinking about gender identity. Ellis believed that d'Eon's passage from man to woman reflected a "pathologic" condition. On the one hand, Ellis contended that d'Eon was acting out an obsessive impulse "to live as a woman." On the other hand, Ellis broke new ground by arguing that d'Eon's effeminate ways had nothing to do with sexual behavior. Furthermore, Ellis perceived that cross-dressing was only one small part of the condition: "The inversion here is in the affective and emotional sphere, and in this large sphere the minor symptom of cross-dressing is insignificant." Finally, Ellis speculated that the original cause of d'Eon's condition had nothing to do with the events that occurred during his life, but was probably organic, involving a "disturbance in the balance of the play of hormones."[19]

The story of the Chevalier d'Eon therefore became the paradigmatic case in the burgeoning field of gender identity disorders, whose origins go back to Ellis and his followers. After the Second World War, when psychologists had refined their research into psychosexual disorders, d'Eon was no longer labeled a transvestite, but became history's best-known "transsexual." In contrast with a transvestite, who feels compelled to dress as a woman, a transsexual is a person who believes that his or her own sex has been misassigned: he or she feels trapped in the body of the wrong sex. Hence a transsexual's gender identity is at odds with the sexual parts of his or her body.[20]

During the 1950s and 1960s, several transsexuals who underwent sex-reassignment surgery became celebrities. One of them, the British travel writer Jan Morris, had no doubt that the Chevalier d'Eon suffered from the same problem: "He was four years older than I was when I entered the same experience, and a good deal worldlier, but what happened to him, happened to me."[21]

The problem with pinning a psychosexual disorder on d'Eon is that it minimizes his own will and cognition in the process of his own gender transformation. Interpreting d'Eon as a transsexual renders him fundamentally passive. His gender transformation is seen as something that happened to him, the result of a genetic defect or childhood experiences, rather than a process that he freely brought upon himself as a mature adult. Instead of an active intellect, aware of his choices, and even trying to change his society, d'Eon is portrayed in this interpretation as a victim of an illness whose only fate is to suffer.[22]

At any rate, it is clear from the basic facts of the story that d'Eon was neither a transvestite nor a transsexual. By definition, a transvestite is someone for whom cross-dressing is a compulsion.[23] There is no evidence whatsoever that such was the case with d'Eon. As we shall see, d'Eon did not cross-dress at any time during the years before England and France declared him to be a woman; even after that, he went through a two-year struggle with Louis XVI to retain the right to wear his (male) military uniform. D'Eon, in short, began to dress in women's clothes only after his king forced him to.

Likewise, a diagnosis of transsexualism is dependent on the individual despising his own genitals and desperately wanting those of the other sex.[24] Again, there is simply no indication that d'Eon hated his own body or that he wanted, or even imagined he would be better off with, the body of a woman. Indeed, as I hope to show in part V of this book, what d'Eon wanted was to have the concept of gender transcend body altogether, so that manhood and womanhood were abstract signifiers that indicated something about one's character, not about one's body.[25]

My interpretation of d'Eon's gender transformation can be summarized as follows:

First, d'Eon's switch was not a compulsion but an intellectual decision that he made between 1766 and 1776, after careful thought and reading. Of course, it was also emotional, but it was neither inevitable nor determined by a peculiar childhood or family history. D'Eon did not become a woman to trick others; rather, he chose to become a woman because he deeply admired the moral character of women and wanted to live as one of them.

Second, the "cause" of d'Eon's transformation was his alienation from French political life. His career as a diplomat and spy having reached a dead end, he searched for a way to win back his honor and regenerate his own soul.

Third, d'Eon was heavily influenced by early modern feminist writing that called into question patriarchal gender roles; likewise, he was keenly aware of the political criticism leveled against the Old Regime by Enlightenment philosophers and their followers. One of the goals of this book is to highlight these texts and the debate over gender boundaries that produced them.

Fourth, shortly after d'Eon transformed himself into a woman, he also became a fundamentalist Christian, and these two new aspects of his personality colored each other. Thus during the thirty-two years that he lived as a woman, he developed a fascinating and pioneering ideology of gender identity that I call a "Christian feminism." While his Christian feminism did not *cause* his gender transformation, his new Christian ideas about manhood and womanhood gave him the justification to remain a woman long after the French Revolution had destroyed the Old Regime.

Finally, d'Eon did not invent these ideas in a cultural vacuum. His story must be read in the context of an aristocracy that was intensely debating appropriate boundaries between the sexes. D'Eon's life was played out against the backdrop of other kinds of gender experiments that tested and challenged relations between the sexes and the nature of manhood and womanhood. In this sense, the peculiarities of European culture near the end of the Old Regime provided d'Eon with resources that allowed him to make a difficult journey across the gender barrier.

Monsieur d'Eon
Is a Woman

Part I

A FRENCH CHEVALIÈRE

Orlando had become a woman—there is no denying it. But in every other respect, Orlando remained precisely as he had been. The change of sex, though it altered their future, did nothing whatsoever to alter their identity. Their faces remained, as their portraits prove, practically the same. His memory—but in future we must, for convention's sake, say "her" for "his," and "she" for "he"—her memory, then, went back through all the events of her past life without encountering any obstacle.

—*Virginia Woolf,* Orlando

Maiden Voyage

IT WAS A PERFECT DAY for crossing the English Channel. The warm winds of high summer had blown away any bad weather, and it took the Chevalière d'Eon only a few hours to sail from England to France on 14 August 1777.[1]

D'Eon was finally coming home. For fifteen years he had, at least from his point of view, served his sovereign faithfully in England, and now the King had provided d'Eon a life pension that would allow him to enjoy the sumptuous style of a wealthy French aristocrat for the rest of his life.

With one very important twist, of course. When d'Eon had left France for England in 1762, he was known as a man. Now, upon his return, all Europe believed that d'Eon was really a woman who had disguised herself as a man early in life in order to serve the French king in the diplomatic corps. "Of all the women who have acquired renown by assuming the appearance of the other sex," wrote Simon Linguet in his popular newspaper, "perhaps the most peculiar in every respect is Charles-Geneviève-Louise-Auguste-André-Thimothée d'Eon."[2] Nor was this merely the opinion of one Gallic gossip. The same judgment can be found in Edmund Burke's more sober *Annual Register*, which claimed that "she is the most extraordinary person of the age. We have several times seen women metamorphosed into men, and doing their duty in the war; but we have seen no one who has united so many military, political, and literary talents."[3]

Since about 1770 there had been rumors that d'Eon was really a woman, but for more than five years no one—especially d'Eon—could or would confirm his sex one way or another. Then, rather dramatically, in 1776 Louis XVI publicly announced d'Eon's female identity. In a carefully worded agreement, negotiated by the well-known playwright Pierre-Augustin Caron de Beaumarchais, Louis XVI acknowledged that d'Eon had been a woman since birth, and decreed that she return to France in peace and freedom.

Even after this declaration, however, d'Eon continued to appear at parties in London dressed as a man, and would refuse to discuss the matter. Then one year later, in July 1777, on the eve of his departure for France, London's highest court reached the same conclusion in a highly publicized trial between two parties who were suing each other over a bet wagered on d'Eon's real sex. Now that Europe's two most powerful governments had decreed that d'Eon was a woman, the forty-nine-year-old bachelor bowed to, if not welcomed, the inevitable: he finally admitted that he was, indeed, a woman.[4]

Despite this admission, d'Eon continued to wear the clothes he had worn since the 1750s: the officer's uniform of a captain in the elite corps of the Dragoons. But his clothing clearly put him in a situation that rapidly became, in his own words, "no longer tenable." He wrote, "I could not go out without being surrounded and hounded by a curious and boisterous crowd, and exposing myself to the severity of the law."[5] D'Eon was not sure whether he was at last voluntarily returning to his beloved homeland or fleeing a situation that had gotten out of hand.

D'Eon's trip across the Channel was thus more than a return home. It marked as well his maiden voyage across the gender boundary, a barrier much better defended and more impenetrable than any national border. As far as the world knew, d'Eon was returning both to his original country and to his original sex. But he himself was well aware of the more frightening and exciting truth: He was returning to his homeland in a gender role that he had consciously chosen.

D'Eon had good reason to anticipate his approach to Boulogne with a certain amount of trepidation. At the age of forty-nine he had rescued himself from a once-promising political career that had reached a miserable dead end in London. Only much later, when he was approaching eighty, did d'Eon realize that he had lived roughly half his adult life as a man and half as a woman—a kind of symmetry still very much appreciated in the neoclassical Age of Enlightenment.[6]

What kind of woman was d'Eon? During the eighteenth century, the question of appropriate gender roles for elite women was intensely debated. There was no such thing as a Platonic sense of womanliness.[7] And this was d'Eon's most immediate problem. Since Europeans wanted to believe that d'Eon was a woman, he would have no trouble convincing them he was. But more troubling, how would he allow becoming a woman to affect the kind of person he had been and wanted to become? What did living as a woman have to do with his fundamental character and personality? D'Eon could anticipate what it might feel like on the outside to live as a French noblewoman near the end of the Old Regime. But no man, not even he, who had read and thought so carefully about gender issues, could imagine in those first days as a woman how difficult the process would be both to decide for oneself and negotiate with others how a woman should live.

Foreign Minister Vergennes

W HEN D'EON LANDED in Boulogne, he was a noblewoman free to live as he wished. But personal liberty was a privilege in Old Regime France, not a right. While the government allowed him to go where he wanted, it watched his every move. Informants wrote almost daily about d'Eon's activities to Charles Gravier, the Comte de Vergennes, Louis XVI's capable Foreign Minister.[1]

D'Eon made his way toward Paris, stopping for a night in the outlying town of Saint-Denis, famous for its stunning Gothic cathedral and noted throughout the country as an important religious center. Months earlier, d'Eon had received an invitation from Saint-Denis's Carmelite nuns to stay with them. Its spiritual leader was the pious Mme Louise, eldest daughter of Louis XV, who had entered the convent in 1771 after the death of her mother and in disgusted reaction to the King's liaison with Mme du Barry.[2]

Before proceeding to the nunnery, d'Eon called on Dom Boudier, abbot of the town's Benedictine monastery. Boudier, surprised to find d'Eon still dressed in male garb, knew he now had trouble on his hands. He could not, of course, allow a female dressed in male military garb to sleep in the nunnery. Immediately he ran over to confer with Mme Louise.[3]

"Alas," Mme Louise exclaimed when she saw how d'Eon was dressed, "has she forgotten that her name is Charlotte-Geneviève-Louise-Auguste-Marie d'Eon? When she wears her dress again, she may return. I will welcome her then with pleasure."

"Madame," d'Eon replied, "don't charge me with this sin. I was raised like this. Your illustrious father knew it and he used me. But now that he is dead, I have become a useless servant. However, our dead King is worth as much as a living king. I know what I will do. I will get up and go to my mother and tell her: 'My good mother, I have sinned against heaven and before you, and I am no longer worthy to be called your son; but soon my sin will be taken away, and she who was hidden among the Dragoons and the army's volunteers will soon, either voluntarily or by legal edict, be called your dear daughter and your beloved in the court and in the city. Now my salvation is closer than when I left London. The darkness of my night is over, and the light of my day is coming when I will be stripped of my Dragoon skin, my weapons, and my accomplishments in the dark. I will soon wear the light and the virtues of your dress in order to behave honestly and in the light of day.'"

Mme Louise then said: "Mademoiselle d'Eon, kindly go into the next room. I want to speak to Dom Boudier."

A few minutes later Boudier informed d'Eon that Mme Louise was writing her grand-nephew, King Louis XVI, urging him to immediately force d'Eon to assume women's clothes.

D'Eon replied to Boudier: "If I continue to visit the holy men and women of Saint-Denis, I will soon be excommunicated ipso facto. People will greet me at the door of the church with the words *sancta sanctis foris canes* [dogs (should be) outside the holy of holies]. If I go see Voltaire . . . he is going to tell me: *The clergy are not what a vain populace thinks they are; our gullibility constitutes their entire knowledge.* I don't know what to do nor to what male or female saint to dedicate myself."

"Take care not to see Voltaire," Boudier warned. "He will corrupt you. You should consult the Church. Outside the Church, there is no salvation."

"This is an awesome stroke of grace for my heart and a destructive blow to the drawbridge that is my pants."

"Don't talk this way, Mademoiselle. What Madame Louise said to you is more serious than you think. Let's go into the choir of our church to pray at the tomb of Louis XV. We will ask God to intercede and make clear the new road you must take."

Later that day, when Boudier and d'Eon were sharing supper in private, d'Eon confided to him that he thought he might return to London that very night. After all, if Mme Louise reacted to him so poorly, what could he expect from Vergennes and the King?

"God protects you from such a plan," Boudier replied. "You are no doubt unaware that since you got off the boat from England, you have been closely followed. If you backtrack, you will be quickly arrested. Men's clothing has wounded your spirit and brings death to your soul. Wear your dress once again: it will return your life to you while subordinating you to your duty. It delivers you from your temptations and all your hardships. It will make you find pardon before God, the King, and the Queen. It will find for you a significant place in the pious Madame Louise's heart and in the Archbishop's [the Archbishop of Paris, Christophe de Beaumont]. You will become once again a Christian girl. The Lord will be with you. He will shower you with gifts and glory. All this I foresee for you."

"I accept your words as words of life," d'Eon replied. "I will no longer stubbornly oppose the spirit which inspires you. I will do as you have told me. I see that I have crossed the Rubicon. I will be like Caesar; I will not retreat. It's not a matter here of saving the Republic. It's only a question of a pitiful girl who was protected by the deceased King. I have never run away from a field of battle. I have never acted like my friend Horace, *relicta non bene parmula* [not wisely having left his shield behind]. I will not run away on the road to Versailles. I am assured of finding in Versailles a generous King and his beneficent ministers."

D'Eon's surrender seemed to please Boudier. "Since I have placed your heart back in its proper place, I want to offer a toast of some good wine from your region of Tonnerre. I will invite Dom Roussel, who was just recently named the chaplain of the former Benedictine abbey of Saint-Michel at Tonnerre, and who is a friend of your mother, your sister, and your whole family, to have dinner with us. It's only been a month since his return from Tonnerre to Saint-Denis."

Naturally the discussion turned to religion. "I am curious to know which prayer Mademoiselle d'Eon said at the foot of Louis XV's catafalque," Boudier said. "Tell us your prayer."

"Here it is: 'Lord, forgive the sins of the good Louis XV, who equally committed both good and evil. His ministers and his favorites are more guilty than he is. Have pity on me, who could do neither good nor evil.'"

Dom Boudier told d'Eon: "This is a good prayer, but it is very short. It is prickly."

D'Eon answered: "*In vino veritas! Brevis oratio penetrat cielos, longua potatio ebriat potos* [There is truth in wine. A short prayer penetrates the heavens; a long drinking-bout leads drinkers to inebriation]. If you want me to compose a prayer as long as that of a pious Benedictine or an emaciated Carthusian, then I'll direct these spoken words to heaven, *Deo optimo maximo* [For God, the greatest good]. 'My God, our Creator and Protector, Supreme Being, royally Good and Almighty, I offer you, I give you, I devote to you my heart. Please take it so that no creature may take it and run off with it. Glory be to the Father, the Son, and the Holy Spirit, as it was in the beginning, and as it is now. . . .'"

Not knowing quite where to have d'Eon spend the night, Dom Boudier finally decided on private apartments in the monastery usually reserved for visiting sisters and mothers of resident monks. But when word spread that d'Eon was about to sleep there, the monks broke from their routines and clamored for a look at the famous Chevalière. The situation was calmed only after Boudier's direct intervention. "Stop being scandalized, my brothers. The Captain of the Dragoons and the Volunteers of the Army, who so boldly enters this sacred apartment, is the courageous Chevalière d'Eon on her way from London to Versailles."

The next morning, just before d'Eon left for Versailles, Dom Boudier confided his frustrations to one of d'Eon's traveling companions: "I have done a very imprudent thing by bringing Mademoiselle d'Eon in her men's clothing to the home of Madame Louise without her permission. Mademoiselle d'Eon for her part unwisely took advantage of the freedom to roam around in our garden, our cloister, our chapter, our refectory, and dormitory without my being aware. She indeed demonstrated the curiosity of her gender. I must immediately write a note to the King apologizing for this matter. . . . Our captain is a lady who doesn't use her sleeve or her foot when she blows her nose. She replies quickly and smartly to everything one asks of her. Her spirit is not easily maneuvered. No doubt she will become more flexible when she redons her cornet, dress, and skirt; when she is with other women in a convent or in a respectable home in order to acquire the modesty and decorum appropriate for her sex. I hope that she will lose the attitudes of a captain of the Dragoons and the Volunteers of the Army."

D'Eon, need it be said, would do nothing of the kind. For almost fifty years he had listened only to the voice in his own heart, and he was not about to start taking advice from a princess, much less a monk. But the issue of d'Eon's clothes would not go away. When he entered Paris a few days later, a firestorm of gossip made him the star attraction on the capital's aristocratic stage. "Everyone talks incessantly of M. or Mlle. d'Eon," wrote Mme du Deffand to her British penpal, Horace Walpole.[4] Immediately a small industry mushroomed that mocked d'Eon's determination to wear his military uniform. In the Palais Royal, center of Parisian cultural activity, vendors hawked songs, broadsides, and prints that made fun of the Chevalière. Even the literati were swept into the frenzy. At the Comédie italienne a play called *Sans dormir* (Sleepless) was hastily put together, which the venerable critic Baron Friedrich Grimm described as a hilarious "vaudeville," where "the principal artifice of the author is to change the role of women to men, and that of men to women." Obviously, Grimm noted, the plot was a parody on d'Eon.[5]

The government was not amused by this sort of gender confusion under its nose. For Louis XVI, the Chevalière d'Eon was nothing but a reminder of the extraordinary decadence and mismanagement of the reign of his grandfather, Louis XV. Like his royal counterpart in England, George III, Louis XVI had begun his reign as an ardent reformer, bent on addressing the vast problems left over from his grandfather's administration. Louis XVI had allowed d'Eon to enter France as a woman because he thought it would put an end to d'Eon's controversial political career and silence him forever. But so far, as d'Eon paraded around the capital in the clothes of a military officer, it was having the opposite effect.

We usually think of the last years of the Old Regime as hopelessly backward, a time when the absolute monarchy of Louis XVI was rigidly tied to a feudalism that had long ago ceased to benefit France. Such a picture, however, was painted not so much by contemporaries as by the Jacobins who destroyed the regime during the Revolution. Now, after decades of research, a new picture is emerging of an administration that was reforming the country at a pace that was in many cases too quick for the population, most of whom were, of course, overworked and impoverished peasants.[6] The ministers of Louis XVI were sympathetic to the ideals of the Enlightenment, and even succeeded in co-opting many of its philosophers, such as Voltaire. For example, Louis XVI's first Finance Minister was the philosopher and administrator Anne-Robert-Jacques Turgot, who had contributed to the great *Encyclopédie* and was an important influence on Adam Smith. But by the time d'Eon returned to France, Turgot had already fallen from office and the chance for fundamental reform was beginning to wane.

At any rate, these champions of modernization, as the historian Simon Schama has recently dubbed them, did not have much regard for d'Eon's gender antics.[7] They were willing to tolerate him up to a point, but they certainly did not want to put themselves in the position of endorsing his behavior. Thus the more d'Eon appeared in the public eye, the more pressure the government felt to do something about him.

This is what led Foreign Minister Vergennes to summon d'Eon to a meeting at Versailles. D'Eon had every reason to anticipate the meeting with excitement and optimism. For years under Louis XV, the Foreign Ministry had been in the palm of the Duc de Choiseul, who despised d'Eon and his patrons. Vergennes, on the other hand, had always gotten along with d'Eon and his friends. When Vergennes had served as ambassador to Constantinople and to Stockholm many years earlier, he had taken his cues from the Comte de Broglie, who was at the same time d'Eon's principal patron. Therefore, since Vergennes's appointment as Foreign Minister in 1774, d'Eon had felt much sympathy for him. Indeed, it was only because d'Eon trusted Vergennes that the deal could be struck which permitted d'Eon's return to France in the first place.[8]

The meeting started pleasantly enough. The two diplomats compared notes about various statesmen they had known. This pleased d'Eon, and perhaps it was not completely unreasonable for him to hope that Vergennes might offer him a new diplomatic assignment. But then came a bomb from Vergennes that put d'Eon, as he later described it, "in a state of confusion without any parallel."[9]

"Mademoiselle," Vergennes began. "I beg you to retake immediately your dress or submit yourself to the law. You will win the affection of women and the respect of men. This indispensable change will allow your character and your behavior to become sufficiently moderate assuring your tranquillity and happiness." And then, if only to underscore the importance the government placed on the matter, Vergennes handed the shocked d'Eon a hand-signed order from the King himself commanding him to "retire the uniform of a Dragoon" and forbidding him "to appear anywhere in the kingdom in any other garment than those suitable to females."[10]

D'Eon immediately protested the order and tried to get it rescinded. He reminded Vergennes of his great service to France and to his King. Had he not served valiantly under the Maréchal de Broglie in the Seven Years' War? Had he not won accolades in his tenure as a diplomat to the court of the Russian empress, Elizabeth? Had not the King freely made him a captain in the elite corps of the Dragoons? Had he not been instrumental in negotiating the Peace of Paris with England in 1763? And had the King not rewarded his service with the office of Plenipotentiary Minister to London? Finally (and most astonishing for a woman), had not d'Eon received the rare and coveted Cross of Saint-Louis for his public service? Given that record, d'Eon asked, why should he be forced to dress in female clothes? There was no reason, he insisted, that his admitting to having been born female should permanently exclude him from future diplomatic activities.[11]

This challenge merely piqued Vergennes's curiosity. Rather than respond directly to d'Eon's arguments, he asked how d'Eon could "hide your sex for so long and fight with so much courage among men." "M. le Comte," the Chevalière replied, "all I did was to hide myself from the eyes of girls and women, boys and men, soldiers, officers, generals, ambassadors, ministers of war and foreign affairs. They are not the ones who decode the messages . . . but it was my job to do such decoding for them."[12]

Meanwhile, the royal court realized it could not simply let d'Eon go free and expect that he would carry out the order. The King's order, it was understood, would have to involve an entire program to retrain d'Eon in the ways of womanhood. He was invited to stay at the Versailles home of Edme-Jacques Genet, the chief administrator at the Foreign Ministry. With the guidance of Genet's wife and his three daughters (two of whom were ladies-in-waiting to Marie-Antoinette), d'Eon was assured of a crash course in proper etiquette. He agreed to stay in the Genet household, but only after a visit to his mother in Tonnerre.

More important, the King made funds available for d'Eon to acquire a new wardrobe, one in keeping with the status of a noblewoman. Queen Marie-Antoinette authorized her wardrobe director, Rose Bertin, to supervise the various steps in making d'Eon a new set of clothes. "The Queen has commanded me to provide you with all that is necessary for your change of state and condition," Bertin announced the next day as she met with d'Eon to take his measurements. "Let us work together to determine exactly what it is that you need."

"Truthfully, Mademoiselle," d'Eon confessed, "I do not yet know what I need. I only know in general that I need all the extras that you have and especially your kindness, your patience, your wisdom, and your prudence. I only know that it is more difficult to equip a lady than a company of Dragoons from head to foot."[13]

Tonnerre

A FEW DAYS AFTER MEETING with Vergennes, the Comte de Maurepas, Interior Minister, granted d'Eon permission to visit his mother in his native Tonnerre, a town of 3,700 poor souls located in northern Burgundy, about 200 miles east of Paris. D'Eon had not been back to Tonnerre since his father had died in 1749. Still, there is no indication that d'Eon had any particular desire to visit Tonnerre before the King's latest decree. More likely, he needed a respite from a public that was addicted to the kind of gossip he inevitably produced. "The Chevalier d'Eon has met with the King in a special audience," one secret agent wrote from Versailles to the Russian court as d'Eon went speeding off to Tonnerre. "His Majesty required in no uncertain terms that this amphibious hero retake the clothes of her sex . . . I believe that M. d'Eon has again fled France, and must be returning to England."[1]

D'Eon had not left France, nor did he have any intention of returning to England. But he did need to escape Paris, if only to contemplate his situation. The King's decree ordering him to dress in female clothes, he later wrote, "was regarded at Versailles, Paris, as well as throughout France and Europe as the judgment of Solomon." On the one hand, d'Eon realized that the decree implied a kind of death, and simultaneously a rebirth. Louis "killed in her the old Dragoon captain," d'Eon later recalled. "Such a change completely transformed her mind, her heart, her conduct, her manners, her habits, and her inclinations. It forced her to come alive, move forward, and act as an entirely new creature . . . resuscitated to all the decency, wisdom and dignity of her sex."[2]

In some respects, being reborn as a woman was precisely what d'Eon was after. But he wanted it done on his terms. "Only my extreme desire to be irreproachable in the eyes of the King and of my protectors, such as yourself and the Comte de Maurepas," he wrote to Vergennes, "can give me the necessary strength to conquer myself and assume this character of meekness suitable to the new existence *I have been forced* to adopt. The role of lion would be easier for me to play than that of the sheep; and that of Captain of Volunteers in the army [would be easier] than that of a timid and obedient maiden."[3]

But if d'Eon thought he could use his stay in Tonnerre to ponder his situation in peace and seclusion, he was mistaken. A celebrity in Paris, he was treated like a goddess in Tonnerre. Everyone in the town was eager to see the controversial Chevalière who had become more famous than any-one else—then or since—in the town's history.

Sometime during the first week in September 1777, d'Eon's coach finally pulled into Tonnerre. When Mme d'Eon saw that her child was still dressed in the uniform of a Dragoon captain, she fainted directly in front of the house. "My good mama, it's really me," d'Eon blurted out during a tender and tearful embrace. "Don't be afraid."[4]

D'Eon was so exhausted from traveling that he soon retired for the night. Later, when the servants had gone to bed, Mme d'Eon came in to her son's room so that she could talk to him alone. She fervently wanted him to dress in female garb.

"Upon your return to France, everyone believed and passed on from ear to ear that you would be obliged to wear a dress again. If you are prudent and intelligent, as I think you are, my dear daughter, follow my advice: Stay quietly in your bed, pretend to be ill for two or three days. During this time, Mademoiselle La Tour, my seamstress, her sister, and I myself will silently prepare a room upstairs and all that is necessary for your change and embellishment. We must do everything we can to put an end to your agitated life [dressed as a man], which is raising such a hubbub in the world, and which fills me with such fear for you and fright for me."

"Do you believe that in my situation I would have come here like a madwoman?" d'Eon asked. "I have in my pocket a valid permit from the Court. Here it is. Read it." D'Eon hoped that during his absence from the Court, his powerful friends and patrons "will have convinced the King to grant me the indulgence of allowing me to remain in uniform since I have retained the Cross of Saint-Louis and all my pensions. In a month I must return to Paris or Versailles to make use of the wardrobe that the Queen is planning for me. Now you see why I am so despondent day and night despite my apparent happiness today. Soon I'll have to bend to the will of the King. What makes me so despondent is that [Vergennes] wants me to be presented to the King, the Queen, and the Court in order to invest me legally with my new dignity. They say that this introduction will give a stability, harmony, and respect that you cannot give me even though you are legally my mother."

"The Court is absolutely right," his mother exclaimed. "I cannot conceive of why you would want to continue wearing your uniform. Can't you see that people are laughing at you? Since everyone knows that you were declared to be female in London and in Paris, this masquerade serves only to perpetuate rumor and scandal. You have to be either one or the other. You are destined to be female; accept it. Since you had the weakness to wear a uniform into war, you have to have the strength to wear a dress during peacetime. How can you still have the folly to think that you will be exempt from this universal law?"

"What?" d'Eon retorted in anger. "Even my mother is against me today! She who in my youth put me in pants today wants to hurry me along to put me into a skirt. . . . Since, according to you, the Court is always right, you must therefore mourn the coming death of your pitiful Dragoon. His days are numbered. He only has several weeks left to live in a man's clothes."

"Blessed be God, may his will be done, as well as that of the King and of the Law," Mme d'Eon sobbed, tears flowing from her eyes. "At this moment I would rather see you dead than in men's clothes."

"I prefer even more, dear mother, to live with you wearing a coif and a skirt than never to see you again if I wore a hat and pants."

"You are still my dear daughter sitting in the darkness and the shadow of death. But you will be reborn, my daughter, without fear or reproach to live and die peacefully near your mother who loves and will always cherish you. For your salvation and our mutual happiness, I have long prayed for the misfortune that befalls you."[5]

How could d'Eon's mother refer to her son as a "daughter"? This conversation, like many featured in this book, comes from d'Eon's autobiographical manuscripts. We may infer at least part of these reminiscences of d'Eon are fictional, since Mme d'Eon, of all people, knew her child was male. D'Eon's autobiography was written for a reader who believed him to be a woman, necessitating the fiction.

The next morning, d'Eon was called out of his mother's mansion to watch a long parade that had been organized in his honor. When d'Eon appeared dressed in his Dragoon uniform and wearing his precious Cross of Saint-Louis, the large crowd loudly expressed its "universal and excessive joy. The bells rang, guns were firing all day; and every demonstration that the day would well permit took place on that occasion."[6]

The pageant itself reflected the basic political structure of a provincial town during the Old Regime. First came the mayor along with the members of the city council, "all very happy to see me and waving palm branches." Then came military officers from various companies, in order of rank and status, who represented the nobility. They were decked out in their finest uniforms, covered with medals and regalia garnered in war. Finally came members of the First Estate, the highest ecclesiastical officers in the region, from abbots to hospital administrators. The fact that the First Estate brought up the rear of the pageant may indeed reflect the decline of the Church's authority in this Age of Enlightenment. Although the division of the realm into three estates was theoretically eternal, the truth was that power was shifting in late-eighteenth-century France away from traditional elites and more toward those who could exploit new economic conditions.[7]

Still garbed in his own military uniform, d'Eon stood at attention in front of his mother's home with mixed emotions. He enjoyed the attention, especially from the military officers who saluted d'Eon as they passed by, but he suddenly felt more like an animal on exhibition at a zoo than an aristocratic notable. The throngs of townspeople crowded in to get a look not at the paraders, whom they could see every day, but at d'Eon. They were struck by how much he looked like a woman, even in his military garb. "He is forceful, but he doesn't have any facial hair nor any beard," one woman remarked. He doesn't appear to have much of an Adam's apple, another spoke up. And "without his uniform" one could make out a girl's figure nice enough to "honor all the mothers of our good town of Tonnerre where all the girls have as warlike a spirit as the boys."

During the next several days a "small civil war" broke out among the residents of Tonnerre over whether d'Eon should get rid of his uniform and wear the normal clothes of a woman. On one side were the clergy who "wanted the Court to force me to retake my female clothes. On the other side were local notables and military men who passionately hoped that the Court would allow me to maintain the privilege of wearing my uniform in order to continue my military service."[8]

To read only d'Eon's account, one would think that these military officers were supporting the introduction of women into the French army. Rather, they were upholding the dignity and status of one of their own. An appointment to the officer corps of the Dragoons was considered a lifetime commitment. One was expected to wear the Dragoon uniform every time one went out. For such an honor to be rescinded was unheard of. It was, after all, the law as set down by an absolute king. Could that king violate even his own laws? That, eighteenth-century aristocrats thought, was precisely the difference between a legitimate monarchy and a despotism: The former was ruled by laws, the latter according to the whim of the monarch. If Louis could take away d'Eon's rank and office, he could do so to anyone.

"Our brave compatriot Dragoon Captain," one military officer exhorted d'Eon, "continue to wear a uniform that you have honored in our presence in war. Know for certain that in whatever costume you appear before our eyes, you will always be dear to the hearts of your brave compatriots of the town and region of Tonnerre." Such fan mail could not have made d'Eon's struggle any easier. The "civil war" d'Eon describes in the town obviously reflected the one taking place in his head.

He also received mail from aristocratic ladies who urged him to go through with his transformation. Why are you delaying a process that is obviously to your advantage and ultimately to our glory, one female correspondent wrote to "our dear and brave heroine. The ladies of Burgundy stand ready to welcome you not only through the doors of their homes, but through their naturally affectionate hearts as well."

D'Eon's supporters also put on a service in Tonnerre's Cathedral of Notre Dame, where a *Te Deum* was chanted in his honor. "An immense number of people attended upon the occasion. Every mouth uttered 'long live the heroine of Tonnerre.'" Each man and woman displayed a white ribbon or handkerchief that signified their solidarity with d'Eon.[9]

The local clergy were offended at this display of support. They warned d'Eon "to no longer visit our churches in the clothes of a man or uniform, because all of the attentions of the faithful that are due only to God are being directed toward our Chevalière, who despite her virtue and her courage has not yet been canonized by the Church of Rome."

This view was loudly echoed by Tonnerre's parish priest, Father Labernade, who visited d'Eon a few days after the parade, hoping to get d'Eon to take confession from him. Labernade was well known to the d'Eon family. Eighty-four years old and still going strong, he was not only the confessor to d'Eon's mother and sister, he had been the confessor to d'Eon's grandmother forty years earlier. Given that track record, it was not unreasonable for Labernade to ask d'Eon, "Why are you not letting me hear your confession? I could offer some help for your condition."

"My reverend father," d'Eon replied coldly, "I have not prepared myself for that. I make my confessions to God before confessing to other men; for there is no man that I have wronged."

"But yours is a habitual sin," countered the priest, "which I would want to see you rid of."

"And what is that, my reverend father?" d'Eon sarcastically asked.

"It is to wear the clothes of a man. You must yourself suspect," Labernade added, "that your birth and education are no mystery to me."

"Do not judge solely on a person's appearance," d'Eon warned, "but judge with good reason."

The conversation then digressed into a theological dispute over the origin of confession. D'Eon took the old view popularized by Protestant theologians, as well as by some Enlightenment philosophers, that the Catholic form of confession was a rather late introduction which "has been a great source of strife among Christians here on earth." To Labernade's dismay, d'Eon insisted that "Saint Peter had been dead more than 400 years before auricular confession was founded and invented."

Labernade was no match for d'Eon's profound intellectual skills, and tried to return the discussion to more personal terms. He reminded d'Eon again that he had been the family's confessor for decades, and noted that by refusing confession d'Eon might be dishonoring the other women in his family who had chosen him as their confessor. As for mother and grandmother, d'Eon coolly responded, "they have their models and I have mine."

Exasperated with d'Eon, Father Labernade threw up his hands and shouted: "My good Chevalier or Chevalière! You are really more learned than I, who studied theology for ten years!"

While Labernade may have failed with d'Eon, he had a close ally in d'Eon's mother. "She tormented me day and night," the anguished Chevalière exclaimed, "and to encourage me, she gave me all her beautiful dresses and lacework."[10] Yet it is not hard to understand her attitude, even through the necessary fictions of her son's later prose. Under these strange circumstances she, like any mother, only wanted what was best for her son. And from her viewpoint that meant a life lived in safety and comfort. The only way to achieve that stability, she reasoned, was by assuming the dress and manners of an aristocratic lady. Revealing himself an anatomical male would embarrass the government so much at this point that such a declaration was out of the question. Likewise, Mme d'Eon could see no advantage at all in behaving as something between the two genders—as a masculine woman.

"I would like you one hundred times better wearing a dress," she told him one day, "than to see you suffering and being the silent object of public scandal. A little kindness is soon passed. Put on your dress . . . and you will live happy and at peace near me."

D'Eon fervently, if anxiously, tried to explain to his mother that he was not made for a tranquil life. God had given him special talents. Whatever his gender status, he felt a calling for political life. "I have the rare advantage," he told her, "of having seen many men in the city and many ordinary and extraordinary dealings both in war and in peace, and I have seen ministers who did not know how to read and ambassadors who did not know how to write." What sense did it make for d'Eon to waste his own God-given talents?

Eventually, however, his mother's pleas and prayers seem to wear down his resistance. She also convinced d'Eon to realize that the Court would not change its mind. "I see that regarding my dress, I cannot expect any indulgence from the King. I know what I will do. I will make my decision as a brave captain. I will go in retreat to a convent in prayer to await there the accomplishment of God's, the King's, and the law's plans. There the memory of good works never perishes. This is the most honest, honorable, and safe decision for me. But I want only my mother to know this, and I'll leave Tonnerre without saying anything to anybody. Many years ago, Regulus, a prisoner of war, on his word of honor returned to Carthage certain of being placed in a barrel pierced with large arrowheads and hurled down from his city's highest point. I came to Tonnerre to visit my mother, having given my word of honor to return to Paris. Do you think a Christian maiden will be more timid than the pagan Regulus to go into a pierced barrel! I will go where honor calls me and pushes me, even if my heart should be pierced by a thousand darts."

D'Eon's mother jumped up to hug him. "I recognize today that you are the worthy daughter of your father and mother, who did not raise you to be timid. Follow the road of honor, and may nothing stop you. When your initial confusion is over, you will bless the day when you put your dress on again. Your affliction today will be your consolation tomorrow."

"Mother, you have taught me everything. I will recall your precepts in order to realize them without procrastinating any longer. Your Charlotte-Geneviève-Louise-Auguste-Andrée-Thimothée d'Eon de Beaumont, through the power of her emancipation and her coming-of-age and by the authority of the law and the King, as much the King of England as the King of France, will thus finally become a maiden, using and rejoicing in her rights. *Ad majorem Dei gloriam!* [For the greater glory of God!]"

D'Eon had come to Tonnerre to avoid the limelight and to rest with his family. But within a month, he had had enough. In his confused state, he couldn't tolerate remaining in this little town of his youth, besieged by petty clergymen and family friends. He decided to leave; indeed, he decided to escape. He secretly wrote to Louis-Jean Bertier de Sauvigny, the Intendant (royal administrator) of Paris, who was relaxing at his chateau in Fontainebleau. When Bertier extended an invitation, d'Eon hastily prepared to leave.[11] One night he rose at 3 A.M., ordered his servants to pack his things and prepare his coach, kissed his mother goodbye in her bed, and sped off for Fontainebleau.

D'Eon's Patrons

D'EON WAS FIGHTING the government for his right to dress as a man. He did not view this right as natural, but rather he thought he deserved it because of his military service to France. Vergennes and the King did not dispute his military heroism. Indeed, the fact that d'Eon—a woman—had fought bravely as an officer during the Seven Years' War made a deep impression on everyone. Rather, the issue boiled down to whether having now acknowledged his womanhood, d'Eon could still retain his Dragoon uniform. The King was firm in his opposition. D'Eon wanted to find a way to pressure the King and his ministers to change their minds.

During the Old Regime, aristocrats used patronage as a traditional means of lobbying the government. A patron was someone with a superior place in society who could facilitate the course of a client's career, winning for him office, rank, and pensions. In return for such favors, the client owed the patron loyalty and service. From his earliest days, d'Eon learned that he had to acquire the most influential patrons possible. In a world where public law was minimal and largely ineffective, and in which rank, order, status, and power were almost always hierarchical, a nobleman's access to power came through his patrons.[1]

D'Eon's use of patronage was at once terribly old-fashioned and remarkably innovative. On the one hand, patron–client systems were being challenged and attacked throughout the Atlantic world during the 1770s. In England, where d'Eon had spent the past two decades, radicals had led a long assault on patronage as the epitome of corruption. Indeed, it was one of d'Eon's closest British friends, the radical Middlesex Member of Parliament, John Wilkes, who led the most virulent campaign against dominant Whig magnates during the 1760s. Likewise, the dramatic political events occurring in America in no small way revolved around antipathy to patronage. Courtiers like d'Eon were assailed by John Adams as appealing to the most vicious side of humanity: "to the Passions and Prejudices, the Follies and Vices of Great Men in order to obtain their smiles, esteem, and patronage and consequently their favors and preferments."[2]

And yet d'Eon's use of patronage was unique in that he was now identifying himself as a female client appealing to male patrons. Such an arrangement was not unknown in certain social sectors, such as the literary world, where a well-known man of letters might help a female client publish her manuscript, but it was certainly unusual in the more exclusive spheres of statecraft and diplomacy. D'Eon, then, was simultaneously embracing and redefining an old-fashioned social institution.

D'Eon's most important and established patron was Charles François, the Comte de Broglie. Broglie came from an Italian family (Broglio), originally from Piedmont, who had begun to work for French kings during the early seventeenth century. In the Seven Years' War, d'Eon served under his older brother, the Maréchal de Broglie, one of France's most gifted military leaders. The Comte had then helped to bring d'Eon into the diplomatic corps during the 1750s. From those early days, d'Eon had squarely identified his own career with Broglie's: their fortunes were tied together—whoever helped the Broglie brothers was d'Eon's friend; likewise, whoever became their enemy could count on d'Eon's vengeance.

D'Eon tried to get Broglie to see the problem from his vantage point. The government had perpetrated its own "public indecency by wanting to force into skirts a former Chevalier de Saint-Louis and Plenipotentiary Minister of France!" What was at stake here, d'Eon insisted, was a matter not of gender, but honor.[3]

But not simply honor. It was also a question of freedom. D'Eon was also afraid of what female clothes might imply about how he would be treated. To put it bluntly, he feared "the complete destruction of my liberty." "A girl easily accustoms herself to obey and my obedience to the Court is the order of the day," he later explained. But "blind obedience is the mother of despotism and superstition, of fanaticism and ignorance."[4] D'Eon's aversion to women's clothes, then, was based on a theme familiar to eighteenth-century aristocrats such as the Broglies (from their reading of Montesquieu's *Spirit of the Laws,* to mention only the greatest account): The loss of any noble person's honor and freedom was itself a sign that France was becoming despotic.

Broglie tried to act on d'Eon's behalf, but he was quickly rebuffed. The King, Broglie was told, feels very strongly about the matter. France had been carefully rebuilding the tarnished image of her army since the Seven Years' War, and d'Eon was a genuine embarrassment in that effort—in the eyes of Europe, his sex dishonored the French military. Louis XVI could not afford to have the French military become the butt of jokes and scandal.

For one thing, the English were astonished at how easily the government permitted d'Eon to wander around the country. For some Englishmen, d'Eon seemed to symbolize the effeminate character of the French military. Copies of a letter reputedly written by British Lord Chief Justice Mansfield to his nephew, Lord Storsmund, then visiting Paris, were themselves strengthening the resolve of the French government. "The public is scandalized," Mansfield reported, by d'Eon's "arrival and reception at Versailles at the present juncture. The existence of Mlle d'Eon in man's clothes" must "be reprobated as contrary to every principle of religion, and every dictate of morality in these circumstances."[5]

D'Eon set his highest hopes on converting Bertier de Sauvigny to his side, and arrived at Bertier's chateau near Fontainebleau on 19 October 1777.[6] As the Intendant of Paris, Bertier was one of the most powerful men in France. Fortunately, he was also one of d'Eon's oldest patrons, the first nonrelative who had helped launch the young d'Eon's career. Bertier had long been friendly with d'Eon's father, and had even stayed at the Tonnerre home for six weeks during d'Eon's boyhood. When d'Eon moved as a teenager to Paris, he found that his Uncle André was a close client of Bertier's. Consequently André found d'Eon an honorific post in Bertier's office, where d'Eon doggedly worked long hours without receiving any immediate compensation. What he was after, of course, was Bertier's long-term patronage.[7]

When d'Eon arrived, Bertier was disappointed to see that he was still dressed in his military garb. "Despite your uniform," Bertier told him, "I am obliged to call you Mademoiselle; for it is urgent that you wear female clothes; it is the top priority in the cabinet of the prime minister." Still, Bertier welcomed him as an old client, and treated him well. He tried to get d'Eon to see the bright side of his situation. By remaining a woman-dressed-as-a-man, d'Eon was destined to remain a freak, one not well tolerated by those executing the royal will, but by assuming a more orthodox female identity, "your glory as a maiden will begin to become evident. Otherwise," he warned, "you run the great risk of being sent for a long time to a dreary convent."[8]

Having failed to make any progress through his major patrons, d'Eon tried a more direct method, with strongly worded appeals to government ministers. He insisted that his case was special. Whoever heard of a woman serving her country with such courage and with such success? To one minister, d'Eon predicted that perhaps only "four cases in a thousand years" would resemble his case. Given the extraordinary circumstances, d'Eon believed he was not out of line to ask for a special exception. Nonetheless, these appeals were little more than futile acts of desperation. Without an aggressive patron, d'Eon had no threat, no stick, no incentive for the ministers to change their minds. D'Eon's hopes for keeping his Dragoon uniform were fading.[9]

Rose Bertin

B
Y THE THIRD WEEK in October 1777, Queen Marie-
Antoinette's wardrobe director, Rose Bertin, had finished creating
d'Eon's new couture. Although the specific bills for this project are
lost, other receipts remaining in both d'Eon's archives and Bertin's business records show that the cost must have been huge, probably running
into several hundred livres.[1]

Not only were the nobility's clothes usually expensive, Rose Bertin was
no ordinary dressmaker. Her rise from her low birth as the daughter of a
policeman to the heights of social power and influence is itself one example of how a few ambitious, talented women might—with luck, patience,
and determination—break into aristocratic court life.

Born in 1747, Bertin spent her younger years as a seamstress in the
Norman town of Abbeville, where she developed an excellent reputation
for her work as a dressmaker. In 1773, she moved to Paris, where she did
so well that in a few years she was employing more than thirty seam-
stresses. For five years, from 1774 to 1779, she collaborated so closely with
the Queen that gossips remarked how Bertin was treated on the same
level as the princesses of the court. More than anyone else, Rose Bertin
determined French (and consequently European) fashion during the first
years of Louis XVI's reign. Thus d'Eon was dealing not simply with a
dressmaker, but with one of the most ambitious and successful women in
France at the peak of her career.[2]

As soon as Bertin had completed d'Eon's wardrobe, the government
began applying more pressure on him. Through Bertier de Sauvigny,
Ministers Maurepas and Vergennes let d'Eon know that if he continued
to refuse to adopt female dress, they would issue an arbitrary warrant, a

lettre de cachet, for his arrest. With his family and patrons against him, d'Eon found himself without any room to maneuver. He had no alternative but to pack away his uniform and put on clothes appropriate to what everyone believed to be his biological sex.

That finally happened the morning of 21 October 1777, in the Versailles home of Foreign Affairs administrator Edme-Jacques Genet. But it wasn't simply a change of dress. It was a remarkable transformation, a coming out, in the presence of the Genet family and a few close friends. Until this day, d'Eon's gender switch had been incomplete. He was, so to speak, standing with one foot in each world. He had done everything possible to encourage the public to think of him as a woman, but he had never dressed as one, maintaining the fine suit of a Dragoon captain. Likewise, he still signed all correspondence *Le Chevalier* d'Eon. The significance of 21 October 1777 is not simply that it was d'Eon's debut dressed as a woman, but it was a preview of a further transformation in the way he would from then on present himself. When d'Eon had written to Vergennes on 29 August, he signed his name *Le Chevalier d'Eon,* but a letter of 3 November is signed *La Chevalière d'Eon.*[3]

Rose Bertin had prepared a "blue satin skirt like the Virgin Saint Mary's" for the unique occasion. "This passage," d'Eon later wrote in his memoirs, repeating a favorite military analogy, was comparable to "that of the Rubicon." But surely it took Caesar's army less time to cross that river than it did for this chevalière to don her new garb. "My first toilette at the hands of the chaste Bertin and her modest ladies-in-waiting [the Genet daughters] was accomplished in nothing short of four hours and ten minutes!"[4] During this time, d'Eon and Bertin had an opportunity to talk in private:

"I have lived for forty-eight years," d'Eon explained. "Thus, my life will not go on much longer. I await impatiently the great transformation which must change us, rendering us eternally equal."

Mlle Bertin tried to make him feel good about his decision. Of course you realize, she told him, that they could not have "every day in Paris a famous maiden in a Dragoon uniform publicly giving fencing lessons." No one could allow that. What was happening should not be considered as a loss but as a gain: "The bad boy must become a good girl."[5]

Still, d'Eon did not see matters that way, and felt himself forced into the change to female clothes. "You can speak with such certainty," he told Bertin, "just as a cannon discharges its missiles. But when I reflect on my past and present condition, I would never have had the courage to go out in public the way you have dressed me. You have illuminated and adorned me with color that I do not dare look at myself in the little mirror you have brought me."

"After this conversation," d'Eon tells us in these autobiographical fragments, "I left . . . the room and locked myself up in my bedroom, where I sobbed bitterly." Mlle Bertin ran after him, and tried to comfort him with handkerchiefs and kind words. But nothing she did could calm him down. "I could not stop crying until I ran out of tears."

Later Mlle Bertin told d'Eon that she had visited the Queen to discuss his condition, and had informed her that "by removing my Dragoon skin, she was able to see if I was as good a maiden as I had been a good captain."[6]

That night d'Eon had to sit through a sumptuous dinner given in his honor by Mme Falconnet, the wife of a wealthy lawyer. D'Eon had still not climbed out of his depression. "You have killed my brother the Dragoon," he told Mlle Bertin. "I am in great pain over it. My body is like my mind. It cannot be content with being embroidered in lace." This was d'Eon's metaphorical way of describing the anguish he felt at being forced to relinquish his manhood completely. He did not want to give up the hope of serving his government in some public capacity, probably an absurd notion at this late juncture, but one nonetheless close to his heart. "My sustenance is that I do the will of the King in order to serve the law."[7]

D'Eon was now in female clothes, but it didn't feel right to him. "Despite the complete change in my clothing," he later wrote, "my heart did not feel any different. Insofar as gender agreements in the language were concerned, I simply followed the example of good Irish gentlemen who always put feminine endings on everything."[8]

No one expected that d'Eon's transformation "back" to womanhood would be swift and effortless. The ladies at Versailles thought of d'Eon as something akin to the wild boy of Aveyron, who was found living among wolves in a French forest, and then returned to civilization to start an education at the age of ten. They fought over the opportunity to teach d'Eon the art of being a lady. "Allow me to do whatever is necessary in the extraordinary case of Mlle d'Eon," the Comtesse de Maurepas, wife of the Interior Minister, requested, "and in less than two years, I promise to change your bad boy into a good girl."[9] What Rousseau did for his Emile, she would do for her d'Eon.

D'Eon's training period would, in fact, take much less than two years, though Mme de Maurepas would have to share him with several other tutors. For the next several months, from the fall of 1777 through the spring of 1778, d'Eon lived primarily at the Genets' in Versailles, taking regular trips to Paris, but mainly staying among Mme Genet, her three daughters, Rose Bertin, the Comtesse de Maurepas, and the Duchesse de Montmorency-Bouteville. Together these women taught d'Eon "to imitate them in the mysteries, usages, habits, duties, and virtues of her sex."[10]

Still, d'Eon was an extremely reluctant learner at first. He let it be known that this "novitiate" would not be easy for him. At the very least, he did not enjoy the change in diet. At the Genets' he ate less meat and more fresh eggs, and he drank water instead of wine.[11] But most difficult were the clothes. D'Eon simply did not like women's clothes and it took him a long time to get used to them. He exclaimed how tight stays hurt the shoulders, stomach, and groin. "I find women's clothes too complicated for dressing and undressing promptly," he later wrote. "Full of inconvenience, unseasonable for winter, impractical for all occasions except those uniquely suited for embodying vanity, luxury, and vice."[12]

At the end of October 1777, he wrote the King that while he deeply resented this "condemnation," and would fight it if he could, he nonetheless recognized that it was the sovereign's will, and so he was resigned to it. To the powerful minister Amelot, d'Eon was even more ambivalent: "I swore in my anger that I would never change into dresses nor skirts." Amelot warned, "Your change of status has been determined legally in England and in France on an irrefutable basis."[13]

A few weeks later, d'Eon's mood had grown even worse. "Don't remind me, Madame," he wrote to his closest new friend, the Duchesse de Montmorency-Bouteville, "about the errors of my youth, nor the happy follies of my military career, for the problems found in the midst of a war were more pleasing to me than the tranquillity of being in the midst of the Court during peacetime. In actuality, I live here in the respectable home of Mme Genet as an honorable prisoner of war." Although d'Eon wanted to be known as a woman, he was having trouble defining the kind of woman he might become. Patriarchal France was intent on forcing him to accept a narrow gender role that meant giving up his military and political career.[14]

Marie-Antoinette

ABOUT A MONTH after d'Eon first dressed as a woman, he was presented to the King and Queen at the palace of Versailles. "The Chevalière d'Eon has made his metamorphosis," wrote one journalist who apparently had not yet become accustomed to referring to d'Eon as a woman. "He appeared at Versailles in female clothes with the Cross of Saint-Louis. This curious outfit, as well as the real and extraordinary merit of this individual, has made a tremendous impression on the public. Everyone tries to catch a glimpse of him in all the places where he might be likely to be found: at the theater, on walks, etc."[1]

The event was also important for d'Eon. His ambivalence was most painful at this point. But the royal meeting gave him a renewed conviction that his passage from manhood to womanhood was absolutely the right thing for him. Accepted by the King and Queen of France as a woman, d'Eon wanted to believe it to be his destiny. Marie-Antoinette, in particular, was fascinated by d'Eon, and took a decided interest in his case.

"How does Mademoiselle d'Eon find her new uniform?" Marie-Antoinette asked him.[2]

"Madame," d'Eon humbly replied, "I am pleased to wear it because it admits me to the Regiment of the Queen, which in all times and in all places is totally devoted to the service of our good King."

"Mademoiselle, if the regiment was composed of only demoiselles," the Queen responded, "who but d'Eon could command it?"

"Madame, it would rather be Marie-Antoinette of Austria," d'Eon said.

The King refused to interrupt them, but couldn't help laughing out loud and even applauding their bantering.

"Madame," d'Eon continued, "in my new peacetime service, the injuries are not any less dangerous than in war. Nighttime battles are the most bloody. When one is too courageous and wants to sacrifice one's life, one dies."

"Mademoiselle, who made you so knowledgeable?" the Queen queried.

"Madame, it is my mother, and above all my grandmother, who had twenty-two children."

"Mademoiselle, you are a good citizen. I hope you have as many."

"Madame, my education has been deficient. I have lost my fertility and my time doing what I should not have done."

"Mademoiselle, there is always time to repair one's faults. I will provide you with another education that can make up for whatever is lacking. The King has given you a good pension from his royal treasury, and as for myself, I have ordered Mademoiselle Bertin to take care of your wardrobe and to give you the first ladies of the court to show you how to wear your dress with suitable decency until such time as we can find for you a Versailles household where your instruction concerning your new life can be perfected."

"Madame, your generosity far exceeds my gratitude, and Mademoiselle Bertin's generous heart has treated me in a manner that honors you. Suffice it to say that she has dressed me richly and carefully. My clothes are so low-cut that soon she will make me go out nude in order to conform to the ordinary standards of the court."

"Mademoiselle, in every country it is necessary to conform to the accepted practice. You are under the authority of the law; be an adult woman using and enjoying your rights. Use them soberly, but the more you get used to your dress, the more you will find what a pleasure it is, and the more you will be integrated into the company of the white skirts of my regiment."

"Madame, since I have worn it, the shadow of the sun has become white as snow."

"Mademoiselle, continue as you have begun and all will go well for you."

"Madame, how can I fulfill your faith in me? Alas, if you stoop to cast your eyes upon me, I will quickly come to understand the road down which I must go; and the load that burdens me today will feel light to me tomorrow."

"Mademoiselle, do not consider today as the last one of your life. It is the start of our happiness together and the height of your glory."

D'Eon then wiped away the tears of joy at his unsought glory at court.[3]

"Mademoiselle," Marie-Antoinette continued, "submission to the law is an absolute necessity in all countries. Your transformation has surpassed our hope for achieving your happiness. Everyone is astonished and your enemies are dispersed and confounded. What more do you want? Watch how everything will go well for you."

"Madame," d'Eon responded, "today I realize that the death of my past condition gives life and glory to my present state and to the future for eternity. Allow me to swear that I will remain a prisoner of war in skirts, in faith and in homage to the law. For faith is the first theological virtue; without it we are but a drum echo in the air."

"Mademoiselle, what you say is the pure truth."

Franklin and Voltaire

D'EON'S RECEPTION by the King and Queen lent much credibility to his new image as one of the most accomplished women of his age. Before d'Eon's arrival in France, Vergennes had expected to remove him from the public eye. The Foreign Minister had hoped that, transformed into a fifty-year-old woman, d'Eon would retire with his mother in Tonnerre or, better yet, into a convent. Not only had Vergennes underestimated the intense interest of the public, he was completely taken off guard by the reaction of the courtiers at Versailles. Overnight d'Eon became the darling of those ladies closest to the Queen, and they refused to let him go. The monarchy itself had signaled the nation that its most famous cross-dresser was a heroine, not a pariah or a freak. It is safe to say that in 1777 and 1778 few stories circulated faster than this one.

In addition to holding a coming-out ceremony for d'Eon before the royal court, the monarchy took two other actions that dashed Vergennes's hopes of silencing him. First, by recognizing his new title of "Chevalière," the King and Queen were inventing a new kind of gender category for the nobility. Presumably all other French chevalières had acquired the title through marriage: they were chevalières only because their husbands were chevaliers. But d'Eon had earned the honorific. The monarchy had fully recognized him as a chevalier only in 1763, when Louis XV awarded him the title for acts of bravery in the Seven Years' War (until then he had been known by the less exalted but still noble title "Sieur d'Eon"). Thus by transmuting the title to its feminine form, the monarchy was indicating to the public that d'Eon's change of gender had no effect on the monarchy's views about his previous military accomplishments.

The same message was conveyed by the government's decision to allow d'Eon to continue wearing the Cross of Saint-Louis. The confusing sight of this rare military medal being displayed on the dress of a woman symbolized the ambiguous status d'Eon had achieved.

Consequently, d'Eon did not have to worry much about making the right social connections in Paris. Everyone wanted to meet this chevalière who had managed, it was thought, to overcome the usual limitations of womanhood and achieve such distinction as a soldier and diplomat. Throughout his residency at the Genets', d'Eon made frequent visits to Paris to attend the various parties and salon gatherings organized by the capital's most illustrious socialites.[1]

Among the most notable rendezvous of this period was d'Eon's meeting with that other famous newcomer to the Paris social scene, Benjamin Franklin. In town to gather support for the American War of Independence, Franklin exploited an entirely different kind of popular image, the rustic philosopher. Armed with bifocals rather than a sword, without any wig or other accoutrements of male aristocracy in France, he played up to the great noblemen by donning a leather coat and fur hat.[2] Thus Franklin and d'Eon were something alike, insofar as each in his own way mocked the stylized dress of the French establishment. And for at least one brief historical moment these two diplomats became an odd couple.

In February 1778 Franklin invited d'Eon to a dinner party at his Paris residence. Conversation, of course, revolved around colonial America's struggle with England, France's archenemy. Who was in a better position to speak authoritatively than a former envoy to England, one who had just returned from a thirteen-year residency there? Franklin liked what he heard. D'Eon spoke vehemently against England, urging France's entry into the war. He praised the rebels for their courage and virtue, urging everyone to join him in a toast to America's success.[3]

A few days later there appeared in Paris and London a scurrilous but popular little pamphlet under the title *History of a French Louse*, which followed the sad life of a Parisian louse, whose first misfortune was to find a home in the wig of a clerk to the Parlement of Paris.[4] From there it went in clothes to a laundress, who happened to be ironing a blouse for the Chevalière d'Eon. After biting the laundress on the bosom, the dirty louse "penetrated into the shirt sleeve which belonged to a lady, well known throughout all Europe for the singularity of her adventures. . . . Never before had I beheld a woman whose manners were so absurd, so masculine, and unsuitable to her sex; always in motion, full of grimace, awkward in the habit, and impatient of the conversation of women."

Conveniently, the louse was residing on d'Eon when he went for supper at Franklin's Paris home. After thirteen toasts made everyone drunk, d'Eon went over to Franklin's seat and sang "some verses of her own composing." The intelligent louse "plainly observed" Franklin expressing "his gratitude to his Apollo by an ardent kiss, but without quitting his spectacles; at the same time he whispered in her ear, *shall it be this evening, my goddess?*" But the affair was never consummated because d'Eon was too drunk, the louse concluded.

The pamphlet's main purpose was to discredit the American patriot, a notorious womanizer, through a recounting of his various romances since his arrival in Paris. Its target was Franklin, not d'Eon. The tract accepted d'Eon's female sex as a given, even when commenting on his extraordinary masculinity, accusing him merely of illicit heterosexual love affairs—hardly a rarity in the capital.

Franklin was not the only Enlightenment eminence who sought d'Eon's attention. France's greatest philosopher, Voltaire, had for years been following d'Eon's career with keen interest. Although Voltaire had corresponded with d'Eon's father, he had never met d'Eon. Nonetheless, during the 1760s he had ridiculed d'Eon's career as a diplomat in England, using it as a kind of paradigm for the inept foreign policy of Louis XV. Still, not even Voltaire's imagination could have come up with what happened to d'Eon during the 1770s. Once the great sage caught wind of d'Eon's female identity, he immediately tried to learn whatever he could. "Someone has sent me an engraving of the Chevalier d'Eon as Minerva," he wrote to a friend in the spring of 1777, "featuring a supposed royal certificate that gives this Amazon a pension of 12,000 livres and which orders him to keep a respectful silence in the same terms that were used in the case of the Jansenists. This will make a grand problem for history. What Academy of Inscriptions will prove the case to be authentic? D'Eon will be a *pucelle d'Orléans* who will not have been burnt. It will be seen how soft we have become."

What most surprised Voltaire was not d'Eon himself but the reaction of the King. Far from assassinating or arresting d'Eon, they were rewarding him with a pension! The *pucelle d'Orléans* was, of course, a reference to Joan of Arc, who was called by that name. Far from ridiculing d'Eon as he had done a decade earlier, Voltaire seems to acknowledge a grudging kind of respect for what d'Eon had achieved. Likewise, "Amazon" is here used as a term of respect, acknowledging d'Eon's talents, not a term of ridicule as it would become during the nineteenth century.[5]

Like so many at the apex of French society, Voltaire was not repulsed by d'Eon's gender ambiguities, but attracted to him, despite the fact that he had been disgusted by d'Eon's political antics some ten years earlier.

D'Eon idealized as the French Minerva, the Amazonian Roman goddess of war. This 1791 engraving commemorates a fencing exhibition in London featuring d'Eon. *(Courtesy of the Bibliothèque Nationale, Paris)*

Just before d'Eon had left England for France, Voltaire received more information from George Keate, a friend in London. "Today no one discusses or speaks of the Chevalier d'Eon except under the title of Mlle de Beaumont." Keate reminded Voltaire about d'Eon's "extraordinary talents, a well-cultivated genius, decorated with all kinds of erudition as his writings have well proved; a brilliant mind, joined with a gaiety of heart that makes everyone want to get to know him."

Keate insisted that the fact d'Eon was a woman should make him an object of praise, not scorn. "Like me, you will believe that every woman in Europe must build to d'Eon an altar for having done so much for the honor of their sex." For them d'Eon "proved that it is possible to cultivate all the political arts, acquire the military glory of the conquerors, and sustain one's virtue in the midst of the greatest temptations." Like Joan of Arc, this eighteenth-century "Amazon" might become an inspiration to all women.

Keate ended his letter by noting that d'Eon had told him he would very much like to meet Voltaire when he returned to France. After explaining to the philosopher how to get in touch with d'Eon, Keate urged him to invite d'Eon to his estate at Ferney. "I am persuaded that the great role that she has played so well during these many years, and the great talents demonstrated during that time, would inspire in you the desire to know a person whom nature and fortune have so distinguished, and who wants to see you." As if that weren't forward enough, Keate put the matter in an even more concrete manner: "It is the most famous maiden in Europe who would like to talk with a man who has been for almost a century its greatest ornament."[6]

Voltaire took Keate's suggestion and wrote to d'Eon as soon as the latter reached Tonnerre. "The honest and amiable Mr. Keate writes to an old and dying man that he may before his last day have the honor to see a very famous lady Captain. The old man longs after that pleasure. He presents his respect to the lady Captain."[7]

D'Eon went to see Voltaire in May 1778, when the latter returned to Paris on the eve of his death. "Mlle the Chevalière d'Eon came yesterday to see M. de Voltaire and the arrival of this celebrated woman did not rouse less curiosity than the old man she visited," one journalist reported. "All the domestics, or rather the entire household, lined up to contemplate her on her way in. She looked in some way ashamed, holding her muff beneath her nose and keeping her eyes downcast. She did not stay long."[8]

Public Perceptions

NOT EVERYONE WAS a Franklin or Voltaire; for every invitation d'Eon accepted, he turned down many more. There was simply no way he could satisfy everyone's curiosity in person, so most of the literate public had to learn about him through newspapers, prints, and songs.

In France, with its well-organized system of censorship and state repression, there were few daily papers, and their authority to report the news was limited. This void was filled by illicit gossip rags, many written by Grub Street journalists in exile, printed in cities like Amsterdam and London and smuggled into France. Because these organs were produced by writers with a political bent, they tended to be sensationalist and rather irresponsible. Among the most successful was *L'Espion anglais* (The English Spy), edited by Pidansat de Mairobert.

"Since the return to France, My Lord, of the Chevalier d'Eon, of this amphibious being, male in London, female in Paris," a correspondent for *L'Espion anglais* wrote in a comprehensive article titled "On the Chevalière d'Eon," "I have focused all my efforts on verifying the condition and the adventures of this celebrity, and my greatest attention has of necessity been to distinguish between the fantastic stories to which a subject such as this lends itself so easily, and the simple truth, the most precise truth, that is already so incredible."[1]

Like similar stories appearing in other journals, this article presumed that d'Eon was a biological female whose parents had desperately wanted a son. The girl's desires soon matched the father's, so that by adolescence, d'Eon clearly hoped to continue the masquerade in order to enter the military and diplomatic corps. D'Eon, the paper presumed, wanted nothing less than to be the first woman to become a minister of state in Europe. This story made sense, and far from being condemned, d'Eon was praised for his ability to pull the hoax off. What the correspondent could not understand was why Louis XV permitted the cross-dressing to go on inside his government. It was inconceivable that this absolute monarch could not have been aware of d'Eon's true sex.

Mairobert had no doubt that d'Eon was really a woman. But the correspondent realized that some readers still couldn't believe it. "On the one hand," Mairobert wrote, "can one imagine that if Mlle d'Eon were really of the masculine sex the government would have had such a bizarre and absurd idea, contrary to all good taste and law, to suggest that he pass himself off as a woman, when his entire appearance would speak against it; and not simply propose it to him, but require it of him under penalty of the government's official disgrace and the loss of its support? Can one believe that Mlle d'Eon, a man, would have had the cowardice to take on a role that would place him in constant difficulties, that would deprive him for the rest of his life of all the pleasures of his true sex, that would make him the subject of speculation to his fellow citizens and foreigners? Could we, in a word, silence the crowd of witnesses who would come forward, and it would be impossible that they not do so if she were really a man, and who would testify against his ridiculous transformation and who would announce his repudiated gender? However, one must admit that among the number of nonbelievers, there is no one that claims to have seen her as a man, nor even knows anyone who has had any physical proof." The implausibility of other explanations (implausible for purely cultural reasons) made this one plausible. The fact that there were no serious challenges to d'Eon's status as a woman during his residency in France is evidence that this argument was accepted by most readers.

Of course, those readers were dying to know what d'Eon looked like. "I have not been any less assiduous, My Lord, in gazing upon this astonishing maiden: I had formerly known her in London, during the time of her adventures; but her sex not then being under any suspicion, her face completely escaped me. I was invited to dine with her in different homes, and one must admit that she has even more of an air of a man since she has begun dressing as a woman. Indeed, can one believe that an individual of the feminine sex shaves, has a beard, has the stature and muscles of Hercules, who can ascend and descend a stagecoach without help; in short, a most nimble chevalier, who climbs a staircase four steps at a time, who, when approaching a fire, pulls her armchair forward, with her hand between her thighs; in a word, who relieves herself like a man.* Moreover,

_____

*Mlle d'Eon urinates standing up and without squatting [original note in *L'Espion anglais*].

the sound of her voice: its external tone belies her clothes; one is tempted to think that it is a masquerade. She herself seems to give credit to this opinion by the ridiculous quality of her dress. She wears old skirts, as some widow in the era of Louis XV. Her hair is slicked down with pomade and powder, topped off with a black cap, in the manner of pious women. Not used to the narrow and high heels of women, she continues to wear her heels low and rounded; she often forgets to put on her gloves, not being used to them either, revealing the arms of a Cyclops. Her chest is covered up to her chin so that one cannot see if there is any deficiency."[2]

There was an even better way for readers to learn what d'Eon looked like: they could buy engravings at any local bookstore. In an era before modern visual media, the circulation of prints was a huge industry. These prints would often be sold as part of a magazine or separately. Every eighteenth-century bookseller offered not only books, pamphlets, and journals, but popular illustrations as well. Some of Europe's greatest artists, such as Hogarth, distributed their work as engravings and made much money from them. Just as in literature, the line between the elite culture of painting and the commercial culture of prints was not always clear. Illustrations meant for a popular audience were always more than simply natural representations. The subject's clothes, expression, actions, and visual context often transformed the prints into editorials, especially when they carried captions.

Among the most successful engravings was the one included in the frontispiece of the *London Magazine* for September 1777, which included a long article on d'Eon. But the print is far more interesting than the article (see next page). Here d'Eon is drawn as one person, but with a kind of gender line running vertically down the middle of his body, from above his head to below his feet. His right side is dressed as an aristocratic woman, perhaps on her way to an evening salon. Her rococo hairstyle is the most striking feature of the print. Female hairstyles during the reign of Louis XV were among the most eccentric of any period before or since. And d'Eon is pictured in a style that is eccentric indeed.[3]

The left side is dressed as a mirror image, in terms of social class and fashion. The sword and britches indicate a nobleman. The wig is simple and elegant (in contrast to earlier styles), as are the shoes and stockings. The frock coat fans out just a bit, almost like a skirt, and is held by steel stays.

This print graphically reflects the gender ambiguity that lay at the bottom of the d'Eon story: Was he a man or woman? The caption emphasizes this problem: "Mademoiselle de Beaumont, or the Chevalier d'Eon. Female Minister Plenip[otentiary]. Capt. of Dragoons. . . ." But far from

MADEMOISELLE de BEAUMONT, or the
CHEVALIER D'EON.
Female Minister Plenipo. Capt. of Dragoons &c.&c.

D'Eon as half noblewoman and half nobleman captures the public's confusion surrounding his gender identity during the 1770s. *(From* The London Magazine; or Gentleman's Monthly Intelligencer, *September 1777)*

resolving the gender confusion, this way of naming d'Eon only increased fascination, because it clearly begged the important question of how a woman could acquire the title of chevalier and become an ambassador and soldier.

A similar statement was made by Bradel's attractive twin engravings that appeared in Paris stores around the same time (see insert following page 228). In one print, d'Eon is a woman dressed in a blue coat with a striking magenta band in her hair. In the corresponding print, the same person has become a man, wearing a green frock coat and red shirt. The poem at the bottom of the male print makes it clear that the artist was not trying to ridicule d'Eon, but praise "her" for her marvelous journey from womanhood to manhood:

> Toi l'honneur de ton sexe et qui réunis
> Les talens littéraires aux travaux de Bellone*
> Immortelle d'Eon, puisse-tu ressentir
> Autant de vrais plaisirs que ta presence en donne

> [You, the honor of your sex and who brings together
> literary talents with the works of Bellona
> Immortal d'Eon, may you experience
> as many true pleasures as your presence gives]

Most prints on the subject, however, did not show d'Eon in the garb of both sexes, but tried to focus on one remarkable aspect of the story. In Pruneau's drawing of 1779 (next page), as in many others, d'Eon is presented as an Amazonian warrior. With one bared breast revealing her womanhood, and a wild headdress symbolizing her bravery and courage, she is compared to Pallas, the Greek goddess who protected Athens:

> Son esprit vaut son coeur:
> C'est Pallas elle même!
> Long-temps on la craignit,
> et maintenant on l'aime

> [Her mind is as worthy as her heart
> She is Pallas in person!
> For a long time she has been feared,
> and now she is loved]

Likewise, in Bradel's portrait (see insert following page 100), where the Cross of Saint-Louis covers the right breast, the artist has used the story to make a patriotic statement about French women, comparing d'Eon to "the memory of the French heroines Joan of Arc, [the fifteenth-century defender of Beauvais] Jeanne Hachette, etc. etc."

---

*Bellone/Bellona was a Roman goddess of war.

D'Eon as an Amazonian goddess, by N. Pruneau, 1779. *(Courtesy of the Brotherton Collection, University of Leeds Library)*

D'Eon reacted nervously to this mass distribution of his likeness. On the one hand, he collected those that he liked and even sent some to friends. But this was a publicity medium he could not control, and he did not like the way some shops, particularly those in London, seemed to be exploiting him. "Such is the conduct of some of the editors of the public prints," he wrote in one autobiographical fragment, "that they seize with avidity every opportunity to disseminate their poison with malignant pleasure."[4]

Like the prints, the songs and poems that were spread throughout Europe dwelled on his mobility from one sex to the other. The following one focused on the extent to which d'Eon's personality remained the same despite his change from manhood to womanhood:

Spinster & minister, knight & dame
Monsieur & mademoiselle
D'Eon in male and female fame
By turns has borne the bell

Adroit to act on either plan
Smile nymph, or hero vapour
And pass with ease from word to fan
From pistol to thread-paper

Genius meanwhile, alert, tho' strange
Preserves its equal claim:
Tis mere *dexterity of change*
Proves d'Eon is still the same[5]

This poem seems to suggest that personality controls gender and not the other way around. There is a "d'Eon" who is essentially the same person whether male or female. His gender is quite literally thought to be a role that the personality uses and discards when a change is needed. Such a view might have pleased d'Eon; he kept a copy of this poem in his personal collection.[6] But there were others that took the opposite view, such as this song that followed d'Eon from England to France:[7]

Du chevalier d'Eon
Le sexe est un mystère.
L'on croit qu'il est garçon:
Cependant l'Angleterre
L'a fait declarer fille,
Et pretend qu'il n'a pas
De trace de béquille
Du père Barnabas.

Qu'il soit fille ou garçon
C'est un grand personnage,

Dont on verra le nom
Se citer d'âge en âge;
Mais pourtant s'il est fille,
Qui de nous osera
Lui prêter la béquille
Du père Barnabas?

Quoiqu'il ait le renom
D'être une chevalière,
Aux yeux de l'Angleterre
D'une petite fille,
Ce qu'on ne feroit pas,
Sans avoir la béquille
Du père Barnabas?

[The sex of the Chevalier d'Eon
is a mystery.
It is believed that he is male:
yet England has declared
him female,
and claims that he has no
trace of the crutch
of Old Barnabas.

Whether female or male
he's an important individual,
whose name will be cited
from generation to generation;
but if he is, however, female
who among us would dare
to lend him the crutch of
Old Barnabas?

Although he has the reputation
of being a chevalière,
in the eyes of England
he is a little girl,
What one would not do,
without having the crutch
of Old Barnabas?]

Here it is clearly the sexual organ that determines everything. D'Eon may be a unique character, one who will be remembered "from age to age," but he won't get very far without a penis. The song assumes that d'Eon needs a penis, anyone's penis, to achieve real greatness. In addition, the song makes a slightly jingoistic comment. The French may treat d'Eon as a kind of heroine, but for the English he will always be a "little girl."

D'Eon on d'Eon

"TODAY I BEGAN TO READ the biography of Mme Geoffrin," wrote the wealthy salonnière Mme du Deffand in a letter about one of her rivals, "but it's nothing more than a bunch of fluff for a soufflé. . . . It is on Mlle the Chevalière d'Eon that I wish someone would write a biography, and not these other eulogies and gossipy portraits."[1]

Mme du Deffand was not alone in hoping for a biography of d'Eon. The public wanted more than songs and anecdotes about its favorite chevalière. Here, it was thought, was one of the most fascinating women of all time. Everyone wanted to know how d'Eon got to be this way; what were the origins of the gender transformation? Although European folklore was littered with women who dressed as men, none had achieved such renown and been in the public eye for so long.

Wherever d'Eon went, he was asked about himself. Rumors circulated regarding his childhood, parents, and early diplomatic career. He was asked to confirm the stories and to provide details. Sometimes he was put on the defensive by a scurrilous pamphlet. But more often, ladies wanted to know his story because they admired him. In short, everyone was willing to accept d'Eon's transformation from chevalier to chevalière, but they needed some explanation.[2]

Thus from the start of his life as a woman, d'Eon was, in a real sense, writing his autobiography. Every day he told stories about himself, and since his name had become a household word in aristocratic salons, every detail of those stories needed to be consistent if d'Eon's change was to stick. As people clamored for more information about his life, d'Eon found himself developing anecdotes about his childhood in letters to women friends such as the Duchesse de Montmorency-Bouteville. Then in 1779 a biography was published, purportedly written by a friend named La Fortelle (but certainly with the collaboration of d'Eon himself). For many years this short book, *La Vie militaire, politique, et privée de Mademoiselle d'Eon*, came to be used as the standard account of his life.[3]

After d'Eon's return to England in 1785, he spent much of his time preparing longer drafts of his memoirs for publication. Here he elaborated on the stories he had been telling. While he added new anecdotes and went into various issues in greater detail, later embellished accounts rarely contradicted earlier testimony.

D'Eon's autobiographical writings were based not so much on a lie as a wish. He wanted people to believe that he had always been a woman because he wanted to live out the rest of his days as a woman. To be sure, he neither was nor ever wanted to be an ordinary kind of eighteenth-century aristocratic lady—his resistance to wearing appropriate clothes demonstrates that. D'Eon knew that his actions were nothing short of an extraordinarily brazen attempt at self-fashioning.[4] He wanted the best of both worlds: he hoped to be known as a biological female who had convincingly dressed and acted like a man. What he needed, then, was an explanation—a myth—derived from an imaginary childhood that might explain why an aristocratic lady would expect to participate in the spheres of political intrigue and war on a par with men.

D'Eon blamed the origins of his gender confusion on his father. Louis d'Eon de Beaumont was born in 1695 and died in 1749, when his son was twenty-one. A nobleman of relatively low rank, he rose from a local attorney and mayor of Tonnerre to become Sub-Delegate of the Paris Intendancy. Intendants were royal officials who were responsible for seeing that the King's policies were carried out in the provinces. Their authority grew dramatically in the seventeenth century, and by d'Eon's time, intendants often supervised tax collection, agriculture, judicial disputes, and welfare. In times of trouble, such as during a famine or an epidemic, their role could be crucial to the survival of the community. The father's jurisdiction included 30 villages surrounding Tonnerre, as well as about 180 parishes in the region. Thus he was a big fish in a rather small pond.[5]

In 1723 Louis d'Eon married Françoise de Charenton, a noblewoman from an old and wealthy southern French family. But according to d'Eon, his father squandered whatever he found in his wife's dowry, and by the mid-1720s was in debt up to his ears. The way out of debt, it turned out, was to have a son. Françoise's family will stipulated that a large inheritance of some 400 louis would go to the d'Eon family only if Françoise had a son. Unfortunately, the first child born to her and Louis turned out to be a girl. In 1727 they had a boy, Théodore, but their luck soured when the child died within six months.[6]

Even before the death of Théodore, Françoise became pregnant once more. According to d'Eon's memoirs, this time Louis made it clear that she had to have another son, if only to assuage his broken heart. A daughter would simply be unacceptable. "My dear wife," Louis instructed Françoise, "if you give me another girl, I will make her into a boy in order to replace my only dead son and to punish you."[7]

For the next several months, d'Eon claimed, a "great domestic quarrel" raged in his parents' household over the sex of the child. Louis supposedly clung to the crazy idea that they might raise the child as a boy whatever the infant's ascribed gender. Françoise wanted a boy, but she was also perfectly content to have a girl. Whereas a boy would obviously be a financial boon to the family, a girl could offer the family important moral and religious benefits, because, as Françoise pointed out, girls were much more likely to remain virgins than boys, and virginity was "like a heavenly treasure." Thus, as d'Eon repeatedly stated in his autobiographical manuscripts, "my father wanted me to become a bad boy and my mother wanted me to become a good girl."[8]

When d'Eon was born in October 1728, he wrote in his memoirs, Louis forced Françoise to go along with his wishes. Although born female, the new infant was to be raised from the start as a boy, and consequently, the parents had the baby baptized as Charles-Geneviève-Louis-Auguste-André-Thimothée d'Eon de Beaumont (the use of female middle names being commonplace in the eighteenth century). Thus according to d'Eon, he was born female, but he never knew what it was like to exist as a girl because from his first breath his family raised him as a son.

Hiding the child's natural sex was not easy, d'Eon stated in his fictionalized version of events. The father swore d'Eon's sister to the strictest secrecy. The baby could not be put out to a wet nurse or raised by nannies, as was commonplace at the time. Both parents took charge of d'Eon's upbringing on their own. They carefully screened his childhood friends, and did not let him play outside with his sister.

D'Eon was "born with a weak constitution" and only overcame a sickly childhood by, in his words, strengthening himself by "the good food and the good wine of Tonnerre."[9] At the root of his medical difficulties may have been a problematic urinary tract. "Until the age of ten years, I was under the yoke of an involuntary urinary flow," d'Eon wrote. "This infirmity gave my mother the pretext to keep me in a *fourreau* [a special undergarment for babies] until I was six years and sixty-four days old.

When [people] asked her why she waited so long to wean me from the *fourreau,* she responded, 'I am not rich enough to give him new pants every day . . . he is fine as he is.'"[10] But d'Eon's father finally put his foot down when the lad was seven years old, and forced him to wear pants.

Because d'Eon's activities were so circumscribed, he spent a great deal of time alone in the huge home that today serves as a bank in the center of Tonnerre. There he learned to read at a very young age, and reading became his favorite activity, as it would continue to be throughout his long and varied life. By the age of twelve d'Eon had absorbed just about all he could from local teachers and books. Louis found himself confronting a rather restless preadolescent. Rather than work on his Latin lessons, d'Eon would now sneak off to be with his mother, or play with his sister's friends in the fields surrounding the town. Françoise's response to her child's mild rebellion was ambivalent at best; she started to undermine Louis's plans by encouraging d'Eon to spend more time with her.

Louis decided that the time was right for d'Eon to move away from his mother and the stifling atmosphere of a small Burgundian town. Louis had a brother, André-Thimothée d'Eon de Tissey, who for years held the important office of Inspector General of the Police in Paris. D'Eon went to live with his uncle in Paris, and entered the prestigious College Mazarin, where he studied liberal arts and law.

At Mazarin, d'Eon discovered his love of learning. When he went off with his friends to the Bois de Boulogne, the other boys would play games in the forest, while d'Eon would find himself a comfortable meadow, where he would sit and read for hours. He excelled at languages and won school awards for memorization—among the most prized skills taught in eighteenth-century schools. D'Eon could recite by heart more passages from the Gospels and Roman authors than anyone else in the school. Thus when he received a law degree from the college in 1749, he had already acquired a reputation as a splendid scholar.[11]

The Hopes of a Good Patriot

T HE FACT THAT d'Eon himself composed this myth about being born female and his parents raising him as a son reveals much about the way he wanted to present himself to the world. By situating the origins of gender confusion at his birth, d'Eon shifts any moral responsibility for upsetting natural gender arrangements from himself to his father. No one who reads d'Eon's account can blame him for being a woman who wants to live as a man. As a child, he found himself under the thumb of a strong father who offered him little choice. His father had died in 1749, so blaming his condition on him was safe and convenient.[1]

D'Eon's story was also a variation on a somewhat familiar theme in early modern folklore. During the seventeenth and eighteenth centuries, hundreds, perhaps thousands, of women disguised themselves as men on a temporary basis. Recently two Dutch scholars have traced 119 such cases and concluded that "passing oneself off as a man was a real and viable option for women who had fallen into bad times."[2] Thus eighteenth-century readers of d'Eon's childhood myth would have understood and sympathized with such an explanation.

More specifically, eighteenth-century France was familar with similar stories. D'Eon himself told the tale of another Burgundian family, the Gurgys, who raised their daughter as a boy until the age of eighteen, when she assumed the identity of a woman and married one of d'Eon's relatives. What impressed d'Eon so much about this case was how liberal the government's reaction was to Mlle Gurgy's gender transformation—they took no action whatsoever against her parents.[3]

D'Eon's version of his childhood would seem believable to an audience reared in Enlightenment thought because it illustrated theories central to eighteenth-century psychology. At the end of the seventeenth century, the great British philosopher John Locke had speculated that environmental factors were critical in the formation of character and intellect. In contrast to the followers of Descartes, who operated within a Christian and Platonic framework, Locke argued that most of our ideas about the world come from the information absorbed by our senses. It did not take long before many of France's greatest philosophers, including Voltaire and Helvétius, applied Locke's ideas to psychology, education, ethics, and politics.[4]

Perhaps the greatest example of Locke's influence on the French Enlightenment was Jean-Jacques Rousseau's *Emile* (1762), the century's most important educational treatise, which followed the development of a boy's character and intellect from birth through adolescence. Rousseau not only popularized Locke, he used Locke to attack the French establishment. Since environment counted for everything, Rousseau argued, it was wrong for aristocrats to leave child care to others, especially to wet nurses, who were ignorant and uncivilized. Parents must, then, become active in every part of the child's life. They must teach by example, and protect the child from evil by gaining exclusive control over the child's environment.

D'Eon insisted that he had experienced a truly Rousseauian education, even though d'Eon was born thirty-four years before the publication of *Emile.* "Although during my childhood the works of Jean-Jacques the Citizen of Geneva did not yet exist, my father, since he had been educated in Paris at the Collège des Quatre Nations, acted the philosopher and had me brought up by my mother according to the doctrines of Jean-Jacques, with the exception of allowing children to run around on their hands and knees."[5]

In his own mind, d'Eon's childhood seemed to prove Rousseau's theories correct. Indeed, d'Eon saw himself as a kind of Emile. What he seems to be suggesting is that any father who had the will, time, and patience could overcome the barrier of sex and choose his child's gender. At the very least, in this story d'Eon projects many of his own feelings onto his father. After all, it wasn't Louis d'Eon who remolded his daughter's gender in the 1720s; it was d'Eon himself who refashioned his own gender shortly after the publication of Rousseau's *Emile.*

Of course, d'Eon was taking Rousseau's environmentalism down a path where the great philosopher would never have gone himself. Rousseau, whose notions about gender were complex, would hardly have approved of a father spending so much time rearing a daughter, much less a female being raised as a male, even if he thought it theoretically possible. His creation of Sophie in the fifth part of *Emile* was designed to highlight differences between male and female education. In this sense, d'Eon perhaps took too much liberty in his memoirs when he remarked that Marie-Antoinette's ladies-in-waiting referred to him as "Mademoiselle Sophie."[6]

Complicating the story even more is d'Eon's claim that he had suffered in childhood from a urinary tract disorder. As a rhetorical device in the autobiography, this important "fact" moves us to sympathize with him, removing him even further from any blame or responsibility. Likewise, it may tempt us to view his childhood medical problem as a cause of his later transsexualism. But surely there have been thousands of children who have had such problems and have maintained ordinary gender roles. The story about the urinary tract disorder may explain not so much why d'Eon wanted to become a woman, but rather, why he was asexual and remained a virgin throughout his life. Perhaps the disorder left some physical or psychological discomfort that lingered in later life.

These ruminations on d'Eon's character, of course, are based on what he says himself in autobiographical writings. Independent evidence is necessary to verify this version. Unfortunately, such evidence is thin. Despite the fact that many of d'Eon's family papers are today preserved in the Tonnerre municipal library, they yield precious little that sheds any light on the nature of his childhood. As far as we are able to ascertain, d'Eon seems to have had an upbringing fairly typical of eighteenth-century noble boys destined for careers in public service.[7]

During his early career d'Eon made friendships that were honest and intimate. Letters furthered these friendships by discussing ideas and feelings of profound importance. One of his close friends, Turquet de Mayenne, complained to d'Eon that his family had sternly rejected his choice for a spouse. A year later, d'Eon received a sensitive letter from Turquet, who was now mourning the sad death of his father. "The more I examine the vicissitudes of life," Turquet wrote, "the more I am convinced of its meaninglessness. Everything disappears, my dear d'Eon, everything is eclipsed. The inevitability of the end of being is the greatest truth."[8]

The intimacy of these male friendships occasionally engendered emotional pain or discomfort. For example, one married friend, La Seuze, scolded d'Eon at one point for treating him shabbily: "It is necessary to love our friends for themselves and not for ourselves," he preached to d'Eon. And then after signing the letter with the formulaic "your very *humble* and very *obedient servant*," La Seuze added: "When you treat me more cordially, I assure you that I will erase the three words that I have underlined in the signature of this letter."[9]

D'Eon's youthful letters, filled with a *Sturm und Drang* that prefigured Goethe's *Sorrows of Young Werther* (1774), reveal no apparent psychopathologies, merely the normal carrying on of close adolescent friends of a particular intellectual subculture. The fact that d'Eon rose so swiftly in the Paris literary scene after college as a young man of letters attests that whatever his peculiarities, he had learned how to get along with influential people well enough. Through his uncle André-Thimothée d'Eon de Tissey, he secured a spot in Bertier de Sauvigny's office, where he was given the time and resources to complete his first book on French government finance.[10] From there, Bertier got him a position as a royal censor, which provided d'Eon a healthy salary for doing little more than reading new books. Under the very liberal Director of the Book Trades, Chrétien-Guillaume de Lamoignon de Malesherbes, royal censors could spend much of their efforts educating themselves in their own chosen fields rather than in protecting the public from so-called dangerous works—that ugly task was more often left to the Church.

In his juvenilia, d'Eon comes across as an eager, ambitious, optimistic reformer ready to work hard for an enlightened minister. In his essay "The Hopes of a Good Patriot," he described a dynamic, progressive government, led by a strong monarch, that would focus its attention on France's vexing social and economic problems. "I hope that commerce will become free throughout the kingdom," he wrote, "because affluence makes the people happy and a happy people makes glory for the state and its prince."[11]

Apart from his own fictionalized autobiographical writings, then, there is little in what we know about d'Eon's early years that would indicate anything unorthodox about his personality or behavior. The clues that d'Eon himself left behind at a much later stage in his life lead to a dead end. The "cause" of d'Eon's gender transformation lies not in anything that took place during his childhood or adolescence, but in his failed political career. Put simply, the hopes of this good patriot were not realized. D'Eon's desire to become a woman was the result of a political crisis that he found himself in during the 1760s and 1770s, when he was already an adult. In order to understand d'Eon's motivation for changing gender, we need to pay somewhat less attention to the psychodynamic factors operating during his youth, and focus more on the particular forces that shaped his career as a statesman.

Part II

THE RISE AND FALL
OF A STATESMAN

It is in the public records at [the Departments of] Foreign
Affairs and War, and in the special papers of Louis XV, that
one must learn the truth about the public and secret history of
this unfortunate maiden . . . d'Eon de Beaumont, who as a victim was sacrificed in what was a pure holocaust.

—d'Eon, Leeds manuscript

Louis XV's Diplomacy

WHEN D'EON ENTERED politics during the 1750s, five states governed European relations: France, England, Prussia, Russia, and Austria. These same five would continue to dominate Europe at least until 1918, when Austria came apart. However, while the basic architecture of European diplomacy was the same as it is today, the substance arguably was more Machiavellian. "One must regard as a fundamental maxim and incontestable principle," wrote Louis XV's foreign policy adviser and d'Eon's principal patron, the Comte de Broglie, "that the credit or the consideration of a prince, his government, his reputation, and his preeminence, and his ultimate authority in the political order, is necessarily founded on power; and that such power can be envisaged under two faces: troops and alliances, military power and federative power."[1]

Broglie's view was hardheaded, but not unusual. Monarchies were expected to either grow or decline. "The spirit of monarchy," Montesquieu wrote, "is war and aggrandizement." The fundamental purpose of foreign policy was, therefore, to increase the territorial holdings of a sovereign. As Frederick the Great, the master of such policies, stated on the eve of assuming the Prussian crown: "The fundamental principle of princes is to expand their territory and their power as much as possible."[2]

After the sixteenth- and seventeenth-century wars of religion, and especially after Louis XIV's failure to create a vast Catholic empire, Europe settled down to a secular age that by and large avoided the religious strife of the previous era. All eighteenth-century rulers agreed that Europe ought to be governed by several large states. Yet this consensus did not mean that monarchs respected the balance of power. While rulers may not have tried to destroy other great states, they felt absolutely no hesitation to chip away at them when self-interest warranted. Each monarch realized that only by weakening one's neighbor could one strengthen oneself. Thus it was one of the ironic hallmarks of this "age of reason" that, while the century largely avoided the fanaticism and destruction of earlier and later centuries, there were at the same time few years in which at least two of the major states were not at war. Here was an age in which war was seen purely as a tool of diplomacy.[3]

The goal, then, of an eighteenth-century diplomat such as the Chevalier d'Eon was not strictly peacemaking. He was expected to act on behalf of the personal interest of the King, and the line between diplomacy and espionage was not very clear.

For almost a century France had been the leader in this game, and for a time, it made the rules—and broke them at will. France had greater resources than any of its neighbors: the largest population, the richest economy, and the most extensive military in Europe, and among the largest territories of any European state. These enormous riches had combined to make France's bid for total hegemony nearly successful during the long reign of Louis XIV (1643–1715). This sovereign represented the epitome of a successful king, and his palace built at Versailles became the emblem of French greatness throughout Europe. Even though Louis failed to crush Protestant Europe, he expanded France's borders eastward to include Alsace-Lorraine, and he created a band of satellite states in Central Europe.

In retrospect, the most important rival of France during the eighteenth century was England. In nearly every major war, from Louis XIV through Napoleon, France and England were enemies. But this view of a "superpower" rivalry is one that grew slowly during the century, and was not clearly evident until after the end of the Seven Years' War in 1763. For most of the century, France's attention was focused on finding ways to expand to the east, to Germany and Poland. During the regency for Louis XV (1715–1734), for example, the French cooperated with the British, and even signed agreements with them that helped to keep the peace in Europe. As for Louis XV, he was much more interested in eastern Europe and only reluctantly came to see the colonial rivalry with England as central to France's interests. A similar awareness can be seen in d'Eon himself, who began his political career in Saint Petersburg and ended it in London.[4]

It is often said that the trouble with absolute monarchy is that genius cannot be passed on to one's progeny. Louis XV was doomed to live in the shadow of his brilliant great-grandfather, the Sun King. But Louis XV's perceived mediocrity was not simply the result of comparisons with his illustrious predecessor. Rather, it was during the great-grandson's reign that the tide turned against France. At least on the military front, France lost much ground during this period, and the crisis that would eventually culminate in the French Revolution of 1789 evolved directly from the reign of Louis XV (1734–1774).

Louis XV was a complex man, whose shyness and reclusiveness led people to underestimate his intelligence and interest in politics. He often shunned the elaborate social life that noblemen had come to expect from a great king. Rather, he preferred to take his meals alone, or with a select group of friends. But he was not lazy. He worked constantly in the privacy of his own study on political affairs. He voraciously read reports from ambassadors around Europe, and spent the small hours of the night writing secret instructions to his ministers.

Because Louis XV spent his time with so few people, the aristocracy became obsessed with the issue of who those people were. And curiously, Louis felt more comfortable spending his time with women than with men. After 1738, when his relations with his Polish-born queen, Marie, ceased, he nearly always had a mistress for his bed. While he was probably no more promiscuous than other kings, his critics soon began to use his sexual behavior as a way to attack the entire regime, perhaps because of a fear that his favorite mistress played more than just a sexual role. Indeed, Mme de Pompadour became a shrewd political adviser who helped to shape French policy. By the time the Victorian writer Thomas Carlyle referred to the regime as a "harlotdom," the idea had already become a cliché.[5]

While Mme de Pompadour played a major political role, she had to compete with more traditional advisers. Among the most colorful during the reign of Louis XV, and of crucial importance to the Chevalier d'Eon, was Louis-François de Bourbon, Prince de Conti. First cousin of the King, Conti was among the wealthiest and most powerful princes in Europe. He owned over a thousand paintings, and his collection of four thousand rings and eight hundred snuffboxes was particularly renowned.[6] A devotee of the liberal arts, he protected Enlightenment authors from persecution. And he was also known for his good looks. "I could never accustom myself to his manner, nor get rid of the embarrassment with which his presence affected me," the charming Mme de Genlis wrote. "His face, person and manners were imposing; no man could say obliging things with more delicacy and grace."[7]

This talented man, head and shoulders above the other Princes of the Blood, harbored enormous political ambitions. Indeed, France would surely have been better off if he had been king himself. Yet just as Conti knew he could never be king of France, so Louis XV knew he had to find him an outlet for his unusual talents. Louis might manipulate his cousin to serve his own ends, but he also had to satisfy Conti's thirst for power.

Conti's abilities made him a genuine hero during the War of the Austrian Succession (1740–1748). In this typical Old Regime war, France's traditional allies—Prussia, Sweden, Spain, and the Ottoman Empire—ganged up on Austria, attempting to reduce its power as much as possible. Austria, for its part, won help from Britain and Russia, and a group of smaller states such as Piedmont. At first, Louis XV banned any Prince of the Blood from fighting on the front lines. But Conti directly violated this decree and went to the Italian front anyway. Soon Conti had maneuvered himself into a position where he demanded command of a regiment. He was given 30,000 troops and assigned to fight the Piedmontese in northwest Italy. He scored an impressive victory there at the Battle of Coni in 1744, a success that followed him his entire life. At the age of twenty-seven, Conti became the most popular nobleman in France.[8]

After the war, Conti often visited the King at Versailles, where they would shut themselves up in one of his private apartments and talk in secret for hours. By the early 1750s, these visits became so regular that they began to disturb the courtiers, who were naturally jealous of Conti's access.

The most jealous of all was Mme de Pompadour. From the beginning, she considered Conti a rival for influence over Louis. Here, after all, was a man completely outside her control, whose ties to the King were based not simply on noble reputation but, more essentially, on blood.

The discussions between Conti and the King focused on foreign policy. The recent war against Austria had resulted in a frustrating stalemate for France. Austria lost the valuable province of Silesia, but to Prussia, not France. And further to the east, Russia's support for Austria had paid off handsomely in that country's pretensions to great power status. The French had come away with little from this expensive war, and Louis could only look forward to a resumption of hostilities in the future.

Meanwhile, a group of Polish noblemen had approached Conti with the idea of his becoming the king of that war-torn country. Such an idea was not completely ridiculous. The Polish throne, wrote Frederick the Great, "is an object of trade like any other commodity on the public market."[9] For centuries the Polish monarch had been chosen by noblemen in periodic elections that were often fraught with violent campaigns between hostile factions. In 1697 Conti's grandfather François de Bourbon (1664–1709) was elected king after many bribes to Polish noblemen from Louis XIV. But when Conti's grandfather arrived in Poland, he found that Augustus II, Elector of Saxony, Poland's western neighbor, had already taken over the monarchy by force. François de Bourbon was obliged to return to France without the crown. There began a long period of Saxon control of the Polish monarchy.

Eighteenth-century Poland was clearly important real estate. It was a huge and wealthy country that included Lithuania, making it roughly twice the size of today's Poland. Outside of Austria and France, it was the largest country west of Russia. If a Bourbon ruled Poland, French hegemony in Europe would be assured for many decades.

Conti's candidacy had to be handled with great sensitivity. On the one hand, openly endorsing it would be disastrous for France. Louis's support of Conti would alienate even the King's own immediate family, including the Queen and the Dauphin.[10] But more important to French interests, open support for Conti would drive the Saxons straight into the arms of Austria, or even worse, Russia. A policy that supported Conti had the real danger of resulting not in France gaining Poland, but rather in France losing Poland to her enemies. The gamble hardly seemed worth it.

On the other hand, given the notorious instability of Polish politics and the talents of Conti, the plan had a fair chance of working. And it would solve the problem of what to do with Conti. The Polish crown was ideally suited to him: it would get him out of the King's hair and put him in a position to further French ambitions in eastern Europe. Conti tried to persuade Louis that this was the best chance he would have in his reign to influence the course of events in Poland.

After hours of secret discussions with Conti, Louis decided to have it both ways: He gave his approval for Conti to seek the Polish throne, and offered Conti certain crucial political and financial resources toward this goal. Yet at the same time, Louis maintained that this new policy had to remain absolutely secret, even from his own Foreign Minister, and certainly from the Versailles court. Officially, as far as the French Foreign Ministry was concerned, no change of policy had taken place.[11]

Therefore, from about 1750 on, France had two contradictory policies toward Poland: an official one that supported the Saxon throne and Polish independence, and an unofficial one that was committed to transforming Poland into a French satellite with a Bourbon king. The conduct of international relations was considered the King's personal business; no one in eighteenth-century France challenged his power to formulate foreign policy however he pleased. Thus what is so peculiar about the situation is to find two contradictory policies stemming from one supreme source: Louis XV.

In the short run, such behavior might allow Louis to keep his options to himself and avoid difficult decisions. But in the long run, a secret policy that was established to undermine the official one could only damage French prestige and the King's power.

The King's Secret

THE DECISION TO INITIATE a separate foreign policy under the Prince de Conti spawned a network of spies that by the end of Louis XV's reign numbered close to twenty, in various capitals throughout Europe. This system, known as the Secret du Roi (the King's Secret), was kept hidden not merely from courtiers and chroniclers, but from nearly all government officials as well. The moment Louis XV's grandson Louis XVI found out about the Secret upon taking the throne in 1774, he ordered an end to it. Only much later, when French Revolutionary activists discovered Louis XV's voluminous correspondence shelved in secret closets, did the public learn about this strange but very influential organization.[1]

Among the first men Conti brought into the Secret was d'Eon's future patron Charles-François, the Comte de Broglie. In effect, the King appointed Broglie to two positions in 1752: France's ambassador to Poland and spy for the Prince de Conti. The first was public and official, the second extremely clandestine. In both, Broglie was serving the interests of the King. Between the King and Broglie, however, were two separate supervisors: the Prince de Conti and the Foreign Minister, who knew nothing of the Prince's involvement. Which of these two superiors took precedence was made clear in a letter from the King to Broglie dated 12 March 1752: "The Comte de Broglie will put faith in whatsoever Prince de Conti shall say to him, and will not speak of it to a living soul."[2] He left no doubt that Broglie really worked for Conti and not for the Foreign Minister.

As a new ambassador, Broglie naturally received detailed instructions from the Foreign Ministry concerning his mission in Warsaw. The Foreign Minister told him to use every opportunity to oppose any alliance between Poland and Austria or Russia. The best way to avoid such an alliance, he insisted, was to preserve the independence of the Saxon dynasty. Thus the ambassador should promise to sustain the dynasty in all circumstances, and promise French support in any effort to defend its integrity.

Meanwhile, Broglie received a very different set of instructions from Conti, who wanted him to undermine the Saxons by encouraging a Francophile opposition. Conti and Broglie discussed how Broglie could carry out these orders without violating those of the Foreign Minister. They decided that Broglie should never ask the Foreign Minister for orders. When Broglie received orders that contradicted Conti's, Broglie should delay by requesting clarification. Nonetheless, Broglie recognized that he was walking a dangerous tightrope, with no safety net under him. "How can I take upon myself to speak to the Saxon Minister in the tone which Your Highness thinks I may assume," he once asked Conti, "without leave from the [Foreign] Minister, whose directions to me are exactly the contrary?"[3]

By establishing the King's Secret, Louis revealed a weakness in his personality that would eventually tarnish the Bourbon monarchy itself. For the Secret pitted one part of the government against another. Those who worked for the Secret could have nothing but contempt for the Foreign Ministry. And while such contempt might begin with one government department, there was no reason it should be limited to just that one. There was every reason for a spy in the Secret to think himself above the King's own government; to believe that the government's policies and laws did not pertain to him; to feel as if he had his own special relationship with the King. Such attitudes on the part of powerful noblemen holding state secrets could prove extremely dangerous to Louis XV and to French interests if the King ever lost control over the Secret.[4]

After all, under older men like Conti and Jean-Pierre Tercier, chief administrator in the Foreign Ministry, were younger noblemen who were getting their start in diplomatic life as spies in the Secret. What attitudes would they develop about traditional monarchical institutions? How would they react when Louis XVI shut down the Secret? Some, such as the Comte de Vergennes, made the transition quite easily from serving as Broglie's spy in Constantinople and Sweden to becoming Foreign Minister under Louis XVI. But others, such as the Chevalier d'Eon, who likewise began his diplomatic career as one of Conti's spies, did not fare nearly so well.

Conti and Russia

M AJOR CHANGES were taking place on the central stage of European diplomacy that would affect Conti and Louis's plans. Everyone expected a new war to break out at any moment, and the need for reliable allies became acute. In 1755, England was searching for a new protector of Hanover, the north German principality that was considered home to England's eighteenth-century kings. Since the recent war had exhausted its traditional ally Austria, England considered improving relations with Russia, which until this time had played only a marginal role in European affairs.[1]

No country had been traditionally more hostile to Russian political ambitions than France. By 1755, France had seen more than a decade of no diplomatic relations with Russia. But the French now had cause for concern. If Britain could win Russian support with hefty subsidies, the Russian army might use the pretext of a new war to invade Poland. Not merely Conti's plans but suddenly all of France's foreign policy in eastern Europe was in jeopardy. These factors led the French to reconsider their policy toward Russia. Besides, Empress Elizabeth I, who had ruled Russia since 1741, had long harbored pro-French sympathies. Rumors had circulated for years about her interest in opening up relations with France.

Among those impressed by such political gossip was the Prince de Conti, who wanted to exploit the new possibilities between France and Russia for himself. Elizabeth ruled over the semi-sovereign Duchy of Courland, which lay just to the northeast of Poland (in what is today Latvia). If a new war would soon break out, as all expected, Elizabeth would need a commander for the troops based in Courland. No one, Conti thought, would be more appropriate for the post than himself.

After a successful war, further French subsidies would induce Elizabeth to name him the Duke of Courland. From there he would be in a superb position to become a candidate for the neighboring throne of Poland, still his ultimate ambition.

During the spring of 1755, Conti won approval from Louis XV to send the Chevalier Alexander Douglas, a Scotch Catholic living in France since 1745, to Russia as a spy to determine how close the British were to signing their own treaty with Russia, and the extent to which a pro-French faction existed in the Russian court.[2]

The King and Conti instructed Douglas to make the trip as a Scottish "gentleman traveling solely for health and pleasure," gathering information on Russian troop positions, the financial status of the government, "Russia's designs on Poland at the present moment and in the future," and especially "of the Empress's attitude toward France." In addition, Conti told Douglas to stop in Courland to get a sense of the political situation there and of Conti's chances for assuming power.[3] Douglas left France in June and arrived in Saint Petersburg in the first days of October.

Douglas arrived too late. In Saint Petersburg he discovered that England's ambassador and Russian Chancellor Bestuzhev were very close to an agreement on Russian troop subsidies. Bestuzhev's program was not hard to surmise: By taking British gold, Russia would have enough money to garrison 30,000 troops on its western borders, ready for a war against Prussia and France. The commencement of hostilities would allow Russia to go on the offensive, attacking France's traditional allies: Sweden, Turkey, and, most important, Poland. It was a shrewd strategy, one well within the aims of Russian interests.

There was nothing Douglas could do but return home. French hopes seemed dashed until January 1756, when Prussian King Frederick the Great surprised all Europe by producing his own alliance with England. Clearly the British had decided that in the event of war, Prussia was in a better position to protect English interests on the continent and give France a hard time. Such developments put Franco-Russian relations back on track.

Upon hearing of the Anglo-Prussian treaty, Louis sent Douglas back to Russia. This time Douglas would work both for the Secret and as a chargé d'affaires for the Foreign Minister. As an official representative of the French government, his mission was to convince Empress Elizabeth how badly the British had betrayed the Russians, and urge that they retaliate by refusing to give England troops in the upcoming war. Likewise, as a spy for the Secret, Douglas was to exploit every possible opportunity to secure for Conti the command of Russian troops and the Duchy of Courland. The crisis in Anglo-Russian relations fueled Conti's ambitions to use these positions as a back-door route to the Polish crown.

Douglas's job was now much expanded. In 1755 he had been a spy who basically gathered information and used his influence to become familiar with powerful aristocrats. But now that he represented the French government, he was sought after by a variety of important people. He needed help. In June 1756, the French government sent Douglas a secretary: the Chevalier d'Eon.

In the twenty or so published biographies of d'Eon, no aspect of his life is more controversial than his first trip to Russia. From the eighteenth century on, it has become the source of legends that helped to make d'Eon a celebrity during his lifetime and well into the nineteenth century.[4] The myths about this trip to Russia must be distinguished from what actually occurred there. Perhaps the best place to start is with d'Eon's own autobiographical account of the journey.

D'Eon explained how badly Conti wanted the command of the Russian army and the Duchy of Courland in order to slide into the Polish throne. By the first weeks of 1756, the greatest obstacle seemed to be the mutual suspicion between Louis XV and Elizabeth. Thus through Douglas, Conti put forward the proposal that the two monarchs begin a personal secret correspondence that would break the ice between them.[5]

According to d'Eon's later memoirs, the Empress responded favorably to the idea of writing to the French King. But she was also a bit nervous about it. She informed Conti that she needed help with her French if such a correspondence was to be fruitful, and asked him to find her a young lady "neither too young, nor too old, [but] honest, well-informed, prudent, and discreet" to tutor her.[6] This noblewoman's duties would also include putting the letters into a secret diplomatic code that would ensure confidentiality. The Empress offered to pay handsomely for this young lady's voyage and stay in Russia.

In the Chevalier d'Eon, Conti found "the only person" who seemed to combine such a range of talents. Because d'Eon was connected to the Prince's salon, he could be trusted; d'Eon had supreme gifts as a courtier and had already proved himself as an author; and most interesting, d'Eon insists in his autobiographical account that Conti believed d'Eon had been born a girl but had been forced by his parents to assume the identity of a boy. If d'Eon would agree to reassume his female identity, he would be the ideal person for the job!

The Prince went for approval to the King, who told him that he liked the plan, as long as Conti could persuade d'Eon to take on the persona of a young lady. "Leave that to me," the Prince replied. "I will do with her exactly what I wish."[7] Conti added that it would not be an insurmountable problem, since d'Eon had been born a girl and had only become a boy because his parents had forced him to. The King agreed, telling Conti that French interests in Russia depended on d'Eon playing the role of Elizabeth's tutor.

The next morning Conti's secretary, Nicolas Monin, led d'Eon into the Prince's bedroom for a private interview. Conti was still in bed, stretched out like a "grand sultan." He invited d'Eon to sit at the end of the bed. Years later d'Eon recalled the conversation as follows:[8]

"Mon petit d'Eon," Conti began, "I have some news to give you that may upset you for some time, but which should eventually console you. I want you to retake your skirts in the service of a great foreign princess who is rich and powerful and who is aware of your talents and how much I love you and admire you, and how much I look after your happiness and your interests. She wants you for her tutor and private secretary. She will treat you well and will pay you handsomely. In any case, you will render services for me and even for the King for which you will be amply compensated. But in order to do that, it is absolutely necessary for you to put on women's clothes and the habits of a maiden. You may write to your mother that I am going to send you on a voyage in a foreign European court to carry out an honorable mission of the King."

D'Eon's first reaction was stunned silence.[9] Finally, he mustered enough courage to respond directly to the Prince:

"My lord, I cannot cry enough tears that would express to you what a cruel sacrifice it will be for me to leave a protector such as yourself, to abandon my mother and Paris and my male clothes to which I am so attached. If I believed that you had been planning to one day have me retake women's clothes, I would not have devoted my studies to horsemanship or fencing. The more this Princess orders me to do what you say will be good for me, the smaller will become my liberty."

"D'Eon," the Prince replied, "this is not about liberty; it concerns your fortune, your usefulness, and your rendering services to the King and to your country. These three things will always assure your happiness. I am in a better position than you to judge. Besides, this is what the King wants, and I want it too. That should be enough for you to obey in secrecy and in silence, unless you want to finish your days in a convent."

"My lord," d'Eon pleaded, "the more I please your great Princess, the more she will want me to stay with her, and the more likely I will lose you forever and ever and remain a maiden."

"If you render such services for the King and me, certainly you will not be forgotten," the Prince promised. "And if you remain a maiden, so much the better for you: you would become rich and happy. But if you keep the clothes of a young man, and if you go to war as you wish, you could be discovered by getting wounded or by a thousand different accidents, then with bad luck you would be in a state of confusion with regard to your sex, and despite your wishes, you would be forced to retake your dresses. Everything that I have planned for you, and everything that I wish for you, is for your own good. You will drop the name of d'Eon and you will take that of Mademoiselle Auguste, which is one of your Christian names."

"My lord,"[10] d'Eon replied, "I will always submit myself to your orders and to those of the King, since I have nothing to lose and everything to gain."

"When you have put on women's clothes, as Auguste, you will not have the fears that plagued you in the clothes of a young man; you will be like a fish in water," Conti assured him.

"My lord, it is certain that for a maiden a dress is more convenient than a suit and pants. But don't forget that a maiden's conduct must always be more constrained, discreet, and modest. Don't forget that she learns nothing more than a few words of Greek and Latin. Her course of studies and exercises, like her ambition, will be sacrificed by her transformation."

"But you should not forget that pleasing the King, the Prince de Conti, and the Empress of Russia will make your fortune and your glory," the Prince reiterated.

"These are powerful and compelling truths," d'Eon admitted. "If the service to my Prince is natural, the service to a foreign princess is [uncanny] and merits double compensation."

"That is true," Conti agreed. "But already the King assures you compensation from his private funds. . . . And the Empress Elizabeth will add to that."

"My lord, that would be fine, but I am in constant fear that some secret dispatch of your Chevalier du Nord [Douglas] or some private note of Vice-Chancellor Count Woronzow will be discovered and reverse the fragile edifice of my existence like some weathercock on the tower of Notre-Dame de Paris."

Conti reminded d'Eon that such reversals were an inevitable part of any Old Regime diplomacy, which typically depended on court intrigues. Any diplomat was constantly in danger of being outmaneuvered, and had therefore to rely as much on luck as anything else. Diplomacy was not something rational or philosophical, but rather, according to the Prince, a "fickle whore that changes with each change of a minister."

"I will keep silent," d'Eon pledged. "Providence rules according to her will. Her lofty wisdom is not of this world. Man must obey, woman must submit, and maidens should do everything justly and honestly without seeing or saying anything."

"If you do that, everything will go well for the King, the Prince, and Auguste," the Prince predicted. "That considered, I warn you not to wear male suits, vests, pants, boots, or spurs, since your dress has already been made. . . . Your sex is a barrier that you will never easily overcome. It exposes you to great fears, to infinite dangers, to inspections, and to much stress that you force upon yourself. . . . I believe that if you abandon your female dress, you will be abandoning your happiness. We could say much more about this subject, but it is enough that you realize what is in your best interest. You will recognize your errors when you have the proper experience, when you are older. I see that you are dying with envy to wear male clothes. This is something that must be seriously discussed. I will tell you what the King thinks in this regard."

"My lord, sometimes circumstances don't work for me, they serve me quite badly," d'Eon confessed. "Politics is my destiny, and my destiny is my nature. I am like a completely paralyzed being, reacting to events as they come; nothing surprises me."

The Prince ordered d'Eon to remain in Paris at the home of his secretary Nicolas Monin. There Monin would teach d'Eon how to decipher diplomatic codes so that the correspondence between the King and the Empress would be kept strictly secret. At the same time, a Mme Maille, perhaps a relative of Monin's, would give d'Eon lessons in ladylike fashions and etiquette to prepare him for his female role. This apprenticeship was apparently quite successful. Mme Maille told Conti that she could not imagine a better student.[11] And from d'Eon's viewpoint, he developed a new appreciation for his femininity. "I discovered in the weakness of my sex," he writes of this period, "a new strength that resuscitated me to a new natural state and allowed me to pass from darkness to enlightenment."[12]

Having reconciled himself to his mission, d'Eon departed for Russia in June 1756 with only two large footlockers, "one containing men's clothes, the other the wardrobe of a woman."[13] When he arrived in Russia in August, he apparently lived out of both trunks. In his male garb, he was the secretary to the Chevalier Douglas, an employee of the French Foreign Minister. When he assumed his female dress, he became the tutor and confidante of Elizabeth, facilitating her correspondence with Louis XV. He thus supposedly lived a double life, as spy and diplomat, as man and woman.

Myths aside, the correspondence between Louis XV and Elizabeth actually did bring the two states closer together. By 1757, Russia and France had reestablished diplomatic relations, and in 1758 signed a military treaty. The two states were allies during the Seven Years' War and went through a short period of unprecedented cooperation. The Chevalier d'Eon laid the groundwork for this crucial rapprochement.

D'Eon's first trip to Russia was thus a diplomatic success. But how did he feel about his cross-dressing experiences? No one was more curious about this than his partner in diplomacy, the Chevalier Douglas, who, according to d'Eon's version, was the only one in Russia who knew d'Eon's secret. One day Douglas asked d'Eon which wardrobe he preferred. D'Eon told him that this really wasn't such a difficult question. "I would prefer to keep my male clothes," he told Douglas, "because they open all the doors to fortune, glory, and courage. Dresses close all those doors for me. Dresses only give me room to cry about the misery and servitude of women, and you know that I am crazy about liberty. But nature has come to oppose me, and to make me feel the need for women's clothes, so that I can sleep, eat, and study in peace. I am constantly in fear of some sickness or accident that will, despite myself, allow my sex to be discovered. . . . Nature makes a good friend but a bad enemy. If you chase it through the door, it just blows back in through the window.

"On the one hand," d'Eon continued to Douglas, "my goal is to succeed in a diplomatic career so that I can help my mother and sister by paying off debts that my father incurred before his death. Without male clothes, how can I perform such a noble project? But on the other hand, my love for studying, my desire to finish books that I have started and many other projects push me to take dresses for working, living, and sleeping peacefully. Here are the two passions of my heart. The one moves me to the right, the other to the left. I do not know how to escape from this Cretan labyrinth."[14]

The Russian Myth Reexamined

T HERE IS NO DOUBT, of course, that this mission to Russia was the turning point in d'Eon's career as a statesman. But ever since the stories about his cross-dressing escapades in the court of the Empress Elizabeth first circulated at the end of the 1770s and early 1780s, they became the stuff of legend, transforming him into a kind of hero. Even today, many scholars and biographers accept his memoirs as factual, and marvel at how "disguised as a woman, d'Eon became the intimate friend of the Empress Elizabeth, whom he persuaded to make a secret alliance with France."[1]

Nevertheless, the story about d'Eon dressing as a woman to become the tutor of the Empress Elizabeth is not at all true. He made it up, probably in 1775 or shortly thereafter.[2] Scholars first got wind of the truth over a hundred years ago, when the French Foreign Ministry archives were opened to the public. Surely if this deception had taken place, it would be mentioned in the secret correspondence among Louis XV, Conti, their assistants, and d'Eon. While there is some discussion of d'Eon's work for the King's Secret in Russia, we find no mention whatsoever of d'Eon's cross-dressing, gender identity, or personal relationship to Elizabeth.

Why would d'Eon invent such a story? As we have seen, Louis XVI was determined to force d'Eon out of public life. The King and the court viewed d'Eon's 1777 transformation from man to woman, and his subsequent return to France, as his definitive retirement from statesmanship. From Vergennes's viewpoint, this was the entire reason they had entered into a formal contract with d'Eon in the first place. Thus the government explicitly linked d'Eon's sex to his ability to remain active in politics.

D'Eon, however, disputed this equation. After his return to France in 1777, he did not think that his newly won official status as a woman necessarily meant the end of his political career. In that sense, his refusal to give up his Dragoon uniform was not merely histrionics, but was a symbolic struggle over his right to continue his political and even his military career.[3]

D'Eon's tale about the Empress Elizabeth must be understood within this context. During his stay in France between 1777 and 1785, he was repeatedly compelled to argue that women could and did make important contributions in public affairs. Women, he insisted, could be more than courtiers, nuns, and salonnières. Some of them might even become soldiers and statesmen, if given half a chance. The myth about the Empress Elizabeth greatly facilitated this goal insofar as it presented the French sovereign and his closest adviser giving just such an opportunity to a woman. According to the myth, Louis XV and Conti had asked d'Eon to go to Russia knowing that d'Eon was a woman. Furthermore, they needed d'Eon to perform sensitive diplomatic assignments as a woman. In d'Eon, Conti supposedly had found a personality who combined the feminine charm, Amazonian courage, and Machiavellian ingenuity necessary for such a significant assignment. In short, the myth about d'Eon in Russia seemed to offer France a very strong example of a contemporary woman who had achieved heroism as a statesman.

Thus d'Eon hoped to use the Russian myth to affirm his patriotism and to undermine the gender exclusivity of the diplomatic and military officer corps. That d'Eon's story was so easily believed during his lifetime is itself remarkable. Casanova was typical of the many well-connected noblemen who were convinced that d'Eon had earlier performed secret diplomatic missions as a woman, and that Louis XV himself had sponsored such transvestism.[4] As absurd as it may sound to us today, the story made sense to a European public which not only saw international relations increasingly dominated by female rulers but also had heard all kinds of strange stories and rumors regarding spies, intrigues, and double-crossings. Indeed, the very existence of the King's Secret is in its way no less absurd than the story d'Eon eventually fabricated.

D'Eon may not have become a female tutor to the Empress Elizabeth, but he was initiated into Conti's Secret and did become the secretary to the Chevalier Douglas. He indeed arrived in Saint Petersburg some time during July 1756.[5] He was immediately struck by the power and charm of the Russian women who surrounded the court. He found them beautiful, shrewd, tough, and smart. These "brilliant" ladies, d'Eon wrote to Jean-Pierre Tercier, chief administrator in the Foreign Ministry and also a spy for Conti, "are really like a small squad of nymphs."[6] Elizabeth chose them herself, and was their inspiration and leader.

The court of the Empress Elizabeth was among the most lavish in Europe. She owned perhaps as many as 15,000 dresses and changed clothes several times a day.[7] In her younger years she was known as a gorgeous woman, with an attractive figure and beautiful face. Such features did not go to waste. Although Elizabeth went through periods of religious devotion, her morals were more often rather lax, and she was rarely without a lover, and sometimes had more than one. Those around her sought to imitate her behavior, and by 1750 her court had a reputation for debauchery.

Elizabeth chose her lovers carefully, apparently on the basis of physical attraction rather than political considerations. Thus her most favored one was Aleksei Razumovskii, a handsome Ukrainian of peasant stock who came to the Empress's attention while singing in the court choir. Her paramour for several years, he eventually rose to the rank of count in 1744 and then was named General Field Marshal, though this latter title was purely honorary.[8]

Of course, this mixture of sex and politics could not have been too surprising to a Frenchman from the court of Louis XV. In both courts, sexual promiscuity was often associated with political ambition and intrigue. We have already seen, for example, the influence wielded by Louis XV's mistress Mme de Pompadour. What was different in the Russian court was the role reversal: a woman was the ruler, choosing a man to be her lover and giving him political rank and power.

During the eighteenth century, Russia was dominated by female monarchs. Between the death of Peter the Great in 1725 and the end of the century, Russia was ruled by empresses for all but four years. Nor were these women mere figureheads. In the brutish political culture of early modern Russia, they had to be ruthless as well as charming. Nowhere is this more clearly seen than in the case of Elizabeth's successor, Catherine the Great (1762–1796), who murdered her husband in order to gain the throne.

D'Eon's fascination with the women of Elizabeth's court was due, then, to their power, not merely their fine looks. But they themselves were highly conscious of their status as women political figures, and developed odd social rituals that reinforced female authority. "Every Tuesday there was a sort of masquerade at Court," Catherine relates in her memoirs about Elizabeth's reign. These balls, clearly the high point of the court's elaborate social life, were restricted to those aristocrats who had personal invitations from the Empress; the guests rarely numbered more than 200. Given Elizabeth's fascination with everything French, d'Eon probably attended these masquerade balls when he resided at the court in 1756 and 1757. At the very least, he would have heard much about them.

And what he would have heard, if not seen, would have been most intriguing. For Catherine tells us that the Empress Elizabeth ordered all the men "to be dressed as women and all the women as men. . . . The men wore whalebone petticoats, the women the Court costume of men." Cross-dressing on a regular basis like this reinforced the fact that women controlled the court.[9]

Masquerade balls were in vogue throughout Europe, and it was not uncommon at these events for men to dress as women and vice versa. But for the monarch to decree that every participant cross-dress was unprecedented. Moreover, according to Catherine, the Empress also ordered every guest to appear without a mask, a practice that was completely different from other masquerades, where aristocrats of both sexes wore masks until the end of the evening. By eliminating the masks, Elizabeth was significantly altering the meaning of the masquerade. Ordinarily, a person who came to such a party posed as someone (s)he was not. The implicit deceit made the evening fun and exciting, as guests played at guessing one another's true identities. By making men and women cross-dress without masks, Elizabeth put everyone in a kind of ambivalent status. Noblemen would masquerade as a female version of themselves: they might cross-dress, but their identity was never in question.

Let us suppose for a moment that the Chevalier d'Eon did go to one of these balls. He would have dressed up as a female, but everyone would have known that it was d'Eon. When d'Eon conversed with others, it would not have been as someone else, but as a female version of the Chevalier d'Eon, as, in other words, the Chevalière d'Eon. D'Eon would not have to pose as someone else, but rather, his original self would now be regarded by others as female. In such a situation, both identity and sexuality were constant, but gender was isolated, deconstructed, and reconfigured.

The extent to which gender lines were blurred here becomes especially clear when we look at the behavior of the Empress Elizabeth herself. Catherine recalled: "The only woman who looked really well and completely a man was the Empress herself. As she was tall and powerful, male attire suited her. She had the handsomest leg I have ever seen on any man and her feet were admirably proportioned. She dressed to perfection and everything she did had the same special grace whether she dressed as a man or a woman. One felt inclined to look at her and turn away with regret because nothing could replace her." For Catherine, Elizabeth seemed to represent a kind of cultural hermaphrodite, combining the best features of manhood and womanhood.

"At one of those balls, I watched her dance a minuet; after it was over she came up to me," wrote Catherine, who was then a girl of fifteen. "I took the liberty of telling her that it was lucky for all women that she was not a man, for even a mere portrait made of her in that attire could turn the head of any woman. This compliment was expressed in full sincerity and she accepted it with grace, replying in the same tone and in the sweetest manner, that had she been a man, it would have been to me that she would have given the apple."

Catherine also recalled that many of the noblemen resented these balls, and even she grew tired of them. Nonetheless, Catherine did not do away with them completely after she became empress in 1762. She continued to hold many masquerade balls, but unlike those during Elizabeth's reign, Catherine's were conventional masked affairs where participants posed as other people. Catherine herself derived much pleasure from dressing as a man and keeping her true identity a secret.[10]

The context of masquerade balls puts d'Eon's Russian story about cross-dressing in an entirely new light. D'Eon was not simply making up a fantasy out of thin air. He was playing on a particular refrain that was well known during his lifetime. Contemporaries and nineteenth-century readers were willing to believe d'Eon's story in part because it fit with what they knew about Elizabeth's reign. D'Eon was reconstructing facts into a new form, but the gist of his account was not so far from the truth: D'Eon was present at the court of Elizabeth; he no doubt participated in these cross-dressing soirées and others; and he did become the conduit between Elizabeth and Louis XV.

Diplomacy in Russia

IN SEPTEMBER 1756, Prussia's Frederick the Great invaded Saxony, beginning the Seven Years' War. Within weeks, an unprecedented alliance led by France, Austria, and Russia was ready to attack Prussia and its main supporter, England. France's strategy from the outset was to convince Russia and Austria to do most of the continental fighting, so it could devote its resources to routing the British in the Atlantic. The French were hoping for a quick, decisive victory against Prussia. In this respect, as with everything else about this war, the French were to be bitterly disappointed.

The war brought new pressures and new opportunities for the King's Secret. D'Eon and Douglas were in Russia to further French influence and, specifically, acquire the command of Russian troops massing in Courland for the Prince de Conti. If France had shunned Russia in the past, it badly needed the country's cooperation now. Russia's commitment to the war against Prussia would free France to focus on England. To an extent, d'Eon and Douglas relied on the old-fashioned but effective approach of every successful diplomat: bribery. Not only did France offer the Empress Elizabeth subsidies for Russian military participation, the Chevalier d'Eon greased the skids in more personal ways: He ordered French wine for influential aristocrats, such as the Vice-Chancellor Count Woronzow. In 1758 he provided Woronzow with 1,900 bottles of excellent Burgundy from his hometown vineyards. All told, d'Eon got the Secret to pay more than 3,000 livres for wine alone during his trips to Russia.[1]

In November 1757, Elizabeth finally signed on to the agreement concluded the previous March among France, Austria, and Sweden against

Prussia. D'Eon rushed with the treaty back to France, forcing his stage-coach to travel at such speeds that he suffered a broken leg during an accident. But that apparently did not stop him, and he won high marks for continuing on to Paris despite his injury. When he arrived in Paris, he also brought news that Elizabeth was apparently sympathetic to the notion of having Conti lead the Russian forces in Courland.

But just at this important watershed, the Secret confronted a new problem: the strained relationship between Conti and the King. At the start of the war, the three Princes of the Blood were energetically seeking the command of the French army that would soon invade Prussia. Of them Conti was clearly the most qualified, having distinguished himself with such bravery at Coni during the recent War of the Austrian Succession. And given the close relations between Louis and Conti, there was every expectation that the latter would be chosen. But because the King's mistress, Mme de Pompadour, had been jealous of Conti for many years, she persuaded the King to reject his appointment.[2]

"I will never go out of my way for him," the King told the Foreign Ministry's Tercier. A year later, when it seemed that Elizabeth would finally name Conti commander of her army in Courland, Louis XV threw cold water on the idea, announcing that "the whole thing repels me a good deal."[3]

Recently, the historian John Woodbridge has advanced another theory about why the King broke off relations with Conti at this critical juncture. Woodbridge's thorough research makes clear that for many months Conti had been seriously considering taking over the French crown himself through a coup d'état supported by disgruntled nobles, French Protestants, and English soldiers. Once royal spies informed Louis of the rebellious scheme, he became determined to counter all of Conti's political ambitions.[4]

At the end of 1756, Louis recalled the Comte de Broglie to Versailles from Warsaw. One would have expected him to tell Broglie the King's Secret was being shut down. After all, what was the Secret without Conti? The Secret had been created for his benefit, and besides, its internal policy struggles (pro-Poland, pro-Russia) made sense only as alternative outlets for Conti's ambitions. Hidden from the Foreign Ministry, the Secret was a constant danger. It undermined the government's authority, was a potential source of embarrassment if word ever leaked out, and was a constant drain on the crown's finances.

But Louis did not end the Secret. He simply reorganized it, putting Broglie in command. Thus in 1757 Broglie returned to his post in Warsaw as head of the Secret. Without Conti, the organization was pointless; indeed, its principled support of an independent Poland might have the effect of undermining France's newly forged alliances with Austria and Russia. Moreover, Broglie had learned that the Secret was stridently blocked at every turn by Pompadour, who had championed France's rapprochement with Austria. How much she knew about Louis's network of spies is still not clear to this day, but she made it apparent that Conti's protegés would not get far.

Consequently, the Secret drifted for the next three years, its spies bickering among themselves. Meanwhile, d'Eon had a front-row seat from which to view this less-than-noble side of Louis XV's monarchy. These experiences formed his apprenticeship in statecraft. But what was he supposed to learn from it? On the one hand, d'Eon held an official position as secretary to the head of the French delegation, a job he apparently performed with much success. In 1757, official relations between France and Russia were finally restored and ambassadors were exchanged. During that summer the Marquis de l'Hôpital became France's ambassador to Saint Petersburg. Douglas returned to France, but Foreign Minister François-Joachim de Pierre de Bernis kept d'Eon on as l'Hôpital's secretary.

D'Eon also worked for the Comte de Broglie, who as head of the Secret issued orders that often contradicted those of Bernis. Within weeks of his arrival in Saint Petersburg, l'Hôpital was besieged with letters from Broglie telling him precisely how to deal with the Russian court. As France's ambassador to Warsaw, Broglie ordered l'Hôpital not to do anything that might endanger Poland. L'Hôpital took offense at both the tone and the substance of Broglie's letters, and a feud developed between them. D'Eon found himself in the middle of it, but successfully protected his turf. Faithful to l'Hôpital, d'Eon became a popular figure in the Russian court. But he also entered into a secret correspondence with Broglie, supplying him with complete details of l'Hôpital's every move. Increasingly, d'Eon came to view Broglie as his major ally and most important patron.

"Broglie acts more like a foreign minister with me than a fellow ambassador," l'Hôpital complained to the real Foreign Minister, Bernis. He begged the Foreign Ministry to get rid of him. L'Hôpital even convinced the Russian government to issue a formal protest against Broglie in November 1757.[5] But Broglie insisted to Bernis and to l'Hôpital that he was merely trying to protect Polish independence. If Russia had no designs on Poland, why should they be offended by his warnings? Broglie further defended himself in secret to Louis XV: "Come to my aid and let me know your will," he begged the King. "This secret project of five years is not mine in concept. I pursue it because you have wished it." Louis told Broglie to just continue as usual.[6]

This complex situation increasingly bothered Bernis, who of course was completely ignorant that Broglie was acting on the direct orders of the King. Finally, on 1 February 1758, Bernis ordered Broglie recalled to Versailles. Amazingly, Broglie refused the order, and quickly wrote to the King that only he could issue such an order. This put the King in a difficult position, having to choose between the Secret and the Foreign Ministry. Louis sided with Bernis, and Broglie was dismissed from his post in Warsaw. Nonetheless, Louis kept Broglie at Versailles as head of the Secret, and welcomed his lengthy and insightful diplomatic analyses.

Pompadour's grip on foreign affairs tightened during 1758. "She played the role of prime minister," d'Eon later wrote, "and controlled the Foreign Ministry" to such an extent that he held her responsible for the controversial new alliance with Austria, "this surprising revolution in the French political system." One concrete manifestation of her hegemony was the appointment of her protegé, the Duc de Choiseul, as Foreign Minister. "Under the appearance of frivolity," d'Eon recalled about this important statesman whom he grew to despise, "there was a profound genius."[7]

Choiseul probably knew nothing of the Secret, but he was determined to reduce the influence of Conti protegés.[8] In 1759 he scored mightily when Jean-Pierre Tercier, the highest-ranking member of the Secret stationed in Paris, was dismissed from his important and sensitive post as chief administrator in the Foreign Ministry. Tercier had also been the censor responsible for approving Helvétius's scandalous book, *De l'esprit*, an irreligious tract that became one of the classics of the Enlightenment. When the Church reacted sharply to the government's approval of the book, Choiseul conveniently used the scandal as a pretext to dismiss Tercier. But as with Broglie, the King kept Tercier on board as secretary of the Secret, and in that role he continued to coordinate activities and write instructions to those spies, like d'Eon, who remained active in the field.[9]

Unlike Conti, Broglie, and Tercier, whose careers were all sabotaged by the Pompadour–Choiseul faction, d'Eon seems to have successfully exploited his dual role as ambassadorial secretary and secret agent. Although he never lived as a female tutor to the Empress Elizabeth, he was personally responsible for facilitating the secret correspondence between her and Louis XV. As he recalled to the Comte de Vergennes many years later, in 1757 he became the mail courier between the two monarchs, bravely traveling on horseback the long distance between Saint Petersburg and Versailles. The letters were kept in a secret compartment in an altered copy of Montesquieu's *Spirit of the Laws.* D'Eon performed so well that Elizabeth even offered him a post and pension if he would stay on permanently in Russia, an offer he politely rejected. So secretive was this correspondence that d'Eon later claimed even Ambassador l'Hôpital knew nothing about it.[10] Within a short time, both the Secret and the Foreign Ministry recognized d'Eon as an expert in Russian politics. When Elizabeth died in 1762, Broglie and Louis XV immediately turned to d'Eon for an analysis of the political situation there.[11]

D'Eon's success in the Secret is easier to grasp than his feelings about it. Those he kept to himself. On the one hand, the Secret certainly served his career well. It gave him access to great power and privilege; it brought him closer to major French politicians, such as the Comte de Broglie, the Prince de Conti, and the King himself. And it allowed him to cut an international figure as a diplomat in a foreign court. In short, it marked a very successful debut for a young nobleman entering the diplomatic service.

But the Secret itself was a terrible failure, exposing to d'Eon both the impotence and the despotism of Louis's troubled reign. After all, none of its goals were realized during this period. If the Secret was initiated to further Conti's ambition, it had clearly failed there: Conti spent the 1760s and 1770s irritating Louis XV with insubordination. If the Secret was to transform Poland into a French satellite, it backfired miserably: By the end of the 1760s, it was not Louis XV but Russia's new enlightened despot, Catherine the Great, who determined the fate of Poland. Indeed, within a few years Poland itself would be carved up among Russia, Austria, and Prussia. No Bourbon king would ever have any influence over that part of Europe again. Thus the diplomacy practiced by Conti's group of spies had disastrous results.

Moreover, the Secret revealed contradictions in the monarchy itself. Under Louis XV, d'Eon wrote near the end of his life, "everything regarding foreign affairs was performed in such a bizarre fashion."[12] When Broglie refused to take orders from Foreign Minister Bernis, he in effect had rebelled against the King's own government. Clearly, the Secret encouraged cynicism among its spies toward the government, an attitude that was dangerous both for the monarchy and, more personally, for Louis XV. Indeed, the Secret may have contributed to Conti's sense that the monarchy was in crisis and that a coup could succeed.[13]

The deceit that lay at the core of the Secret—indeed, at the center of the monarchy—made everyone mistrust everyone else. Diplomats were routinely asked to sidestep the usual channels and relate directly to the King or to one of his specially chosen delegates. And yet, for all its

Machiavellianism, the Secret had little to show for it. Thus the King's Secret seems to epitomize the political problems of the entire reign of Louis XV. One contemporary French journalist, writing in the free atmosphere of London, summed up what many Frenchmen thought but could not say: "France has schools for all the sciences, except that of administration."[14]

Dragoon Captain

WITH THE SEVEN YEARS' WAR, d'Eon saw that his career could now best advance by joining the army, since noblemen traditionally used military glory to procure future office and pensions. The King appointed d'Eon assistant to the Comte de Broglie, his former superior in the Secret, who himself was the aide to his brother, the Maréchal de Broglie, co-commander of the Army of the Rhine. Louis also commissioned d'Eon at the prestigious rank of captain into the Dragoons, an elite brigade of the army.[1]

When d'Eon reached the front lines during the summer of 1762, the Seven Years' War had nearly exhausted itself. Showing himself to be a supreme military strategist and courageous statesman, Frederick the Great of Prussia had managed to survive six long years of brutal battles with all of his kingdom intact. Far from being cut down to size by a formidable alliance, Prussia would emerge from the war as one of the great powers of Europe.

The French had divided their army in Germany into two separate commands, one under the Maréchal de Broglie and the other under the Prince de Soubise. D'Eon arrived in time to witness the battle of Villingshausen (15–16 July 1761), in which France tried to retake this small but strategic village in Westphalia. The French outnumbered the Prussians both in troops and arms, but they bungled the operation. Somehow—military historians are still not quite sure how—the two commanders misunderstood each other. The result was a terrible defeat that forced the French to retreat: 757 French soldiers died, over 1,000 were wounded, and 1,143 were taken prisoner—almost 3,000 soldiers lost, more than double the number of Prussian casualties. In an age when honor was as much at stake as tactical advantage, Villingshausen was a deep blow to the morale of the French army.[2]

Immediately the recriminations began. In a long letter to the King, the Comte de Broglie blamed the entire affair on Soubise.[3] Nevertheless, the Broglies knew that the Duc de Choiseul, now War Minister, would never buy their story, no matter the truth. Someone had to be held accountable for the debacle, and that someone would certainly not be the Prince de Soubise. Handpicked by Pompadour, Soubise had been chosen over Conti at the start of the war, to the chagrin of the Broglies and d'Eon. For Soubise to admit blame for Villingshausen would have been an embarrassment for Choiseul and Pompadour. The Broglies' fates were pretty much sealed. The "Messieurs de Broglie have made some huge military mistakes," Choiseul wrote to his brother a few weeks later, instructing him that they were no longer "to be considered as our friends."[4] On this important issue, the King was not about to directly challenge his War Minister. The Broglies were permitted to keep their command for the duration of the campaign, but as soon as the war was over, they were dishonorably exiled to their estates in Normandy, where they spent two years under a sort of house arrest.

Amazingly, d'Eon escaped the fate that befell his patrons. Although he was the personal assistant to the Broglies, the war enhanced his own reputation, even with Choiseul. To be sure, d'Eon's wartime career was short: he fought in only one major campaign, and was back in Paris by November. Nonetheless, he had showed both courage and skill as a soldier, and was wounded in the head and thigh. Indeed, the praise lavished on d'Eon by the Broglies—"he has, upon several occasions, given proofs of the greatest intelligence and of the greatest valor"—was warmly received at court.[5] He dwelled on these heroic days for the rest of his life.

During the spring of 1762, the Foreign Ministry had begun to have second thoughts about its ambassador to Russia, the Baron de Breteuil. In December 1761 the Empress Elizabeth had died, and the new emperor, Peter III, was pulling Russia out of the war and realigning himself with Prussia. The French needed someone who could instantly make sense of the Russian political scene, someone who already had developed close personal contacts within the Russian court. In June, Louis decided to appoint d'Eon, and the choice met with approval from those in the Secret.[6] D'Eon began preparations to leave immediately, and he received a long set of diplomatic instructions from the Foreign Ministry. But suddenly, days before d'Eon was to depart, Versailles got word that Peter III had been assassinated and that Catherine, his wife, had taken power. King

Louis decided that the situation in Russia was now too unstable for a change in ambassadors.

The Foreign Ministry soon had other plans for d'Eon. By the summer of 1762, Choiseul had had enough of the naval war against England. French ships were bottled up in their own ports, while the English routed the French in Canada. Meanwhile, the French government debt had doubled during the war, to 2.3 billion livres.[7] Choiseul knew that he needed peace to rebuild the military and reestablish French finances. Thus he ordered the suave and princely Duc de Nivernais to lead a peace delegation, and Choiseul chose d'Eon to be Nivernais's secretary. On 19 August 1762, d'Eon agreed to join the negotiating team, and by 2 September he was off for England. As a special token of his appreciation, Louis gave d'Eon a gift of 3,000 livres before his departure. It would not be the last such gift.[8]

D'Eon's political career is curious because his personal successes came in the wake of colossal political failures. He got his start as an agent for the Secret, whose goal was to put Conti on the Polish throne and turn Poland into a French satellite. By late 1762, France couldn't have been further from this goal. Another aim of the Secret was to manipulate Russia for French interests. But again, even though d'Eon was praised by all in his efforts as a diplomat in Saint Petersburg, the larger picture that emerged was not a pretty one for France. As late as September 1762, Louis XV might boast that "the goal of my Russian policy is to distance Russia as much as possible from European affairs,"[9] but in what can only be described as a complete failure, the opposite took place. Along with Prussia, Russia was the great winner of the Seven Years' War. She acquired significant territory and influence along her western border and, like Prussia, achieved the status of great international power.

Nor can it be said that d'Eon rode the coattails of his patrons. However much patronage was necessary for advancement in Old Regime France, it is not clear that d'Eon's patrons in fact helped his career. The Prince de Conti had bitterly distanced himself from the monarchy. Tercier, who had controlled the Secret from the Foreign Ministry, had been ejected from that important and lucrative office. Meanwhile, the Broglies were forced out of the limelight altogether, exiled in shame to their country estates. If d'Eon succeeded in building an impressive career, it was due not to the generosity of his friends, but to the recognition of his talents by others, such as Choiseul, whom d'Eon himself distrusted. This attests to d'Eon's arsenal of personal charms and diplomatic skills. He was likable; he was dependable; he was enormously skillful as a diplomat; and perhaps most important, he was very intelligent.

By age thirty-four, d'Eon had done everything right while serving a king who had done just about everything wrong. Nowhere was this more apparent than in the war against England. The Atlantic struggle became a fiasco for France. Even though Choiseul recognized as early as 1758 that most of France's energies needed to be directed toward the western front, the kingdom simply did not have the economic and military resources to properly defend her overseas colonies from England, whose wealth and power had grown so dramatically. Louis XV did not enter peace negotiations in 1762 because he wanted to; he did it because he had to. Ironically, therefore, d'Eon's ascent to political power was concurrent with France's decline.

Making Peace

B
Y THE TIME the Duc de Nivernais and d'Eon arrived in England in September 1762 to negotiate a peace treaty, most of the diplomatic work was already done, and there were relatively few issues dividing the two hostile countries. The preliminaries of the treaty were negotiated in a matter of weeks, and signed by both parties on 3 November 1762. Then the treaty went to Parliament for approval. It sailed easily through the House of Lords, but in the House of Commons a vociferous anti-Bute party, led by William Pitt and including such shrewd oppositionists as John Wilkes, bitterly opposed the treaty. Pitt made a three-hour speech from the floor that harangued Prime Minister John Stuart, the Earl of Bute, for effectively selling out British trading interests. Pitt warned that the treaty allowed France to reestablish her power, and the result would be another war. But the British government, in typical eighteenth-century fashion, had done its homework: more than £25,000 were distributed among the members of Parliament to secure their votes, and the results turned out to be a lopsided 319 to 65. Sensing defeat, Pitt was so disgusted that he left the chamber before the vote was even taken. For Bute, the passage of the treaty was a huge political victory.[1]

Some issues were still unresolved which prevented the final version of the treaty from being signed, so that in January 1763, Nivernais and d'Eon worked long hours over tedious but crucial phrasing of certain clauses. The most important of these was the issue of Dunkirk, the port town on the French coast close to English soil. The British were determined to make sure that France could never launch an invasion from a port so close to England. They demanded that France destroy its entire harbor, making a French naval presence there effectively impossible.

Nivernais protested, but to no avail. On this issue the British would not budge, and Choiseul gave his reluctant assent for Nivernais to include the destruction of the harbor in the final version of the treaty.[2]

D'Eon and Nivernais worked together quite well, developing a useful patron–client relationship. The Duc de Nivernais had led an illustrious life as a diplomat, courtier, and man of letters. Handsome and charming, he was a welcome guest at any European court or salon, and was a friend of Mme de Pompadour. He had also served France in two very important diplomatic missions: At the end of the War of the Austrian Succession in 1748, he achieved great success in his negotiations in Rome with the Pope. Less successful, but just as important, Nivernais went to Berlin in 1756 to learn the precise details of King Frederick's new alliance with England.[3]

D'Eon admired the ease with which Nivernais was able to cut a figure among the English aristocrats. "Frankness and gaiety are the principal characteristics of this Minister," d'Eon remarked. "His naturally easy disposition and happy temperament, his sagacity and energy in great affairs, keep disquiet from his mind and wrinkles from his brow. He is little affected by hate or love; for on the one hand he is separated from his wife and does her no harm; on the other he has a mistress and does her little good. In short, he is certainly one of the gayest and most amiable of European Ministers."[4]

Likewise, Nivernais was impressed by d'Eon's talents and energy. "D'Eon is at work usually from morning to night. I cannot sufficiently extol his zeal, vigilance, amiability of disposition, and activity," he wrote to César-Gabriel, Duc de Praslin, the Foreign Minister. "He is very active, very discreet, never exhibiting curiosity or officiousness; never giving cause for mistrust or acting defiantly." And to d'Eon's mother, Nivernais wrote: "I love his personality, and I am impressed by his zeal."[5] Nivernais clearly displayed this admiration when he and Bute agreed to have d'Eon carry the final version of the signed treaty back to Paris in February 1763. Normally such an honor would have been reserved for someone at the level of an ambassador. That even the British would assent to this role for d'Eon is a tribute to his charm and diplomatic skills.[6]

Nivernais wanted d'Eon to be more than just a messenger. The ambassador enjoyed the sport of diplomacy, but he hated the gray humidity of the English climate. In his correspondence with Foreign Minister Praslin, his praise for d'Eon was offset by his complaints about his own health and temperament, which he attributed to the effects of the weather. He begged his superiors to let him come home as soon as possible, and suggested that d'Eon remain in London as France's official representative until a permanent ambassador could be chosen. That the government agreed to this proposal is yet another indication of d'Eon's glowing reputation. Clearly Praslin was very impressed with the work d'Eon was doing in London.[7]

Around the time the treaty was signed, the French government appointed a career military officer, the Comte de Guerchy, as ambassador to England to replace Nivernais. But Guerchy was not expected to start for several months. In the meantime, the government accepted Nivernais's resignation and appointed d'Eon "Plenipotentiary Minister," or acting ambassador. Although not a permanent position, it represented a promotion for d'Eon, placing him in the front row of European statesmen. D'Eon's mother was so filled with gratitude that she wrote to both Nivernais and Praslin thanking them "for all the favors and goodness that you have bestowed upon my son."[8] If only for a short time, d'Eon would be the official conduit between the two most powerful states in Europe.

Once again, then, d'Eon had put on a performance that impressed his superiors. And once again that performance belies the disastrous consequences that befell France. For though the Treaty of Paris may have finally brought an end to a long and terrible war, it spelled for France a humiliating defeat. Despite the celebrations in Paris that marked the end of the war, everyone who was intimately connected with French foreign affairs knew the treaty to be an unmitigated disaster. In his correspondence, Foreign Minister Praslin tried to put the best face on the treaty: "The peace is not good, but it is necessary, and I believe that in the present situation we shouldn't flatter ourselves by thinking that we could have done better." War Minister Choiseul was slightly more candid: "We know perfectly well that this peace will not be glorious nor useful for France . . . but unfortunately the circumstances don't allow us to obtain better conditions." The King agreed: "The peace that we have just signed is neither good nor glorious and no one feels that more deeply than I. But under these unhappy conditions, it could not be otherwise. . . . If we had continued the war for another year, we would have had to accept a worse one." Pompadour put the matter much more bluntly to Nivernais: "I believe that all is lost."[9]

Indeed, the Peace of Paris should be considered among the worst French defeats of early modern history. France had thought of herself as the greatest power in Europe, if not the world. Alliances might keep her from expanding, but no one state could take her on directly. Now the British had almost singlehandedly beat her at sea and destroyed her American empire. "The total exclusion of the French from Canada," one British statesman wrote, "gives Great Britain the universal empire of that extended coast." This was a shattering blow that would take Frenchmen many years to comprehend.[10]

A new kind of state—richer, freer, but seemingly more unstable and prone to public disagreements—had successfully beaten back an old-style absolute monarchy. This is certainly how large segments of the reading public saw the event, at any rate. "Till the peace of 1713, England had but small influence on the affairs of Europe," one Frenchman remarked in the London papers. "England is at present to Europe, what those Grecian Republics, against which the successors of Cyrus spent in vain their utmost efforts, were formerly to Asia." The result, according to this writer, was that "England has found the way to make the seeds of those virtues which were implanted in her to germinate. And from that moment she has seemed to command fortune. In France," on the other hand, "our manners have changed, and our glory has declined." During the age of Louis XIV, France had "inspired one half of Europe with confidence, and the other with terror." Now, while England had become a superpower, France was sinking further into decay.[11]

The Secret in England

T HE DEFEAT ITSELF would have been bad enough. But during
the negotiations the British did not treat their French adversaries
with the respect warranted by a great power; an "insultingly snob-
bish manner" was how d'Eon described it to the Comte de Broglie.
Broglie himself was smoldering in anger and bitterness.[1] Exiled on his
estate miles from anywhere, he kept up a remarkable correspondence with
the King in which he took stock of France's political situation with a
sobriety that reminds one of a Metternich or a Kissinger.

With the appointment of d'Eon as Plenipotentiary Minister, Broglie
realized that having one of the Secret's most talented spies in the ambassador's chair in London presented a golden opportunity. While a direct
attack on England had been impossible during wartime, Broglie thought
it just might succeed while France and England supposedly were at peace.
His idea was that France would place a spy, the thirty-year-old military
officer Louis-François de La Rozière, under the direction of d'Eon. He
would travel up and down the English coasts scouting possible landing
sites and taking note of where pockets of British troops were located.
D'Eon would analyze La Rozière's data, put it into secret diplomatic code,
and send it to Secret spies Tercier and Broglie. In this way, the preparation
for a French invasion of Britain could begin immediately, and the actual
assault on England's coast might take place in just two or three years.
"What we did in a small way in Poland," Broglie wrote of his ambitions
for the Secret, "I want to do in a big way" in England.[2]

Broglie's dangerous plans went even further. With his own man in
London, Louis XV could establish a foothold with the English parliamentary opposition in the House of Commons, bribing politicians and

influencing important votes, just like the British government itself did. "I want to influence the elections and firmly control a powerful party in Parliament," noted Broglie, who dreamed of "nourishing the germ of divisions that already exists there" to the point where the government might fear violence and even rebellion.[3]

Of course, none of these plans, much less anything about the Secret, was to be leaked to ministers Choiseul or Praslin, since the entire project undermined the peace they were making simultaneously with England. Even an unprincipled Machiavellian like Choiseul would never have approved a plan for a direct attack on England at the very moment a peace treaty was being signed by the two kings. Thus if Louis XV approved Broglie's plan, d'Eon would again be placed in the position of working for two separate supervisors: Foreign Minister Praslin and the Comte de Broglie.

On 17 March 1763, Louis XV gave his approval to Broglie's idea. As he later explained to a member of the Secret, France was obligated to challenge the "ambition and arrogance of the English nation."[4] For something this important, Broglie wanted the King's specific written orders, lest he (or one of his spies) later be accused of treason by Choiseul. That order he received on 7 April: "Monsieur the Comte de Broglie," began the King, "my intention is to perform reconnaissance on the English coasts and in the interior of that kingdom in order to facilitate the execution of projects that circumstances will make possible to execute one day soon, I hope. I approve the idea that you have communicated to Sieur Tercier to appoint at this moment a capable and intelligent agent to make all the necessary reconnaissance relative to this goal, which you will explain to him. Thus I am enclosing the order that authorizes Sieur de La Rozière for this work. I order you to maintain the strictest secrecy, and I depend upon all the loyalty that I know you have for my service and my person. I am admitting only Sieurs Durand, Tercier, and d'Eon in the secret, their cooperation in the project being necessary."[5]

Secret spy François-Michel Durand and Tercier informed d'Eon about the new project shortly after his arrival in Paris. This visit to France was also marked by a new honor for d'Eon: In an elaborate ceremony, he was awarded the rare Cross of Saint-Louis. Introduced during the reign of Louis XIV, the Cross was given directly by the Sun King only to those noble military officers who had performed acts of unusual heroism and bravery in war. The award had lost none of its value in the reign of Louis XV. It was unusual for the medal to go to one so young; d'Eon had just reached his thirty-fifth birthday. The Cross also raised him in noble rank:

from now on he would be known as the Chevalier d'Eon instead of the more common Sieur d'Eon.[6]

Of course, in d'Eon's case, even though he was a military officer and had distinguished himself in battle (by physical wounds, if nothing else), the medal was not really for his military services. Rather, it was the King's way of rewarding d'Eon's diplomatic service in Russia and England. In an age obsessed with honor, the Cross would open many doors for d'Eon. He had now become a gentleman whom no one could ignore.

D'Eon returned to England in April to begin his duties as Plenipotentiary Minister. Although Nivernais would not officially leave his post until the end of May, he turned over most affairs to d'Eon and spent several weeks traveling in the English countryside.[7]

In Paris, meanwhile, discussions among Secret members had focused on the strict security measures that had to be taken by d'Eon and La Rozière. The King noted that La Rozière should carry no papers with the King's signature on them because of the possibility of arrest. He instructed La Rozière to leave any secret papers with d'Eon. The concern about security for d'Eon was more complicated because of his double duties as spy and secretary for the new ambassador. As long as d'Eon was acting ambassador, he could play both roles with relative ease. But Broglie was concerned about the impending arrival of the new ambassador, the Comte de Guerchy. The invasion project must be kept from him just as if he were an English statesman. Broglie was worried that d'Eon would inevitably do something that would compromise himself. Every precaution had to be taken to prevent the new ambassador from discovering the project. For example, d'Eon's apartment, Broglie suggested, must be arranged in such a way that a surprise interruption from Guerchy would not pose a problem. He cautioned d'Eon to keep the papers for the secret project completely separate from his more official Foreign Ministry documents.[8]

Like Broglie, d'Eon wanted written orders for a mission of such sensitivity. On 3 June 1763, Broglie sent d'Eon a letter informing him that his orders from the King would arrive immediately: "You will easily understand why the role that you are going to play *will make your presence in England [so] necessary*." That same day in Versailles, the King composed the following handwritten and signed order:[9]

> The Sieur d'Eon will receive my orders through the channel of the Comte de Broglie or M. Tercier concerning the reconnaissances made in England, be it on the coasts, be it in the interior of the

country; and he will conform to everything that he is supposed to do in this regard as if I were directing him myself. My intention is that he keep this affair strictly secret and that he never mention anything of it to any living person, not even to my ministers.

He will receive a secret code for the special correspondence concerning this affair using the addresses provided to him by the Comte de Broglie or Sieur Tercier; and by this secret code, he will send them all the information he can procure on the aims England will pursue, with regard to Russia and Poland as much as in the North and throughout Germany, that he believes will serve my interests, for which I know him to be zealously devoted.

Never mind the Cross of Saint-Louis or the appointment as Plenipotentiary Minister: this brief note confirming his position was by far the most important honor d'Eon ever received in his political career. If privilege and power in Old Regime France resulted from one's relationship to the King, then this note reveals just how close d'Eon had come to France's political nerve center. The King had singled d'Eon out for a project of which only he and four others in the entire kingdom could have any knowledge. But the reason for the secrecy also provided d'Eon with much latent power: If such a secret ever leaked out, the position of the King's ministers, particularly Choiseul and Praslin, would be completely undermined. More important, if England ever discovered this project, the British might immediately invade France in order to finally destroy her navy along the western and southern coasts. One can hardly imagine a state secret more potent during the summer of 1763 than the one d'Eon had in his London safe.

Reversal of Fortune

IN THE SUMMER OF 1763, at the age of thirty-five, the Chevalier d'Eon had already achieved many "hopes of a good patriot." He had worked his way up the diplomatic ladder, attaining high-profile assignments in Russia and England; he had seen battle as a captain in the Dragoons; he had published two books and served as a royal censor; and he had won friends throughout the French political elite. And now, with his appointment as Plenipotentiary Minister to England, he had finally moved up to the premier stage of European diplomatic life. He was, in short, well on his way to becoming a major figure in the royal government, perhaps one day a minister of finance or foreign affairs.

Within three months, however, those dreams were shattered. By the autumn of 1763, d'Eon was considered by many in the French government to be an outlaw, and he actually had cause to fear for his life. Far from dreaming of some future ministerial post, he felt lucky just to survive. His political career had come to a complete and sudden end. For the next several years he would live in England, not so much a diplomat as an exile.

Explaining d'Eon's fall is not easy; nearly all the popular biographies become confused at this point in the story. What occurred during the summer of 1763 will always remain somewhat of a mystery. Indeed, in many ways d'Eon's political demise is even more of an enigma than his gender switch a decade later. Accounting for the first transformation may provide a key to the second, since d'Eon's gender metamorphosis can be traced at least partly to his failure in politics and his subsequent exile.

Certainly his political fall wasn't due to laziness. Without a family or other responsibilities, d'Eon was devoted to his work, thinking about little else from sunrise to midnight. Apart from directing La Rozière's movements for the Secret, the core of d'Eon's work consisted of negotiating issues linked to the Treaty of Paris. These mainly involved prisoner-of-war exchanges in Canada and the destruction of Dunkirk's harbor. The English had captured about 18,000 French soldiers during the war, and demanded compensation from the French for the food and lodging they had provided them. But discovering the precise number and identity of the prisoners, much less their condition, was difficult and tedious.[1]

As to Dunkirk, Choiseul wanted d'Eon to stall as long as possible. Although he had signed the treaty, Choiseul wanted to do everything short of war to avoid destroying this strategic naval harbor. D'Eon played this hand beautifully. He convinced his British counterparts that while Dunkirk's battlements might be destroyed, it was in Britain's own mercantile interests to save the town as a port. D'Eon arranged for London merchants to lobby their politicians with the argument that the destruction of Dunkirk would severely harm English trade with France.[2]

D'Eon was more than a negotiator; he also considered himself an intellectual and writer, and his cogent and informative analyses of international affairs were much appreciated back home. One dispatch, for example, included a twenty-five-page treatise on trade between England and France.[3]

Just as important was d'Eon's ability to gather specific and concrete information about the British political scene to relay to Choiseul and Broglie. In an era when the most important political news was held, even in England, in private hands, and discussed in elite social circles far away from the press, a diplomat had to have the right connections. The French government certainly recognized this fact, and encouraged its diplomats to cultivate a lifestyle that won friends among the politically powerful. Because such friends were invariably noblemen, and often among the wealthiest members of a society, such diplomacy meant spending a good deal of money on a lavish social life. Thus Praslin had already provided d'Eon with four cooks, five kitchen helpers, four household servants, and three coachmen. If the French government was to have access to, much less influence on, Parliament, d'Eon needed to be on good terms with its leaders.[4]

And that is what first got d'Eon into trouble. He had been living in London for nine months when he assumed his ambassadorial duties, so his social life was already on the fast track. Within a short time, he had become more than a success on London's grandest social stage. In May 1763 we find him visiting Strawberry Hill, Horace Walpole's patrician estate, dining there with Lord and Lady Holderness and the Duke and Duchess of Grafton, and attending a private wind ensemble concert with visiting French philosopher Charles Duclos.[5]

D'Eon's first cousin, the twenty-three-year-old Maurice d'Eon de Mouloize, who joined d'Eon in June as his secretary, became aware of his employer's popularity right away. "The number of his friends is great," he wrote to relatives back home. "He has made friendships with all the English counts, dukes, and lords who have any tie to their court. His reputation is perfectly established. . . . The King and Queen like him very much. He has had the honor to go to the court weekly, where he has an audience with them according to the customs of the nation." By the time d'Eon submitted his official papers as Plenipotentiary Minister to George III on 3 July 1763, he was already well known throughout the royal court and the leadership of Parliament.[6]

D'Eon was a great conversationalist, with a keen wit and quick mind, despite his poor command of English. He also had a potent secret weapon that he had been using with much success since his arrival in 1762: wine. D'Eon had a passion for wine, and was most at home—literally—when drinking it, since the best thing about d'Eon's hometown, Tonnerre, was the wonderful white and red Burgundies that came from its golden vineyards. When d'Eon drank a good bottle of *vin Tonnerreois,* it was as if he were drinking the earth of his native province. Tonnerre, and neighboring villages like Auxerre and Chablis, were "three very remarkable towns noted for their excellent wines. Without good wine," he could not help adding in one memoir, "there would neither be good people, nor good poetry, nor good painting, nor good culture." Rarely would d'Eon ever say anything about his hometown without mentioning its outstanding wine.[7]

Wherever he went, whenever he tried to exert his influence, he came bearing generous gifts of wine, and not just any *vin ordinaire* from Burgundy. D'Eon imported a special wine from vineyards near his own estate in the Tonnerrois and Chablis regions, or from neighboring districts such as Beaune. This was more than a way for d'Eon to bring a little of Burgundy with him. Since these particular wines were—and still are—considered among the best and certainly the most expensive in the world, these gifts were warmly welcomed by d'Eon's aristocratic consumers. "The question of Burgundian wine," one British diplomat confessed to d'Eon during the negotiations over the Treaty of Paris, "is a subject at least as important as this peace."[8]

Just how much wine d'Eon bought in 1763 is not clear. But we know that it was enough to upset the British Prime Minister, George Grenville. Normally governments exempted what diplomats imported for their personal use from the usual tariffs and duties. But d'Eon began bringing so much wine into London that the Grenville government threatened to impose taxes on it. Only when d'Eon made a considerable amount of noise over the prospect did the government reluctantly back down.[9]

In fact, throughout d'Eon's stay in England wine became his trademark. There are no records of his wine purchases until the mid-1770s, when he was short of cash. But one invoice, dated 28 June 1774, shows d'Eon buying "10 barriques of vin rouge de Beaune." Each "barrique" contained 280 bottles and cost £15. So for that order alone d'Eon paid £150 for 2,800 bottles of wine. Another invoice shows d'Eon placing an order for 1,800 bottles. Further invoices indicate that for the period from 1768 to 1774, d'Eon bought well over £405 worth of prime Burgundy.[10] If this is what d'Eon spent during a period of financial constraints, how much more he must have bought when he could charge it to the French government!

And that was precisely the problem. Although France was the wealthiest country in Europe, her government was rapidly becoming one of the poorest, at least in 1763. After the war, Choiseul put the government on an austerity budget so that he could devote all extra funds to rebuilding the navy. Besides, there was a real danger of state bankruptcy. This concern over state finances, however temporary, extended to foreign affairs. Broglie explained at length to the King how he had instructed La Rozière to stay within a tight budget.[11]

D'Eon not only spent what government money he could, he also tried to get his superiors to advance him even more. In letters written throughout the summer of 1763, he tactfully reminded Foreign Minister Praslin that he had never been repaid for debts incurred while serving the King in Russia and during the Seven Years' War. He thought the government ought to reimburse him immediately.[12]

In July and August, d'Eon began to receive letters from Praslin criticizing his extravagance. At first, d'Eon responded respectfully by pointing out how much it cost to prepare housing for the new ambassador, the Comte de Guerchy. Praslin looked upon such responses as little more than excuses, and insisted that d'Eon cut back.

On 14 August, d'Eon received a letter from his close friend Claude-Pierre de Saint-Foy, chief clerk at the Foreign Ministry. He informed d'Eon that due to financial constraints, d'Eon would have to give up the title Plenipotentiary Minister once Guerchy arrived, and settle for Secretary to the Ambassador. It is not clear whether this change of title was perceived by the government as routine or as a punishment for d'Eon's free-spending ways.[13]

The demotion offended d'Eon deeply and he let his superiors know it. The tone of his letters became testy. When Guerchy and Nivernais were called in to try to smooth over the brewing feud, d'Eon rebuffed them both. "I am sorry that my impudent letter, as you call it, has caused annoyance to yourself and the Duc de Praslin," he wrote to Nivernais. But as the letter went on, it became apparent that d'Eon was not at all sorry: "That truth which I expose and that justice which I demand are not reasons for two great and enlightened Ministers to feel themselves aggrieved. I have acted with due reflection, as is my wont; and as my intention is always to act for the best, I have never yet repented of my past actions, and I do not anticipate that I shall have to repent of my future actions. I have long been predestined to final impenitence."[14]

Nivernais responded by telling d'Eon that he was very upset by the hostile tone of the letter. He warned d'Eon that it was wrong to complain about these titles and it was especially impolitic to remonstrate to the Foreign Minister. "Calm yourself now," he pleaded. "Be more flexible and more reasonable, my dear friend, be less agitated and less agitating."[15]

But nothing seemed to move d'Eon back to moderation. "This letter touched my heart a great deal," he later wrote, "but it did nothing to persuade my mind."[16]

When the spies of the Secret learned of the growing tension between d'Eon and the Foreign Ministry, they began to worry that d'Eon would jeopardize the entire project. Durand urged Tercier to calm d'Eon. "In the main you are right," Tercier wrote sympathetically, "and it cannot be expected from you that, after having been Plenipotentiary Minister of the King, you should descend to be Secretary every time that Guerchy goes to England, and that when he leaves you should resume the rank of Minister; such a thing has never been seen. M. Durand and I agree that on this point you are right. But the form of your letters really pains us. Your intrepid spirit, the loftiness of your sentiments, and your disinterested philosophy certainly deserve much praise, but we think you ought to act with more reflection. I beg you to abstain from jests, excellent of their kind, but which cannot be taken in good part, and which have a worse effect than the thing in itself. There is, also, another important reason, and that is, that you are not free to give yourself up to what your sentiments may prompt you to. You cannot fail the King, who, because he has counted on you, has confided a most important affair to you. Too high an opinion is entertained of your zeal to let it be believed that you would allow such a great undertaking, whose success promises such results to yourself, to perish at its outset. We know the taste you have for great things, and your talent for bringing them to a successful termination. Take care, then, that you do not embroil yourself; there is no remedy if you do, and we cannot believe that you would prefer a small personal motive to that which the strictest duty and also your own renown dictate to you. The Comte de Broglie would be inconsolable if the affair that he has commenced so well were to fail. Send me, by the first opportunity that presents itself, news likely to give him satisfaction."[17]

This letter was a masterpiece of rhetoric, appealing simultaneously to d'Eon's rational appreciation for good argument, his economic self-interest, his political aspirations, and his hope for future rewards. Friendly in tone, it was a thinly veiled warning that if the Secret fell apart, everyone was prepared to blame d'Eon—and the consequences could be grave.

D'Eon's friend Saint-Foy saw d'Eon's iconoclastic behavior as philosophical: "This is the moment to choose between philosophy and politics," he accurately told d'Eon. "If you go for philosophy, I am telling you, my friend, with whatever authority that my heart has any power to move yours, you will be sorry, you will be duped, and you will lose whatever friends have been pleading your case."[18]

On 25 September, d'Eon responded to this pressure with a barrage of letters to Praslin, Choiseul, Nivernais, Guerchy, Broglie, and others. To Saint-Foy, he expressed agreement that the choice was between philosophy and politics, and announced that he was definitely choosing philosophy. It was as simple as that: "I myself am more familiar than anyone with all the difficulties, all the grief, all the headaches of politics; and the decision that I am making today is nothing but the result of how this experience has put my knowledge into action."

To Nivernais's secretary, his outburst was even more emotional: "I will always go my own way, fate has determined that; the bomb must burst; the fuse is at the end of the wick. Too bad for those who get splashed with mud or hit with pieces. Those with the most fear will pull back. The devil take me if I retreat."[19]

To Broglie, d'Eon wrote: "If I refuse to behave more complaisantly, it is because they want to dishonor me. This affair is not about money due me, it is about honor and justice. I have kept my honor intact, and no one can take it from me."[20]

Because of his own political exile, d'Eon's most intimate and important patron, the Comte de Broglie, real chief of the Secret, did not immediately hear about what was going on with him. In early October, however, Broglie finally drafted a long letter that tried to put d'Eon in his place:

"I think, with your other friends, that you are wrong, very wrong, both in the nature of your pretensions and in the manner in which you have advanced them; in the former, because you have nothing to complain of in regard to your treatment. I acknowledge that the alternating from minister to secretary is somewhat extraordinary, and neither becoming to your-

LA CHEVALIERE D'EON.

Née à Tonnerre le 5. 8.ᵇʳᵉ 1728.

"La Chevalière d'Eon," by J. Condé, first published on 1 March 1791 in the *European Magazine*. It is a fairly realistic portrait of d'Eon in his late fifties, living as a woman but with the Cross of Saint-Louis on his left breast. *(Courtesy of the Bibliothèque Nationale, Paris)*

D'Eon idealized as Pallas, the Greek warrior goddess who protected Athens, by B. Bradel. Note the Cross of Saint-Louis on the left breast. *(Courtesy of the Bibliothèque Nationale, Paris)*

The Prince de Conti was among France's most celebrated and controversial heroes during the reign of Louis XV. D'Eon identified him as a principal patron. *(Courtesy of the Brotherton Collection, University of Leeds Library)*

Intellect, music, and culture mix with fashion at the salon of the Prince de Conti, where, according to d'Eon, he won friends and influence early in his career. Portraits of important women look on from above. *(Courtesy of the Brotherton Collection, University of Leeds Library)*

The Russian Empress Elizabeth held masquerade balls in which courtiers cross-dressed without masks. During the 1750s, d'Eon's diplomacy resulted in closer relations between Louis XV and Elizabeth. *(Courtesy of the Brotherton Collection, University of Leeds Library)*

autre coſte de la VILLE TONNERRE.

D'Eon's hometown, Tonnerre, was known for its wonderful Burgundian wine. *(Courtesy of the Brotherton Collection, University of Leeds Library)*

Mme de Pompadour was Louis XV's favorite mistress, and her influence upon French foreign policy was without parallel. D'Eon believed that she despised him. *(Courtesy of the Brotherton Collection, University of Leeds Library)*

The Duc de Choiseul was France's most important minister during the 1760s. D'Eon perceived him as a bitter enemy. *(Courtesy of the Brotherton Collection, University of Leeds Library)*

The last will of Pierre-Henri Treyssac de Vergy confirmed that French ministers had conspired to assassinate d'Eon. Vergy died in 1794. *(Courtesy of the Brotherton Collection, University of Leeds Library)*

A view of Golden Square, London, where d'Eon lived for most of his residence in London. *(Courtesy of the Brotherton Collection, University of Leeds Library)*

King Louis XV, who reigned between 1734 and 1774, employed d'Eon as a spy and trusted him with state secrets. *(Courtesy of the Brotherton Collection, University of Leeds Library)*

British Chief Justice Lord Mansfield, a Scottish jurist famous for his intellect, heard several cases involving d'Eon. *(Courtesy of the Brotherton Collection, University of Leeds Library)*

The Comte de Vergennes was a Foreign Minister under Louis XVI. He ordered d'Eon to dress as a woman. *(Courtesy of the Brotherton Collection, University of Leeds Library)*

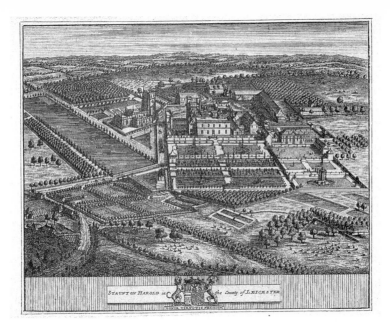

Between 1771 and 1777, d'Eon regularly escaped to the secluded estate of Staunton-Herald, owned by his friend Washington Shirley, Lord Ferrers. *(Courtesy of the Brotherton Collection, University of Leeds Library)*

The Chevalier d'Eon as he probably looked when he was Plenipotentary Minister from France to England. *(Courtesy of the Bibliothèque Nationale, Paris)*

This idealized engraving of a young and feminine d'Eon is reputed to have been made from a painting by Angelica Kaufmann. It is based upon a myth, since no one saw d'Eon dress as a woman until he returned to France in 1777. *(Courtesy of the Bibliothèque Nationale, Paris)*

Le Chevalier D'Eon

A young Chevalier d'Eon wearing a three-cornered hat not usually associated
with the Dragoons. *(Courtesy of the Bibliothèque Nationale, Paris)*

self nor to your office, while it seemed reasonable enough that you should be left in London in the same capacity as that which M. Durand filled at Warsaw with me. . . . All this is true, and it was right to represent it to M. de Praslin, sticking to the good reasons which exist for it, but not to offer a threat of resignation. . . . I will not repeat all that you have said and written; I can only tell you that if you had written to me in the same style, although I love you with all my heart, and believe you to be in every way capable, I should have ordered you at once to leave one of the secretaries in charge in London and to return, never to be employed again. . . . To these reasons, which appear to me irrefutable, I will add that on this occasion you have been doubly to blame to risk your recall from a post in which you know that you are useful and agreeable to His Majesty. He has confided to you, specially and secretly, the conduct of the most important of all affairs, and just at the time that it is being put in action, you run the risk of frustrating it; for you cannot be ignorant that the secrecy he is pleased to maintain in the matter would not permit him to oppose your recall. Truly, you could not have been yourself when you acted as you did, for I know the love and respect you have for the King, and that you would give your life a hundred times over for him; how much more should you be willing to sacrifice your dislikes, and put up with a little inconvenience, all the more because we know that he can make it up to you. To such a powerful motive I will not add the little share I have in this. I know your attachment, your friendship for me. Would it be worthy of that friendship to abandon a task in which I am a participant, and which I am unable to conduct without you, a work which, while it contributes to the welfare and safety of the State, may also contribute to my satisfaction?"[21]

Recalled

ON 4 OCTOBER 1763, Praslin finally issued d'Eon's Order of Recall. D'Eon was to present the official letter to George III, and then leave England immediately upon the arrival of the new ambassador, the Comte de Guerchy, who was soon to depart Paris. D'Eon was to come directly to Versailles, where "you will report your arrival to me, and there, *without coming to Court,* await further orders which I shall address to you." The meaning of this curt letter was clear enough: D'Eon was fired, his political career was finished. At best he would be exiled in the manner of his patron the Comte de Broglie, but Praslin might have him thrown into the Bastille for insubordination. Tercier wrote Broglie about the recall, noting that Praslin was "sending [d'Eon] home in poverty." As for d'Eon himself, he recognized the recall for exactly what it was: a "complete disgrace."[1]

The recall order put the entire invasion plan in jeopardy. If d'Eon followed the order and left England, that would be the end of the project. Clearly the decision about the fate of the Secret was neither d'Eon's nor Broglie's: it belonged to the King. Immediately after learning of Praslin's order, Tercier wrote a tactful letter to the King informing him of it and asking his advice with regard to its implications for the Secret. Louis's response was clear: D'Eon's behavior was entirely unacceptable. No one should act toward the King's ministers in such an insolent manner. Louis supported Praslin's recall order and commanded Tercier "to take whatever precautions you need to maintain the secrecy" of the project once d'Eon was back in France. Clearly the King was concerned less with dropping the invasion project than with the risk that it might leak out either to the British or his own ministers.[2]

The new ambassador, the Comte de Guerchy, finally arrived in London on 17 October 1763. When Guerchy met with d'Eon, he reiterated Praslin's instructions as outlined in the Order of Recall. Incredibly, d'Eon ignored these orders. He told Guerchy that since he had been named Plenipotentiary Minister directly by the King, he would only accept a recall from the same source.[3] On the one hand, such direct resistance to the Foreign Minister was a breach of all diplomatic etiquette. On the other hand, seen from the viewpoint of the Secret, where spies had conflicting loyalties, d'Eon's behavior was not so different from Broglie's a decade earlier in Warsaw.

D'Eon received a second letter from Praslin a few days later, demanding that he leave London immediately and that he turn over his diplomatic files to Guerchy as well. Again, d'Eon ignored the order. "I have learned with the greatest surprise," Praslin wrote on 29 October, "that you have refused to follow the order I gave you on the 19th of this month to remit to the ambassador of the King all of your papers that concern His Majesty, all of his ambassadors, ministers, and chargés d'affaires. . . . I order you again on behalf of the King, under penalty of insubordination." D'Eon likewise ignored this third attempt by the Foreign Minister to dismiss him.[4]

D'Eon's refusal to abide by the Foreign Minister's Order of Recall placed him in a new category as far as the government was concerned. It made him a virtual outlaw, subject to charges of treason. What is so incredible about this affair was that it was so unnecessary. The matter at stake struck most people at the time, and perhaps us today, as rather petty and personal—issues of honor and ego, rather than state. Why, then, did d'Eon continue to fuel the wrath of the Foreign Minister? Why did he insist on a showdown?

In London and Paris drawing rooms the most common reason offered was insanity. "What is become of d'Eon?" asked Lord Hertford, England's ambassador to France (and thus d'Eon's counterpart), of Horace Walpole. "I suppose he fears the Bastille more than the *petites maisons* [asylums], which is the most charitable way of treating him in his present circumstances." Walpole agreed with his correspondent, offering to Hertford details of d'Eon's supposed madness.[5]

Nor was this just the opinion of the English. Guerchy and others subscribed to it as well. And, at first, so did the King. Certainly there is some firsthand evidence that d'Eon's behavior was different from usual. But La Rozière, who knew him as well as anyone, repudiated the charge of madness. While he admitted that d'Eon's behavior might be eccentric, La Rozière insisted his friend was as lucid and rational as ever.[6]

What Lord Hertford didn't know, of course, was that d'Eon's role as a spy, his membership in the Secret, his clandestine orders to scout an invasion against Britain, all gave him a feeling of invulnerability. As long as he possessed those secret instructions, d'Eon figured, he held a guarantee of his freedom and security. Given such important orders, it seemed "impossible that Louis XV had consented to my recall."[7]

However, granting that d'Eon had achieved a position of invincibility does not explain why he would use it to such extreme ends, alienating most of his friends and his king. To understand d'Eon's motivation, we need to examine his duties and relationships.

The double roles of Plenipotentiary Minister and royal spy were always seen by the leaders of the Secret as closely related. Only an official position in London could give d'Eon the cover and the independence to direct La Rozière's activities. However, well before the Comte de Guerchy arrived in London, Praslin's government had encroached on d'Eon's autonomy by criticizing his profligacy. D'Eon would have felt somewhat justified believing that as a spy for the Secret, even more than as Plenipotentiary Minister, he would need to pursue a sumptuous lifestyle, sprinkling wine and money in the right places to nurture close relationships with the leaders of Parliament. After all, what d'Eon was doing in London was little different from the role Broglie had played earlier in Warsaw.

Even if d'Eon's behavior was at times "mad," there can be no doubt that the French government must bear some of the responsibility, because it had placed him in a "mad" situation: Having to take orders from two superiors, Praslin and Broglie, and having to work both under Guerchy in one role but above him in another created unusual difficulties.

And then there was the problem of Guerchy's own mediocre reputation. The decision to appoint Guerchy to the post was never popular, even among the French ministers themselves. "I am much concerned about this poor man, Guerchy," wrote Praslin to Nivernais, "and I really do not know whether we have done him a good turn by making him Ambassador to London. He is not liked in that country. I dread his dispatches as I do fire. You know how much badly written dispatches tell, against both the work and the man; and one judges a minister less by the manner in which he transacts affairs than by the account he renders of them. I think our friend will do well, but he cannot write at all—about that there is no mistake."[8]

As Nivernais's secretary, d'Eon not only read this letter from the Foreign Minister, he made a copy for himself (which he later published). Certainly Praslin's criticisms of Guerchy fed d'Eon's own overblown sense of himself. The talent for writing—and thinking—was exactly what distinguished d'Eon in his own mind from other diplomats. In contrast to Guerchy, d'Eon had published two books on political economy. He was more than a statesman—his writings had made him a political philosopher as well. In addition, d'Eon had more diplomatic experience than Guerchy. Before his appointment to London, Guerchy had never held a diplomatic post; he had never even been involved in any negotiation between states. He was a complete political novice. Consequently, d'Eon believed himself far superior to Guerchy and would not take orders from him.

D'Eon's resistance to Guerchy was also fueled by his perception that Guerchy was loyal to Praslin and Choiseul. Indeed, d'Eon perceived what happened to him during the summer and fall of 1763 as being part of a great power struggle between two wings of the French government—the Secret and the Foreign Ministry—over control of foreign policy. On the one hand were Choiseul, Praslin, and subordinates such as Guerchy, all under the general tutelage of Mme de Pompadour. Against them were Broglie, Tercier, Durand, and d'Eon—the group whose allegiance went back to Conti.[9]

This Manichean struggle for power between the followers of Louis's mistress and the Secret had a substantive policy component as well. The leaders of the Secret were critical of the 1756 "diplomatic revolution" that had allied France with Hapsburg Austria. For Broglie, this marked the culmination of France's retreat from eastern Europe. Conti and Broglie wanted France to return to its more traditional policy of supporting Poland, Turkey, and Sweden against Austrian and Russian ambitions.[10]

During the summer of 1763, d'Eon's patrons had failed to recapture the ground they had lost during the Seven Years' War. Conti and Broglie were both still banned from the capital, while Tercier and Durand had been stripped of their official positions. Thus it is hardly surprising that when Praslin began criticizing d'Eon's spending habits in July and August of that year, the latter perceived the attack as part of a Pompadour–Conti power struggle, of which he was apparently to become the latest victim. Would he, too, go the way of Broglie and Conti? This feeling of political persecution, intensified by d'Eon's relative isolation in a foreign country, was bitterly reinforced when he was demoted from Plenipotentiary Minister to Secretary. Such insults from the Praslin–Choiseul faction could not be borne without a fight, especially since he was in England as a personal emissary of the King. D'Eon's role in the Secret gave him the psychological motivation and the political clout to fight back.

Thus d'Eon was not crazy, but considering his peculiar political status, he had good reason to be a bit paranoid. Certainly, at least, his closest friend and first cousin, Maurice d'Eon de Mouloize, who was his own secretary during this period, knew he was not crazy, but rather very nervous and agitated. "These various happenings have considerably upset his health," d'Eon de Mouloize wrote to his father. "The constant turmoil affects his character, changing it considerably. I speak to you truthfully and objectively."[11]

Louis XV, growing increasingly concerned about the fate of the instructions in his own handwriting which were in d'Eon's possession, decided to take two bold steps to get them back. The first involved writing Guerchy about the existence of the secret papers. The new ambassador, of course, knew absolutely nothing about the Secret, and the King was careful to tell him only as much as he needed to know. He informed Guerchy that d'Eon had secret papers that were very important to the King. Guerchy was to obtain those papers immediately, by whatever means necessary, and then lock them up in a safe at the embassy. Under no circumstances should he show the papers to anyone.[12]

The second step Louis took was even more daring: He began the legal process of requesting extradition of d'Eon through the British government. "I warn you," Louis wrote directly to d'Eon on 4 November, "that a demand for your extradition, signed with my stamp, has been addressed today to Guerchy, to be transmitted by him to the Ministers of His Britannic Majesty. This demand is accompanied by officers of the Paris Police to assist in its execution. If you cannot save yourself, at least save your papers."[13]

Until now, the d'Eon dispute had obsessed the officials of the Foreign Ministry and d'Eon's friends who surrounded Broglie, but it had remained largely a private, secret affair. Now, however, with an extradition process begun, the British government would have to know about d'Eon's odd status. And once discussed in government circles, it was bound to leak through the press to the public.

The British government began discussing the matter secretly at the highest levels. D'Eon was a popular figure at court, and King George III took a pronounced interest in the affair. In November 1763, after much back-and-forth discussion, the British foreign minister, Lord Halifax, decided that since d'Eon had broken no law, and since England was a free country, he was welcome to stay. However, Halifax also insisted that d'Eon was to be treated as a private person, with no diplomatic privileges, such as invitations to royal ceremonies.[14]

D'Eon was thankful that the British remained true to their free laws and refused to extradite him. But while he now had nothing to fear from

British authorities, such was not the case with the French, who were beginning to view d'Eon as a criminal. He began to fear that with the extradition blocked, the French might resort to other ways of silencing him. They would certainly try to steal his papers, or worse, kidnap or even assassinate him. Nor were such fears unfounded. During the next several months, Praslin and Choiseul did indeed make several attempts to arrange for d'Eon's kidnapping and arrest.[15] So with Guerchy's arrival in London, d'Eon became more cautious about his activities.

One morning around this time, d'Eon was visited by Pierre-Henri Treyssac de Vergy, who identified himself as a friend of Guerchy's and someone who was well known back in France. As was the custom of the day, especially for a diplomat, d'Eon refused to see Vergy until he could provide letters of introduction. When Vergy confessed that he had none, d'Eon became suspicious and had his valet show him out. When d'Eon and Vergy met a few days later at the French embassy, insults were traded, an argument ensued, and a duel was set for a few days after the meeting. When d'Eon recounted all this at a dinner party at the home of Lord Halifax, the latter insisted that d'Eon immediately renounce any intention of dueling Vergy in England. After several hours during which guards barred d'Eon from leaving the dinner party until he agreed with the English foreign minister, d'Eon finally signed an affidavit promising to call off the duel with Vergy. A few days later d'Eon saw Vergy talking with Guerchy at the embassy, confirming his suspicion that Vergy was a spy hired by Guerchy, which Vergy eventually admitted.[16]

More serious was d'Eon's claim that Guerchy tried to have him poisoned. On 28 October, so d'Eon narrates (see chapter 21), he was dining at the French embassy with several other guests, while Guerchy was at the home of Lord Sandwich, one of England's secretaries of state. Guerchy had arranged for someone to slip a heavy dose of opium into d'Eon's wine. But luckily d'Eon did not drink much that evening, so even though he got very sick, the scheme failed.

These incidents convinced d'Eon that, unbeknownst to the King, the Foreign Ministry had hatched a plot to kidnap or assassinate him. He moved out of his apartment and into La Rozière's place on Brewer Street in Golden Square, where he installed a concealed iron safe under the staircase for his papers.

D'Eon, then, did not consider himself a traitor, but a loyalist to his king and to his own vision of French interests. He was convinced that his actions would be supported by Broglie and the King, if only they knew the real facts.

They were indeed about to learn the facts. La Rozière, the army officer who had been d'Eon's fellow spy in England, returned home to France at the end of November to report directly to Tercier and Broglie about d'Eon's behavior. He took with him a long and important letter from d'Eon for the King and Broglie.

D'Eon to Louis XV and Broglie

London, 18 November 1763[1]

M. de La Rozière can tell you all about the tricks, schemes, promises and threats that the Comte de Guerchy has used to try to discover the secret motive of my conduct. He will also explain the way in which I have evaded all his questions and the little regard I felt for his threats and promises. I do not believe it possible to do more than I did or that any ambassador has ever been more humiliated and mystified than the Comte de Guerchy. As for his threats, I laughed at them. Speaking to him personally, I told him I should hold my ground in wait for him, and that if he came at the head of a second brigade of guards, I should not attack him in the streets but, if he tried to enter my house, he would see how I received him at my door. I have at home no fewer than eight Turkish sabres, four pairs of pistols and two Turkish rifles with which to give him a Turkish brawl. My door is narrow and people can only enter one by one. In any case, I am still Plenipotentiary Minister, since I have not taken my farewell audience [with King George III], and, if I wish, I can keep up a diplomatic defense here for a whole year before taking it; it is only a question of having a little money for my lodging, food, etc. La Rozière can tell you, too, that I worked out eighteen crucial points of defense or diplomatic strongholds [to protect my home], and they will have to carry me before forcing me to take my leave. Only La Rozière and I know my defense positions. At the first attack the Comte de Guerchy and Lord Halifax tried to make on me, I revealed my first arsenal and they retreated in disorder. . . .

On Friday 28 October, the Comte de Guerchy went to dine with Lord Sandwich, and I dined at the French Embassy where there was only the Comtesse de Guerchy, her daughter, M. de Blosset [a French military officer and diplomat], the Chevalier d'Allonville [French military officer who later emigrated to England during the French Revolution], and M. Monin [Conti's former secretary, Nicolas Monin, was sent to London to try to mediate the dispute between Guerchy and d'Eon]. Immediately after dinner, the Comtesse and her daughter went out to make some visits. I remained with these gentlemen, who began to chatter like magpies. Shortly afterwards I felt sick and very sleepy. As I was leaving the house, I found a couch, which they pressed me to take; I refused it. I fled home on foot where, in spite of myself, I fell asleep in a chair by the fire. I was obliged to go to bed early, for I felt even worse, as if my stomach was on fire. I went to bed and, though I have always risen by six or seven o'clock, I was still asleep at midday when M. de la Rozière came and woke me up by banging loudly at my door. Subsequently I have discovered that M. de Guerchy caused opium, if nothing worse, to be put in my wine, calculating that after dinner I should fall into a heavy sleep, that they would put me, still asleep, onto a couch and, instead of my being carried home, I should be carried down to the Thames where probably there was a boat waiting ready to abduct me. For nearly a fortnight I have felt extremely ill; even now I have burning pains in my head and stomach and an irritable bile. La Rozière can certify this.[2]

The day after I had drunk this cocktail, M. Monin came to see me and dine with me. I told him how sick I felt. He told me he had had almost the same symptoms, but not so violent. A few days later, the Comte de Guerchy came to see me before nine o'clock, accompanied by his two aides-de-camp. They examined my little lodging very closely and, as there were four engravings in a little drawing room representing the King with Painting, Sculpture, Music, and Architecture, the whole set dedicated to Mme de Pompadour, the Chevalier d'Allonville began by saying: "Ah, M. le Comte, you see M. d'Eon has engravings dedicated to Mme de Pompadour on his walls!" I replied: "Why not? Do you think I fear Mme de Pompadour? She has never done me either good or ill. I am not afraid of beautiful ladies." Later, the Ambassador asked me what was the matter with me. I replied with Burgundian frankness: "Ever since I dined at Your Excellency's house on the 28th, I have felt extremely ill. Apparently your cooks are not careful to clean their saucepans properly. That is the trouble of running a house on a grand scale; one is often poisoned without knowing it." (I had said the same thing to everyone who had been to see me, as well as to my doctor and my surgeon.) The Comte de Guerchy replied: "I have told my kitchen manager to supervise the cooking. These gentlemen also felt indisposed and so did M. Monin." Afterwards, the Ambassador said to me: "We were going to walk to Westminster Abbey," which is on the bank of the Thames. "If you had not been indisposed, I should have asked you to come with us."

The visit so early in the morning of the Ambassador and his two aides, the overbearing way these gentlemen demanded admittance, the suggestion they *had made and their close scrutiny of my apartments, all announced some trouble for which I was well prepared, for I am always prepared. Luckily, one of my friends, who happened to be in my bedroom, upset the military plans of the great General Guerchy. . . . Finally seeing that he had been foiled, the Ambassador stayed only a short while and departed. . . .*

Broglie to Louis XV

BROGLIE, 9 DECEMBER 1763[1]

It is difficult for me to express to Your Majesty the extreme embarrassment I feel by rendering an account of such a strange affair, one so unique and in which so many persons have been compromised. . . .

I ought to have the honor to confess to Your Majesty that in the entire case the Sieur d'Eon has offered concerning his conduct, I have seen no trace of mental illness that many have asserted. . . . I find, I say, all his dispatches and his ministerial conduct marked in the end by zeal, enlightenment, and the experience that I have always seen in him; and if sometimes his expressions are too strong and his advice too emphatically enunciated or supported, it is proof that Your Majesty will be able to recognize in all of his adventures the same character as always, and that this does not seem to me worthy of condemnation other than he displeases those who might be less loyal to the truth.

I do not pretend to excuse even some of the proceedings and uncontrolled behavior with his superiors. . . . But I would beg Your Majesty to sympathize with weakness that is inherent in the human condition: one rarely finds men exempted from all the weaknesses that belong to them, and I do not think that Your Majesty disapproves if I take the liberty to implore his indulgence for faults that are redeemed by essential qualities, valuable services, and tireless zeal.

The letter that the Sieur d'Eon had the honor of writing to Your Majesty explains the motives for his disobedience to the orders of M. the Duc de Praslin and M. the Comte de Guerchy. One must admit that he must have been in a cruel embarrassment in receiving no order from Your Majesty nor by my channel nor that of M. Tercier; [the note in] the proper hand of Your Majesty that we thought Your Majesty sent to M. Guerchy to give to him was, in fact, never sent.[2] M. de La Rozière has assured me of this fact. Given this general silence, it was logical for him to think it essential and indispensable to remain in London. The ways [for us] to reach him were difficult and those who were employed for getting him to return his confidential letters were so mismanaged, and following his reports, full of such humiliations, that one can understand easily enough how things developed. It is certain that he could not support himself with ordinary and natural procedures in such circumstances. It was necessary to resort to unusual pretexts and means, and I believe that with a little less animosity against him one would have avoided a part of the furor that this unhappy affair has produced. . . .

It seems to me that Your Majesty has only three choices under which his stay [in London] could take place:

1) If it pleased Your Majesty to retain the title of Plenipotentiary Minister, in spite of the presence of M. the Comte de Guerchy, and revoking the recall that he [Guerchy] has already announced.

2) If Your Majesty judged it more appropriate to send him a secret permission to remain there as an ordinary Frenchman. . . . He then would profit from all the important happenings in order to give information to us that would be perhaps more useful than what might come from an official minister.

3) If through the failure of these two ways and in despair of losing the protection and the esteem of Your Majesty, he threw himself into the arms of the His British Majesty and regarded as a means of revenge the revelation of the important secret that has been confided to him.

One cannot begin to realize how difficult it is to choose between these choices and to avoid all danger. Since I have the honor to serve Your Majesty in the career of a political agent, I believe it necessary to remark that he has been very careful to conserve there the mystery such that the usefulness of his service has suffered. There is no doubt that it is necessary to draw the curtain on this mystery in wanting to retain for the Sieur d'Eon, after all that has happened, the title of Plenipotentiary Minister in London. However, in order to avoid this inconvenience, one only needs a direct and strict order to M. de Guerchy, and, even if it would be secretly leaked to M. de Praslin, as would be quite realistic, they would both submit themselves to the will of their master. Thus the only thing to fear would be the diminution of their zeal to carry it out.

As to the second alternative, the only inconvenience I see is that of the correspondence to establish it and the difficulty to ensure that an isolated man will be sheltered from the abuse that can happen to a stranger. I am not familiar enough with the English constitution to have a clear opinion in this regard, but the Sieur de La Rozière assures me that all individuals in London are protected from all illegal enterprises and that he cannot be arrested except by the channels of justice which would not allow any violence upon him. As to the correspondence, [La Rozière] also believes that through Calais it could be established with security, perhaps through him, perhaps through some other person that he could easily find. . . . I must add here that in this last case, it is absolutely necessary to assure for him an honest subsistence and that he could not possibly stay in London, where everything is so expensive, without protecting him from need and without having to support himself in the company that he is accustomed to, so that he could usefully perform the services and carry out the views of Your Majesty. . . . I have always found in [d'Eon] an objectivity and a distinguished integrity, but if he finds himself abandoned by Your Majesty, expatriated and without any resources for his subsistence, what would he have to fear?

If, in light of what has happened and because of his need to live a decent life, he makes [the King's order of 6 June 1763] public or gives it up to the British ministry, who knows what might happen? Would it not be correct to fear that the sacred person of Your Majesty might not be compromised and that a declaration of war on the part of England might not inevitably follow? It is incontestable that the Sieur d'Eon has been reduced to despair, and that without the benevolence of Your Majesty, he can only expect something very bad from the French, and that [his secret orders] are his only sure means of making a good living in England. By all reason, I would implore Your Majesty to stop the pursuits of M. de Guerchy and M. the Duc de Praslin under the pretext that it pleases him to immediately return the Sieur de La Rozière to England in order to deliver [new] orders to the Sieur d'Eon. . . .

Scapegoat

T HE MOST AMAZING THING about this extraordinary exchange of letters is that the Comte de Broglie accepted d'Eon's
version of this bizarre political mess. Of course, Broglie did not
want to appear gullible. He noted to the King that d'Eon was rude and
insubordinate. But Broglie basically excused d'Eon's outrageous behavior
by viewing his protégé as d'Eon saw himself: as a victim of political
infighting. And like d'Eon, Broglie regarded the entire brouhaha as linked
to the struggle with the Pompadour–Choiseul faction for control of foreign affairs.[1]

For Praslin, Choiseul, and Guerchy, the matter was fairly straightforward: By refusing Praslin's Order of Recall, d'Eon was committing an
act of profound insubordination, if not treason. Broglie thought otherwise. He presented d'Eon as an intelligent, zealous, hardworking diplomat and spy with noteworthy talents. From his vantage point as leader of
the Secret, Broglie could understand why d'Eon would resist Praslin's
order and insist on a direct order in the King's hand. After all, years ago,
when Broglie had been both a diplomat and spy in Poland, he too had
resisted the orders of the Foreign Minister. For Broglie, then, d'Eon's
recent behavior did not necessarily mean that his career was over.

Of course, Broglie was most worried about what he refers to in the letter as alternative no. 3. If France abandoned d'Eon, there would be nothing to stop d'Eon from selling his papers to the British government for a
handsome annuity that would allow him to live well in London for the
rest of his life. Here Broglie candidly tells King Louis that if England got
hold of the plan for a secret invasion, the result would be war. The King
later responded that he did not believe the British would attack even if

they discovered the plan. But French honor would nonetheless be tarnished, and there would certainly be a deterioration in relations between the two countries.[2]

Clearly two of Broglie's choices were out of bounds: Cutting d'Eon off would create an international crisis with the British, while renaming d'Eon Plenipotentiary Minister and vindicating his behavior would undermine the King's authority at home. Broglie, therefore, offered another choice: Give d'Eon enough money to live comfortably, and tell him to remain in London without official capacity until the storm blew over. The entire letter, in fact, can be seen as one long argument to make the King see the efficacy of this strategy.

Broglie's rhetorical success is evident in the fact that Louis accepted his recommendation: the King would prevent Praslin from arresting or murdering d'Eon; he would secretly guarantee d'Eon's safety from French aggressors; he would offer him a large amount of money. D'Eon would be stripped of his formal diplomatic title, but the King would secretly order him to remain in London as a spy, without any official political capacity. The King accepted Broglie's argument not because he approved of d'Eon, but because he became convinced that d'Eon was not insane and therefore all the more dangerous. "I really don't think he is mad," Louis wrote Tercier, "just extremely haughty and egotistical." At any rate, this meant that while d'Eon would leave the diplomatic corps, he would maintain his more significant position in the Secret.[3]

Broglie had urged the King to act fast, and the King indeed did so. Immediately he ordered Broglie and Tercier to prepare the Sieur de Nort for a mission to England to negotiate with d'Eon, and approved 200 ducats for Nort to give d'Eon. However, the members of the Secret allowed themselves to become bogged down in the details of the visit. Many hours were spent during the next few months figuring out how to keep Nort's journey a secret, not from the British, but from the French Foreign Ministry.[4]

Unfortunately, the Secret could not afford to stall. In England, the story was beginning to leak out to the press, posing the threat of a significant embarrassment. In mid-November, the Comte de Guerchy's own spy, Vergy, wrote a pamphlet criticizing d'Eon, which elicited a vigorous response from d'Eon, attacking Guerchy. Guerchy countered with a pamphlet against d'Eon's broadside, written by the polemicist Ange Goudar.[5] This small pamphlet skirmish quickly spread, with several newspapers picking up the story and following it with great interest. A dispute that had originated within the French government now threatened to spill over into public mudslinging.

Louis tried desperately to stop the scandal from spreading to France. On 30 December, he authorized 6,000 livres for members of the Secret to buy up all remaining copies of these tracts.[6] But this effort was, of course, futile. The important if underground French periodical, the *Mémoires secrets,* published an account of the affair before the end of the year. The article clearly sided with Guerchy, seeing the struggle as purely a feud between Guerchy and d'Eon, in which the latter had overstepped his authority.[7] Knowing d'Eon's proclivity for writing, his need for money, and his intense regard for his reputation, French statesmen worried that he might continue to write pamphlets hostile to Guerchy, which would rub salt in what had quickly become a wound in the belly of the monarchy.

As 1763 turned into 1764, the situation became more dangerous. Even though the King had decided to satisfy d'Eon's basic political demands, d'Eon was unaware of that critical fact. The Secret, mired in the details, left d'Eon in the dark. In the meantime, Broglie and Tercier had stopped writing to d'Eon, and consequently, he felt abandoned by the Secret. By March, d'Eon realized that it had been months since Praslin's Order of Recall, and neither Tercier, Broglie, nor the King had come to his aid. As far as he was aware, he had been left alone to defend himself against the French Foreign Ministry.

There was also the issue of money. The Foreign Ministry renewed its claims that d'Eon owed thousands of livres for improper use of funds. Not only did d'Eon refuse to give anything back, however, he insisted that the Ministry owed *him* money. Complicating the situation was the rumor that Praslin was about to cut off a pension awarded d'Eon in 1759. This rumor plunged him further into a state of alienation.[8]

At the end of February 1764, a dramatic turn of events occurred in French politics: Mme de Pompadour, who had been ill for several years, was now on her deathbed. Louis took this moment, on the eve of her death, to publicly announce the political rehabilitation of her two enemies, the Comte and the Maréchal de Broglie. His exile finally over, the Comte returned to Paris, where he resumed direct control over the Secret.[9]

One would think that d'Eon would have been thrilled at the news of Broglie's release. At first, d'Eon assumed that such a development would certainly mean his own rehabilitation. But when he still did not hear from Tercier or Broglie, he began to despair. This definitively proved, d'Eon reasoned to himself, that the Secret had turned him into a kind of scapegoat.

It is very sad, he wrote Tercier in March, that after all the "useful and important services" he had rendered to the King, he could be so easily "sacrificed." Promising that he would never "abandon the King nor my country," he vowed to do everything in his power to protect his own life, as well as his security and his career. After all, in the kind of Hobbesian state of existence to which he was now reduced, that was his absolute right. "I will not pretend with you, Monsieur," he confessed to Tercier. The British were offering him money—lots of it—to switch sides and work for them. And although d'Eon loved his king, the more abandoned he felt, the more inclined he was to make a deal with his British hosts.

"The chiefs of the opposition," he continued, "have offered me all the money that I would need, provided that I give them my papers. . . . I open my heart to you and you know just how much this kind of expedient action is repugnant to my character. But, well, if I am abandoned, what would you expect me to do? As to the papers of the Advocate [Louis XV] and his Substitute [Broglie], I guard them now more than ever. I have all of them and those of La Rozière. . . . But if I am abandoned totally, and if, from now until 22 April, Easter, I do not receive a signed promise from the King or from the Comte de Broglie that the entire affair with M. de Guerchy has been resolved, well then, Monsieur, I will declare formally and truthfully that all hope is lost for me, and that in forcing me into the arms of the King of England, his Prime Minister, and lords, it is obvious that you will be determining the fate of the next war, of which I will certainly be its innocent author, a war that will be inevitable. The King of England will be constrained by the nature of circumstances, by the cry of the nation and the party of opposition, who will become increasingly more powerful. . . . Thus your grand project, so glorious for the King and so advantageous for France, will turn against you."[10]

With this letter d'Eon finally admitted what had previously only been implied: He was prepared to blackmail the French government to gain his own freedom and security. Despite his insistence that he remained loyal to the King, his threats spoke otherwise: If d'Eon had sold the papers of the Secret to the English, the monarchy of Louis XV might have split apart, with or without a war. At the very least, it would have meant the worst scandal in Louis's reign. This was to be avoided at all costs. And d'Eon himself was willing to avoid it, at least until 22 April 1764, or so he said. But for now he wanted the King to know that he was the one who held the trump card.

The Lettres, mémoires, et négociations

D'EON IMMEDIATELY FOLLOWED the blackmail threat with a bombshell designed to overcome any suspicion that he might be bluffing. On 23 March 1764, he published in England the *Lettres, mémoires, et négociations,* a 200-page documentary history in French of his alleged overspending and subsequent recall, reproducing the secret diplomatic correspondence of d'Eon, Guerchy, Praslin, Choiseul, Nivernais, and others. The book naturally sent shock waves through the French government and transformed the nature of the affair. For weeks, diplomats on both sides of the Channel could talk of little else. "It is divided into three parts," Guerchy quickly wrote to Nivernais. "The first is simultaneously sort of historical memoir and libel against our friend [Praslin] and me. There is also the question of your role, with some nice phrases, but joined with other remarks of a different sort. . . . The second part is a collection of several of your private letters to M. de Praslin and many of his responses. . . . The third part includes letters to different people and some responses that he received. He announces that he will publish an entirely new volume in three months. I am, as you can imagine, extremely upset from all of this, which is going to become the subject of every conversation in London." Nivernais's reaction was completely predictable: "I am equally scandalized, shocked, and embarrassed by it!"[1]

It is impossible to overstate the sensational reception this book received. Within five days of its publication even King George III could talk of little else. "When Mr. Grenville went to the King," the British Prime Minister wrote about himself, "he found him very uneasy, and expressing great eagerness upon the publication of M. d'Eon's book." Indeed, Guerchy's prediction that it would become the topic everywhere in London was proven to be entirely too restrictive; it became the topic of conversation anywhere in Europe where politics was discussed. Naturally, the most upset were officials of the French Foreign Ministry—"a master-piece of insolence and perfidy" was Praslin's angry description. By the second week of April, the French newsletter *Mémoires secrets* was already writing that the book "was making a very great sensation in this country," even though copies were hard to find.[2]

The publication of the *Lettres* transformed d'Eon from someone known primarily among the intelligentsia and in diplomatic circles to a household name—at least in aristocratic households. Infamous or other-wise, few statesmen were as well known as d'Eon after the spring of 1764. Within a few months of its publication, d'Eon's book wasn't simply debated by powerful men at court, or even by the bourgeoisie in their cafés and newspapers, it was even discussed at home between mothers and daughters, as this fascinating excerpt from a letter from a sixteen-year-old aristocratic girl to a teenage friend testifies. (Because so many of us in the twentieth century would doubt that teenage girls during the eighteenth century would be interested in politics and intellectual life, the reader will forgive me for including such a lengthy citation.)

"After lunch I took my design lesson, finished Locke and started Spin-oza. After the lesson, I finished my writing assignment, and we took a walk on the rampart where we go practically every day. Yesterday, after Mass, unhappy at not having seen you, I practiced writing in Spanish and Italian, and then came lunch. I stayed in my mother's apartment until five o'clock. When everyone started to play, I retired. I worked on a play about the power of education and read [Montesquieu's] *Spirit of the Laws* until six o'clock. . . . This morning I took my Italian and Spanish lessons and read twenty-three pages of Plato. We ate lunch, and now I am taking the most comforting recreation in writing to you. At this moment my mother is reading the memoirs of M. d'Eon. What insanity! Or even more, what treasonous impudence! This work is forbidden and can't be found in Paris; one is obliged to order it from England. He promises five volumes, of which the first has appeared. There he limits himself to mocking the con-duct of M. de Guerchy, but they say that in the other volumes he clearly divulges state secrets."[3]

One thing is clear: The readers of d'Eon's shocking book were over-whelmingly hostile to what he had done, concurring that he had commit-ted a serious crime by publishing it. Indeed, the act of publishing the book completely overshadowed the Guerchy–d'Eon affair itself. "The indignity of his procedure," noted the *Mémoires secrets*, "the incongruity of his conduct and his style in his account, indicates either evil or madness." Horace Walpole was of the same opinion. Even d'Eon's curious counterpart, the British politician John Wilkes, whose own similar political problems in England had caused him to go into exile in Paris, wrote that Versailles's feeling of betrayal was due not so much to d'Eon's arguments but to the fact that he "published the secrets of his negotiations."[4]

Wilkes's analysis reminds us that d'Eon's book was not subversive simply because it lacked the required approval of the royal censor. After all, by the 1760s French censorship had already begun to break down. In 1764 alone, only 40 percent of the 1,548 titles published in French even requested such approval.[5] Technically, then, the majority of books published in that year could be described as subversive. But, of course, they were not. Rather, what made d'Eon's book especially scandalous was its public presentation of secret diplomacy. The act of publishing such a correspondence was a brazen political act; d'Eon was, in effect, submitting King Louis XV to the judgment of a higher authority: public opinion.

In the annals of European history since the Renaissance, it is extremely rare, if not unique, to find a diplomat publishing contemporary secret correspondence. D'Eon had crossed the line between private and public in a way that radically challenged the status quo in Old Regime Europe. During the early modern period, diplomacy between one state and another was very much the private business of the sovereign. In the case of France and most other countries, this meant the business of the King and the King alone. Practically no one during the eighteenth century challenged the government's right to control these kinds of state secrets.

D'Eon's actions must be seen within the context of developing notions of public opinion that were adopted by different factions in eighteenth-century French political life to circumscribe the absolute power of the monarchy. During the 1750s and 1760s, the French parlements and tax courts began using appeals to public opinion to challenge Louis XV's authority over religious, fiscal, and judicial policies. For example, the Parlement of Paris appealed to the public instead of to the King in its struggles over the "refusal of sacraments," an important religious issue. Similar fights broke out over economic policies, especially with regard to the government's plans to reduce regulations of the grain trade. Under the cover of such appeals, these bodies began to publish their own remonstrances and broadsides that aimed to convince a public outside the government that the monarchy's policies were wrong. The goal of some leaders of the parlements was nothing short of becoming the kind of loyal opposition that already existed in England. Indeed, these developments posed a serious enough challenge to royal authority that in 1764, the same year as the publication of d'Eon's *Lettres,* the King firmly outlawed the printing and sale of any such works.[6]

D'Eon was certainly aware of these developments and found himself enamored of English liberty. In this sense, the publication of the *Lettres* constituted an attempt to extend the tribune of public opinion to foreign affairs. And yet d'Eon's meager attempt was doomed from the start. Not only were there precious few Frenchmen prepared to accept a formal role for public opinion in the shaping of foreign policy, d'Eon did not really believe himself to be the political radical that his publication implied. In this case, he only wanted to publicize a secret correspondence in order to defend his own political turf. Still, as is the case throughout d'Eon's life, what may have been motivated by old-fashioned and conservative concerns (in this case honor and reputation) mutated into a kind of radical subversion of the status quo.

The development of the authority of public opinion shaped events in both France and England. In 1764 the English were absorbed in their own political scandal, concerning a British politician who had used the power of the press to appeal to public opinion over the heads of both the King and Parliament, and who, as a result, had fled into exile in Paris to escape arrest. This was the famous case of John Wilkes, and its particulars were so similar to those of the d'Eon affair that the two causes célèbres were often spoken about together.

Wilkes was born three years before d'Eon, in 1725, to a wealthy and pious London distiller. In 1747, he married a friend of the family, who provided him with wealth and a daughter, Polly, in 1750. But by 1756 the couple had separated, though Polly remained under her father's guardianship. Neither father nor daughter married while Wilkes lived, and Polly became the best friend that John never found in his wife.[7]

In 1757, during the Seven Years' War, Wilkes was elected to the House of Commons from his home town of Aylesbury. From the beginning of his political career, he was a protégé of William Pitt, supporting a vigorous foreign policy to expand the empire throughout North America and to defeat French interests wherever possible. When Pitt lost his majority in the House of Commons, forcing him to resign ministerial office, Wilkes joined him in the parliamentary opposition.

During the summer of 1762, on the eve of d'Eon's arrival in England, Wilkes began his own periodical, the *North Briton,* to oppose the peace negotiations and to paint the new Prime Minister, the Scottish Lord Bute, as a traitor. By December, when the negotiations with Nivernais, d'Eon, and their team had been completed, Wilkes's rhetoric had become extremely vitriolic. "It is with the deepest concern, astonishment, and indignation," Wilkes wrote in one vicious attack, "that the *Preliminary articles of the Peace* have been received by the public. They are of such a nature, that they more resemble the ancient treaties of friendship and alliance between *France* and her *old, firm, ally, Scotland,* than any which have ever subsisted between that power, and her *natural enemy,* England. The *Preliminaries,* which were communicated by a Scotsman to the *London Chronicle,* . . . are in many respects, less adequate to what England has *now* a right to expect. [In contrast,] Mr Pitt seems to feel the most sincere benevolence, and disposition to do good to the *people of England.*"[8]

By April 1763, when Parliament reconvened after the peace treaty had been signed by both parties, the government had had enough of Wilkes's paper and was ready to suppress it. Each session of Parliament began with a traditional speech by the reigning monarch. Of course, for decades such a speech was written by the Prime Minister, and everyone knew it. This year's speech, written by Lord Bute, naturally praised the government for negotiating the Peace of Paris and celebrated the end of the war against France.

Within days, Wilkes's *North Briton* no. 45 was off the presses, attacking the speech for its pro-French sympathies. Wilkes was careful to distinguish between King George and his ministers; he explained that while the King had given the speech, everyone knew it to be Bute's words and that *he* was Wilkes's target. Nonetheless, since Bute was, after all, acting as the King's agent, the government accused Wilkes of treason and libel, and issued a general warrant for the arrest of anyone connected with the paper. Consequently, in the middle of the night of 30 April–1 May 1763, nearly fifty people, including Wilkes, were dragged off to jail.

In a hearing before Britain's Chief Justice, Lord Mansfield, Wilkes attempted to transform his own trial into a debate over the nature of the British constitution. "The liberty of all peers and gentlemen, and, what touches me more sensibly, that of all the middling and inferior set of people, who stand most in need of protection," Wilkes proclaimed to the court, "is in my case this day to be finally decided upon."[9] Lord Mansfield ruled that Wilkes's status as a Member of Parliament prevented his arrest on all charges except those in which he might endanger national security.

Wilkes was free, famous, and a hero among the opposition. That made the Bute government all the more determined to seek revenge. A few months later, in the autumn of 1763, British government spies discovered copies of a pornographic poem (*An Essay on Woman*) that Wilkes had written and printed privately for the entertainment of his friends, not for publication, much less profit. Nonetheless, the announcement that such a poem was found in Wilkes's home was enough to alienate Pitt, who now denounced his old student.

More serious, on the first day of its autumn session the House of Commons voted that both the *Essay on Woman* and the *North Briton* no. 45 were grounds for charges of defamation and obscenity, and moved that a new trial proceed under Mansfield. Two months later, on 20 January 1764, the House of Commons expelled Wilkes. This time Mansfield's court found Wilkes guilty and issued a writ for his arrest. A few days earlier, Wilkes had absented himself from the trial, and indeed from England. Having been expelled from the House and proclaimed an outlaw, Wilkes began a period of exile in Paris that lasted four years.

The Wilkes affair, then, took place at the same moment the d'Eon–Guerchy affair was erupting. In a sense, the two cases developed along parallel lines, and everyone who talked about politics felt they had much in common—except for Wilkes and d'Eon themselves. "The affair of d'Eon is infamous," Wilkes wrote to a friend. "His affair is always mentioned as bearing some relation to mine, though there is not the least resemblance." Similarly, when the *Gazette d'Utrecht* joked that both Versailles and Westminster were now taking orders from "their sovereigns Mr. Wilkes and the Chevalier d'Eon," it was d'Eon who insisted that "there can be no parallel" between the two situations.[10]

But there was in fact a great deal of resemblance between the *North Briton* no. 45 and d'Eon's *Lettres, mémoires, et négociations*. Like d'Eon, Wilkes had taken foreign-policy issues directly to the public. It would have been one thing if the *North Briton* had dealt with matters in which the English people had felt directly involved, such as a gin tax or the price of grain. But Wilkes sought nothing less than a comprehensive public review of the negotiations that had led to the Peace of Paris. Both Wilkes and d'Eon, then, challenged the right of eighteenth-century states to conduct foreign policy secretly and demanded a role for the public.

Moreover, like d'Eon, Wilkes was not simply a journalist who had gotten his hands on secret documents; he was an insider who himself played a significant role in the government. As a member of the House of Commons, his right to oppose the government's foreign policy from the floor of the House would not have been disputed. It was Wilkes carrying his attack beyond the walls of Parliament that English aristocrats found objectionable. In d'Eon's case, no one would have questioned his right to privately remonstrate against his superiors; what became offensive was his appeal to the public through print.

Even the British government recognized the similarity between the two cases. When Guerchy pushed Prime Minister Grenville to arrest d'Eon, Grenville responded by comparing d'Eon to Wilkes. Grenville reasoned that if the English king could not arrest Wilkes for the *North Briton* no. 45, he certainly could not arrest d'Eon for a publication that, from England's viewpoint, was far less offensive.[11]

There were differences between the d'Eon and Wilkes cases, however, especially in the two kingdoms' political cultures. If these controversies revolved around issues of personal and press liberties, there can be no doubt that England was well ahead of France in this regard. Britain was, after all, a constitutional monarchy in which George III shared power with Parliament. Wilkes attempted to open up this already liberal system to encompass a much wider and more diverse constituency. France, on the other hand, was still very much stuck in its absolutist system, in which the crown recognized no loyal opposition, and political struggles often took the shape of court intrigues.[12]

Another way to chart the differences between France and England is to note the effect each affair had on its own political culture. The Wilkes case resulted in greater press liberties and the suppression of general warrants, and was also responsible for bringing new support to the cause of parliamentary reform. Neither d'Eon's scandal, nor any other like it, stimulated such reform in France. After the death of Louis XV in 1774, the monarchy of Louis XVI became even more despotic in its handling of foreign policy and the press. During the 1770s and 1780s, Foreign Minister Vergennes assumed an even more aggressive posture toward journalists, restricting the range of news and opinion more than his predecessors had during the hardly liberal reign of Louis XV.[13]

The affairs of d'Eon and Wilkes, however, were not simply two stories that came to the attention of the European public at the same time, and thus were compared to one another. D'Eon's relationship with Wilkes was actually more concrete than that. The two men became good friends. In fact, it would not be an exaggeration to say that d'Eon became closer to Wilkes than to any other English politician.

Despite his exile in Paris (where he sometimes dined with Broglie and Tercier), John Wilkes was, after all, one of the leaders of the parliamentary opposition to Bute's administration that d'Eon had referred to in his letter of 23 March ("The chiefs of the opposition . . . have offered me all the money that I would need"). Why would this faction want to bribe d'Eon? What did it need from him?

Following Pitt, the opposition strongly believed that if the Seven Years' War had continued, Britain would have gained even more territory from France and Spain. Thus they were bewildered that Bute and his ministers accepted a peace treaty in 1763, when total victory seemed within reach.

Specifically, they could not understand why Bute had conceded rights for French fisheries in Newfoundland. They suspected that the French had bribed Bute, but they had no evidence to make their charges stick. If anyone could provide such evidence, certainly it would be d'Eon, who knew as much about the negotiations surrounding the Treaty of Paris as anyone. When d'Eon refused an Order of Recall from his own Foreign Minister, the British opposition was ready to take him (and his secret papers) into their fold.

Thus Wilkes and his friends did everything they could to establish intimate ties with d'Eon. Even more important, they made sure that d'Eon remained safe in London, no easy task since rumors regarding plots against his life were circulating in both capitals. "I expect every day to hear of his death by assassination, or poison," Wilkes noted to a friend.[14]

One important element of the opposition's support for d'Eon was the way it was able to use crowd activities to help him. As we have seen, during the winter and spring of 1764 d'Eon lived in terror of being kidnapped from his home in Golden Square. The opposition therefore organized crowds to mill around his home, and when d'Eon went out on errands or social obligations, these crowds would cheer and protect him.[15]

In this way, d'Eon, like Wilkes himself, became the darling of the London mob, who recognized the close relationship between the two causes, as their chants—"To the health of d'Eon! To the health of Wilkes!"—attest. They saw in d'Eon a victim of government oppression who dared to publish tracts his government did not like. For these working people of London, d'Eon represented integrity and honesty. One French journal reported that d'Eon was known in London as "Mr. Truth."[16] Outraged that the French would dare to try to kidnap him in a free country, they were just as determined to prevent their own government from abusing its laws, as in the Wilkes case.

"Seeing therefore that our laws can no way justify us in sending the Chevalier d'Eon out of the kingdom," wrote one "Timothy Watchful" in a London newspaper, "it must of course follow, that they can by no means protect any persons of a different nation, who attempt to seize and carry him off by force: On the contrary, such an attempt would be the most flagrant violation of those rights and liberties which render us the envy as well as the admiration of the world, and must excite the whole thunder of our indignation against any one daring enough to set it on foot. Abstracted from all this, the Chevalier d'Eon is, as an officer, a person of approved bravery; as a minister, a person of acknowledged abilities; and as a man, a person of probity and honor: qualities that must excite our humanity in his defense, if he was even unprotected by our laws."[17]

The relationship between d'Eon and the followers of Wilkes was not one-sided. D'Eon needed the leaders of the opposition as much as they needed him. On the one hand, his proximity to them served as an implicit threat to his government that he stood ready to sell his secrets if necessary. Even more important, d'Eon's close relationship with Wilkes's supporters enhanced his value as a spy for the Secret. Louis XV was intensely interested in Wilkes and his democratic movement. For a time, he believed that Wilkes might bring down the British government and even spark a rebellion in England. Louis wanted to help fuel anything that might undermine George III's authority. Ironically, then, the closer d'Eon became to Wilkes and the opposition, the more valuable he became to Louis XV as a spy.

Libel

D'EON'S PUBLICATION of the *Lettres* constituted a challenge to, perhaps even a rebellion against, his own government. On the other hand, he knew that Louis XV was well aware of what he had chosen *not* to publish in the book. Conspicuously absent to those familiar with d'Eon's correspondence were any letters from the members of the Secret: None of the letters from Broglie or Tercier, even those on innocuous subjects, were included. Nothing from the King, nor most especially, nothing about the Secret's plans to invade England, was revealed in the book. "I am innocent and I have been condemned by your ministers," d'Eon anxiously wrote to Louis a few weeks after the book's publication. "Be convinced, Sire, that I will die your faithful subject, and that I can now, better than ever, serve Your Majesty in his great secret project."[1]

The Foreign Ministry tried to do everything it could to get rid of d'Eon. Guerchy applied constant pressure on the British government. He demanded that George III issue orders to arrest d'Eon and turn him over to French authorities. And indeed, much of London's ruling elite, including George III and the diplomatic community, were embarrassed by the *Lettres,* and wanted d'Eon punished. Nonetheless, George's own ministers concluded that there wasn't much that could be done about it. They explained to Guerchy that in England, any person, even a foreigner, could be arrested only if the government was certain the person had committed a crime; so far, the government could not find a law that d'Eon had broken. D'Eon's book may have been outrageous, they admitted, but it was legal for someone to publish the correspondence of foreign diplomats, especially if he had copies of the letters in his possession.[2]

Perhaps the most difficult thing for the French to accept was the inability of a British king to extradite a French subject to France. Over supper one evening in Paris, Broglie talked for hours with David Hume, then secretary to the British ambassador to France, about why the British government could not simply deport d'Eon. In France, Broglie argued, nothing could stop the will of the King in a matter of this kind. The famous philosopher reminded Broglie that in England the King was not sovereign, the laws were, and while everyone who lived in the kingdom was subject to those laws, no one could be held against his will unless there was evidence that some law had been violated. Broglie went home that night amazed that a monarchy could develop strong political institutions based on such strange notions.[3]

By now, Louis XV had lost all patience with d'Eon. He wanted d'Eon back in France any way possible, and was willing to risk disaster to make that happen. In the heat of anger, he temporarily shelved Broglie's plan to retain d'Eon as a spy. Rather, Louis decided to pursue two complementary strategies. First, he approved Praslin's plan to kidnap d'Eon and return him secretly to Paris. Second, he approved Guerchy's plan to implement proceedings against d'Eon for libel. Presumably if d'Eon was found guilty of libel, the French government would then have the legal means to extradite him from England.[4]

Broglie himself was ambivalent about what to do, and as d'Eon's acknowledged patron, felt responsible for the current situation. He complained to the King that none of this would have happened if "my wishes for sending Sieur d'Eon to Saint Petersburg upon the death of the Empress Elizabeth" had been heeded. Indeed, having been rehabilitated by the King so recently, Broglie's political career was threatened once again by the publication of the *Lettres,* as Praslin and Choiseul could blame the entire affair on him—a possibility that terrified him. At first, Brogile wanted to treat d'Eon gently. "We must calm him and make him believe that we don't hold him responsible," Broglie urged the King in early April. But once the King's violent reaction was made clear, Broglie accepted his master's more aggressive strategy.[5]

Guerchy even picked on d'Eon's secretary and cousin, Maurice d'Eon de Mouloize. He wrote to Mouloize's father urging him to compel his son to leave d'Eon and come home. But such pressure only served to harden the resolve of both d'Eons. "You don't know anything about it," Mouloize wrote to his father, "and so I believe that it would be inappropriate for you to speak a word of this to anyone other than ourselves."[6]

After weeks of pressure, Guerchy finally scored a victory when the British government announced that it would prosecute d'Eon for libel. A trial was set for early July. D'Eon attempted to put it off, claiming that Guerchy had "sent away some of the witnesses, which it was necessary to have in his defense."[7] D'Eon published a brief pamphlet in which he called upon Chief Justice Mansfield, William Pitt, the Earl of Temple, and Lord Bute to dismiss the libel proceedings as essentially a political trial that violated his rights. He also informed them of various plots to kidnap him, and declared that English law alone ought to guarantee his safety, since "liberty . . . forms the basis of English government."[8]

None of d'Eon's efforts had any effect. The court overruled his motions for dismissal, finding that his printing of Guerchy's private letters had injured the ambassador's reputation. As was common in English law, sentencing was delayed until the next court session a few months later. By then, d'Eon had gone into hiding, fearing for his life, trying to find some way out of the trap Guerchy had set for him. Rumors were circulating that when the British nabbed d'Eon, the government would make a deal with Paris to trade him for Wilkes (still in French exile). The free laws of England had stopped working in d'Eon's favor.[9]

D'Eon reportedly stayed in London at a friend's home and wore female clothes whenever he went out—at least that is what one informant told Broglie. This is the first mention of cross-dressing that we know of in d'Eon's life, but we should not make too much of it. He was not presenting himself to anyone, but hiding himself from everyone. Cross-dressing for the purposes of disguise was a common enough practice in d'Eon's time. We need look no further than John Wilkes for confirmation: It was reported that when Wilkes fled British authorities for France in 1763, he eluded the London police by dressing in women's garb.[10]

During this brief period of hiding, the tables turned yet again because of another remarkable development that shocked everyone involved, including d'Eon himself. In October 1764, one of d'Eon's bitterest enemies, Pierre-Henri Treyssac de Vergy, confessed to d'Eon that he had been part of a conspiracy to murder him—a plot organized by the Comte de Guerchy. More important, Vergy was willing to go public with the story. In November he offered under oath the most minute details about the plot during two separate court hearings, and then he immediately published a pamphlet addressed to the Duc de Choiseul that repeated the entire story. Even on his deathbed in 1774, Vergy stuck to this version of the story.[11]

In his testimony, Vergy pointed his finger at Foreign Minister Praslin as the ultimate ringleader of the plot against d'Eon. Vergy claimed that Praslin, during a meeting in Paris, had told him that d'Eon had to be removed from office and that Vergy would eventually become Guerchy's new secretary. Next, Vergy corroborated d'Eon's story about the poisoning. Not only had Guerchy tried to have d'Eon poisoned at a dinner party on 28 October 1763, but when that failed, the Ambassador then allegedly ordered Vergy to assassinate d'Eon—an order that Vergy claimed he refused to obey. Vergy also confirmed that Praslin's ultimate goal was not so much d'Eon as the Broglies. "We want to strengthen the enemies of the Maréchal [de Broglie]. . . . For that, d'Eon is useful," Praslin is said to have told Vergy.[12]

Once again a word-bomb had exploded among Europe's senior diplomats. "Shall I tell you anything about d'Eon? It is sending coals to Paris," Horace Walpole wrote to Lord Hertford, England's ambassador to Versailles. "You must know his story better than me; so in two words: Vergy, his antagonist, is become his convert: has wrote for him, and sworn for him,—nay, has made an affidavit before Judge Wilmot, that Monsieur de Guerchy had hired him to stab or poison d'Eon."[13]

This shocking turn of events constituted nothing short of a coup d'état for d'Eon, and everyone knew it. Vergy's confession took the wind out of any libel prosecution by Guerchy, gave new life to d'Eon's old charges of attempted murder, and, just as important, demonstrated, without revealing anything of the Secret, that the feud between d'Eon and Guerchy was actually grounded in the power struggle between Praslin and the Broglies.

"Finally, Monsieur," d'Eon wrote confidently to the Comte de Broglie, "The horrible conspiracy is discovered: I can now say to M. de Guerchy what the Prince de Conti said to the Maréchal de Luxembourg before the Battle of Steinkerque: 'Sangaride, this day is a grand day for you, my cousin. If you can get out of this one, I will acknowledge how clever you are.' Nobody is more interested than you and M. the Maréchal to take all possible means to defend yourselves against the enemies of your household. The King cannot now keep from seeing the truth; it has been made clear today. I have done my part. I have notified the Duke of York and his brothers of the truth and of the blackguards who have conspired against you, the Maréchal de Broglie, and me. They will inform the King, the Queen, and the Princess of Wales. Already M. de Guerchy, who had been received quite badly since his return [from a short visit to France], is in the most troubling confusion, despite his audacity, and I know that the English King is disposed to render justice to M. le Maréchal and me. Do your part, M. le Comte, act accordingly and do not abandon me, whatever you do. I will defend myself until the last drop of blood, and, by my courage, I will serve your house despite you, for you have abandoned me, you have not sent me any money, even though I have fought for you. Do not abandon me, M. le Comte, and do not reduce me to despair. Send me a sum sufficient for supporting your war and mine, if you do not want to be stamped out under the feet of injustice. I have spent more than £1,200 for my war, and you have sent me nothing: that is abominable. Allow me to tell you, M. le Comte, that I would have never thought that possible."[14]

D'Eon's new clout was demonstrated when less than a month after receiving this letter, Broglie convinced the King to approve £1,200 for d'Eon's immediate use, and negotiations on a reconciliation with d'Eon continued at a more intense pace, with d'Eon's valet Hugonnet shuttling between England and France. Toward the end of 1764, the King approved d'Eon's demand that Broglie himself cross the Channel and negotiate with d'Eon in person; by the beginning of January, Broglie was pleading with the King to order Guerchy to withdraw the libel suit altogether.[15]

From his side, d'Eon came forward with six specific demands to resolve his status: first, setting up an official meeting with the British king and queen, in which he could resign his post as Plenipotentiary Minister in an honorable fashion; second, allowing the prosecution of the Comte de Guerchy for attempted murder to proceed; third, dismissing the libel prosecution against him; fourth, recognizing d'Eon's titles and assuring safe passage in France; fifth, the sum of £30,000 (more than 650,000 French livres), of which d'Eon would presumably live off the interest; sixth, reinstating and promoting his assistant, Maurice d'Eon de Mouloize. When these six conditions were met, d'Eon promised, he would turn over all diplomatic papers to Broglie.[16]

CHAPTER 26

Indictment

D ESPITE THIS HAPPY REVERSAL of his political fortunes, d'Eon suffered a terrible personal tragedy. In January 1765, his closest friend, cousin, and loyal assistant, Maurice d'Eon de Mouloize, died of smallpox at the age of twenty-eight. Since the summer of 1763, when Mouloize had come to London as d'Eon's secretary, he had largely sacrificed his own career for the sake of his older relative.

D'Eon was especially shaken because the death was so unnecessary. "He never wanted to inoculate himself," d'Eon tearfully wrote to the Comtesse de Massol. Inoculation was a new and controversial procedure in eighteenth-century Europe. Recently learned from the Turks, it seemed an absurd and barbaric practice to many stubborn Europeans—including Catholic Frenchmen. When Voltaire became an advocate, inoculation became another cause célèbre of the Enlightenment. D'Eon himself was pulled into the controversy during his tenure as Plenipotentiary Minister, when the French government publicized English enthusiasm for inoculation. The more d'Eon learned from the English, the stronger his advocacy for the procedure became. Still, d'Eon's cousin was proof that there were many intelligent Frenchmen who refused the advice of scientists. Mouloize "always persisted in the vain opinion that he would never get smallpox," d'Eon wrote, "because his grandfather reached the age of 90 without contracting it. He died a martyr to such prejudice."[1]

Six weeks later, d'Eon was jolted out of this mourning period by an indictment lodged by the British government against Guerchy for hiring Vergy to "kill and assassinate" d'Eon. It described the Ambassador as "being a person of cruel mind and disposition, not having the fear of God before him, but moved and seduced by the instigation of the devil, and having conceived the blackest malice against . . . d'Eon."[2]

Guerchy an alleged conspirator in an assassination plot—again scandal shook the European diplomatic world, thanks to the Chevalier d'Eon. For the French, everything about the indictment was insulting—that the official representative of the French king could be tried for attempted murder seemed a clear violation of diplomatic immunity. Besides, in France, where indictments were controlled by the crown, the prosecution of a diplomat could happen only if the monarch intended it as an act of war. David Hume again patiently explained to a skeptical Broglie that the English political system was different from the French. Laws in England were immutable. If a law was violated, Hume boasted, the government had the obligation to prosecute the criminal, no matter his status. In contrast to France, whose Old Regime was based on the notion of privilege— literally, private law—in England, no one, at least in theory, was above the law.[3]

English public opinion was bitterly divided. On the one hand, George III and his ministers were embarrassed by the indictment, seeing it as an unnecessary insult to Louis XV. They immediately took the case out of the lower court and referred it to Chief Justice Mansfield's higher Court of King's Bench. There they moved to dismiss the case with a *noli prosequi*. But the Attorney General decided that the evidence against Guerchy was simply too great for the court to do so. Not only was there Vergy's powerful testimony, but Guerchy's valet, the one who allegedly had slipped the opium into d'Eon's drink, had fled town fearing prosecution, further incriminating Guerchy.

The parliamentary opposition wanted to exploit anti-French sentiment whenever possible. For them a trial would highlight the despotic activities of the Choiseul regime against even its own subjects. Alongside these Pittites were many of the working people of London, who never tired of celebrating d'Eon as their favorite, demonstrating their attitudes in the street. At one point, they mobbed Guerchy's carriage, pelting it with stones, nearly killing him. They viewed a *noli prosequi* as a campaign waged by the government to appease the French king, which would ultimately destroy British liberty. D'Eon acknowledged the power of these political forces when he described himself in a letter to Broglie as being "under the protection of the Tribune of the People."[4]

The result was a stalemate. While Guerchy's trial was not dismissed, neither did it move forward. The prosecution simply sat on it. And clearly Vergy's indictment also put the libel suit against d'Eon in limbo. Meanwhile, d'Eon continued his intense negotiations with Broglie and Louis

XV to resolve the crisis that had now been going on almost two years. During 1763 and 1764, Louis not only wanted his secret instructions of 3 June 1763 returned to him, he also wanted d'Eon himself returned to France and probably imprisoned. But by 1765, Broglie had managed to persuade Louis that while securing d'Eon's secret papers was essential, it would be in France's best interests to keep d'Eon in England.

After 1763, Louis XV was convinced of two things regarding England: first, that it had now become France's greatest rival in Europe and that to a great extent, France's prosperity would depend on Britain's decline; second, that the English political system, filled with its noisy opposition and aggressive public, was prone to instability, and perhaps even revolution. With seven Prime Ministers rising and falling, the decade of the 1760s was the most tumultuous of the century.[5] The French in particular could not distinguish between an opposition that was loyal to the regime, but would do almost anything to gain power, and an opposition that was genuinely revolutionary. This inability to appreciate the subtleties of British politics convinced many intelligent Frenchmen, such as the Comte de Broglie, that French policy could hasten a homespun British rebellion during the 1760s or 1770s.

When d'Eon went to London in 1763, the members of the Secret thought he could help facilitate a French invasion. Ironically, d'Eon's troubles with his own government made him more attractive to certain British politicians. Pitt and Temple, for example, wanted d'Eon to become a naturalized Englishman, and were willing to sponsor him in the House of Commons. They and their followers courted d'Eon, inviting him for dinners and weekends at their country estates, as well as seeking his advice on matters of substance and administration.[6]

By the summer of 1765, Broglie had persuaded Louis XV that d'Eon's "intimate relations" with such important statesmen provided the Secret with a unique opportunity. Ironically, since d'Eon was openly despised by the French Foreign Ministry, he would continue to gain the confidence and affection of the British establishment. But since he was working secretly for Broglie and the King, France would have placed an intelligent spy in the very bosom of the enemy.[7]

Following this logic, Louis changed course in 1765. Instead of "firing" d'Eon from the Secret, he allowed Broglie to retain him as a spy in London. By the spring of 1766, Broglie had worked out a covert arrangement between d'Eon and Louis that was acceptable to both parties. From d'Eon's viewpoint, many of the essential points he had raised in December 1764 were included: He would receive an annual pension of 12,000 livres for the rest of his life; his titles of Chevalier and Dragoon Captain, along with his military honors, would remain intact; and he would not be prosecuted by any French court. He would also retain a special relationship to the King, through Broglie, as a spy for the Secret, and in that capacity he would write confidential reports to Broglie about British politics. But he could not return to France, at least not until Choiseul and Praslin had retired from the government. The King understood that d'Eon would surrender his 3 June 1763 instructions. Thus by occupying d'Eon in England, Louis avoided the worry about what to do with him in France.[8]

Royal Decree of 1 April 1766

IN COMPENSATION FOR *the services that the Sieur d'Eon has rendered to me in Russia as well as in my armies and other commissions that I have given to him, I gladly want to assure him an annual pension of 12,000 livres, that I will pay to him exactly every six months, in whatever country he is, except in a country at war with me, and until I decide to appoint him to some post whose benefits are more considerable than the present ones.*

At Versailles, this 1 April 1766
signed: **Louis**

I, THE UNDERSIGNED, *Plenipotentiary Minister of the King in this court, certify on my honor that the above promise is truly written and signed in the proper hand of the King my master, and that he has ordered me to remit it to M. d'Eon.*

London, the 11 July 1766
signed: **Durand**[1]

Part III

INSIDE D'EON'S LIBRARY

He—for there could be no doubt of his sex, though the fashion
of the time did something to disguise it . . .
                                        —*Virginia Woolf,* Orlando

D'Eon to Jean-Jacques Rousseau

London

20 February 1766[1]

Monsieur,

It is only recently that I have learned in my isolation of your arrival on this island. If I had known earlier, I would have already welcomed you, and if I had had the honor of knowing you personally, I would have written you a long time ago inviting you to come more promptly to this isle of liberty.

The knowledge that I have of your character and of your virtue from your works, those I have read in Paris and in London, makes me think that you will be a little less disgusted with London than Paris, that you will live much more freely, more peacefully, and take better walks in some seclusion a bit removed from the capital. You could retire to the province of Wales, which is the Switzerland of England; I could arrange some good friends for you there, and you could go there and see it. If you like hunting and fishing, you could live there, without depending on anyone, with the same liberty and innocence of our forefathers.

May these reflections express everything that I feel about your situation, things which I find particularly moving because they relate to mine: Our misfortunes have almost the same common origin, however different the causes and the effects. They say that you love liberty and truth too much. They burden me with the same reproach, and they add that we would make ourselves much happier by calming down, you in humiliating fewer scholars, and me in disputing less with the Ministers. I agree that you have suffered terrible humiliation in the eyes of philosophy, but I can say the same regarding my dispute with the Ministers. I recognized their authority, but that did not take away what I

believe is my right to defend myself against the barbarity of a novice ambas-
sador who violates positive and natural law, human rights and public charac-
ter, and who in my opinion has ruptured and lacerated all of the parts of your
Social Contract.[2]

In order to convince you of all this, I am sending you what I have published
on my affair. I send it to you not because of the distracting furor it caused
throughout the world, nor to render a judgment about the atrocious injustices
that I have proven, but because it is natural for the afflicted to search out one
another. It is to alleviate my sorrows that I place these publications under the
eyes of a man such as you. There are only a few sages and a particular enlight-
ened public who could judge in silence the crimes of certain great men who
believe themselves to be above all laws. I have read your Lettres écrites de la
montagne *[Letters Written from the Mountain (1764)], and all the distin-*
guished replies of your adversaries. Allow me, therefore, to persuade you to read
my responses as well. I would be humiliated if, after defending to the best of my
abilities the rights of honor and of humanity, there remained prejudices about
me in the mind of a man as virtuous, as enlightened, who I loved and respected
as much as you. I have no way to learn of such a judgment on your part; how-
ever, it is principally in your works that I have learned that the conservation of
my integrity was the fundamental law of nature, and precedes the obligation of
all other laws when they are in conflict; that this natural law is independent of
all human conventions. Thus whatever the dignities and the character of my
enemy, he can never acquire any right on my life; no more than I can have one
on his or that of my neighbor.

One could in many ways make a parallel of the strangeness of your situation
and mine. You, Republican and Protestant, for having published Emile *in a*
Republic, you were outlawed without having a fair hearing.[3] Me, a French
minister, for having published a defense against another French minister who
attacked me, I have been condemned in a Republic without having been heard.
If I have not appeared at the King's Bench, it is certainly not because of any con-
tempt for English laws, which in general are much more just than anywhere
else. It is that I know that, because of political complaisance, they would con-
demn me and not judge me. They refused me the necessary time to defend myself
and also my witnesses. When I had had them ready for the following term,
someone tried to kidnap me and send me to France for refusing a summons to
appear before a tribunal. Prudence obliged me into hiding, and during this
time, they condemned my book as a libel without any hearing. On the one hand,
they condemned my defense, and on the other, they suspended the verdict of the
Grand Jury of England, who had found my enemy wrong and guilty of crimes
of poison and assassination against my person. Not being able to defend him
[Guerchy] with the truth, they sought to subvert the severity of the laws, to

exploit their authority by requesting in the final instance a Noli Prosequi. *Is not this request itself the best evidence of a crime? Despite English liberty and equity, I can not obtain full justice, because my poisoner and my assassin is still officially in power. His crimes will rank in history among the great unpunished crimes. Alas! My dear Rousseau, my old colleague in politics, my master in literature, companion in my misfortune, you who, like me, had proof of the caprice and injustice of many of my compatriots, it is to you that I can say with truth that I would have never dared, following my relatives, to serve the King and my country with such zeal and love as I did, if I could have believed that slander, poison, and the dagger would be in the end my only compensation for my services and my wounds. Don't say anymore that you are the only truly unhappy man, that the strangeness of your destiny belongs only to you. I agree that there have been many extraordinary misfortunes in the course of your life, but admit that the star of my birth has not been happy either. However I was born with the Caul [with the amniotic sac intact; a sign of good luck], I have belied the proverb. Nothing like that must sadden us up to a certain point, our conscience regrets nothing, and we know by our proper experience the malice of men.*

However it seems, I am not complaining about the misfortunes that have happened to me. Providence (thanks to English liberty and my vigilance) has permitted only that the innocent fall under the axe of his prosecutor. The heavens have given me virtue, the unjust man cannot blacken me. I have embarrassed calumny, I have shut the mouth of the liar, and that of the impostor who would let loose against me. My enemies are already covered with ignominy, and wear shame as their topcoat. In my oppression my heart is at peace, in my poverty I am in abundance. There are still here the English lovers of justice, zealous defenders of liberty, illustrious and generous English who keep watch over my safety, and I do not doubt that many of them, touched by your virtues and your rare talents, won't avenge your misfortunes and your enemies.

I will finish, Monsieur, by confessing to you, with the good faith of which I have worked to make clear my whole life, that I am always naturally taken to support the validity of your philosophy, except certain points on religion that it is not permissible for me to adopt, by which I submit (only in a certain number of extraordinary cases) my reason to faith.[4] I don't comprehend any more than you the mysteries that you examined; I don't seek to investigate them for my happiness in this world, and in the other. If one requested of me 100,000 écus to make me understand and believe a mystery, I would neither believe nor pay; but on the one hand, no one asks anything of me, and on the other hand, so much is promised me. It is therefore more advantageous to believe in the words of Jesus Christ who cannot deceive us, to have confidence in the promises that are manifest in the hearts of men, happy or unhappy, this tender consolation, and the soothing hope of a happy and durable future. For all that I cannot understand in the Holy Bible, whose majesty and authenticity no one until the present has better depicted than you, I write with Saint Augustine: O Altitudo! *I am not, however, among the number of those fanatical Catholics who believe everything because they understand nothing. I burn no one, neither on earth nor in the heavens. Please God, my dear Rousseau, may my actions respond to the purity of my faith, and please God that your faith be also simple and also as pure as your actions. The Christian religion would need a man such as yourself, who had the righteousness of your mores, the objectivity of your conduct, the force of your logic, the enlightened eloquence, joined to the sublimity of your genius. Soon you will strengthen the spirit of the weak, you will support the walls of the forts. You will dispel and sweep away this ant-hill of little authors who are one hundred times more incredulous than you, without being able to develop the least of your arguments.*

I have the honor to be, with all the esteem and attachment that inspires your virtues, your talents, and your misery,

Monsieur,

Your very humble and very obedient servant,
The Chevalier d'Eon

Rousseau's Disciple

T HESE TWO very different documents—the King's concerning d'Eon's pension and d'Eon's letter to Rousseau—help delineate d'Eon's odd political status for the next decade, until his transformation into a woman in 1776. By the spring of 1766, when the smoke from his political feuds had cleared, d'Eon had at least achieved a partial victory, which was itself an amazing feat. He had managed to humiliate Guerchy, had won a handsome annual pension from the King, and was still working for the Secret as a spy. Indeed, during the next decade d'Eon became France's best source of intelligence about British politics. When, for example, John Wilkes returned from his exile in France to run for Parliament, d'Eon sent regular reports about his activities back to Broglie.[1]

But d'Eon's victory, if one can call it that, came at too high a price. He had struggled so hard against such daunting odds, he had come to know danger so intimately, that his triumph was a painful one. Besides, what had he really achieved? D'Eon had not entered political life to remain a spy in virtual exile; he had looked forward to a career that might climax with a ministry. Any French nobleman in political life hoped to work at some point in Versailles. But in 1766 d'Eon seemed as far from an appointment at Versailles as ever; in his own country he was still regarded by many as an outlaw.

D'Eon's greatest problem remained: Praslin and Choiseul still were ministers, and their hold on power seemed more secure than ever. Two years earlier, when Mme de Pompadour had died and Broglie was recalled from internal exile, d'Eon had believed a shakeup in the ministry to be imminent. But that prospect soon fizzled; Choiseul had now become, in d'Eon's words, "more despotic than all the Grand Visirs of Constantinople."

Choiseul's cousin Praslin, who as Foreign Minister dealt more directly with d'Eon, was no improvement: "an abusive and arrogant man; the inventor of misery." It was they more than anyone else who were responsible for allowing d'Eon "to vegetate in the hope of a better future."[2]

The longevity of the Praslin–Choiseul government frustrated d'Eon no end. He had to watch his every step. He could not manage his financial affairs in Burgundy properly; he could not return to France even for a visit. More painful, he could not explain his situation candidly to his own mother, for fear that such letters would be intercepted by the police. "It is necessary to maintain one's patience for the present," d'Eon wrote to another relative, "and to suffer the bad with the good." But sooner or later his patience would run out.[3]

To Rousseau, d'Eon had written of a heart guided by virtue. But the letter also reveals that d'Eon's heart was as much guided by hatred for his "enemies" as anything else. Elsewhere, he blamed all his troubles on "despotic ministers." Drawing on an old theme that would renew itself in the era leading up to the Revolution, d'Eon insisted on the goodness of the King, claiming only that Louis was being deceived by "monsters" seeking to undermine his authority and policies. "I don't complain about the King, who is the best of masters, who has only treated me kindly, I complain solely about these enslaved puny royal underlings at the court."[4]

D'Eon might not blame the King personally for his misfortunes, but he increasingly came to blame the political system that nurtured such a weak monarch. Earlier, political life had offered d'Eon enormous opportunities—in the spring of 1763 there had been promises of wealth, power, and glory. But from his viewpoint in 1766, the system had betrayed him. As far as he could tell, his patrons had used him to further their own interests, and when he was no longer of any use to them, they tossed him aside. During this period, d'Eon had a recurring dream that he was a human cannonball fired in battle from his side over to the enemy.[5] The dream reveals his feeling of helplessness, of being an agent of someone else's policy, of being used as a weapon in the struggle between England and France.

Slowly d'Eon began to understand that political life itself, rather than any particular people, was responsible for his sad situation. He came to believe that the political world of the Old Regime did not offer an arena where a person could display virtue; to the contrary, it constituted a polluted public space in which the worth and honor of a gentleman were too often disregarded, and where falsehood and betrayal were the norm.

The feud with Guerchy was the final proof for d'Eon that Montesquieu had been right about the direction of French politics: The country was becoming a tyranny regardless of whatever good intentions King Louis may have had. "The history of the entire world," d'Eon wrote in the *Lettres, mémoires, et négociations*, "has never furnished us with a better example of this MINISTERIAL DESPOTISM."[6] With Montesquieu dead, the greatest challenger to French absolutism was d'Eon's "master," Jean-Jacques Rousseau.

These potent political attitudes—feelings that were relatively new to d'Eon, and that he did not quite know how to express—spilled out, however unintentionally, in his letter to Rousseau. D'Eon did not simply admire Rousseau; he did not just feel the need to make Rousseau his judge; he repeatedly identified his life with Rousseau's, and saw their two careers as parallel: "Our misfortunes have almost the same common origin, however different the causes and the effects." Indeed, among all the papers by or pertaining to d'Eon, no other living figure was ever described in such mimetic terms—"my old colleague in politics, my master in literature, companion in my misfortune." To understand d'Eon's feelings about himself and his situation, we must know a bit more about Jean-Jacques Rousseau.

D'Eon states that just as he had been tricked by despotic ministers, so Rousseau had been tricked by narrow-minded scholars and philosophers. The early careers of Rousseau and d'Eon were in fact quite similar. Both men were well known in political and intellectual circles at an early age. Rousseau had been secretary to the French ambassador to Venice in 1743 and 1744. After that experience, he returned to Paris, where he cut such a figure among Enlightenment philosophers that Jean Le Rond d'Alembert, an editor with Diderot of the *Encyclopédie*, described even a young Rousseau as among the greatest minds of the age.[7]

Despite Rousseau's reputation as a young genius, he grew increasingly disenchanted with both the political world of the Old Regime and the intellectual world of the Enlightenment. In a series of works that culminated with three classics in 1761–62 (the *Social Contract*, *Emile*, and *La Nouvelle Héloïse*), Rousseau reached enormous fame as perhaps the most important writer of his day, but curiously, at the same time, as Europe's greatest iconoclast. At the core of Rousseau's works is the conviction that European political and cultural life was organized in such a way as to make a virtuous life impossible. A virtuous man, he argued, would seem ridiculous in London or Paris.

Rousseau's own life exemplified such pessimistic claims. While his books were met with adulation from readers, the political and intellectual establishments often scorned him. His native Geneva expelled him, and France more than once threatened to throw him into the Bastille. Indeed,

Rousseau accepted David Hume's invitation to England only because of an impending arrest by the French authorities.

D'Eon had read all of Rousseau's major works carefully, especially the most recent *Lettres écrites de la montagne.* He identified less with the arguments developed in those books and more with Rousseau's life struggle: the ability of one virtuous man to write the truth in a world of artifice and deceit. D'Eon's promise to readers in the preface of the *Lettres, mémoires, et négociations*—"my politics is finally that of an honest man who always tells the truth"—comes directly from Rousseau.[8]

D'Eon's identification with Rousseau also makes clear the extent to which his own political career had reached a dead end. How could he live a life of virtue as a spy in London? How could he expect any sort of advancement or rehabilitation? Like Rousseau, he saw himself as absolutely alone, charting a course for himself that was not at all clear, filled with unpredictable pitfalls. Rousseau was a refugee from the world of letters, d'Eon from the world of politics. Neither man could find a secure foothold in the Old Regime.

In a letter to his mother, d'Eon explained this position in language lifted directly from Rousseau's *Discourse on the Origin of Inequality:* "As to those who will tell you that your son is 'a wild beast reared in the forests of Burgundy'—as M. de Guerchy has already said—reply to them with me and my friend Jean-Jacques that nature treats all animals left on their own with predilection." Just as dogs and cats were "stronger, more vigorous, and more courageous in the forests than in our houses, losing these advantages when they were domesticated . . . so it is with man himself. In becoming social and the slave of the high-and-mighty, or those who ape greatness, he becomes weak, timid, and servile, while his lifestyle becomes soft and effeminate."[9]

Thus both d'Eon and Rousseau confronted an existential problem: how to live in a world that had made them celebrities, yet had no place for them. For Rousseau, by the end of the 1760s the answer seemed to be to become the establishment's pet radical. He accepted offers from wealthy aristocrats, including the Prince de Conti, to live on the grounds of their chateaus, where, often in sumptuous isolation, he wrote his last works in relative peace.

At first, d'Eon tried a similar kind of compromise. During the decade after 1766, he spent many hours each day reading in his study, ostensibly researching his old area of expertise, government finance and taxation. And indeed, in 1774 his thirteen-volume *Loisirs du Chevalier d'Eon de Beaumont sur divers sujets importans d'administration, etc. pendant son séjour en Angleterre* (Reflections of the Chevalier d'Eon de Beaumont on Various

Important Subjects of Administration, etc. During His Stay in England) was published. But unlike Rousseau's, the words that d'Eon wrote during this period did not reflect his political experience or personal crisis. They are academic works, written in a scholarly and distant style. Rarely do they touch on topics of much controversy. These writings, in short, did not exhibit the kind of psychological intensity found in Rousseau's books or in d'Eon's own unpublished manuscripts. Thus, despite d'Eon's identification with Rousseau, despite his similar feelings of political persecution and alienation, the influence of Rousseau on d'Eon is best seen in d'Eon's behavior rather than in his published writings.

D'Eon's Library

WITHOUT THE RESPONSIBILITIES of a family, the upkeep of an estate, the rigors of military life, or the demands of political office, d'Eon had a great deal of time on his hands. To some extent, he spent it studying government finance and taxation in preparation for the *Loisirs*. But d'Eon also read other things; indeed, he seems to have read everything.

D'Eon tried to work out his Rousseauian alienation from Old Regime politics by reading. He had been a voracious reader since boyhood, and as an adult he became a compulsive buyer of books. During this period in London, between 1762 and 1777, he built an extraordinarily large private collection. For example, during one ten-week period in 1764 he purchased more than 200 books. By the time he returned to France in 1777, he had amassed some 6,000 books and 500 rare manuscripts.[1] In an era when books were much more expensive than they are today, this constitutes an amazing feat for one man. His pension allowed him to live very well, but he spent so much of his discretionary income on books that many of his letters to French officials include requests for even more money.

When the French Revolution threw d'Eon into poverty, he was forced to put his library up for sale. Although the sale did not take place until his death, a catalogue was prepared by the auctioneer Christie. This catalogue, along with a second one that was put together just before the actual sale, offer a good indication of what d'Eon was reading before his return to France in 1777.[2]

For the most part, there are few surprises. He had an extensive collection of works on European law and government. He owned dozens of manuscripts by the seventeenth-century French military strategist the Maréchal de Vauban. While in England, he bought 557 copies of Horace's works, constituting the largest single collection of that Roman author in the world.[3]

The great number of reference books reveals that this was a working library for a serious scholar. D'Eon owned countless dictionaries and encyclopedias, some general, some on specific topics, including a first edition of Diderot and d'Alembert's *Encyclopédie,* the most important work of the French Enlightenment. In addition, he owned many grammars and foreign-language dictionaries, including several for Hebrew alone, plus hundreds of religious books and manuscripts, including more than forty bibles, a fifteenth-century Greek manuscript, and a Latin manuscript dating from the year 998.

D'Eon, of course, owned editions of nearly every major political author of the eighteenth century, including Voltaire, Montesquieu, Helvétius, Locke, Mably, Raynal, and especially Rousseau: "This edition is the most recent," explains a note in the first catalogue about the 1769 Amsterdam edition of the *Oeuvres de Rousseau,* "the most beautiful, and the most complete, supervised directly by the author."[4]

When we compare d'Eon's library to other large private libraries of the era, such as those of Montesquieu or the philosopher and government minister Turgot, for example, we find many of the same kinds of books.[5] D'Eon may have been less interested in scientific questions than those better-known bibliophiles were, but he seems to have been more committed to mastering ancient languages. For the most part, d'Eon's library seems fairly typical of an eighteenth-century *philosophe.*

There was one group of books, however, not found in the libraries of Montesquieu, Turgot, or apparently any other large private collector of the day. This was a section of forty to sixty books about women. They ranged from multivolume encyclopedias to small pamphlets; from devotional works meant for pious Catholic women to militant feminist manifestos.[6] Outside the largest public collections, such as those that would become the British Library or the Bibliothèque Nationale, we know of no other person who assembled so many historical and contemporary books about women. It is a unique collection.[7]

Like the other volumes in d'Eon's library, the majority of his books on women date from the period before 1777, the year he returned to France as a woman. While it is possible he had bought some of these books before coming to England in 1762, it is unlikely that he would have shipped more than a few volumes across the English Channel. Thus,

Astell, Mary. *Some Reflections Upon Marriage*, 4th ed. (London, 1730) [1: 58]*

Aublet de Maubuy, Jean-Zorobabel. *Les Vies des femmes illustres de la France*, 6 vols. (Paris, 1762–68) [6: 546]

Biographium Faeminem. The Female Worthies; or Memoirs of the Most Illustrious Ladies of All Ages and Nations Who Have Been Eminently Distinguished for Their Magnanimity, Learning, Genius, Virtue, Piety, and Other Excellent Endowments, 2 vols. in 1 (London, 1766) [6: 651]

Boudier de Villemart, Pierre-Joseph. *Le Nouvel ami des femmes, ou, La Philosophie du sexe* (Amsterdam and Paris, 1779) [6: 545]

[Drake, Judith.] *An Essay in Defense of the Female Sex*, 2nd ed. (London, 1696) [6: 645]

Du Bosc, Jacques. *L'Honneste femme* (Paris, 1647) [6: 164]

Fauques, Marianne Agnès. *The Life of the Marchioness de Pompadour*, 4th ed., 2 vols. (London, n.d.) [6: 666]

Female Rights Vindicated (London, 1758) [1: 44]

Galien de Chateau-Thierry, Mme. *Apologies des dames appuyée sur l'histoire* (Paris, 1737) [6: 550]

La Croix, Jean-François. *Dictionnaire historique portatif des femmes célèbres*, 3 vols. (Paris, 1769) [6.551]

La Porte, Joseph. *Histoire littéraire des femmes françaises*, 5 vols. (Paris, 1769) [6: 102]

La Vallière, Louise-Françoise, Duchesse de. *Lettres de Madame la Duchesse de la Vallière, morte religieuse carmelite* (Liege and Paris, 1767).

The Lawes Resolutions of Women's Rights or the Lawes Provision for Women (London, 1632) [2: 42]

Le Moyne, Pierre. *La Galerie des femmes fortes*, 5th ed., 2 vols. in 1 (Paris, 1665) [6: 557 and 585]

Lenglet du Fresnoy [also Dufresnoy], Nicolas. *Histoire de Jeanne d'Arc dite la Pucelle d'Orléans*, 3 vols. (Amsterdam, 1775) [6: 555]

Le Roy, Alphonse. *Récherches sur les habillemens des femmes et des enfans; ou Examen de la manière dont il faut vêtir l'un et l'autre sexe* (Paris, 1772) [6: 548]

Portia. *The Polite Lady; or A Course of Female Education* (London, 1760) [6: 650]

Serviez, Jacques Roergas de. *Les Femmes des douze cesars; contenant la vie et les intrigues secrètes des imperatrice et femmes des premiers empereurs romains; ou l'on voit les traits les plus interessants de l'histoire romaine* (Paris, 1758) [6: 547]

Thomas, Antoine-Léonard. *Essai sur le caractère des moeurs, et l'esprit des femmes dans les différens siècle* (Paris, 1772) [6: 554]

Vertron, Claude-Charles Guyonne de. *La Nouvelle Pandore, ou, Les Femmes illustres du siècle de Louis le Grand. Recueil de pièces academiques en prose et en vers, sur la preference des sexes*, 2nd ed., 2 vols. (Paris, 1703) [6: 549]

Walsh, William. *Discours sur les femmes, adressé à Eugenie et suivi d'un Dialoge philosophique et moral sur le bonheur* (Paris, 1768) [6: 553]

Warder, Joseph. *The True Amazons; or, The Monarchy of Bees: Being a New Discovery and Improvement of Those Wonderful Creatures* (London, 1713) [6: 647]

---

* Bracketed numbers indicate section and page number in *Catalogue of the Scarce Books and Valuable Manuscripts of the Chevalière d'Eon . . .* (London, 1791).

when we integrate the dates of publication with facts about d'Eon's life, it is safe to assume that most of the volumes were purchased during his London residency between 1762 and 1777.

Is it simply a coincidence that one of the most avid collectors of women's books became the first known man in European history to live half his life as a woman? The facts are as follows: D'Eon was buying and presumably reading books about women during the same decade (1766–76) that rumors about his gender identity began spreading in London and Paris. By 1777, d'Eon himself was willing to admit publicly that he was a woman. Is it too far-fetched to suggest that d'Eon's reading had something to do with his adoption of this new gender identity? Still, before we can accept the notion that his gender transformation was aided by intense reading during this period of alienation, we first need to explore what these texts said regarding gender roles in the early modern world.

D'Eon owned at least six multivolume encyclopedias of "women worthies," two from the seventeenth century and four published during the 1760s. The oldest and probably the best known was a model for what subsequently became a genre: Pierre Le Moyne's *Galerie des femmes fortes*, first published in 1647 and translated into English in 1652 as *The Gallery of Heroick Women*. And a gallery is exactly what it is. The two illustrated volumes contained short articles on famous women throughout history. In a lengthy introduction, Le Moyne bemoaned the fact that women had been largely left out of history, resulting in a lack of appreciation for what they might offer to society. Throughout the encyclopedia, Le Moyne used the articles didactically to demonstrate the significant contributions women had made to civilization. Their virtues, he wrote at one point, were "as beneficial to the public as [those] of men."[8]

Claude-Charles Guyonne de Vertron's *La Nouvelle Pandore* (The New Pandora) restricted its purview to women famous during the author's own day. Like Le Moyne, Vertron noted that elite women had risen to prominence during the reign of Louis XIV (1643–1715), and Vertron believed they were in no small way responsible for its glory. Indeed, the notion that French women reached a zenith of influence, power, and virtue during the early years of the Sun King pervades these encyclopedias.[9]

Vertron, like Le Moyne, began with a preface that spilled over into polemics. He included a dialogue between one man who passionately believed that women were at least the equals of men and another man who was convinced of their natural inferiority. Clearly Vertron's sympathies were with the feminist. At one point, Vertron even reinterpreted Genesis and the Gospels in ways that reveal a feminist imagination. He argued that God's order of creation followed a hierarchical pattern: first God created lowly creatures, then moved on toward more complex higher forms of life. For example, God created fish before mammals. So, Vertron argued, when God created Eve, "woman was formed from a material more pure" than man. As a result of this difference, women did not experience the original fall into sin as men did. In another biblical example, concerning the life of Jesus, Vertron found that "women are more faithful than men." Indeed, throughout his iconoclastic text, Vertron equates women with virtue and men with bestiality: "the virtue of women reestablishes what the vice of men have corrupted."[10]

The four "worthy women" encyclopedias that were published in the 1760s imitate their seventeenth-century predecessors in several ways. Jean François La Croix's *Dictionnaire historique portatif des femmes célèbres* featured "courageous and militant women," while Joseph La Porte's *Histoire littéraire des femmes françaises* demonstrated the vast contribution women had made to French literature since the Renaissance.

The anonymous *Biographium Faeminem*, published in London in 1766, went even further by developing a kind of theory regarding gender inequality. In a spirited introduction, the author claimed that nature determined no "disparity between the two sexes"; women were the intellectual equals of men, and were capable of any achievement worthy of civilization: "The intellectual powers have no dependence upon, or connection with, the sex of the person who possesses them."[11]

The most ambitious of the encyclopedias in d'Eon's collection was Jean-Zorobabel Aublet de Maubuy's six-volume *Les Vies des femmes illustres de la France* (The Lives of Illustrious Women of France), which did not hesitate to attack all forms of misogyny as prejudiced and unenlightened. Many of the great women featured in this book, Aublet argued in the standard polemical preface, had been given unusual opportunities because of their class and family backgrounds. If other women had access to such educational opportunities, they too would be able to achieve great things. The blame for keeping women ignorant fell entirely on men, Aublet reasoned: If men regard women as "soft, effeminate, and without strength," that is only because women have been educated by men to be so. He asked his male readers to "dispose of your vanity, your egoism, even for just a moment." After all, the physical differences between men and women were not so important when compared to more essential similarities, he wrote. "The example of each and every individual tells me that, woman or man, they have one soul, one heart, one mind, one faculty of judgment, of understanding, of feeling, one imagination. . . . Why nourish a prejudice so bad for ourselves?"[12]

These encyclopedias of famous women were part of a greater body of literature that focused on celebrating feminine virtues and improving the condition of elite women. This genre, today known as the Querelle des Femmes (Argument About Women), included hundreds of pamphlets, plays, treatises, and dialogues about the nature of gender differences. Early modern Europe had its own intense debate over feminist theory.[13]

The Querelle des Femmes began around 1400, with Christine de Pizan's *The Book of the City of Ladies,* regarded as the first feminist work in Western civilization. Although his library catalogues offer no evidence that d'Eon owned a copy, he was certainly familiar with it. By the eighteenth century, articles on Pizan were featured in all of the volumes on "worthy women," and *The Book of the City of Ladies* was reprinted in various formats. While d'Eon may not have owned *The Book of the City of Ladies,* he did own the manuscript of another masterpiece of early Renaissance feminism, Martin Le Franc's *Le Champion des dames,* written between 1440 and 1442 and first printed in 1485. Like its more famous predecessor, it "defended" women by arguing for the superiority of their character. Later in his life, d'Eon would draw on this text to write his own history of medieval female transvestites.[14]

In recent years, literary historians have charted the rise of the Querelle des Femmes in early modern European culture. Joan Kelly's pioneering research has been confirmed by other scholars, who describe the importance of this literature during the seventeenth century, when texts that valorized female character became influential. For example, Jacques Du Bosc's *Honneste femme* (1647), owned by d'Eon, helped to spread the notion that the attributes usually associated with virile noblemen should apply as well to their female companions. By the end of the seventeenth century, there was already a rich tradition of feminist criticism firmly rooted in Cartesian philosophy, and best exemplified by François Poulain de la Barre's *De l'é-galité des femmes* (1673), a classic polemic on gender equality.[15]

The vigorous Querelle des Femmes literature of England was also well represented in d'Eon's library. For instance, he owned a copy of Mary Astell's *Reflections Upon Marriage.* Astell, often called England's first feminist, argued for a major reform of England's sex/gender system. She recognized that few options were open to women outside of marriage: a woman could attain status and wealth only as the dependent of a successful husband. Astell criticized this social system as inherently sexist. "That the custom of the world has put women, generally speaking, into a State of Subjection, is not denied," she bitterly remarked. "But the right can no more be proved from the fact, than the predominancy of vice can justify it."[16]

D'Eon also owned Judith Drake's *Essay in Defense of the Female Sex,* a powerful polemic thought in d'Eon's day to have been written by Mary Astell. Like Astell, Drake hoped to convince her readers that English women lived in a peculiar state of oppression; that they were tyrannized by men in a brutal way, and that such tyranny had been going on for so long that women accepted it as normal. Drake argued that this state of affairs was neither normal nor natural, but was instead a historical phenomenon. Like many of the Querelle des Femmes authors, Drake posited a golden age in the past when women and men had existed in a kind of primitive equality. This epoch had been brought to an end by men concerned only with their own self-interest. "As the world grew more populous," Drake wrote, "and men's necessities whetted their inventions, so it increased their jealousy, and sharpened their Tyranny over us, till by degrees, it came to that height of severity, I must say cruelty, it is now at in all the Eastern parts of the world, where women, like our Negroes in Western Plantations, are born slaves, and live prisoners all their lives."[17]

This kind of gendered slavery, Drake argued, was quickly spreading to Europe. The French, for example, had once respected the authority of women, but during the early Middle Ages they had excluded females from holding the throne—a brazen example of male oppression. French men "knew well enough, that we were no less capable of reigning, and governing well, than themselves; but they were suspicious, that if the rebel power should fall often into the hands of women, they would favor their own sex, and might in time restore them to their primitive liberty and equality with the men, and so break the neck of that unreasonable authority they so much affect over us."[18]

As a more positive example of what women were capable of, Drake pointed to the Dutch, the wealthiest and most civilized state of her day, whose women managed not only domestic affairs but often the finances as well—"doing all the business, even the nicest of merchants, with as much dexterity and exactness as their, or our men can do."[19]

Astell and Drake's ideas were picked up by a number of other English authors, including some men, such as William Walsh and Joseph Warder. In Walsh's "Dialogue Concerning Women," which pitted Philogynes against Misogynes, the Philogynes clearly won the debate with their invocation of the achievements of Queen Elizabeth as an example of the great things women could accomplish if only they were given appropriate opportunities and a good education.[20]

Warder used the metaphor of a beehive to argue for the inclusion of women in politics, citing the example of Queen Anne as proving that women were, like the queen bee, even better able to govern than males.

"Her absolute power over the rest is not procured by any Tyranny or cruelty by her exercised over her subjects, but from an innate loyalty natural to these creatures, not to be diverted by envy nor faction, towards this their lawful sovereign."

One day, Warder tells us, the queen bee was kidnapped and the males were left to themselves. Almost immediately this all-male republic turned into "anarchy," splitting off into contentious factions.[21]

Recent scholarship on the Querelle des Femmes literature has focused almost exclusively on the Renaissance and the seventeenth century. The eighteenth-century participants have been overlooked by scholars, probably because many of the great writers of the period ignored them. But as d'Eon's library shows, the Querelle des Femmes did not disappear after 1700; if anything, it became even bolder. The number of titles published or reprinted during the 1760s constitutes something of a revival in the Querelle.[22]

Among the most powerful myths developed by Querelle des Femmes writers was the "Amazon," the female militant who could match a man's virility in war or statecraft. Virtually all the feminist tracts in d'Eon's collection celebrated the achievements of the Amazons, the ancient group of women warriors who through excellence in the martial arts and discipline won battles against the Greeks and Scythians, according to Herodotus.[23]

The Amazons provided early modern feminists with proof that a state run by women was not only possible, it had already happened in history. Although today most scholars accept the view that the story of the Amazons is mythical, several Querelle des Femmes authors believed it provided strong women—*femmes fortes*—with a history of their own.[24]

One book in d'Eon's library that celebrated contemporary public women as modern Amazons was the Abbé Guyon's *Histoire des Amazones anciennes et modernes,* published in 1740. In a lengthy preface, Guyon explained that his purpose was not simply to report history, but to convince the reader "that women are capable of governing a state with wisdom, skill, and glory."[25]

Guyon tried to link the ancient tradition of women warriors with the modern experience of queens and exemplary women. He began by citing Herodotus on the Amazons. Guyon argued against the view of some skeptics that Herodotus was simply retelling myths, and that there had never been an Amazonian nation. Asserting the historical reality of the Amazons, he charged that any doubt regarding their veracity was itself a form of prejudice on the part of men whose own conceit prevented them from accepting strong, militant women. Guyon did not simply want to prove that an Amazonian nation had really existed, he clearly wanted to celebrate this "gynecracy." After all, he contended, even Plato hoped to minimize sexual differentiation by creating "a perfect republic where men and women would share the same activities from birth."[26]

Guyon recognized that contemporary life was characterized by such hardened patriarchal authority, most women were limited in their capacity to express their masculine inclinations. Typical of such repression were France's Salic laws, which forbade women from ascending the throne. But sometimes exemplary women transcended their limitations. One such heroine for Guyon was Queen Elizabeth of England. "Although governed by a woman, the nation lost none of the glory acquired under the previous kings."[27]

Guyon, then, recognized that in many ways modern Amazons were nothing like their ancient counterparts. Herodotus's Amazons were a warrior nation that was a constant threat to the more cultured Greeks. Enemies of men, they were primitive foes of civilization. Modern Amazons, by contrast, were men's leaders, not their enemies. Nor did they try to work in groups. Usually, modern Amazons acted alone; their virility was singular. Neither did they constitute much of a threat to civilized society. Indeed, in the early modern reworking of the Amazonian myth, the Greek goddess of war, Pallas Athena, became an archetypical Amazon.[28]

Perhaps the best representative of these eighteenth-century feminist/ Amazonian works in d'Eon's collection was the anonymous English pamphlet of 1758, *Female Rights Vindicated.* Published half a century before Mary Wollstonecraft and the Marquis de Condorcet and a century before John Stuart Mill—that is, well before the supposed birth of modern feminism—this small tract argued passionately that women and men were absolutely equal, and that political life ought to reflect this fact. All sexual inequality, its author maintained, was the result of tyranny and oppression.

"My first Proposition," declared the "lady" author of *Female Rights Vindicated,* "is that women, considered according to the principles of sound philosophy, are as capable as the men of all kinds of knowledge, as good sense is of no gender. . . .

"My next proposition is that women are not less capable than men of filling the employments in society. . . .

"Hence it may be concluded, that if both sexes equally labored, and took the same exercise, they would, perhaps, be equally vigorous; this was formerly the case in a republic, where wrestling and other gymnastics were practiced by both sexes."[29]

Pompadour and La Pucelle

A T THE CENTER of this eighteenth-century revival of the debate about the value of women in public life were two women in particular, whose lives were scrutinized in France perhaps more than any others': Mme de Pompadour and Joan of Arc. In the encyclopedias of "worthy women" owned by d'Eon, Joan was portrayed as the first national hero of France, who helped her country in its laborious struggle against England. Likewise, Pompadour too tried to save France from the British, probably accumulating more influence on foreign affairs than any other French woman of non-royal blood. And like Joan, Pompadour was a self-made woman, one who imposed herself on the crown from the outside. Whatever she achieved was due solely to her character and abilities. Even today Joan and Pompadour remain the best-known non-royal women in French history before 1800.

The two women used radically different aspects of their womanhood to rise to the top, however. Joan was, first and foremost, a virgin who dressed as a man in order to go to battle against the English. Where Joan denied her sexuality, Pompadour made the most of hers, dressing to the hilt and making herself the most prized sexual object in France. Where Joan helped to legitimize one king's throne, Pompadour helped to "desacralize" another. Where Joan offered virtue to Charles VII, Pompadour lent Louis XV an unprecedented reputation for licentiousness.[1]

D'Eon owned the most important eighteenth-century biography of Joan, Nicolas Lenglet Dufresnoy's three-volume *Histoire de Jeanne d'Arc*, first printed in 1753. When Lenglet died in 1755, d'Eon published an admiring eulogy of the author in *L'Année littéraire*, praising his treatment of the heroine. Prior to Lenglet, most French biographies of Joan had comfortably endorsed the view that her mystical visions of a new France were real, that she had heard and heeded the voice of God. Lenglet himself had held this view earlier in his career. In this work, however, published when he was in his mid-seventies, Lenglet abandoned the view that Joan was part of any supernatural phenomenon directed by God. Instead, he argued that her fantasies were the result of an unusually compelling and forceful imagination. Joan's vision was actually her own "internal persuasion, a reflective meditation that struck, agitated, and animated the imagination."[2]

Like most early modern commentators on Joan, Lenglet was also impressed by her virginity. She marched, ate, fought, and slept among soldiers and yet managed to keep it intact. While today some might find this insignificant, early modern commentators regarded it as a miraculous achievement. Even her nickname, *La Pucelle,* means "the virgin."[3] Joan's ability to renounce her own desires, as well as her ability to make the men around her disregard her as a sexual being, attested to a personality of unique integrity. "She was a virgin, and even at the age of eighteen years old, she was not yet subjected to her sex's ordinary inconveniences," d'Eon wrote. What especially impressed him was that Joan's supreme moral discipline ruled over her physiology to the point that she could even retard her menarche. And because Joan—a French girl from an ordinary background—could achieve this kind of greatness, it proved, in the words of Pierre Le Moyne, "that women are capable of the most vigorous and illustrious actions."[4]

But Joan was not only a virgin and a pious Christian, she was also a soldier, who was said to have led her comrades in battle against the English and, as it turned out, gave up her life in that cause. Even more than the image of *La Pucelle,* Lenglet and many other writers of Querelle des Femmes literature emphasized Joan's Amazonian qualities: her vigor, militancy, courage, and prowess. Eighteenth-century writers stressed that Joan dressed as a man not only because she needed to for battle, but also because she wanted to: when she was offered male clothes in prison, she readily put them on; when on another occasion she was offered a dress, she refused it.

"She demanded," the Abbé Guyon wrote in his history of Amazons, that Charles VII "permit her to wear men's clothes and to take up arms among the French troops." Likewise, Le Moyne admired her transition from "a shepherdess into an Amazon": "Would you not say that she is born in a Magazine of Arms, and that she is trained up in a Camp? That

Joan of Arc dressed as an Amazon, leading French troops into battle. This eighteenth-century image had a profound effect on d'Eon. *(Courtesy of the Brotherton Collection, University of Leeds Library)*

she is come to us from the Country of Amazons?" For Philippe-Joseph Caffiaux, Joan's example proved that "military skills are neither too difficult nor too rough for women. The heart, which is the essential organ for bravery, is no smaller in women than in men." The "lady" who wrote *Female Rights Vindicated* thought Joan illustrated the kind of military skills many women could acquire if given the opportunity. And William

Walsh asked his proto-feminist readers in 1691, "Should I carry you into France, and show you a warlike virgin (at least an unmarried woman) whose memory is still annually celebrated by one of their chiefest towns [Orléans]?"[5]

Joan wasn't born an Amazon. Everyone knew that she had been born an ordinary peasant girl in the sleepy village of Domrémy and had transformed herself. For Querelle des Femmes writers, fifteenth-century Joan was a model for eighteenth-century French would-be heroines. In 1761, when the artist Pigalle was approached by the town of Orléans to create a statue of Joan for the town square, his plans called for her to be dressed in battle clothes "as Pallas, having a leopard lying at her feet." This, then, was the image of Joan presented to d'Eon and his contemporaries a decade before d'Eon displayed a similar image to his own king.[6]

As for Mme de Pompadour, the Chevalier d'Eon did not need to read a book—he knew enough about her firsthand. Raised in a bourgeois Parisian family, Jeanne-Antoinette Poisson rose to prominence in high society due to her intelligence, charm, and beauty. She met Louis XV at a masked ball, and by 1745 was living at Versailles as his mistress. She became much more than his lover, however, winning the King's trust and friendship as well. By the mid-1750s, she became one of the King's most important political advisers, and was at least partly responsible for the diplomatic realignment that resulted in a Franco-Austrian alliance. When she died in 1764, Pompadour may no longer have been playing the role of royal lover, but she was still King Louis's best friend.[7]

D'Eon may not have needed any book for these facts, but the most important biography of the period, Marianne-Agnès Pillement de Fauques's *The Life of the Marchioness de Pompadour*, which was in his library, did much more than just restate them. Fauques cited sexual intrigue and scandal to indict the entire regime of Louis XV: the mingling of extramarital sexual activities and politics inherent in the relationship with Pompadour was no aberration or sideshow, but revealed the extent to which immorality had soiled the French throne.

Fauques's basic approach was to depict Pompadour as a monstrous whore who had made it her life's work to snare the King. Before we are even ten pages into her long but engaging biography, we learn that Pompadour's father was "hanged in effigy for a rape" he had supposedly committed shortly after his own wedding. He was forced to flee France, and stayed abroad until much later, when he won a pardon through the influence of his daughter.[8]

Or so-called daughter. One of the charges Fauques makes at the beginning of the book is that Pompadour was illegitimate: "Her mother, who was one of the most beautiful women in France, did not, in the absence of her husband, deliver herself up to a vain barren affliction." She was simultaneously the mistress of two corrupt tax collectors, so not only was Pompadour an illegitimate child but, according to Fauques, there is no way to know exactly who her father was. Fauques's Pompadour was thus born and raised in sin and crime.[9]

The King was not a bad man, but in Fauques's analysis he was certainly a weak one. He was no match for Pompadour's seductive charm. "Louis XV could not resist the calls of his constitution, which was naturally an amorous one; he, like a torrent that had been before restrained by its banks, overflowed all fields of licentiousness." Jealously guarding her newly won power, Pompadour disposed of any rivals for the King's affections. As for the Queen, Pompadour had the "insolence in thus forcing herself upon the Queen" by sitting with the King in her presence at official functions.[10]

But Pompadour's greatest achievement, according to Fauques, was to become even more intimate with the King after her days of sleeping with him were over. First, she became, in effect, his pimp, bringing him young women whom he could bed, but who posed no threat to Pompadour's political authority. Second, Pompadour began to exert this authority to an unusual degree. By the start of the Seven Years' War, she could "at will make and unmake Generals; [could] pull down Ministers, and set up others in their place; [could] raise a little Abbot to a cardinalship, a scoundrel to a blue ribbon, or sink a Grand Monarque into the lowest of characters."[11]

According to Fauques, the greatest victim of Pompadour's foray into the public realm was the Prince de Conti, who "vexes her the worst of all, and he most openly declares his high contempt of her. He knows perfectly well how far he can show it to her, without affecting the King by it; and therefore frequently finds and takes opportunities of mortifying her excessive pride. The Marchioness, in her turn, finds means of avenging herself on him, as far as she can so on a Prince who is respected and beloved by the whole nation." Fauques publicized what d'Eon already knew to be true.[12]

Fauques's method of combining sexual and political intrigue into a synthesis that essentially blamed the failures of Louis's reign on debauchery spawned a virtual literary industry during the second half of the eighteenth century. French hack writers of various stripes took up residence in

England to lambaste their King. Among the most prominent was Charles Théveneau de Morande, whose *Gazetier cuirassé* (1771) was a scathing portrayal of decadence at the court of Louis XV. Likewise, Pidansat de Mairobert's biography of the Comtesse du Barry, Louis's most significant lover after the death of Pompadour, showed a tyrannical and sex-crazed monarch more in the style of Nero than Louis XIV. Pidansat himself was editor of *L'Espion anglais,* an underground newspaper published in London that offered a potent cocktail of sexual and political gossip, convincing readers that the French court had certainly lost its way. Finally, the claim that France's political and diplomatic failures somehow originated in court licentiousness was already a cliché by the time Mouffle d'Angerville published his *Vie privée de Louis XV* on the eve of the French Revolution.[13]

In a series of fascinating articles, the historian Robert Darnton has charted how this kind of political pornography undermined the legitimacy of the absolute monarchy in the years before the French Revolution. Arguing against the notion that the great ideas of the Enlightenment philosophers caused the Revolution in any mechanical sense, Darnton claims that the works of these "gutter Rousseaus" were actually much more popular than the classics of Voltaire, Montesquieu, or Rousseau. Eighteenth-century readers may or may not have appreciated the latter's abstract arguments, but they were obviously impressed by the graphic depictions of debauchery at the court of Louis XV. By the 1780s, Darnton states, many sectors of French society had lost any sense that the monarchy was a sacred office.[14]

Both Joan and Pompadour, then, involved themselves in activities from which women were usually excluded, Joan by acting like a virile man, Pompadour by acting like a loose woman. In terms of the limitations of early modern culture, Joan showed what women could do when allowed to exercise their abilities, while Pompadour demonstrated for observers such as Marianne Fauques how women degrade themselves and others around them when constrained to act in "womanly" ways. Joan's entry into the public sphere brought France virtue, while Pompadour's brought debauchery. The dichotomy had become so formulaic that when Voltaire dared to publish a satirical poem about Joan around 1762, Fauques asserted that the poem was really about Pompadour.[15]

We know that d'Eon bought and owned these biographies of Joan and Pompadour, and we can be reasonably certain that he read them. However, aside from his article on Lenglet, d'Eon left little record of his reactions to these books. All we have to go on is what he would much later write about the two women in his autobiographical fragments. Although they were written between fifteen and thirty years later, these fragments echo the body of Querelle des Femmes literature in general and, more specifically, its focus on Joan and Pompadour.

We have already seen how d'Eon dealt with Pompadour. In the autobiographical papers, he portrays her as his sworn enemy. First, like Fauques and other writers, he sees her as the foe of his patron, the Prince de Conti. But d'Eon goes further. Writing for a readership that is convinced he is a woman, d'Eon explains that during his trip to Russia in 1755, he carried on a secret correspondence with Louis XV, who also knew at that time that he was a woman. One night Pompadour secretly went through the King's papers and found a letter from d'Eon. Pompadour was immediately sent into a fit of jealousy by this woman who had entered public service, and she resolved to ruin d'Eon's career as soon as possible. To hear d'Eon tell it, her chance came during the summer of 1763, when d'Eon was Plenipotentiary Minister in England. Thus, in essence, d'Eon portrayed Pompadour as his greatest political rival.[16]

In contrast, d'Eon identified with Joan of Arc as a model of what he himself was trying to become. Like her, he had dressed as a man to enter the King's military service against England; like her, he had sought to live a life of virtue, at the cost of risking his neck and sacrificing his career; and like her, he increasingly came to rely on his Christianity as a source of solace and strength. At the University of Leeds, in an unmarked file, is a draft in d'Eon's hand of a title page for his unpublished autobiography: *La Pucelle de Tonnerre*.[17]

During the 1760s and 1770s, then, the Chevalier d'Eon seriously studied early modern notions of womanhood and manhood, aided by a resurgence in the Querelle des Femmes literature. These books guided him toward what kind of a woman he would become. At the core of the Querelle des Femmes, d'Eon found two women who represented different types of womanhood. Pompadour was sexuality embodied: she used her charms and passions to influence the government. For d'Eon, this kind of woman also represented his past: in his mythology he laid blame for the failure of his career on her passionate jealousy. In this Manichean vision of womanhood, Joan of Arc stood for the other kind of woman, the kind who hid or restrained her sexuality so that she could transcend desires of the flesh. By renouncing her sexuality, Joan became a patriot. In exchange for her fertility, she mothered a nation. By becoming a modern Joan of Arc, d'Eon would be able to regenerate his soul, returning to the original idealistic intentions best stated in the title of his early essay, "The Hopes of a Good Patriot."

Contra Rousseau

URING THE 1760S, the Chevalier d'Eon worked out his alienation from politics by reading especially those publications that were part of the Querelle des Femmes revival sweeping Western Europe in the third quarter of the eighteenth century. His transformation to womanhood, then, was a cognitive reaction to a specific social situation brought about by his odd political status. His identification with Jean-Jacques Rousseau, however, presents a conundrum. For in Rousseau himself, we have perhaps the eighteenth century's greatest opponent to "female rights."

Throughout his major works, Rousseau developed notions of womanhood that not only stood opposed to Cartesian feminists like Poulain de la Barre and Mary Astell, but established an ideology of sexual differentiation that would have enormous influence on the social elites who took power during the French Revolution and especially afterward, during the nineteenth century. Although a democratic thinker with respect to politics, when it came to gender Rousseau's ideas were profoundly reactionary.[1]

What made Rousseau's ideas about gender so significant was that he linked them to his ideas about politics. In his 1758 *Lettre à M. d'Alembert sur les spectacles* (Letter to M. d'Alembert on the Theater), Rousseau blamed many of the problems of Old Regime France on women. He noted how active some women had become in cultural and political life, and argued that their participation had ruined public discourse. "There are no good morals for women outside of a withdrawn and domestic life," he insisted. "I say that the peaceful care of the family and the home are their lot, that the dignity of their sex consists in modesty." By becoming power brokers in the public sphere, women had sullied themselves; worse, their soft manners had spread throughout society, transforming an aristocratic elite from warriors to weaklings. "Unable to make themselves into men, the women make us into women," Rousseau proclaimed.[2]

It was a commonplace of Enlightenment thought that the role and status of women improved with the progress of civilization. Everyone knew that an aristocracy which minimized the martial arts in favor of more cultivated interests such as table manners, conversation, music, and literature was more civilized than a warrior class. Indeed, by the eighteenth century an older, more virile model of the courtier had been tamed by the court, and the nobleman was less a warrior who showed off his virility than a "sincere gentleman" (*honnête homme*) who prided himself on his social intercourse with women.[3]

Rousseau's genius was to identify the feminization of male elites as the central factor explaining the corruption of political life. In 1761 and 1762 Rousseau laid out a more positive, though no less disturbing, proposal for the role of women in a revitalized French society. In his classic educational treatise, *Emile,* as well as in his popular romantic novel, *Julie, ou La Nouvelle Héloïse,* Rousseau presented what he believed to be a superior notion of gender relations. "The whole education of women ought to relate to men," he expostulated in *Emile.* "To please men, to be useful to them, to make herself loved and honored by them, to raise them when young, to care for them when grown, to counsel them, to console them, to make their lives agreeable and sweet—these are the duties of women at all times, and they ought to be taught from childhood." What the "lady" author of *Female Rights Vindicated* had identified as an ancient prejudice, Rousseau transformed into an avant-garde philosophy.[4]

How could d'Eon, who would later claim to be a feminist, who owned perhaps the largest private collection of Querelle des Femmes books— indeed, who would soon transform himself into a woman—how could he identify himself with Rousseau? Surprisingly, in this regard d'Eon was not exceptional. For years, scholars have been baffled by the fact that many of Rousseau's warmest admirers were women and feminists.[5]

There was a tendency to read Rousseau as a polemicist, whose overall style and goals were to be admired but who got carried away with his own arguments.[6] These readers could commend Rousseau's integrity, as well as his utopian portrayal of gender relations, without believing that he meant every word. In an aristocratic world that had not yet completely separated work from home nor the public sphere from the private, notions regarding an ideal of female domesticity may have seemed novel and subversive, and their implications were not perceived as they are today.

Nonetheless, there were some Querelle des Femmes books that directly challenged Rousseau. Aublet's encyclopedia condemned him for "wanting to place women in the class of domestic animals." In 1779, a Belgian work attacked Rousseau's characterization of Sophie, the fictional female character in *Emile*, asserting that women who received the same education as men could achieve great things; the authors even used the life of d'Eon (by then perceived to be a woman) to prove it![7]

In fact, Rousseau's ideas about gender are not so much misogynistic as fundamentally ambivalent. His fear of female power in the Old Regime comes from a recognition of women's authority, influence, and similarity to men. "In everything not connected with sex, woman is man," he remarks in a well-known passage from *Emile*. "She has the same organs, the same needs, the same faculties. The machine is constructed in the same way."[8]

It is no accident that this remark, like many others in his works, sounds like phrases out of the Querelle des Femmes literature. After all, early in his career, probably during the 1740s, Rousseau had begun to compose an essay on women that clearly imitated works like Le Moyne's *Galerie des femmes fortes* by describing "women deprived of their liberty by the tyranny of men." He saw this deprivation as wrong, and he advocated female participation in public life: "We see in the other sex models as perfect [as men] in all types of civic virtues and morality." If women had been as active as men in running governments, Rousseau went on to claim, political empires would have been that much more glorious.[9]

During the 1740s, Rousseau was also the personal secretary to Mme Dupin, who herself was then writing a large book on women that idealized the Amazonian tradition and Joan of Arc in the polemical style of a typical Querelle des Femmes treatise. "Today we continue to see in the world," Mme Dupin dictated to Rousseau, "an oppressive inequality between men and women that does not seem to be founded in nature or upon any other truth. The goal of this writing is to examine its origin, character, and effects." Although the book was never published, hundreds of manuscript pages survive today, many in Rousseau's handwriting. While there is no way to tell whether Rousseau agreed with the ideas of his employer, the existence of this work is itself evidence that Rousseau, like d'Eon, was deeply engaged in eighteenth-century feminist polemics.[10]

Thus there is good reason to speculate that Rousseau's thinking about gender developed from an earlier position close to that of Querelle des Femmes feminists. Like his relationship to the great philosophers of the Enlightenment, whom he first joined only to oppose later—one thinks of his turbulent history with Voltaire, for example—his philosophy of gender may have taken a similar route.

Supporting Rousseau were many less famous authors who seem to have had similar intellectual trajectories. Among those represented in d'Eon's library was Pierre-Joseph Boudier de Villemart, whose *Ami des Femmes* was published in two separate French editions (1759 and *Le Nouvel ami des femmes* in 1779), translated into English, and even published in America. Boudier thought of himself as a pro-woman writer in the tradition of Poulain de la Barre. He admired women who could achieve great things, and his 1779 edition included an alphabetical listing of 300 French women who had contributed the most to public life (the Chevalière d'Eon among them).[11]

But Boudier's feminism had its limits. While women had made strides, they had done so at the expense of men, he said. Boudier explained that among the elite classes during the Dark Ages, the sexes were necessarily segregated. Because warfare was incessant, and was carried on among private armies of aristocrats, warriors naturally came to define much of male aristocratic life. Gradually, virile qualities such as strength came to differentiate men from women. This trend changed during the Renaissance, when the monarchical state imposed its authority on a feudal society. According to Boudier, warfare became less frequent, and armies were controlled by the king and were increasingly composed of mercenaries. In short, while aristocratic men still fought in wars and cherished high military office, warfare no longer defined male aristocratic life.

Boudier argued that aristocratic men filled this void by taking on feminine interests as their own. Salons, conversation, fashion, and games increasingly defined aristocratic life for both sexes. "Softness having feminized everything," Boudier commented, "the contrast established by nature between the two sexes has disappeared."[12] By the mid–eighteenth century, there were no longer two contrasting genders—one masculine, one feminine—but rather two feminine genders.

Rousseauians like Boudier, then, agreed with Querelle des Femmes feminists that European society had become more feminized. But unlike the feminists, who thought of such a trend as heading toward refinement and further civilization, the Rousseauians believed the situation had gotten out of hand and had become perverse. However paradoxical, their support for improving the status of women was offset by their worry about confusing gender roles.[13]

In a sense, the Rousseauians differed from the feminists not so much in their view of women as in their view of men. They were profoundly ambivalent about whether the feminization of aristocratic men was a good thing or not. After all, even for Rousseau, the most dangerous aspect of Amazonian women was their feminizing effect on men. Nowhere was such ambivalence better expressed than in Patrick Delany's *Reflections Upon Polygamy*, a 1737 British religious work also found in d'Eon's library. Delany claimed that too much social and sexual intercourse with women resulted in a medical disease, "eviration," in which men literally became women due to the withering away of their genitalia. Essentially, then, it was the fear of "eviration," rather than any overt hostility to women, that excited Rousseauian passions.[14]

Precisely how d'Eon negotiated this ideological battlefield is impossible to tell, since his notions about gender were quite fluid and unsystematic, at least until the 1780s, when he began writing his autobiography. This much can be said, however: D'Eon borrowed a great deal from both the Rousseauians and the Querelle des Femmes authors. He agreed with Rousseau that women were to blame for much of the corruption of the French monarchy—but not all women. D'Eon's ideas about the evil doings of Pompadour can be read as a kind of Rousseauian sermon on what happens if a certain kind of woman—that is, lewd, irreligious, and autocratic—achieves power. Given the contemporaneous accession of Catherine the Great to the Russian throne, this type of woman seemed to many observers to have acquired unprecedented political power in Europe.

But d'Eon also agreed with the Querelle des Femmes authors that such women were far from representative of their sex. Indeed, in a patriarchal world that favored political ambition and sexual immorality, women like Pompadour and Catherine were the only kind that could succeed. Unlike the Rousseauians, d'Eon and the Querelle authors did not conclude from a few notorious examples that all women should be excluded from public life. Rather, they turned to a different model of femininity, best represented by earlier women, such as Joan of Arc. They tended to idealize women who were chaste, if not virgins; who, like the noblewoman Mme de Caylus (1673–1729), rejected the political world of the court for the religious world of the convent, but who nonetheless maintained their presence in the public sphere by writing pious tracts for other women and helping to expand the role of convents in French society.[15] Such women were not examples of Rousseauian domesticity, but were celebrated for their courage, militancy, patriotism, and determination to change the face of their society.[16]

Thus we can find sources for d'Eon's conception of womanhood among both the Rousseauians and their adversaries. It is, however, far more difficult to trace d'Eon's ideas concerning manhood. There was no eighteenth-century writer who systematically addressed the feminization of men in terms that were wholly positive. The feminist Querelle des Femmes authors remained ambivalent at best, while the Rousseauians imagined a generalized epidemic of "eviration." In this respect, d'Eon was boldly original. If actions speak louder than words, then willfully transforming himself into a woman was the ultimate celebration of male feminization. However, actions don't speak louder than words; words may indeed have a life that is far more enduring. By keeping his autobiographical writings unpublished and maintaining the fiction that he was an Amazonian woman, d'Eon severely diluted the strength of his own ideas regarding manhood.

Part IV

THE TRANSFORMATION

A DISCOVERY HAS lately been made on this continent that will astonish the whole world. Our great and excellent General Washington is actually discovered to be of the female sex.

—*(London)* Daily Advertiser,
25 January 1783
(D'Eon's clipping)

Contexts

THE QUERELLE DES FEMMES BOOKS in d'Eon's library were not part of some escapist or utopian genre that interested only a few eccentric intellectuals in their leisure time. Across Europe, gender roles had become a burning subject of debate. Just as with the development of d'Eon's ideas we have found a fertile cultural context, so there was also a social context for what he was trying to do.

At the start of 1763, when d'Eon was in London putting the final touches on the Treaty of Paris, Britain's most popular actor, David Garrick, starred in a London production of *The Discovery* by the woman playwright Frances Sheridan. D'Eon could well have been in the audience on one of the seventeen nights the play ran. He wrote to friends about other Garrick plays at the Drury Lane Theater, and even sent back an engraving of Garrick for an acquaintance who shared his fascination with the actor.[1]

If d'Eon had been there, he would have seen the play begin with Garrick emerging from the wings dressed as a woman, and speaking the following monologue:[2]

A female culprit at your box appears,
Not destitute of hope, nor free from fears.
Her utmost crime she's ready to confess,
A simple trespass, neither more nor less . . .
The fault is deemed high treason by the men
those lordly tyrants, who usurp the pen;
For women, like state criminals, they think,
should be debarred the use of pen and ink. . . .

Our author, who disclaims such Salique laws,
to her own sex appeals to judge her cause:
she pleads Magna Carta on her side,
that British subjects by their Peers be tried . . .
Ladies, to you she dedicates her laws:
assert your right to censure or to praise:
Boldly your will in open court declare,
And let the men dispute it—if they dare!

Garrick's transparent transvestism was performed here at the expense of
women; insofar as it was women who were being mocked, one could
interpret this speech as fitting into a tradition of misogynist satires so
common in early modern English literature.[3]

But the fact that Garrick was speaking the lines of a woman playwright
makes the speech something other than comic misogyny. Garrick may
have been pretending to be a woman, but the playwright herself was
boldly announcing that she had written this play as a woman, and
demanding that the audience know that and judge her on that basis. The
speech, then, is both a satire and a defense of women in the public sphere.
Garrick was simultaneously a carnivalesque clown playing a woman and
the most famous male actor of his day, who insisted on performing a play
written by a woman. The prologue, then, recognizes that the issue of gender roles and identities is a problem for the actors and the audience.

While the bulk of *The Discovery* does not deal directly with these
issues, in the Epilogue Sheridan resolved the gender confusion expressed
here. On the stage stands one of the main characters, Mrs. Pritchard, who
complains to the women in the audience about Sheridan's creation of her
character:

I told her (for it vexed me to the heart)
"Madame—excuse me—I don't like my part:
'Tis out of nature—not the least High-Life;
of quality!—and such a passive wife!
Such females might have lived before the flood
But now, indeed, it is not flesh and blood
so mild a character will seem too flat!"

"My friend"—she cried—"must I new-plan the part,
and make my pen run counter to my heart?
Too oft has Ribaldry's indecent mien,
tricked out by Female Hands, disgraced the scene.

Let me to this *one* merit lay my claim,
not to debase my sex, to raise my name."

Now there could be little doubt as to Sheridan's intent. Unlike so many male playwrights, she would not have her women characters indulge in affairs to pique the amorous desires of the men in the audience. Such behavior might make for more popular plays, and more appealing characters, but they "debased" her sex.

Here Sheridan resolved some of the gender ambiguities by asserting that her mission as a woman playwright overshadowed other factors. She did not care to write a play as a man would, even though she obviously had the talent. Her gender offered her special opportunities and responsibilities. She wanted to create characters from a woman's viewpoint, characters who honored womanhood, not degraded it.

In Sheridan's *The Discovery*, the rhetoric of eighteenth-century feminism is revealed despite the satirical constraints of the genre. There is a remarkable self-consciousness about how female actors and playwrights have something special to offer to the theater. And indeed, during the seventeenth and eighteenth centuries, at least in England, women participated in the theater in ways that undermined traditional gender roles even further. For example, women actors often played Sir Harry Wildair in George Farquhar's *Constant Couple* (1699), and Shakespeare's Hamlet and even Romeo were sometimes played by women. Likewise, in 1781 a production of John Gay's *Beggar's Opera* (1728) featured men playing all the women's parts, and women playing all the men's.[4]

In other kinds of mid-eighteenth-century fiction as well, gender blurring is everywhere apparent. For example, Henry Fielding's popular short story "The Female Husband" spoofed the true story of a woman who had lived her life as a married man. Mary Price, the wife, swore before a court of law that she never knew her husband was a woman until she was arrested. When asked if "he" had treated her as a husband ought to treat a wife, Mary answered strongly in the affirmative.[5]

More typical of eighteenth-century male authors was their use of female protagonists as first-person narrators. The best example of such "literary transvestism" is Samuel Richardson's *Pamela, or Virtue Rewarded* (1740), among the most popular novels of the century, and particularly influential among French writers such as Rousseau. Through a series of letters written by chambermaid Pamela Andrews to her parents, we learn of her resistance to the seductive ploys of her master, Mr. B., and her eventual marriage to him. *Pamela* is much more than the story of a romance. Instead of presenting Pamela as a temptress who manipulates an aristocrat into marrying her, Richardson is able to paint her as an agent of virtue by telling the story through her own voice; indeed, she is the only agent of virtue in the book. Pamela not only holds on to her virginity until her wedding, but her strong moral character slowly transforms her master. Mr. B., the decadent aristocrat and playboy, is reformed by the good-hearted servant girl.[6]

In *Pamela,* class and gender are displaced in revolutionary ways. Virtue has little to do with its etymological cousin, virility, and much more to do with the combination of moral discipline and generosity of spirit that characterizes the maiden. In many respects, Pamela Andrews was an eighteenth-century Joan of Arc. Like Joan, Pamela was a *pucelle*—a maid, a virgin, who made those who had sexual designs on her feel ashamed. Like Joan, Pamela asserted her will without being an egotist. While never straying from her own goals and interests, she nonetheless cared deeply for other people and was ready to sacrifice much to improve their moral status.

Rarely has a male author celebrated the moral superiority of women more effectively than Richardson. Some recent feminist scholars have claimed that Richardson's efforts resulted in more patriarchy, not less, since a man invented Pamela Andrews.[7] But such a reading treats the novel as if it were Victorian instead of Augustan. Whereas the late nineteenth century was tainted with a deep-seated misogyny, Richardson's attitudes toward women were fresh and sincere, and readers of the era knew it. Women wrote Richardson to ask his advice on various matters, and he wrote back to them with care.[8]

Behind Richardson's literary transvestism was a culture that believed men and women's roles were converging. Women were seen as more "masculine," men as more "feminine." France and England were still intensely patriarchal societies, but, it would seem, a bit less so than before. "The sexes have now little other apparent distinction, beyond that of person and dress," the divinity professor John Brown wrote in 1757. "Their peculiar and characteristic manners are confounded and lost. The one sex having advanced into *boldness,* as the other have sunk into effeminacy."[9]

If English etiquette books can be believed, women wore pants whenever they could get away with it, as, for example, while riding horseback. Before the eighteenth century, the hunt was an exclusively male sport; it too was now apparently invaded by the ladies. "On meeting a company on horseback now-a-days," wrote the author of an etiquette book published in 1769 and owned by d'Eon, "one shall hardly be able to distinguish, at first sight, whether it is composed of ladies or gentlemen. . . . They should be called Amazons."[10]

The extent to which European women among all classes assumed men's clothes and went off to war—sometimes to follow their men, but sometimes just for the adventure—is quite surprising, given our assumption that warfare was monopolized by men. More interesting, eighteenth-century popular literature made heroes of such women. Hundreds of songs about female warriors—true Amazons—flourished throughout the century at both the popular and elite levels. Not surprisingly, many of these ballads refer to Joan of Arc as one who exemplified female prowess.[11]

Among the cultural elite, an effeminate style dominated male fashion, at least until the last quarter of the century, when neoclassical Rousseauians unleashed a powerful backlash. During the first half of the century, for example, men's clothes became more and more like women's. The frock coat included metal stays, and gradually the stays flared out, resembling the skirt of a woman. Commentators remarked, perhaps only half in jest, that if the trend continued, one would soon not be able to tell a man from a woman. "I believe the gentlemen will wear petticoats very soon for many of their coats were like our mantuas," observed Sarah Osborne in 1722. "Lord Essex has a silver tissue coat, and pink color waistcoat, and several [others] had pink color and pale paduasoy coats, which looks prodigiously effeminate."[12]

The most exaggerated examples of effeminate manhood were the Macaronis, who achieved notoriety during the 1760s and 1770s, at the same moment d'Eon was making his move from manhood to womanhood. The Macaronis were young men who had finished their grand tour of the continent and were identified principally by their exaggerated dress and hairstyle: baroque buckles on their dainty shoes, extra embroidery on their hose, fancy garter belts, very wide stays on their coats, but most of all, enormous curly wigs, as only women had worn previously.[13]

To their critics, the Macaronis were clear evidence that European male aristocrats had become thoroughly effeminate—that they had already become women, a vivid example of Delany's "eviration." John Brown warned that taking the grand tour before puberty increased an aristocrat's risk of effeminacy. Such a critique may have inspired the odd lyrics to "Yankee Doodle": English soldiers making fun of their American counterparts for trying to act like Macaronis.[14]

The most prominent example of a male afflicted with "eviration" was apparently King Louis XV himself. The political pornography of France's spiteful Grub Street exiles spread the notion that the King's promiscuity had rendered him effeminate and impotent. While in his earlier life his virile sexual appetite might have reinforced his manliness, by a mature age

Pompadour and the others had satiated it to such an extent that the King's maleness had withered away. "Since 1760," one contemporary courtier wrote, "this monarch was simply lazy in the eyes of Europe and the French people. One hurried hour in the morning given to the work of his ministers, another in the evening in boredom with his counsel was the only royal work done by this effeminate prince. The hunt and nightly orgies occupied the rest of his time. The reins of government, that his weak hands could not or would not direct, floated between those of his ministers."[15]

Another example of gender blurring among Europe's elites during the 1760s and 1770s was the popularity of masquerade balls where the participants cross-dressed. The vogue for them in Russia has been noted in chapter 14. In England, masquerade balls came over from Italy around the turn of the century, and the fad lasted until the era of the French Revolution. Certain shops specialized in clothes for these balls. The British socialite Horace Walpole, for one, "had a large trunk of dresses" available for such occasions. Indeed, it is no exaggeration to say that by the 1770s every European nobleman with any sort of social life would have known what it was to dress as a woman, and conversely, every noblewoman would have known what it was to dress as a man.

Masquerade balls were more than just occasions of fashion and fun. They were opportunities for social experimentation, when conventional elites could play with new gender roles. And for many, the result was liberating: "I love a masquerade because a female can never enjoy the same liberty anywhere else," one British woman wrote. Similar sentiments were echoed in 1777 in the *Lady's Magazine* of London: "A masquerade is one of the most entertaining diversions that ever was imported; you may hear and see, and do everything in the world, without the least reserve—and liberty, liberty my dear, you know, is the very joy of my heart."[16]

Thus during the 1760s and 1770s, Europe was in the midst of what can be described as a crisis in its "sex/gender regime."[17] London was certainly one center of the debate over gender roles, but all agreed that France had become the capital of European gender bending. The roles of French women and men had overlapped to such an extent that it was sometimes impossible to tell the two sexes apart. "At all times it has appeared to me," wrote the English bluestocking Elizabeth Montagu, "that the French women have too much of the male character, the men of the female."[18]

For one thing, many French aristocrats continued to cultivate the reputation of Amazonian women who eagerly participated in public life. They remembered the women who had fought in the Fronde, the aristocratic insurrection against Louis XIV. And they honored the salonnières, the women at the center of the Enlightenment, who organized important gatherings of artists, intellectuals, and statesmen. "It is principally in France that women can profit from these advantages," wrote Joseph La Porte in 1769 about what he viewed as the privileged position of French upper-class women.[19]

When French novelist Marie-Anne de Roumier Robert imagined a female utopia in 1765, she described a world that had obliterated all "distinctions of sex"; a world so androgynous that only one sex was acknowledged, and love, sexual liaisons, and even marriage were all forbidden.[20]

In 1779 William Alexander claimed that French women, having spent too much time with men, had lost their femininity and had become just like men. He observed that French women had no sense of modesty when they traveled by coach in mixed company: when they needed to go to expel their waste, they simply asked the driver to stop, took a few steps outside, did their business in full view of the carriage, and returned to their seats "without the least ceremony or discomposure."[21]

Twenty years after he produced *The Discovery*, David Garrick put on another play written by a woman, Hannah More's *Percy: A Tragedy*. Confusing gender in both form and content, Garrick himself wrote the Prologue, but specifically for a female narrator. It mocked the increasing number of women who had violated their supposed boundaries—including the Chevalière d'Eon:

To rule the man, our sex dame Nature teaches;
Count the high horse we can, and make long speeches.
Nay, and with dignity, some wear the breeches
And why not wear them?—We shall have your votes,
While some of t'other sex wear petticoats.
Did not a lady knight, late Chevalier
A brave smart soldier in your eyes appear?
Hey! Presto! Pass! His sword becomes a fan,
A comely woman rising from a man.
The French their Amazonian maid invite;
She goes—alike well skilled to talk or write,
Dance, ride, negotiate, scold, coquet, or fight
If she should set her heart upon a rover
And he prove false, she'd kick her faithless lover.[22]

Rumors

S OMETIME DURING THE YEAR 1770, rumors began to surface
that the Chevalier d'Eon was actually a woman. Given the nature of
rumors, it is impossible for the historian to determine their origins
with any precision. "The first rumor that the Chevalier was a woman," an
early biographer wrote in 1777, "passed only through the circles of the gay
and polite about St. James's and Westminster." The first written record that
we have of this rumor comes from none other than the King of France
himself. "Do you know," Louis XV wrote in October 1770 to one of his
generals, "that M. du Châtelet is convinced that d'Eon is a girl?"[1]

Châtelet was France's new ambassador to England, having arrived only
a year earlier. Certainly the rumor did not start with him. Châtelet hardly
knew him; as of the spring of 1769, in fact, d'Eon had never spoken to
him.[2]

Next, the historical record picks up the rumor a notch down on the
social scale, in correspondence between two aristocratic celebrities, the
English gossip Horace Walpole and the French salonnière the Marquise
du Deffand. In December 1770, at the end of a long letter about other
matters, Deffand wrote the following from Paris to Walpole in England:
"I almost forgot to tell you that M. d'Eon is a woman." And then she adds
as an afterthought to what is already an appendix: "That's what is passing
as fact."[3]

One month later we find Deffand's fellow salonnière, Louise d'Epinay,
passing the rumor on to her friend, the Italian philosopher the Abbé
Galiani: "Do you know the nonsense that has just been told to me this
very minute? It is the number of letters from England saying that d'Eon,

who has been there forever, is a woman, truly a woman. Note, I tell you, the weight of the evidence:

"First, his friends know nothing because they have never seen him dress himself. First proof.

"His washerwoman knows it for sure because she says so. Second proof.

"All the world says it. Final incontestable proof!"[4]

These three statements from the King, Deffand, and d'Epinay share certain characteristics. The writers assume that their correspondents know d'Eon well enough that he needs no introduction. Because of his political activities, d'Eon was indeed already a celebrity. Second, they treat the matter rather lightly. In none of these letters is d'Eon's gender headline news. While worthy of telling, it is remarked upon as a curious anecdote, almost an afterthought or joke—"I almost forgot to tell you." Third, the rumors are remarkably vague. In these reports, as in others, no one ever describes a particular incident or event that made Londoners or Parisians suddenly believe d'Eon was a woman. Rather, as d'Epinay's letter indicates, for some unknown reason people just seemed to be perceiving d'Eon differently. Fourth, while each of these letters expresses skepticism over the possibility that d'Eon is female, each also is impressed with the extent to which the rumor is taken seriously by others—even the French ambassador is convinced, as the King reveals. Finally, one cannot but notice the important rhetorical difference here between the male correspondent, who refers to the new d'Eon as a "girl" (*fille*), while the two female authors use the word *femme,* or woman.

In a couple of months, the wild story hit the London newspapers. The *Public Advertiser* reported d'Eon's female status as a fact: "The discovery of her sex was occasioned by her lately discharging a favorite footman, [to] whom she had entrusted the secret." A rival paper claimed that d'Eon's female sex was acknowledged in the private correspondence between d'Eon and the Duc de Nivernais, "now in our Premier's possession," in which Nivernais supposedly addressed d'Eon as "ma chère Chevalière." "A report prevails at the West end of the town," went one story in the *London Evening Post,* "that a celebrated Chevalier (D'—n) has, within a few weeks past, been discovered to be of a different sex."[5] The London journalistic community, the most intensely competitive in the world, knew a good story when it found one, and for several months, indeed years, rumors of d'Eon's sex would appear at irregular intervals.

As important as journalism was to London, it paled in comparison to the city's business community. During the 1770s, London was the financial capital of the world, a center of bustling commerce that was about to launch the first industrial revolution. One way or another, everything in London related to business, and in this most expensive city in the eighteenth-century world, business meant the business of money.

The rumor regarding d'Eon's sex was no sooner before the public than London businessmen began placing bets on the highly charged question. On the first Thursday in March 1771, gamblers gave 3:2 odds that d'Eon was a man, though one day later, bookies were giving only "even money." "This very extraordinary phenomenon," one journalist commented, "is the conversation of all our *beaux* and *belles esprits*." A few days later the betting spread to Garraway's pub, "and several other coffee houses" in the neighborhood of the stock exchange, where bookies were giving 10:1 odds that d'Eon was a man. According to one news item, £800 "was *done* at the rate above mentioned" on just one day, March 15. According to another, one nobleman wagered £500 that d'Eon was a woman.[6]

Most of the time, larger bets were made not with cash, but with life insurance policies used as collateral. Since insurance policies were often sold by stockbrokers, they took bets at pubs and restaurants near the stock exchange. While it is impossible to estimate the total amount of money waged on d'Eon's sex, one newspaper claimed that by May 1771 the sum had reached £60,000.[7]

Many sophisticated Londoners were skeptical about the whole affair. They reasoned that d'Eon and certain unscrupulous stockbrokers had concocted a scheme to rid rich financiers of their loose change. Such, at any rate, is the meaning behind a popular print, featured in the *Oxford Magazine* and sold at bookstores throughout London, "The Chevalier D'Eon Returned or The Stock Brokers Outwitted." In this print (facing page), d'Eon arrives at a gambling room to collect his money and have some laughs at the expense of those financiers he has taken. The same charge was made by the *Morning Chronicle*, which even printed a bogus letter in which d'Eon orders his stockbroker to wager £2,000 on his being a male. Needless to say, d'Eon himself repeatedly denied participating in these bets himself, and offered to swear it under oath in any court of law.[8]

What were d'Eon's feelings during this crucial period? It is impossible to know for sure. He did not leave a straightforward account of how the rumors began. Nothing in his correspondence with the Comte de Broglie or anyone else during the fall of 1770 or winter of 1771 gives any hint as to what is about to happen. For example, a March 1771 letter to his mother contains only an urgent request to send 200 livres' worth of good Tonnerre wine.[9]

Once d'Eon got wind of the gambling, however, he exploded in anger. He was outraged not so much that someone might think he was a woman,

CHEVALIER D'EON RETURNED, OR THE STOCKBROKERS OUTWITTED. [*See note, p. 287.*]

This British cartoon plays on the rumor that d'Eon was participating in the bets placed on his sex in the 1770s. *(Courtesy of the Brotherton Collection, University of Leeds Library)*

but that financiers would bet on his sex in public. Never mind that England was, in his words, a "country of gamblers." It was one thing, he noted to Broglie, to have to endure "all the extraordinary reports coming from Paris, London, and even Saint Petersburg about the uncertainty of my sex." But it was something else altogether to witness gambling "for considerable sums at the Court and in the City on so indecent a subject."[10]

On Saturday 23 March, d'Eon finally went to the taverns around the stock exchange. Dressed in his uniform of a Dragoon captain, and showing off an expensive cane, he found a banker by the name of Bird who was apparently the first to have arranged a bet over d'Eon's sex. D'Eon challenged Bird to a duel on the spot, and announced that such a challenge was open to anyone who dared to bet on him. Obviously, none of the shocked businessmen drinking in these coffeehouses would accept d'Eon's challenge. Everyone was polite to him and tried to reason with him. Bird himself apologized, but tactfully reminded d'Eon that in England it was legal to draw up such bets on anyone except the King, the Queen, and their children.[11]

But if d'Eon thought he had successfully put a stop to the gambling, he was sorely mistaken. Indeed, if anything, his dramatic entry into the gambling dens had the opposite effect. By May, Lloyd's Coffee House alone had arranged bets totaling close to £6,000. Apparently, excited financiers were all the more eager to wager insurance policies on d'Eon's sex, despite the fact that at least some Lloyd brokers viewed "this Policy as the most idle and nonsensical Policy that ever was opened there."[12] Nor was there really anything d'Eon could do about it. His challenges to duel had a ridiculous quality about them, like something out of *Don Quixote*. Bourgeois London was not aristocratic Paris: businessmen felt no shame in refusing to duel, especially if there was any chance that d'Eon might turn out to be a woman.

The press continued to have a field day with the d'Eon story, competing for the most outrageous anecdote. One newspaper printed a letter from "Marie d'Eon de Beaumont," admitting finally that she was truly and definitively a woman. Another report, dated 17 April, noted that the infant recently abandoned in the lobby of the House of Commons was actually the child of John Wilkes and "the Body of Madame d'E-n." Like all satires, this one was not composed out of thin air, but played on the well-known friendship between the two celebrities.[13]

Speculation regarding d'Eon's sex also gave rise to the charge that he was actually a hermaphrodite. "Many persons, since the Chevalier d'Eon's sex has been the universal topic of conversation," the *Gazetteer* noted, asserted that there was no such thing as a hermaphrodite. However, at least one physician, "Dr. William Cadogan, Fellow of the College of Physicians, publicly declares that in the course of his practice, he has known and seen many cases of confirmed Hermaphroditism." Still, other readers disagreed. One cited the experience of Alexander Pope and a physician friend of his, Dr. Arbuthnot, who were summoned to be present "at the examination of a certain person of great quality, whose sex, like that of the Chevalier d'Eon, was somewhat problematic." Like d'Eon, this person had been raised as a male since birth. At first glance, the person's genitals were clearly female. But "a deeper examination by men of science" found that the muscles and glands were like those of a man. The experts concluded that the person was not a hermaphrodite, but a woman with extraordinary masculine features.[14]

Meanwhile, as the betting increased, d'Eon began to worry about his personal security. After all, no one who wagered would be paid until the public could determine d'Eon's sex without ambiguity.[15] Since d'Eon refused to walk around London nude, or make any other public display of his sexuality, he and his friends became concerned that he would be kidnapped by thugs hired by a businessman wanting his winnings. As long as d'Eon refused to help the public resolve the matter of his sex, he no longer felt safe on London streets.

So it is not surprising that by the first week of May, d'Eon was gone. No one, neither his friends nor even his own servants, knew anything of his whereabouts. After a few days, his close friends Peter Fountain and Humphrey Cotes put a missing-person notice in the newspapers. They said that d'Eon had last been seen leaving his house on the afternoon of Tuesday 7 May. He was wearing a coat "scarlet faced with green with his Cross of St. Louis, had a plain new hat, with silver button, loop, and band, with his sword, but without his cane. He went out alone, leaving orders with his servant to call for him at a friend's house at ten o'clock, but had not been there, nor been heard of since." Fountain and Cotes promised a "handsome reward" to "whoever can give intelligence of any such conceal- ment or violence."[16]

No one responded to the advertisement, nor did d'Eon show up any- where or contact anyone. After a month, friends became increasingly wor- ried that d'Eon had not been simply kidnapped, but killed. Perhaps some- one who had wagered great sums had discovered the "truth" of d'Eon's sex and decided to dispose of his body rather than pay off his bet. Or perhaps, as the *St. James's Chronicle* speculated, the French authorities had finally succeeded in kidnapping him. "He was seized by six men, who put him on board a boat in the River, in which he was conveyed, as it is thought, over to France." At any rate, for a few weeks d'Eon's disappearance was the talk of the town.[17]

This new turn of events gave a new lease on life to that ridiculous rumor about d'Eon's pregnancy. One reporter recycled the story about d'Eon giving birth, announcing that readers "may find Lady d'Eon at a private Lying-in Hospital, in Oxford Road, where on Thursday, two Days after absenting herself, she was brought to Bed of a fine Boy with remark- able Features. . . . She had a hard labor, and is not yet past Danger, being very weak."[18]

D'Eon's disappearance caused much volatility in the insurance policy market. Many investors who had gambled on d'Eon's sex now had second thoughts. On Monday 13 May, nine young "men of fashion" who had bet on d'Eon gathered to talk about his fate at Almack's Coffee House. After "comparing notes," they "discovered that a most iniquitous plot was laid to rob us of three or four thousand pounds." Tricksters were offering the gentlemen wagers at a 30 or 40 percent discount, knowing full well that since d'Eon was missing, the bettors would have no way of cashing in.[19]

Suddenly, on Thursday 20 June, six weeks after his disappearance, d'Eon reappeared at his home "in good health." He claimed that he had taken a trip to Germany, and while in Hamburg had read notices of his disappear- ance with sadness and alarm. He returned to London immediately and apologized to his friends.[20] Actually, not even this was the true story. In secret letters to Broglie, d'Eon confessed that he had intended to reach Ireland where, for a few months, he would travel under another name. Unlike Germany, where he had traveled earlier in his life, Ireland was someplace he'd never been; he would not be recognized there. But d'Eon didn't make it to Ireland; in fact, he never left England. When he read about his disappearance in the papers, he decided to go back to London.[21]

D'Eon's return caused even more hoopla than his disappearance had. Now there were charges that certain parties had paid him a handsome sum to leave town, in a scam to influence the wagers.[22] Accusations flew at d'Eon from all sides. To stem these verbal attacks, on the morning of 29 June he went to London City Hall to swear an affidavit directly before Brass Crosby, Lord Mayor of London. The statement had three parts: first, d'Eon swore that he never "had and never will have any Part directly or indirectly in the Policies of Insurance that have been made relating to my person." Second, he swore that he had never taken any bribe whatsoever from anyone concerning these bets, nor ever discussed such a bribe with anyone. Finally, he swore that he had not "received directly or indirectly any sum or promise to make this voyage: That I made it voluntarily, as well to avoid all suspicions and the vexation that this public jobbing [betting] has involuntarily occasioned to me." Curiously, however, d'Eon swore nothing whatsoever regarding his gender status, the cause of all the trouble.[23]

D'Eon spent much of the summer of 1771 shut up in his house. If he went out at all, he took bodyguards or friends with him. Safety, though, was only part of the problem. Wherever he went, people wanted to see him, to catch a glimpse of this man who might be a woman. The ambiguity of d'Eon's sex attracted all kinds of attention. Even in seclusion, he received letters from fans begging him to reveal the truth about his sex.[24]

Drouet's Visit

D'EON'S RETURN TO LONDON may have calmed his nervous friends, but he soon realized that it was a mistake. The same discomforts that had led him to flee the capital were now even more pronounced. He was followed wherever he went; crowds would gather as soon as he was recognized; the press was still full of awful rumors. He knew he had to find another way to get out of town.

In July 1771 that way appeared in the form of Washington Shirley, the fifth Earl of Ferrers, who invited d'Eon for a long stay at his country estate, Staunton-Herald, situated in Leicestershire, about four miles from Derby. Shirley had been a decorated naval officer, celebrated for his bravery in the War of the Austrian Succession and the Seven Years' War.[1]

D'Eon accepted Ferrers's invitation and left London for Staunton-Herald in October 1771, remaining there through February 1772. D'Eon loved the Ferrers estate, with its large, beautiful trees and meandering meadows. But what d'Eon most appreciated about it was its solitude. He could spend hours reading and preparing the last volumes of his *Loisirs*. And, in his words, he "could live in such magnificence there for free," dining at a sumptuous table provided by Ferrers. As the weeks turned into months, d'Eon found that his acquaintance with Ferrers became a close friendship. Some of d'Eon's favorite moments were spent in evening reminiscences as the two military officers traded war stories.[2]

For the next six years, these long retreats to the country made life bearable for d'Eon. Whenever his situation became too intense, whenever he feared for his own security, or simply wanted a vacation, d'Eon would slip away to Staunton-Herald. Between 1771 and 1777, d'Eon spent nearly half his time at the Ferrers estate.

In March 1772, when d'Eon returned to London, the city was even more convinced than before that the Chevalier was a woman; "for that she is of the *Female* Sex there is now no manner of reason to doubt," one observer claimed.[3] Nor had the boisterous jokes quieted. One newspaper gleefully announced the publication of *The Memoirs of an Hermaphrodite*, "Inscribed to the Chevalier d'Eon." (Needless to say, no such book was ever actually published.)[4]

But d'Eon also had other matters to think about. He was, after all, still spying for Louis XV, and during these early months of 1772 there was apparently much to occupy a spy. D'Eon had heard of a Scottish plot (supposedly led by former prime minister Lord Bute and Chief Justice Lord Mansfield) to exclude the Hanoverian succession after the death of King George III. Now it was d'Eon's turn to spread rumors. He immediately wrote to the Comte de Broglie explaining what he had heard. Obviously such news would be extremely important to policymakers in Versailles.[5]

Broglie was indeed impressed with d'Eon's news. He advised the King that the matter was "of such great importance," he should authorize his own secretary, Jean Drouet, to go to London immediately and find out whether the rumors were true. Broglie also instructed Drouet to get to the bottom of that other rumor floating around London, the one about d'Eon's sex. The King approved Broglie's plan, and preparations were made at once for Drouet's voyage.[6]

Drouet was in London for one month, from 17 May to 17 June 1772, during which he seems to have spent much time with d'Eon, whom he had known since d'Eon's days with the Secret in Russia. When he returned to Versailles, Drouet was able to confirm the validity of both rumors to Broglie. First, Drouet repeated d'Eon's claim of a plot against the Hanovers. Second, Drouet confirmed d'Eon's female status. "The suspicions which were raised last year regarding the sex of this extraordinary celebrity are well founded," Broglie immediately reported to the King. "Sir Drouet, whom I had instructed to do his best to verify the rumors, assures me upon his return that he succeeded in doing that, and that he can certify to me, after having examined and touched with much attention, that the so-called Sieur d'Eon is a girl and is nothing other than a girl, that he has all of the attributes of one and all of the regular inconveniences." Drouet explained that d'Eon had shared his secret with him in the strictest confidence, for, Broglie wrote, "if it was discovered, his [political] role would be entirely finished."[7]

Broglie and Louis XV had reached the truth about d'Eon's sex, they thought. From this point forward, the French government was convinced that d'Eon was a woman. Louis XVI, French Revolutionaries, Napoleon—everyone in the government until d'Eon's death in 1810 accepted his female status as a fact.

What evidence could Drouet have had that led him to "certify" d'Eon's womanhood as a fact before the King of France? What had he examined and touched that had led him to this erroneous perception?

While we can never know for sure, the one logical and inescapable conclusion that must be drawn from Drouet's testimony is that *d'Eon wanted Drouet to think he was a woman.* D'Eon, of course, knew that Drouet would fire back such hot information to Broglie, who would relay it immediately to Louis XV. Thus we can be certain that by the spring of 1772, if not before, d'Eon wanted the French government to think of him as a woman.

Knowing that d'Eon confessed his supposed womanhood to Drouet sheds light on the rumors about his gender status that circulated during the fall of 1770 and winter of 1771. First, we know that they didn't start because d'Eon was discovered dressing as a woman. During the period between 1762 and 1777, no one ever witnessed d'Eon wearing women's clothes. Everyone who suspected d'Eon of being a woman viewed him as "a maiden appearing in the clothes of a man"—in the uniform of a French Dragoon captain, to be more precise.[8] "Neither his looks nor behavior betrayed any womanish symptoms," noted one London journalist in March 1771. Thus the origins of d'Eon's gender transformation had nothing to do with transvestism or with any perceived transvestite episodes. D'Eon would not wear female clothes until the French king forced him to when he returned to France in 1777. Indeed, one British newspaper claimed that d'Eon did not wear women's clothes in England until after he moved back to that country in 1785.[9]

Second, the fact that d'Eon told Drouet he was a woman meant that he also wanted others to think of him as such. Far from being, then, the *victim* of rumors concerning his gender status, we can logically conclude that at some point during 1770, d'Eon himself *initiated* these rumors with deliberate "secret" confessions made, at first, to close confidants. These friends, in turn, told their friends and superiors (which is why the first places we find the rumors are in the correspondence of the King and Anglo-French aristocrats), until the "secret" finally leaked to the press. After all, during the 1760s d'Eon had become a master at leaking diplomatic and political secrets. D'Eon, of course, would never admit that the rumors had begun with him. For such a scheme to work, he had to play the role of victim rather than propagandist.

D'Eon blamed the original discovery of his "true" sex on a Russian courtier, the Princess Daskova, who was visiting London at this time. The niece of a powerful Russian minister under the Empress Elizabeth, Daskova had been at the center of court circles while d'Eon had been in Russia, and had played an important role in the conspiracy that brought Catherine to the throne. D'Eon told Drouet that he had "confided his sex" to Daskova while he was in Saint Petersburg during the 1750s, and that it was she who first betrayed his secret to the public during her visit to London.[10]

However, it is doubtful that Daskova thought d'Eon a woman at the court of the Empress Elizabeth. First, Daskova, born in 1743, was only a child when d'Eon was at Elizabeth's court. There is no mention of her in d'Eon's diplomatic correspondence from Russia. Nor does Daskova mention d'Eon in her memoirs.[11] It is extremely unlikely that d'Eon would have chosen such a young girl as a confidante. Second, no one has ever offered any explanation of why Daskova would have divulged the secret on her visit to London. As far as one can tell, d'Eon and Daskova never met together on her visit. What motive would Daskova have for suggesting such a tale?

Far more likely is the explanation that the rumors had some other source and that Daskova was interviewed about them in one salon or another. What did she think of the idea that d'Eon was really a woman? Had she known him well in Saint Petersburg? Did he exhibit any strange behavior then? To these questions, she very well may have told listeners that she had seen d'Eon dress as a woman, or at least heard from others about his masquerading at parties, and that he indeed made a very convincing woman. In the androgynous culture that defined Elizabeth's court, cross-dressing was a common practice; this fact by itself was hardly an indication that d'Eon was female. However, in the midst of such rumors about d'Eon, and given that Daskova's conversations were probably taking place in French, it is likely that her words were misunderstood or twisted out of context.

The most likely conclusion, then, is that sometime between the summer of 1770 and the spring of 1772, d'Eon decided that he wanted others to think of him as a woman who was passing as a man. This period was a watershed for both France and for d'Eon. By 1770 d'Eon had come to the realization that his exile was far from temporary—that he could spend the rest of his life as a kind of political outlaw, estranged from his beloved

France. Although he was still working for his king, he received no recognition for his services—and recognition meant everything to this eighteenth-century nobleman.

This was also an unusually stressful period in d'Eon's life because of financial troubles. In 1766 Louis XV had promised d'Eon an annual pension of at least 12,000 livres (this figure did not count military pensions, nor his own revenues from his estate in Tonnerre). Consequently, he lived sumptuously, spending huge sums on books. By 1770, however, d'Eon was virtually broke. While Louis XV did not repudiate his financial obligations, he rarely paid his bills on time. In d'Eon's case, the government saved money by delaying the payment of his pension—sometimes for one or even two years—and then stringing it out by sending several partial payments. In nearly every letter d'Eon wrote to Broglie, he begged the government for an immediate cash payment. At various points, his friends had to cover his debts for him.[12]

Momentous, disturbing political changes were also taking place in France during this period. In December 1770, after years of bitter criticism from rival groups of aristocrats and courtiers, especially from his parlements, Louis XV made a clean sweep of his cabinet, replacing his most important ministers. To Interior and Finance came Chancellor René-Nicolas de Maupeou and the Abbé Terray. The King did not want to decide immediately on Praslin's replacement at the Foreign Ministry, so he asked the Duc de Vrillière to step in as acting foreign minister until a permanent one was chosen. Choiseul and Praslin were finally gone.

This Maupeou government soon acquired the most heinous reputation in eighteenth-century French politics. Asserting a brazen form of royal absolutism, Maupeou set out to thwart the political ambitions of French judges who had used the parlements (appellate courts) to curb the King's powers. At his first opportunity, Maupeou exiled these parlementaires, effectively shut down their courts, and established a new judicial system for the country. While Voltaire praised the Chancellor for his reforms, most Enlightenment critics thought that Maupeou was leading France straight into despotism. Relations among political elites worsened, and some of France's best-known nobles, such as the Prince de Conti, flirted with the radical ideas of Rousseau.[13]

However controversial the Maupeou "coup" became, d'Eon welcomed it as a godsend. After all, anything that got rid of Praslin and Choiseul was good news. For many years, d'Eon had been convinced his problems stemmed from the fact that Praslin had long hated him and his patron Broglie. Anyone in his place was bound to be an improvement. But d'Eon had further reason to be optimistic. By early 1771, rumors were coming out of Versailles that the race for Foreign Minister had come down to two men: the Duc d'Aiguillon and the Comte de Broglie. If these rumors were true, and Broglie were chosen, then d'Eon's worries would certainly be over, and a final resolution to his political career would not be far off.[14]

But Broglie did not get the job. In June, Louis appointed the Duc d'Aiguillon as Foreign Minister. Although this was not the outcome he had hoped for, d'Eon did not know how d'Aiguillon would respond to his case.

A year earlier, Drouet had reported to Broglie that d'Eon wanted his female sex to be kept a secret because if it were made public, "his role would be entirely finished." But perhaps that is exactly what d'Eon wanted: to end his role as a dishonorable French spy in exile, and to return to France with dignity and respect.

Passing as a woman could achieve this goal: If the public came to see d'Eon not as a trickster, but as a heroine who had dressed up as a man in order to perform patriotic acts for Louis XV, this perception might provide d'Eon with his ticket to France. D'Eon knew that the government would seek his retirement from the Secret as soon as his female status became acknowledged. But he gambled that the government would not take a chance on retiring him in London, where the English might use him as a spy for their own purposes. If d'Eon was to be retired, he had to be brought home to France.

Of course, once d'Eon was back in France, Louis XV could then take away his pensions or even throw him into the Bastille. But given the state secrets d'Eon knew, this was very unlikely—especially if the government and everyone else were celebrating d'Eon's status as a female. Thus, passing as a woman seemed an effective way to resolve many of d'Eon's political difficulties.

Still, while we can make the case that passing as a woman might seem politically logical, we must admit that such reasoning cannot begin to explain why d'Eon in fact decided to choose this course. After all, there were many, perhaps hundreds of, European aristocrats in political exile from antagonistic governments during the eighteenth century. D'Eon's situation, while noteworthy, was hardly uncommon. Certainly he could have come up with a plan that did not involve anything so drastic as gender transformation. No one before 1770 ever claimed that d'Eon was a woman. The notion of becoming a woman for the second half of one's life had no historical precedent. In deciding to become a woman, not in some episodic transvestite phase but for the rest of his life, the Chevalier d'Eon was engaging in an act of pure invention, refashioning himself radically.

D'Eon's passage to womanhood was more than a means of escaping London and the King's Secret; it was a way to pursue a path toward moral purification; to actualize the virtuous aspects of his personality that had been repressed in a life of devious diplomacy and war. Near the end of his stay in London, d'Eon wrote Drouet that at the core of every politician's heart lies only "vainglory and egotism," which constitute "the two principles of all action."[15] D'Eon's career had reached a dead end, and he longed for a rebirth that would lead him into something different and better.

Macaulay, d'Epinay, and the Femme Savante

ONCE PEOPLE BEGAN to believe that d'Eon was female, they had to come to terms with the kind of woman he was. Not surprisingly, the categories people used to draw a new portrait of him came from the same Querelle des Femmes literature that influenced d'Eon himself. Moreover, since the Querelle was not so much a literary movement or school as an ongoing debate about women, d'Eon became part of that disputation. During the 1770s, he became an object of controversy over the potential of elite women to play a significant role in public life, and Querelle authors manipulated his image for their own purposes. One part of his new role was his reputation as a *femme savante*, or woman intellectual. Here was evidence that a woman could be given a "male" education and go on to produce works of intellectual weight.

The press linked d'Eon to the influential contemporary British historian Catherine Macaulay. Next to that of Hume, her *History of England* was perhaps the most important multivolume history to appear during the eighteenth century. And unlike Hume's conservative tract, Macaulay's was written from a radical tradition that influenced John Wilkes's efforts at political reform. Not surprisingly, the press sometimes associated Macaulay, Wilkes, and d'Eon as part of the same circle.[1]

One London newspaper made the connection between d'Eon and Macaulay even more pronounced by spreading the rumor in March 1771 that bets were now being placed on *Macaulay*'s sex: "The policy which was opened last week in the Alley, for *doing* a (late) French Plenipotentiary Minister, now being quite full, another policy, it is whispered, will be opened in the course of this week, for *doing* Catherine Macaulay; the *manly* style, and muscular abilities of that famous historian, having lately occasioned many doubts of the *gender* of that exemplary and *republican* writer. A certain elderly Dowager in Pall-Mall, it is said, has already given a premium of 300 guineas to receive 3000 on proof of the party in question being of the *male* genius, and she charges herself with the *onus probandi*."[2]

Macaulay and d'Eon's careers did actually overlap. The first volume of Macaulay's *History* was published in 1763, the year d'Eon became Plenipotentiary Minister in London. Throughout the 1760s both names became familiar to the English public. During 1771, when the press reported that d'Eon was a woman and about to publish his *Loisirs*, rumors also spread that Macaulay would take her history up to the present. Both accomplishments seemed amazing feats for women.[3]

Moreover, there was some basis in fact for associating Macaulay and d'Eon. The extent of their friendship is not clear, but it would appear to have been at least cordial. In 1768, just after Macaulay had published the third volume of her *History*, she sent her own annotated copy to d'Eon, asking for his comments and suggestions that she might use toward a second edition.[4]

The issue raised by the d'Eon–Macaulay comparison boiled down to whether a woman could gain citizenship in the "Republic of Letters," the set of cultural institutions including academies, reading clubs, and editorial projects (Diderot and d'Alembert's great *Encyclopédie* being the most famous example) that made up the Enlightenment. D'Eon and Macaulay were presented to the public as two women, one French, the other English, who had managed to get a "male" education in history and politics, and who had published important works in hitherto exclusively male fields. While Querelle des Femmes feminists used these two to demonstrate what any woman could do with a good education, the male *philosophes* of the Enlightenment reacted ambivalently. After all, despite the inferiority of female education, eighteenth-century women managed to make up a large sector of the reading public.[5]

If there was a French contemporary of Catherine Macaulay who aspired to be like her, it was Louise d'Epinay (1726–1783), who in 1774 had achieved fame with her *Conversations d'Emilie*, a work that tried to do for women what Rousseau's *Emile* (1762) had done for men.[6] At precisely the same time that she was writing to the Abbé Galiani about the rumors surrounding d'Eon, d'Epinay was also complaining to him about the tremendous obstacles facing women who had intellectual aspirations. Women were absolutely right, d'Epinay repeatedly told her male friend, "to acquire as much knowledge as possible . . . because that is a sure means of becoming self-sufficient, of being free, and independent."[7]

Galiani found d'Epinay's letters so interesting that he wrote a short "Dialogue on Women," which, while not published, traveled the salon circuit in Paris and was partially read before the French Academy. The dialogue opposed a chevalier and a marquis. The chevalier argued that the only thing women lacked was proper education, while the marquis contended that no amount of education could overcome a woman's "naturally weak and sickly" conditon.[8]

The chevalier's position was taken up by a close friend of Galiani and d'Epinay, Antoine-Léonard Thomas, who published a short book in 1772 (bought by d'Eon, who described him as an "old friend") on female character. Thomas compared the condition of women to that of the American Indian: both were oppressed, exploited, and conquered. He did not doubt that women were weaker than men, nor did he think women were equal with men in every way. But he firmly believed that making women the intellectual equals of men would improve men's moral character.[9]

None of this impressed d'Epinay. She complained that neither Galiani nor Thomas would state directly that "men and women are of the same nature and the same constitution." For d'Epinay, any genuine feminism had to start with that basic assertion. "The proof of this," she lectured Galiani, "is that primitive women are as robust, as agile as primitive men: thus the weakness of our constitution and of our organs certainly belongs to our education, and follows from the condition we have been assigned in society. Men and women, being of the same nature, are susceptible to the same faults, the same virtues and the same vices. The virtues that people wish to give to women in general are almost all virtues against nature, which produce only small artificial virtues and some very real vices."[10]

Among those who attributed false virtues to women was another of d'Epinay's close friends, the *philosophe* Denis Diderot, who had the opposite reaction to Thomas's essay. Diderot thought Thomas oversimplified the fundamental sexual differences between men and women. "He wanted his book to be sexless," Diderot charged, "and unfortunately he has succeeded all too well." For Diderot, men and women were governed by their separate and distinct physiologies. The starting point to understanding female character and psychology was to know something about female sexuality. If the Querelle des Femmes was pointing toward some kind of social androgyny, Diderot wanted no part of it. In his dialogue "On Women" he wrote: "Woman has inside her an organ, subject to terrible spasms, which rules her and rouses up in her phantoms of every sort. In her delirium she goes back into her past and plunges forward into the future, both states being all the while present to her. All her extraordinary ideas spring from this organ, which is peculiar to her sex."[11]

Like Rousseau, Diderot claimed that he too was for improving the condition of women. Men should not be cruel toward women, he believed; they should neither beat them nor abandon them. Nor should civil laws deprive women of property rights. Nevertheless, men should not ignore what women are really like. Diderot urged all men to "remember that, owing to her lack of principles and power of reflection, nothing penetrates deeply into the comprehension of women: notions of justice, virtue, vice, goodness, or wickedness, float superficially above their soul. Remember that women have clung with all the energy of nature to egotism and self-interest. More civilized than us externally, they have stayed simple savages within, all more or less Machiavellian."[12]

With misogynistic criticisms such as these passing for "enlightened discourse," no wonder d'Epinay felt isolated, alienated, and pessimistic. Indeed, the closer one gets to the center of the Enlightenment, the more of an emphasis one finds on sexual differentiation. French Enlightenment *philosophes* such as Rousseau and Diderot longed for a more "natural" society that would recognize the social implications of sexual difference. "There are women who are men and men who are women," wrote Diderot, perhaps thinking of d'Eon's story. "And I admit that I will never make a friend of a man-woman. We have more intellect than women; women more instinct than we."[13]

In the "Supplement to Bougainville's Voyage", another dialogue written in 1772, Diderot argued that primitive peoples understood that gender derives from sexuality, whereas civilized Europeans, being so far removed from anything natural, believed gender and sexuality to be relatively autonomous. Diderot related an anecdote about a steward who was said to have joined the eighteenth-century French navigator Louis-Antoine de Bougainville's journey to Tahiti: "The servant was a woman disguised as a man. Her sex had been kept secret from the crew during the whole voyage, but the Tahitians recognized it at the first glance. She was born in Burgundy." Might Diderot have been thinking of d'Eon, the period's most famous Burgundian female-to-male cross-dresser? If so, Diderot seems to imply that only in a Europe out of touch with its own natural sexuality would d'Eon's gender be mistaken for so long.[14]

Thus when the rumors flew throughout London and Paris that d'Eon was a woman, the issue itself became a rhetorical bargaining chip in the intense debate regarding the place of women in society and, more specifically, the role of women intellectuals. If d'Eon was a woman, he was another Catherine Macaulay, and where there were two, perhaps there was a trend. That is how Louise d'Epinay and possibly many others viewed the situation.

Several years later, in Mary Wollstonecraft's classic defense of feminism, the *Vindication of the Rights of Women* (1792), d'Eon was again held up as an example of what women could become if only they, like the lucky d'Eon, had access to a male education. Wollstonecraft's contemporary Mary Robinson put the case more polemically: As long as d'Eon dressed as a man, his political and military activities won "distinguished honors. But alas! When she was discovered to be a *woman*, the highest terms of praise were converted into eccentricity, absurd and masculine temerity, at once ridiculous and disgusting."[15] D'Eon became an important example in the struggle of eighteenth-century women, and women intellectuals in particular, to attain dignity, if not equality.

Hannah Snell and the Amazons

I own I cannot brook such manly belles
as Mlle d'Eons, and Hannah Snells

—Peter Pindar or Dr. Walcot, 1787 (d'Eon's clipping)

D'EON WAS MORE than an intellectual. Wearing the uniform of a Dragoon captain, he was also a military officer, a hero of the Seven Years' War, one to whom the King had awarded the prestigious Cross of Saint-Louis. When Europeans came to accept d'Eon as a woman, they began to include him among several well-known cases of eighteenth-century women who had disguised themselves in order to enter military service. The most famous of these was Hannah Snell.

Born five years before d'Eon, Snell led a conventional working-class life in England until she was abandoned by her husband following her first pregnancy. When her daughter died at only seven months, Snell became despondent over her double tragedy, and decided to find the louse of a husband who had deserted her. Discovering that he had entered the British navy, she dressed as a man, took the name of her brother-in-law, James Gray, joined the navy, and for nearly five years participated in the War of the Austrian Succession. After leaving military service, she sold her story to a publisher and traveled around England, performing a one-woman show about her career.[1]

More interesting than the story itself, however, is the way contemporary English audiences interpreted it. In their eyes, Snell had committed a major transgression; by impersonating a soldier, she had even committed a

D'Eon was often compared to Hannah Snell, who passed as a male soldier and fought in battle. *(Courtesy of the Brotherton Collection, University of Leeds Library)*

crime. However, in the pamphlets devoted to her, and in the countless retelling of the story, few criticized her. To the contrary, the English considered her one of the great heroes of their age. Newspaper publisher Robert Walker, in particular, praised her for martial characteristics usually found in men. He was proud to call her "our British heroine," and thought she ought to be considered a model for other British women. Comparing her to the protagonist of Richardson's famous novel, Walker claimed that Snell "is the real *Pamela*, the other a counterfeit; this *Pamela* is real flesh and blood; the other is no more than a shadow: Therefore, let this our Heroine . . . be both admired and encouraged."[2]

Through studying the virile exploits of Hannah Snell, British women could appreciate that virtue, honor, and courage were not the monopoly of men. "However, tho' courage and warlike expeditions are not the provinces of the world allotted to women since the days of the Amazons," Walker noted, "yet the female sex is far from being destitute of heroinism [sic]. Cleopatra headed a noble army against Mark Anthony, the greatest Warrior of his Time."[3]

It is significant that Walker did not present Snell as a transvestite, liar, or trickster, even though her career required all three abilities. Rather, for him she was a modern Amazon, and her transvestism was not a means to deceive others, but rather the only way she could successfully prove her courage and "love of glory."

Walker was also impressed that Snell was able to maintain her chastity while living as a soldier in the most crowded conditions. There was no doubt in his mind that if Snell's true sex had been discovered, she would have become the victim of a violent sexual assault. Not only did Snell preserve her own virtue, Walker claimed that she helped other women preserve theirs. When at one point her superior officer boasted that he was going to rape a village girl, Snell managed to forewarn her and the rape never took place.[4]

By placing Snell in the role of Amazon, Walker was playing upon a familiar theme in eighteenth-century European popular culture. At the level of society, Snell was just one of hundreds, perhaps thousands, of women who followed their husbands into battle. The front lines of early modern wars were composed of members of both sexes. Most women at the front provided services ranging from cooking and washing to prostitution. But it was also not uncommon for women to take on the uniform of a soldier in order to be closer to their mates. What Hannah Snell did, then, may have been extraordinary in its duration, but it was merely an exaggeration of a more widespread phenomenon.[5]

Popular stories and ballads featuring Amazonian heroines flourished in eighteenth-century England, revealing the extent to which women warriors were admired by common folk in d'Eon's era. At the end of one long ballad, after the woman has returned home from war to marry her man, the minstrel sings

They often think upon that day when she received a scar
When Susan followed her true love on board a man of war.[6]

This celebration of Amazons was both noticed and replicated by some of England's best-known writers, such as d'Eon's friend Richard Brinsley Sheridan. In Sheridan's *The Camp*, a popular play first performed in October 1778, a Suffolk girl pursues her lover to his military camp, where she becomes so enthusiastic about military life that she marries the soldier and stays to fight beside him.[7]

An essay titled "Female Warriors," written near the end of the Seven Years' War and commonly attributed to Oliver Goldsmith, takes a satirical angle on this phenomenon. Noting that the loss of so many men in the war has resulted in an oversupply of women, it argues that the government should balance the sexes by "raising thirty new Amazonian regiments, to be commanded by females, and serve in regimentals adapted to their sex." The author is convinced that British women would make good soldiers because so many of them excel in virile activities on the streets of London. To dramatize the androgynous nature of working-class women, Goldsmith recounts the occasion when he came upon two boxers fighting in a street match. "I imagined the combatants were of the other sex [men], until a bystander assured me of the contrary." Such a satire could not make readers laugh unless they recognized in it a germ of truth.[8]

Thus when rumors began to circulate that the Chevalier d'Eon was really a woman who had dressed up as a man, there was a clearly defined cultural category in which to place him: the Amazon. Like Hannah Snell and the "virago" Catherine Macaulay, d'Eon appeared to be a woman who had empowered herself to act virilely in a man's world. Those who believed d'Eon an Amazon saw the Chevalier not as undermining any sacred norms of sex or gender, but rather as manipulating those norms to get what "she" wanted. Of course, implicit in the eighteenth-century version of the Amazon was a consensus that this behavior was episodic and temporary. Unlike the Amazon of ancient myth, whose warrior ways ended only in death, Amazons such as Hannah Snell returned to their ordinary lives as women upon the discovery of their true sex. This is what was expected of d'Eon.[9]

Contemporary illustrations from this period demonstrate the perception of d'Eon as an Amazon. In "The Discovery of the Female Free Mason" (facing page), d'Eon has just thrown off his frock coat to reveal the very feminine dress of a woman. While d'Eon's physiognomy is portrayed as anything but masculine, his formidable posture as well as three important masculine symbols present him as an Amazon: first, the sword, which only male noblemen were allowed to wear in traditional European societies; second, the walking stick, which had become the phallic symbol

"The Discovery of a Female Free-Mason." This British print satirizes d'Eon's membership in a London Masonic lodge. *(Courtesy of the Brotherton Collection, University of Leeds Library)*

of civilized masculinity by the eighteenth century; and finally, and most noteworthy, the Cross of Saint-Louis pinned to the Chevalier's right breast, which must have been seen by eighteenth-century eyes as the most bizarre visual juxtaposition—France's most coveted medal for military valor displayed on a feminine bodice. Finally, as the title makes clear, the print was meant to make fun of d'Eon's membership in a London Masonic lodge (which he had joined in 1769).[10]

The illustration on page 206, first sold in London and Paris bookstores in 1773, more directly associates d'Eon with the ancient Amazonian tradition by portraying him in a military camp ready for battle in the guise of the ancient war goddess Pallas Athena (here known by her Roman name,

Carola Genovesa Lousia Augusta Andrea Timothea D'Eon de Beaumont.

Knight of the Royal & military order of S.t Louis Captain of Dragoons Aide de Camp to the Marechal Duke de Broglio.

Minister Plenipotentiary from France to the King of Great Britain.

D'Eon imagined as an Amazonian warrior standing outside her military tent ready for battle. The Cross of Saint-Louis is on her left breast. *(Courtesy of the Bibliothèque Nationale, Paris)*

Minerva). While the nobleman's sword and walking stick have been replaced by the Romans' pike and shield, the Cross of Saint-Louis is still pinned to her breast. The Chevalier is dressed in ancient garb capped with the three-plumed helmet associated with Athena. By highlighting (and embellishing) d'Eon's military career, these prints placed the Dragoon captain within an Amazonian tradition.

"She was present in several sieges and battles," the caption below the picture noted, "and has been wounded at the affair of Vetrop, and in the year 1761 near Ostewich being then Captain of a highly praised detachment from the volunteers of the army. She did charge the battalion of . . . Prussian De Lhees so very opportunely and with such an undaunted resolution that she obliged the whole battalion to surrender as prisoners of war in spite of its great superiority."[11]

Europeans welcomed d'Eon as a contemporary Athena. The director of France's School of Design of the Royal Academy of Painting sent the following lines to his heroine:[12]

Pourquoi faut-il que l'on cache
La fleur des héros français
sous ce feminin panache
voile se augmenter trait
à la guerre c'est Achille
Pour un traité c'est Pallas
que maudin sein l'imbecille
qui nous prive de son bras

Why is it necessary to hide
the flower of French heroes
under a female plume
covering a shooting arrow
At war, it's Achilles
At writing a treaty, it's Pallas
May the imbecile who deprives us
of his services be cursed

Of course, d'Eon was no ancient Roman or Greek. Closer to home there was a more appropriate Amazonian model: Joan of Arc. At the bottom of one print, the publishers claimed that "our chevalière" was "a heroine already more conspicuous in her lifetime than Joan . . . the Maid of Orléans."[13]

The parallels between d'Eon's story and Joan's were so striking that nearly everyone connected with the story, including d'Eon himself, identified the Chevalier with the medieval martyr. In an influential article at the time, *Annales politiques* editor Simon Linguet became one of many who referred to d'Eon as a "modern Joan of Arc."[14] D'Eon's image as a new Joan was perhaps most colorfully portrayed in poems that were sent to him:[15]

Toi qui de Jeanne d'Arc autres fois eus le nom
Tu venais aujourd'hui sous celui de d'Eon

[You who in earlier days had the name Joan of Arc
You came today under that of d'Eon]

The comparison between d'Eon and Joan stuck firmly in the public's mind, eventually spreading even to the young United States. In 1794, the valedictorian of the Young Ladies Academy of Philadelphia, Ann Harker, told her fellow graduates that "in the martial field of glory, we have a long list of memorable heroines: the Count d'Eon and the Maid of Orléans shall defend our honor with Amazonian courage." In 1803, when d'Eon, near the end of his life, referred to himself as "a warrior maiden" who had lived a "persecuted life during the last century just like Joan of Arc did during the reign of Louis VII," he was simply using a familiar and even clichéd public image.[16]

Thus much of the reason the public so readily believed d'Eon was a woman is that the story satisfied their desire for proof that a Hannah Snell could appear at the very highest levels of society. Here, it seemed, was the ancient Amazon myth regenerated in the modern world. No wonder d'Eon became an international celebrity, acclaimed throughout Europe. When, a few years later, the cultural entrepreneur George Keate persuaded d'Eon to donate his sword to Keate's London museum, he wrote d'Eon a poem in honor of the event:[17]

La Pucelle de Tonnerre
ayant terminé la guerre
Depose son Cimeterre
chez George Keate son ami
et des muses très cheri
que Dieu soit loué et beni

[The maiden of Tonnerre
having finished the war
Puts down his scimitar
At the home of his friend George Keate
and is a favorite of the muses
may God be praised and blessed]

Morande

"WE ARE IN 1773," d'Eon wrote Broglie at the beginning of that year. "It is time more than ever that His Majesty directs his good attention to putting an end to my unhappiness by publicly recalling me." Now that Praslin had been replaced by the Duc d'Aiguillon as Foreign Minister, d'Eon still hoped that he would soon return to France. As the months went by, however, d'Eon became increasingly frustrated. He repeatedly urged Broglie to take his case to Louis XV. When that didn't work, d'Eon sidestepped his patron and wrote to the ministers and other influential noblemen himself. He blamed his situation on Praslin and Choiseul, proclaimed his loyalty to his King and patriotism to his country, and begged for a legitimate political rehabilitation. "I have been persecuted and in exile since 1763," he exclaimed to Chancellor Maupeou.[1]

Despite the uncertainty over d'Eon's gender, or perhaps because of it, Broglie and Louis XV wanted d'Eon to remain precisely where he was. From Broglie's viewpoint, there was little reason for the government to return d'Eon to France, where, whether man or woman, he could only stir up trouble, and there were sound political reasons for keeping him in London. Since the end of the Seven Years' War, Broglie, like Choiseul and Louis XV himself, had increasingly come to appreciate England's new role in international affairs. While the European state system was still composed of five or six great powers, Great Britain seemed to be in a class by itself. Given France's recent reconciliation with Austria, Broglie had little doubt that new wars would be fought between France and England. Therefore, Broglie reasoned, France needed to focus as many resources as possible on gathering intelligence in England. Nor had anyone in the

Secret given up hope of one day launching a surprise attack on the western coast of Britain. Whatever kind of liability the Chevalier d'Eon had become for France, he was still an extremely valuable correspondent to have in London. During his long tenure there, after all, d'Eon had become a prominent fixture in the city's elite social and political scene, invited to not only the best soirées in the capital but also to some of the most important political gatherings.[2] And there was always d'Eon's unusually close relationship with John Wilkes, still among the most influential political figures in the country.

But neither could Broglie afford to dismiss d'Eon's pleas out of hand. If d'Eon thought there was no chance of rehabilitation, he might sell his services to the British, or some other country, such as Poland or Spain. Indeed, during 1773 d'Eon himself claimed that he had turned down such offers. Thus Broglie continued to string d'Eon along. He wrote d'Eon that the King wanted to reach some sort of reconciliation. But when d'Eon drew up specific terms for such an agreement, they were always rejected.[3]

Broglie and the King also assigned d'Eon new tasks, demonstrating their continued faith in him as an agent still worthy of their confidence. In particular, the mission assigned to d'Eon in early July 1773 was especially delicate and important for the King. The French writer Charles Théveneau de Morande, who had been turned away from d'Eon's home in 1771, had just completed a vicious biography of the King's mistress, Mme du Barry, and was threatening to publish it in London. Indeed, 6,000 copies had already been printed (a large run for the eighteenth century) and were about to be distributed to bookstores. D'Eon's assignment was simple and straightforward: to convince Morande to suppress the book.[4]

Mme du Barry was not yet thirty when she became the King's mistress in 1768, some four years after the death of Mme de Pompadour. While undoubtedly beautiful, she came from a background that would seem to have disqualified her for the court at Versailles. Born into the working class, she had acquired a loose reputation as a shopgirl in Paris during her teenage years, and later, as she made the right contacts among the aristocracy, she became a commodity of exchange among noblemen doing favors for one another. The regime, which since Pompadour had established a reputation for allowing inappropriate lovers into the bedrooms of power, was now besieged with criticism.[5]

The King had good reason to concern himself with Morande's book. By 1773 Morande had become known as one of France's most notorious authors. He had been born down the road from d'Eon's Tonnerre, and d'Eon admitted to Broglie that the families knew each another, but

Charles was something of a black sheep. When he moved to Paris, he spent most of his time hanging around brothels, getting on the wrong side of the law. The police watched him carefully, and finally, in 1768, threw him into the Bastille. Released a couple of years later, he emigrated first to Holland, then to England, where he remained until the Revolution, writing vitriolic tracts condemning the French government.[6]

In August 1771 Morande published his first and most famous book, the *Gazetier cuirassé*, which attacked the Old Regime by defaming the character of its leaders. Inventing a genre that anticipates our supermarket tabloids, Morande wrote short, pithy paragraphs describing the debauchery and moral license among France's most powerful political leaders. Although published anonymously in London, the book was smuggled into France and became one of the century's best-selling books in that country.[7] Morande had proved how dangerous he could be with his pen, and the King had to stop him if he could.

Given the popularity of the *Gazetier cuirassé*, this new biography of Mme du Barry was sure to be a blockbuster. Even without Morande's book, du Barry had a terrible reputation as a slut, whom the King had supposedly picked up off the street. And since she was routinely given the credit for pushing d'Aiguillon and Maupeou upon the King, attacking her was a convenient way of attacking the King's new ministers. In the literature surrounding Louis XV, lurid gossip was never far from political commentary.

Unlike Pompadour, for whom d'Eon had a strong antipathy, the Comtesse du Barry was someone he "never had had the honor to meet nor to see." But when public opinion turned against the King, d'Eon came to his defense. "It is enough for me," he told Broglie, "that the King loves her." Besides, she is "a young and a pretty woman," and if that was what the King wanted, d'Eon felt, then so be it. Although d'Eon had many reasons for sharing Morande's hatred for France, and had himself dabbled in political muckraking, in this case he very much wanted to demonstrate his loyalty to Louis XV by distancing himself from Morande.[8]

Since arriving in London in 1771, Morande had repeatedly sought the friendship of his fellow Burgundian, but d'Eon refused to have anything to do with him. When Morande would call upon him, d'Eon would simply have his servant send him away. But now, d'Eon eagerly took up his assignment, delaying a scheduled departure for his English country retreat. D'Eon and Morande met several times during the fall of 1773 and winter of 1774. At one point, d'Eon read the book at Morande's home, a task that took him past midnight. What he read convinced d'Eon that Morande was a thoroughly despicable character.[9]

Morande tried to justify his behavior. Put yourself in my place, he told d'Eon. You are a bachelor and have no idea of the obligations one owes to a family. Everything I do, he explained, I do for my wife (who is deathly ill) and children, whom I love more than anything else—even more than fame or money. But money I need, and lots of it, in order to pay off my heavy debts. If I don't get a lot of money, and get it quickly, I'll be thrown into prison and my wife and children will be left to fend for themselves. Besides, he added, "there are certainly many other men than I" who have told similar stories without being condemned. Indeed, some of them are men of high rank with large pensions; all I want to do is pay my debts.[10]

The good news, from d'Eon's point of view, was that Morande was up for sale. Neither an ideologue nor an aspiring radical philosopher, Morande was a bourgeois entrepreneur intent on making money. Whether he sold his 6,000 books to the public or to the King of France made no difference to him. The practical result of this stance was to hasten the negotiations with d'Eon; the only thing they needed to argue about was a price.[11]

It took a few months before they reached a preliminary agreement.[12] At that point, the King commissioned a new secret agent to leave Paris with the necessary funds to purchase the manuscript and extant copies of Morande's book. That agent was Pierre-Augustin Caron de Beaumarchais, himself among the Old Regime's most colorful characters.

In Beaumarchais's life one finds many of the Old Regime's contradictions. The son of a watchmaker, he learned his father's trade well enough to invent an escapement mechanism that became a standard part for improved watches. As an artisan, he would never have been able to move far in Paris, but as an inventor, he was sought after as something of a young genius. He was something of a man of letters as well: By 1774, the Comédie française had already put on two of his plays, while two more, *The Barber of Seville* (1775) and *The Marriage of Figaro* (1781), would soon establish his reputation as France's leading playwright. Beaumarchais charmed his way into aristocratic salons, and married a wealthy noblewoman. Meanwhile, he had invested his newfound money wisely and had become enormously rich. But his quick rise had its costs. He became embroiled in lawsuits, and found too often that the court's decisions went against him. The Parlement of Paris condemned him for insulting one of its judges. If Louis XV had not stepped in with this assignment in London, Beaumarchais would have fled France for Flanders. Beaumarchais, then, was a good match for Morande.

D'Eon had laid the groundwork well, so that the final negotiations between Beaumarchais and Morande went smoothly. In a statement dated 24 April 1774, the French government agreed to purchase the manuscript and the entire run of the du Barry biography for 32,000 livres plus a life pension of 4,000 livres a year. This was a whopping amount of money—certainly much more than Morande would have been able to earn from sales of the book.[13]

While d'Eon was reporting to Louis on conversations with Morande, he would naturally use the occasions to plead his own case. When he outlined Morande's terms at the start of one letter, he might conclude by complaining about his own financial condition. For d'Eon, the two negotiations were intertwined.

Although the two cases proceeded along parallel tracks, Morande's was resolved relatively quickly, while d'Eon's situation seemed stalled. The contrast baffled d'Eon. After all, Morande was the incarnation of the eighteenth-century rogue, who had already published diatribes against king and country and was ready to do so again. Here was a man, d'Eon believed, who confused patriotism and pornography, demeaning both love and politics. And yet the French government seemed to reward him for what he had done. Meanwhile, the "good patriot" d'Eon, the secret agent loyal to Louis XV, was virtually ignored by this same sovereign. Certainly the Morande affair could only have increased d'Eon's animus toward the Old Regime.

D'Eon was aware that part of the reason his own case still languished had to do, yet again, with court politics at Versailles. In September 1773, Mme du Barry, who had been responsible for getting Louis XV to choose d'Aiguillon instead of Broglie as Foreign Minister, discovered the secret correspondence between the King and Broglie. D'Aiguillon sent Broglie into another exile on his estate in Ruffec.[14]

D'Eon reacted bitterly to these developments, pouring out his feelings to the impotent Broglie. Before, d'Eon had been willing to blame matters on ministers and forgive Louis XV. But now he was altogether sick of political life and thought seriously of unilaterally severing all relations and correspondence with French officials. "If for fifteen years this monstrous edifice known as politics has never worked honorably, it has been because the French ministers and ambassadors have been the most extraordinary that one could find in history; ministers and ambassadors, who while coming from high birth and favor, have not seen anything coming, have not learned anything, and never will do anything!" To watch Morande succeed while he and Broglie were thwarted by the system was just too much for d'Eon. Now his alienation from political life was complete.[15]

As much as d'Eon resented and despised Morande, he was also intrigued by him. Perhaps he thought he could use a scoundrel like Morande for his own purposes. At any rate, it appears that sometime during the negotiations over Morande's book, probably at the end of 1773 or during the early months of 1774, d'Eon confided to Morande that he was a woman. In one letter, Morande expressed how moved he was that d'Eon would "open yourself up to me," and he promised d'Eon that he would never give away his secret to anyone, especially not in the newspapers or in his own pamphlets.[16]

D'Eon probably divulged his womanhood to Morande for the same reason he had done so in 1770 and 1771 to others: because he wanted the story leaked to the public. We can speculate that he figured the more British and French citizens believed him to be a woman, the more pressure would be exerted on the government to resolve his political status.

Whatever feelings d'Eon had during the Morande negotiations, they were sure to have changed with the news that reached him less than one month later: On 28 April, Louis took ill, and two weeks later he died, on 10 May 1774. Until now, d'Eon's entire career had been in the hands of this one monarch. In an instant, everything was different. Suddenly nothing was fixed or predictable. What Louis's young, inexperienced, but sincere grandson would do regarding d'Eon was anyone's guess, but at least it offered d'Eon new opportunities to resolve his status.

Louis XVI

I T IS DOUBTFUL whether there was ever a French king whose death was less mourned than Louis XV. Indeed, Parisians are said to have cheered when the demise of the old monarch was announced. And today historians corroborate what contemporaries sensed: The reign of Louis XV was one of the great failures of early modern French history. In domestic affairs, Maupeou's efforts to reform the French judiciary were unsuccessful, and the King left the country's finances in a shambles. But the failings of Louis XV are best seen in foreign affairs. The Seven Years' War had shown England's superiority in the Atlantic, and between 1763 and 1774, despite bold plans to rebuild the French navy, Louis could not challenge British hegemony. Meanwhile, the alliance with Austria, symbolized by the marriage of Marie-Antoinette, daughter of Austrian Empress Maria Theresa, to the future Louis XVI, was unpopular. All the marriage seemed to serve, critics charged, were Austria's own aims in eastern Europe. And they had a point: France's impotence in eastern Europe was never so acute as in 1772, when its traditional enemies (Austria, Prussia, and Russia) agreed to partition large parts of its traditional ally, Poland. Such failures were rightly blamed on the old king.[1]

Criticism of the dead king was matched by high hopes for the new one. Certainly Louis XVI was a different entity from his grandfather, whom he was never particularly fond of or close to. Only twenty years old when he took the throne, the young king had little political experience, either in managing the vicious domestic infighting that plagued Versailles or especially in foreign affairs. He would learn on the job.

Just three days after Louis XV's death, the Comte de Broglie sat down to write the new king a memorandum. He sketched a brief history of the

Secret, noting its origins with the Prince de Conti, and emphasizing its awkward relationship to the Foreign Minister. Broglie stressed that the Secret had existed solely because of Louis XV's insistence, but now he stood ready to do whatever Louis XVI wanted.[2]

Two weeks later Broglie prepared a more detailed memorandum on the Secret for the King. This one began with a discussion of d'Eon. "I imagine it is possible that Your Majesty has heard some bad talk about him," Broglie began, "and thus Your Majesty might be surprised to find him included in the number of persons honored in the confidence of the late King." Giving the young Louis XVI what was certainly shocking news, Broglie gently revealed that d'Eon had secretly worked for the government since 1756, when Conti had sent him to Saint Petersburg. Broglie explained how d'Eon had become both spy and Plenipotentiary Minister in England, and how, despite d'Eon's falling-out with Guerchy and Praslin, the King had kept him on as a spy, at an annual salary of 12,000 livres. "This unique being (for Sieur d'Eon is a woman) is, more than anyone else, a mixture of good and bad qualities, and he lurches from one extreme to the other." Realizing that he was raising far more questions than he was answering, and that it was absurd to try to explain all of this in a memo, Broglie finished by requesting a separate meeting with the King to talk about d'Eon. "It is necessary that I have the honor to enter into this subject in much greater detail with Your Majesty, when you have decided definitively on the fate of the secret correspondence."[3]

Louis XVI was, indeed, stunned by what he read. He immediately informed Broglie of his intention to shut down the Secret, and ordered him to burn all the secret correspondence in his possession. Broglie could accept the end of the Secret, but he begged the King to reconsider his decision to have the papers burned. Without those papers, many French statesmen would have no way to defend themselves against charges that might surface in the salons, at court, or in the press. If arrested by ambitious ministers, they would have nothing to support their claims.[4]

Luckily for Broglie (and future historians), one of those vulnerable statesmen turned out to be Louis XVI's new Foreign Minister, the Comte de Vergennes, who for several years had been a spy for the Secret in Sweden. Broglie agreed to turn the matter over to Vergennes, who, in 1775, wrote a long report to the King explaining why the secret correspondence should not be burned. Evidently, the King accepted his recommendation.

The new king insisted, however, that the entire operation of the Secret be completely shut down. He firmly believed that there should be only one foreign policy formulated by the King and his Foreign Minister, and administered by the Foreign Ministry. Louis therefore ordered that the twenty or so spies be retired and given a handsome pension each according to his degree of service. From the beginning, the King recognized that d'Eon was a special problem, due to his political status as an outlaw in England, as well as to the state secrets he still held in his possession. Nonetheless, Louis insisted that some agreement be reached with d'Eon, and that his situation be fully resolved.[5]

By the end of the summer, Broglie and Vergennes had decided on a plan, which was approved by the King in September. The deal they envisaged was surprisingly simple: The King was willing to continue d'Eon's annual pension for the rest of his life, and to escort him back safely to France, where he would no longer be considered an outlaw but would be within the full protection of the King. In return, the King demanded two things: first, that all of d'Eon's secret papers, including the 3 June 1763 memorandum from Louis XV, be returned immediately; second, that d'Eon promise never to say or do anything that might harm the family of the Comte de Guerchy, his former enemy, who had died in 1767.[6]

It seemed astonishingly easy. Louis XVI also scrapped plans for an invasion of Britain. The struggle against England would continue, but it would take a different form. Soon other spies were in London, not to scout the coasts for landing spots, but to encourage the Americans in their rebellion, and traffic arms for them. In this context, d'Eon seemed a rather bizarre relic of a previous administration, and the new diplomatic team wanted him retired at home, where he could make no trouble.

The most surprising aspect of this plan, however, is that it ignored the issue of d'Eon's sex. There is no doubt whatsoever that in September 1774 Broglie, Vergennes, and Louis XVI believed d'Eon was a woman. That they would not make an issue of it demonstrates how urgently they wanted d'Eon's role as a spy resolved. It also shows that they did not think the transgression of impersonating a man to be a major crime, and would deal with it, if at all, after d'Eon was already pensioned and retired in France.

D'Eon rejected the plan out of hand. Having recently watched a rogue like Morande blackmail an experienced king, d'Eon was certain he could squeeze a better deal out of a new one. D'Eon responded with essentially two changes: First, he wanted the capital of his annual pension to be transferred to him personally, in effect making the pension a private annuity; second, he insisted that the government pay off debts incurred in his capacity as diplomat and spy over a quarter-century of service. When d'Eon added up the bill, it totaled some 318,477 livres! He insisted he needed this much money to pay off his creditors in London.[7]

Foreign Minister Vergennes informed the King that d'Eon's reply revealed "the traits of conceit and greed. Indeed, this is a new monument to madness from such a unique mind." But he also warned Louis XVI against cutting d'Eon off from the government altogether. After all, the papers d'Eon had in his possession were still of great interest to France. The Foreign Minister therefore recommended that they firmly and categorically reject d'Eon's claims, but also resume negotiations with him, and meanwhile continue to pay him his annual pension in quarterly installments.[8]

"I return to you, Monsieur, the note of d'Eon," the King replied. "I have never seen anything more impertinent and ridiculous. If he did not have important papers, we would just forget about him; but, as you suggest, we must give a rotten 12,000 livres to him to save the Secret, which will be less important than getting him out of there."[9]

Broglie too was repulsed by d'Eon's behavior, and let him know it. He scolded d'Eon for refusing the King's generous offer, an offer Broglie had worked so hard to get the King to agree to since his first days in office. After all, here was a new, young king ready to offer d'Eon a complete pardon and life pension. Broglie warned that d'Eon could not count on Louis XVI's patience for long. Unlike his predecessor, Louis XVI would not permit this kind of ambiguous situation to go on indefinitely. Either d'Eon would be rehabilitated, or he would be cut off forever from his homeland. Broglie cautioned d'Eon that any further "defiance on your part would be absolutely inexcusable."[10]

Luckily for d'Eon, Louis XVI was determined to seek some settlement with him, and by April 1775 the King had ordered Beaumarchais back to London to negotiate with d'Eon. A year earlier, when Beaumarchais was in London negotiating with Morande, d'Eon would have little to do with him. At that time, in 1774, Beaumarchais had been sought by the Parlement of Paris for criminal financial activities. Since then, his political problems had received at least a temporary reprieve, while his reputation had been transformed by the success of his play *The Barber of Seville*. After circulating around Paris in different versions for many years, it had finally opened at the Comédie française in February 1775. Now Beaumarchais was considered France's new Molière and greeted wherever he went as an ambassador of the Republic of Letters—a position always respected, if not coveted, by the Chevalier d'Eon.[11]

The negotiations between Beaumarchais and d'Eon proceeded along a convoluted track, with fits and starts, and were often broken off because of the slow travel between Versailles and London. Nor did the two parties particularly trust each other. Each knew the other could be shrewd and devious. Back in 1774, Beaumarchais had warned one minister that d'Eon was not ever to be trusted. "D'Eon's secret is to deceive those who want to trap him, pocket their money, and remain in London," he wrote to one minister.[12]

The two negotiators each hired assistants from the underbelly of Old Regime politics. Beaumarchais's was none other than Charles Théveneau de Morande—the person who in 1774 had blackmailed Louis XV was engaged one year later by his successor to help Beaumarchais in London![13]

On d'Eon's side was Jean-Joseph de Vignoles, who had acted occasionally as d'Eon's secretary since at least 1765. Vignoles was an ex-priest who had been forced to flee his French monastery after his lover became pregnant. The couple moved to Holland and married, where after a few years in commerce, Vignoles was forced to declare bankruptcy. He moved on to London, living at the margins of publishing and politics, making ends meet however he could.[14]

D'Eon himself was not above using the methods of a Morande or Vignoles. D'Eon renewed his threat to publish a second edition of his *Lettres, mémoires, et négociations* (first published in 1764) if an agreement was not reached quickly. This time he hired Vignoles to translate the diplomatic letters into English, and to supplement the material with various legal proceedings surrounding the feud with the Comte de Guerchy that had taken place since the mid-1760s. Clearly the French government would want to avoid such an embarrassing publication, especially since it could never be sure whether d'Eon might include even more dangerous material, such as the documents dealing with a surprise invasion of England.[15]

Meanwhile, there can be no doubt that Beaumarchais was thoroughly convinced d'Eon was a woman. During these negotiations d'Eon presented himself as an "unhappy woman" who had performed great services for her country in battle and statecraft, but who now wished only to retire. Morande, already sure that d'Eon was a woman, helped to convince Beaumarchais.[16]

The negotiations centered on three basic areas: money, political rehabilitation, and d'Eon's gender status. As to the first, d'Eon had amassed a huge documentary collection of account books, letters, and memoirs proving that Louis XV had intended d'Eon's annual 12,000 livres to be a life pension, and not simply a salary for services rendered as a spy. Moreover, d'Eon tried to justify his requests that his government cover the debts he had incurred as a spy over the years.[17]

D'Eon also demanded that the government rehabilitate his political and legal status by publicly declaring that in 1763 Guerchy had tried to murder him. D'Eon wanted the government to admit that his actions after that were within the bounds of justifiable self-defense, and that so far as Louis XVI was concerned, d'Eon was not now—nor had he ever been—an outlaw.

Finally, and most interesting, d'Eon demanded that the government publicly recognize him as a woman. He wanted a royal decree concerning his gender status to be part of any agreement. He was aware that the King would have a very difficult time with this demand, because it would make the monarchy seem to have been a conspirator in an act of deceit (that is, in d'Eon's supposed female-to-male transvestism). The King might ignore the transgressions of a noblewoman, but he could not officially condone them.

That, however, is precisely what d'Eon asked Louis XVI to do. At this point d'Eon knew that all of the principal players in the government—from Morande and Beaumarchais to Vergennes and Louis XVI—believed d'Eon was an anatomical woman who for years had impersonated a man in order to participate in politics. What d'Eon needed to do now was to demonstrate to them that the origins of his supposed transvestism (from female to male) lay not with himself, but with others, in particular with his father and Louis XV.

In order to gain the King's recognition of his female status during these negotiations with Beaumarchais, d'Eon apparently invented two fictions crucial for understanding his life. First, he created the mythology of his birth and childhood (see chapter 9): that he was born female but raised as a boy by his father, who had desperately wanted a son. Because of an inheritance that was destined only for a son, d'Eon's mother allowed herself to be overruled by her despotic husband.[18]

Second, it is likely that at this point d'Eon invented the fable regarding his inauguration into diplomatic life that later became so much a part of the lore surrounding him (see chapters 13 and 14): that during the mid-1750s, when the Prince de Conti asked him to perform secret diplomatic assignments in Russia, Conti was well aware that d'Eon was really a woman, and ordered him to take on the identity of a woman during the Russian mission. Thus, so the story goes, d'Eon dressed as a woman and became the confidante of the Empress Elizabeth.

The best evidence for suggesting that d'Eon himself invented these crucial stories as part of his 1775 negotiations with Beaumarchais are two letters d'Eon wrote to Jean-Pierre Tercier, formerly chief clerk at the Foreign Ministry, who for many years acted as secretary for the King's Secret. They are dated within two days of each other (18 and 20 January 1764) and are written in d'Eon's hand.

In both letters, d'Eon reminisces about his earlier trips to Russia. In the first, he claims that Louis XV "sent me in the first instance secretly as a female tutor [*lectrice*] to the Empress of Russia," where he facilitated Eliz-abeth's secret correspondence with the King. D'Eon insists to Tercier that when Mme de Pompadour found out about this secret correspondence, and d'Eon's role in it, she was bitterly angry. Pompadour saw d'Eon as Conti's female protégée, and as such a rival, and was determined to stop his career. Thus d'Eon explained his political frustrations as ultimately stemming from Pompadour's machinations. The second letter reveals less important information, but ends: "My only fear is that the King's Secret and my sex will be discovered." Moreover, at the bottom of the second let-ter there is a "note of 1775," which, while containing nothing of signifi-cance, indicates that this letter, supposedly written in 1764, was somehow reworked or reused eleven years later.[19]

These letters were part of an effort by d'Eon to construct an autobio-graphical narrative regarding his supposed female-to-male transvestism that featured two themes: first, that d'Eon himself was not to blame for his transgressions; second, that his Russian transvestism had been adopted as a spy in the patriotic service of his king.

By giving his supposed transvestism a utilitarian and patriotic purpose, d'Eon hoped to offer the government the necessary rationale for publicly rehabilitating him as a woman. His fabricated story, no more unusual than the truth, would have reinforced his image as a heroine, a modern Joan of Arc, as Beaumarchais and many other contemporaries tended to view him already.

D'Eon's efforts were only partially successful. Vergennes indicated to Beaumarchais that while the government was willing to recognize d'Eon as a woman, there could be no specific public declaration. As Vergennes put it, "the revelation of his sex can no longer be permitted; it would be ridiculous for both [the Versailles and Westminster] courts."[20] On the issue of money, Vergennes was in a mood to compromise. While the gov-ernment was willing to continue d'Eon's 12,000-livre pension, it would not create an independent annuity. Similarly, while it was willing to pay off some of d'Eon's debts, the total would be considerably less than d'Eon hoped.

One month later, in July 1775, Beaumarchais returned to Versailles to reach a preliminary agreement with Vergennes and the King. Despite the ups and downs of the negotiations, d'Eon was confident that his twelve-year exile was very close to a definitive resolution, and that shortly, possi-bly within a matter of months, he would be living in France as a woman. Now he began preparing for his return.

The Letter to Poissonier

ONE OF THE MOST INTRIGUING aspects of this story concerns those people who had seen d'Eon naked, and therefore knew he was male. First among them were, of course, his surviving family members, his mother and sister, who obviously were aware of his sex. Their collaboration with their loved one's deception can be interpreted as a form of family loyalty. But what of d'Eon's friends? Throughout his life as a woman, rumors abounded about boyhood friends in Tonnerre who claimed he was really a man, after all. But no one seemed to pay much attention to these provincial voices. Apparently, as long as no one with any status in Paris had any knowledge of d'Eon's male anatomy he was safe.[1]

There was, however, at least one prominent Parisian who did have direct knowledge of d'Eon's anatomy: Pierre-Isaac Poissonier (1720–1798), one of Louis XV's personal doctors. During the 1750s, Louis XV sent Poissonier to the Empress Elizabeth as a kind of gift to help with her medical problems. For a few years Poissonier stayed in Russia, where he and d'Eon became close friends. On at least one occasion, d'Eon himself required the services of Poissonier, who gave him a comprehensive physical examination. Later, Poissonier returned to France, where during the 1770s he was still an influential figure at Versailles. He and d'Eon had continued to maintain their friendship. In 1773, for example, Poissonier made a short visit to d'Eon in London.[2]

On 15 July 1775, d'Eon wrote Poissonier an opaque, indirect, but nonetheless extraordinary letter. It is a clear picture of d'Eon's mood on the eve of his venture into womanhood. Here he can be seen in a much more candid mood than in his letters to Broglie or Beaumarchais. He was writing to a genuine friend in intimacy.[3]

M. de Beaumarchais, . . . who is leaving for Paris this morning, is informed by our kind Foreign Minister, your compatriot [Vergennes], about the true standing of my physical and political existence in order for me to be paid a part of what the Court owes me, and for my return to France, which I myself desire as soon as I am able to do it safely. As for honor, thank God it is not in any man's power to take that away from me.

I believe it my duty, even through M. de Beaumarchais, to inform you that with respect to me, he was as smart as you and your friend P***, and this by an absolute necessity, or a power of Versailles greater than mine. You know with what unselfishness I myself have acted during this affair, as in all others, in order to acquit myself of my promise before you and to testify before you that I will always be as attached to your interests as you have been touched by my [page torn] . . .

When you see our worthy Minister, our President Jeannin, tell him that I told you how much my heart is moved by everything he has done and wants to do for me. Alas, if his foreign finances were as great as the virtues of his heart or of his mind, he would have soon put me in a position to pay off my creditors in England and I could fly off to join him. I am persuaded that he sees clearly, and with all the force of my innocence, that it was only power I lacked in order to triumph over the major forces that attacked me; that the weaker I found myself, the more I defended myself; it being in my Burgundian nature or in my head of a "Dragoon" to protect myself in war and in peace until death. When one attacks me unjustly, or my weakness, I can only heed the courage that God granted me. I am a ram that Guerchy has made enraged in wanting to hurl him into the river of oblivion.

I beg you to have confidence in M. de Beaumarchais, whose mind, talents, and integrity are well known to you, as much as in my old friend, the virtuous Drouet, who is at the waters of D'lombières with his wife.

Tenderly embrace Mme Poissonier for me; you will no doubt allow me to do it myself when I return, without much concern for the consequences or what people will say. If it results in a second son for you, I will leave him the pension that Louis XV designated for me, and that Louis XVI has preserved for me in his justice.

If one day you destine your son for politics, allow your enlightenment, your experience, and my example to trace the path for him that is the most safe to walk with the high and mighty in such a way that he will not fall into the abyss of their intrigues and their factions.

I feel all the feelings and gratefulness and affection that I have pledged to you for life; your devoted servant . . .

P.S. My health is better and worse, depending on the barometric climate of England and the political climate of Versailles.

The events in America are going still worse for the English; with a bit more of a courageous effort the Americans will be free and will be an independent power. I am in too much of a hurry to tell you about what's going on there, since you know more about it than I.

This letter is perhaps most noteworthy for what it ignores. Nowhere does d'Eon assert that he will return to France as a woman. The only reference to d'Eon's womanhood occurs in the opaque comment in the first paragraph regarding his "physical and political existence." By relating these two aspects of life, d'Eon seems to be telling his old friend that his alienation from manhood was brought about by an alienation from political life. Near the end of the letter, d'Eon hopes that Poissonier will use d'Eon's sad life as an example if his son should ever want to go into politics, again reinforcing the letter's central theme that d'Eon's impending transformation is the best means for his escape from a political cul-de-sac.

D'Eon never pretends that he thinks he is a woman; nor does he expect Poissonier to believe it either. The joke about impregnating Mme Poissonnier serves to assure Poissonier that d'Eon is quite aware of his own biological potential. D'Eon seems to be obliquely reminding his friend that he is leaving manhood not for sexual reasons, but for political ones. D'Eon believed the only way he could avoid a "fall into the abyss of [politicians'] intrigues and their factions" was by living his life as a woman. Indirectly, all d'Eon asks of Poissonier is that he go along with d'Eon's scheme, something the old doctor apparently did.

The Transaction

T HE CONVERSATIONS BETWEEN Beaumarchais and Vergennes went smoothly enough that in August 1775, Louis XVI approved the following plan for resolving d'Eon's situation: First, d'Eon was to surrender all of his secret correspondence and diplomatic papers to Beaumarchais; second, d'Eon was to maintain a strict silence regarding the Comte de Guerchy and members of his family; and third, d'Eon was to return to France as soon as possible. In return, the King agreed to some of d'Eon's demands: First, he agreed to transform d'Eon's pension into a life annuity that would yield 12,000 livres a year; second, the King agreed to pay many, but not all, of the debts that d'Eon could verify with appropriate documentation; third, the King promised that d'Eon could return to France in complete safety, with the King's full protection; finally, and perhaps most important, contrary to what Vergennes had written only a few weeks before, the King was now willing to publicly recognize d'Eon's status as a woman, as long as d'Eon in turn promised to dress in women's clothes immediately after returning to France. But the King refused to acknowledge any diplomatic services that d'Eon may have performed in women's clothes for his grandfather, Louis XV.[1]

A few weeks later Beaumarchais was back in London presenting this plan to d'Eon. D'Eon realized that the negotiations had gone as far as they could, and over some relaxed dinners at John Wilkes's house he decided to accept the government's offer.[2]

On 4 November 1775, d'Eon gave Beaumarchais the iron safe full of secret documents, and the two men signed a contract establishing d'Eon's new status in specific terms. Known as the "Transaction," this statement in which the King and Foreign Minister defined d'Eon's status was considered by him to be the most important document of his life.[3]

The Transaction began by designating d'Eon a woman: "Demoiselle Charles-Geneviève-Louise-Auguste-André-Thimothée d'Eon, mature maiden [*fille majeure*], known until today under the name of the Chevalier d'Eon." Article IV concerned d'Eon's gender status:

"I [Beaumarchais] demand, in His Majesty's name, that the disguise which has until today hidden the person of a maiden [*fille*] under the appearance of the Chevalier d'Eon be entirely abandoned. And without wishing to blame Charles-Geneviève-Louise-Auguste-André-Thimothée d'Eon de Beaumont for the disguise of his condition and sex, of which his parents alone are guilty, and even rendering justice to the modest, wise, and sincere, though vigorous and manly, manner in which she has always conducted herself in her adopted garb, I require absolutely that the uncertainty about her sex, which until today has been an inexhaustible subject of indecent bets and salacious jokes which might be renewed, especially in France, and which her proud nature would not tolerate and which would lead to new quarrels that might perhaps only serve as a pretext for renewing old ones, I repeat, in the name of the King, that I absolutely demand that the ghost of the Chevalier d'Eon vanish entirely and that a public and unequivocal declaration be made of the true sex of Charles-Geneviève-Louise-Auguste-André-Thimothée d'Eon de Beaumont before her arrival in France and her resumption of her women's clothes settles the public's ideas once and for all on the matter."

As one might expect of d'Eon, he signed the Transaction only with certain qualifications and amendments. He agreed to all of the King's requirements, but he remonstrated that "it would have been much more agreeable to me had he deigned to employ me once again in his army or in his diplomatic service." Ideally, d'Eon would have liked to have been recognized by the King as a female military officer and diplomat, rehabilitated to the status of a Plenipotentiary Minister.

Likewise, while d'Eon regretfully submitted to wearing women's clothes, he gave himself an escape clause: "I submit to declaring my sex publicly, to leaving my condition beyond any equivocation and to reassume and wear till death women's clothes, unless, in consideration of my being so long accustomed to wearing my military uniform, and only after long suffering, His Majesty consents to let me reassume masculine ones, should I find it impossible to bear the discomfort of the others."

D'Eon agreed to avoid slandering the memory of Guerchy, and to hand over the crucial memorandum of 3 June 1763. He promised that he would try entering a convent upon his return to France. But he also asked whether he might not be allowed to continue to wear the Cross of Saint-Louis, "whatever dress I adopt," since it was given to him not because he was thought to be a man, but because of the risks "I acquired at the peril of my life in the battles and sieges in which I participated." Finally, d'Eon raised one more important matter: If he returned to France dressed as a woman, he would have to discard his male clothes and at great expense purchase an entirely new female wardrobe. He asked that such an expense be borne by the King.

Beaumarchais responded to these requests in the Transaction's final section. Noting that only the King had the authority to approve d'Eon's request to continue to wear the Cross of Saint-Louis, Beaumarchais nonetheless contributed his personal view, which he promised to convey to the King:

"Considering that the Cross of Saint-Louis has always been regarded uniquely as a reward for bravery on the battlefield, and that several officers, after being decorated with it, have retired from the army and adopted a civil profession, and have continued to wear it as proof of having courageously done their duty in a more dangerous situation than with their civilian dress, I do not believe there could be any objection to allowing the same liberty to a heroic maiden, who, having been brought up by her parents as a man, has bravely fulfilled all the dangerous duties involved in the profession of a soldier. If she did not realize the false attire and status under which she had been forced to live until it was too late to change it, she is not to be blamed for not having done so until now.

"Further considering that the rare example of this extraordinary maiden is unlikely to be imitated by persons of her sex and can lead to no consequences, and that had Joan of Arc, who saved the throne of Charles VII by fighting in man's garb, been awarded some military decoration such as the Cross of Saint-Louis, there is no reason to suppose that when her task was done and the King asked her to resume her feminine dress, he would have deprived her of the honorable reward of her courage. Nor would any gallant French knight have thought that ornament profaned because it adorned the bosom of a woman who, on the field of honor, had shown herself worthy to be a man."

Beaumarchais also agreed with d'Eon's request for funds toward the purchase of a female wardrobe, "on the condition that she shall not bring back from London any of her weapons or male garments, because her desire to assume them again might be constantly tested by their presence." Beaumarchais would only approve "her keeping one complete uniform of the regiment in which she served, together with the helmet, sabre, pistol,

These twin French portraits, each displaying the Cross of Saint-Louis, juxtapose the ambiguity of d'Eon's gender identity. The public, it would seem, endorsed both: "Dedicated to the French Dragoons," reads one, while the other is dedicated "to the memory of French heroines." *(Courtesy of the Bibliothèque Nationale, Paris)*

A French portrait of how d'Eon probably looked in 1777, though it is doubtful that he wore dresses cut so low. *(Courtesy of the Bibliothèque Nationale, Paris)*

George Grenville was England's Prime Minister when d'Eon was France's Plenipotentiary Minister. *(Courtesy of the Brotherton Collection, University of Leeds Library)*

Louis XVI.
le dernier Roi de France
naquit le 23 Août 1754
monta sur le trône le 10 Mai 1774 et sur l'échafaud le 21 Juin 1793
O mon Roi! l'univers t'abandonna!

King Louis XVI put a stop to the Secret du Roi, legitimized d'Eon's status as a woman, and forced him to dress as one. *(Courtesy of the Brotherton Collection, University of Leeds Library)*

"The Trial of d'Eon by Women." This London print, published during the early 1770s, satirizes the controversy over d'Eon's sex by invoking a special trial in which d'Eon would be tried by his peers. *(Courtesy of the Brotherton Collection, University of Leeds Library)*

P. A. CARON DE BEAUMARCHAIS

The famous playwright Beaumarchais was sent by Louis XVI to negotiate with d'Eon over the latter's political rehabilitation. D'Eon grew to despise Beaumarchais's attitude toward women. *(Courtesy of the Brotherton Collection, University of Leeds Library)*

John Wilkes, Member of Parliament from Westminster (London), championed the cause of making British politics more democratic. His colleagues in the House of Commons tried to expel him and forced him into exile in France. His situation was often compared to that of d'Eon, with whom he was a close friend. *(Courtesy of the Brotherton Collection, University of Leeds Library)*

Mlle Bertin.

Rose Bertin was Queen Marie-Antoinette's dressmaker and Europe's most influential fashion designer. She created d'Eon's new couture. *(Courtesy of the Brotherton Collection, University of Leeds Library)*

D'Eon fences in a 1787 exhibition before the Prince of Wales. *(Courtesy of the Brotherton Collection, University of Leeds Library)*

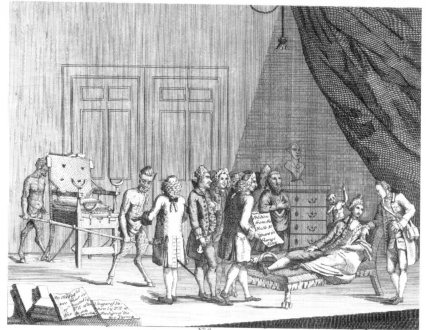

A Deputation from Jonathan's and the Free-Masons

Miss Epicene D'Eon is discours'd in close consultation with its Wine Merchant & Privy Counsellor. The Free Masons beg the Secret of its Sex may be kept inviolable; the Committee of Underwriters on the other hand Petition for the Discovery; & propose that Mons. A shall explore the sex Signature manually after the manner used in the election of a new Pope, for which purpose the Doctor is seen introducing his new invented Night-Chair. Pub'd as the Act directs July 17 1771.

"A Deputation from Jonathan's and the Free Masons," July 1771, sent to determine d'Eon's sex. *(Courtesy of the Brotherton Collection, University of Leeds Library)*

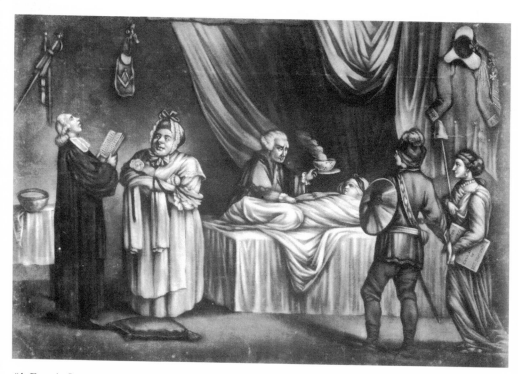

"A French Captain of Dragoons Brought to a Bed of Twins." This 1771 cartoon plays on the odd rumor that d'Eon gave birth to twins. *(Courtesy of the Huntington Library, San Marino, California)*

The Duc de Nivernais had been a military officer and ambassador to Rome and Berlin before Louis XV put him in charge of the team negotiating the end of the Seven Years' War with England. D'Eon became his most valuable assistant in that effort. *(Courtesy of the Brotherton Collection, University of Leeds Library)*

The Duc de Praslin, Foreign Minister from 1763 to 1771, despised d'Eon and ordered him recalled from England. *(Courtesy of the Brotherton Collection, University of Leeds Library)*

Los Angeles mail advertisement from the 1950s. *(From the collection of the author)*

The Comte de Guerchy, French Ambassador to England between 1763 and 1767, feuded with d'Eon and apparently plotted to have him assassinated. *(Courtesy of the Brotherton Collection, University of Leeds Library)*

Charles Théveneau de Morande was among France's most successful authors of scandalous works. King Louis XV used d'Eon to negotiate with him over the suppression of one such manuscript. *(Courtesy of the Brotherton Collection, University of Leeds Library)*

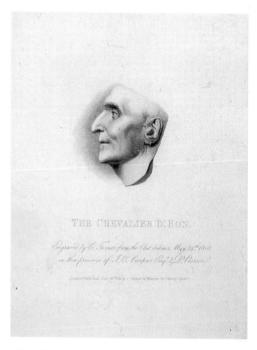

This death mask was made shortly after d'Eon's death in 1810. *(Courtesy of the Brotherton Collection, University of Leeds Library)*

rifle and bayonet, as a souvenir of her past life or as one keeps the cherished relics of a loved object that no longer exists."

Although Beaumarchais and d'Eon signed the Transaction on 4 November 1775, they agreed to backdate the contract one month, to 5 October 1775, d'Eon's forty-seventh birthday—making the Transaction function as a kind of birth certificate. Among the first to congratulate d'Eon was his secretary, Jean-Joseph de Vignoles, who knew how much this day meant to him. "What has happened to us," he wrote d'Eon that day, "is something so extraordinary that I can't explain it." D'Eon was now reborn as a woman, and would live as one for the next thirty-five years.[4]

A few weeks later d'Eon finally made his confession to his old patron, the Comte de Broglie. "It is time to disillusion you. You have had for a Captain of Dragoons and aide-de-camp in war and politics only the appearance of a man. I am only a maiden, and would have sustained my role perfectly until death if politics and your enemies had not made me the most unfortunate of maidens." If his confession regarding his sex was a lie, the way that d'Eon related his gender transformation to his political alienation was from his heart: "You will understand by the ease with which I am able to detach myself from the world that I remained in only for you; and since I may no longer work nor fight under your orders or those of your brother, M. the Maréchal, I would renounce without regret this deceitful world, which in any case never seduced me except in my sadly misspent youth."[5]

Beaumarchais Bets

S HORTLY AFTER SIGNING the Transaction, Beaumarchais trans-
ported d'Eon's secret papers back to Paris. The order of 3 June
1763, which had instructed d'Eon to prepare for an invasion of
England, was treated with particular care. Years earlier, while in Russia,
d'Eon had used a copy of Montesquieu's *Spirit of the Laws* to carry the
correspondence of Louis XV and the Empress Elizabeth, creating a secret
compartment in the inside front cover with special glue. Now, twenty
years later, he used the technique again in the same book to return the
dead king's special order.[1]

Back at Versailles, Beaumarchais presented the Transaction to Vergennes. The Foreign Minister had little problem with the financial
arrangements, but had strong objections to the issues surrounding the
clothes d'Eon would wear. As long as France was prepared to recognize
d'Eon as a woman and guarantee her safety, Vergennes believed that
d'Eon should give up all his male clothes, and everything associated with
them, including his military swords and medals. In this negotiation,
Beaumarchais became d'Eon's advocate, vociferously arguing that while
d'Eon should not be permitted to dress as a man, he ought to be allowed
to wear his military medals, especially the Cross of Saint-Louis, since it
was given to him not because of his sex, but because of his great achievements in the Dragoons. Vergennes remained adamant, and for a few days
the negotiations were deadlocked over this and other minor points.
Finally, Vergennes and Beaumarchais agreed to bring the matter before
the King in a written memorandum, and allow Louis to decide. Beaumarchais's memo went as follows:

Essential points, which I beg M. the Comte de Vergennes to present for the King's decision, before my departure for London, this 13 Dec. 1775; to be replied to in the margin:

Does the King grant to Mademoiselle d'Eon permission to wear the Cross of Saint-Louis on her woman's clothes?

In the provinces only, replied the King.

Does His Majesty approve of the gratuity of 2,000 crowns which I have given to this young lady on her assuming woman's clothes?

Yes.

Does His Majesty in this case leave her man's clothes at her entire disposition?

She must sell them.

As these favors are to be dependent upon a certain frame of mind, into which I wish to bring Mademoiselle d'Eon forever, will His Majesty leave me the power of granting or refusing, according as I may think useful for the good of his service?

Yes.[2]

With the Transaction completed, all parties expected to see d'Eon in France as soon as he could wrap up his affairs in England. Newspapers immediately began to report that an agreement had been worked out with the French government, and that d'Eon would soon be leaving London.[3] That is not at all what happened, however. Within a matter of days, d'Eon felt so betrayed by Beaumarchais that he threatened to cancel the Transaction.

The initial cause of d'Eon's concern was a very brief announcement carried in the London morning papers a week after the signing of the Transaction: "A new policy is preparing in the city on the sex of the Chevalier d'Eon; bets now run 7 to 4 a woman against a man; and a nobleman well known on the turf, has pledged himself to bring the matter to a clear decision before the expiration of fourteen days."[4]

D'Eon smelled a rat: Suddenly he realized that he had been made a patsy by Morande and Beaumarchais. With their knowledge that the French government was about to declare d'Eon a woman, Morande and Beaumarchais, sensing an opportunity to make a sweet fortune, had wagered a great deal of money on d'Eon's sex. Indeed, the two had bet thousands of British pounds, some of it probably on behalf of Paris financiers, the total approaching perhaps £100,000.[5]

D'Eon was outraged that these two men whom he had come to know so well these past months would dishonor him in this humiliating way.

After the suffering he had endured in 1771 and 1772, d'Eon had managed to dampen speculation about his sex only by spending months outside of London, at the estate of Lord Ferrers. Now these two scoundrels were about to stir up the pot again, just when it seemed like d'Eon's situation had been fully resolved. If huge sums were wagered about d'Eon, English investors might not permit him to leave England without some conclusive demonstration of his sex; worse, they might try to kidnap him, or even have him killed. From d'Eon's viewpoint, Morande and Beaumarchais had gone beyond dishonoring him: they had put his life in danger.

D'Eon quickly published a letter in the London papers that tried to quash speculation regarding his gender without declaring anything specific about it. He asked the English to stop wagering any money over it at once, and then informed readers "that there are among the high and mighty in France some that abuse the perfect knowledge they have of his sex, so as to engage certain bankers in London." In other words, d'Eon warned Londoners who insisted on placing bets that they would be swindled. He also informed readers that he would "never manifest his sex, till such time as all policies shall be at an end."[6] Meanwhile, the resumption of gambling over his gender so distressed him that he was overcome by illness—or pretended to be—and he remained in his bed for the next two months, venturing outside on only one or two occasions.[7]

After Beaumarchais returned to London at the end of December 1775, d'Eon was confronted with even worse news, conveyed to him at a dinner party at Morande's. Apparently, when Beaumarchais had visited Paris to gain approval for the Transaction, and perhaps capital for his bets, he had spread the fiction that he and the Chevalière had fallen in love and were seriously considering marriage. The musically talented Beaumarchais composed love ballads about the affair, and even had the gall to sing d'Eon his favorite one after dinner. D'Eon began receiving mail from French friends asking whether the rumors were true. He took great offense at the joke—he did not want to return to a Paris that was laughing at him, but craved above all else the honor and respect due an aristocratic Amazon. D'Eon was so upset by this news that he packed his bags and headed straight for Ferrers's country estate.[8]

D'Eon did not inform Beaumarchais that he was leaving, and the latter became angry when d'Eon was nowhere to be found. After all, they still had delicate business to conduct: It seemed that d'Eon had, in fact, not yielded all his secret documents, and the King wanted the affair wrapped up as quickly as possible. In a letter condescending in its tone (Beaumarchais referred to d'Eon as "my child") and unique in its address (it was the first in which Beaumarchais addressed d'Eon as "Mademoiselle" instead of "Monsieur"), Beaumarchais demanded d'Eon's cooperation.[9]

D'Eon shot back a blistering letter from Lord Ferrers's estate, calling Beaumarchais's behavior nothing short of "revolting" and "despotic," comparing it to the outrageous actions of William Pitt near the conclusion of the Seven Years' War. At stake was "a veritable principle of honor," something an upstart bourgeois like Beaumarchais apparently could not understand about the noble d'Eon. He refused, he told the playwright, to become "the dupe of gamblers, who regard my sex as the means of fortune, like some gold mine in Peru." Besides, when Beaumarchais insulted d'Eon, he was also insulting Louis XV, for whatever d'Eon had achieved in this life—"girl, man, woman, soldier, politician, secretary, minister, author"—he had accomplished in the service of the late king. That Beaumarchais could make light of such service, while himself serving a king, was itself an obscenity.[10]

Beaumarchais's behavior led d'Eon to reconsider certain aspects of the Transaction. He had little problem with its financial and political terms. But now he was less willing to consider his rehabilitation necessarily a retirement from public life, and regretted that Vergennes and the King evidently viewed the recognition of his female gender as itself constituting such a retirement. D'Eon wanted everyone to think of him as a woman, but he did not want to be forced to wear women's clothes, nor did he want to abandon diplomatic work or retire from the Dragoons. He told Beaumarchais that what he really desired was to be reinstated as a Plenipotentiary Minister and Dragoon captain, with the privileges normally accorded to both. He also explained that it would not be safe for him to travel in France in female clothes—he would have no way to defend himself against insults and jokes. Under no circumstances, he informed Beaumarchais, would "I give up my [Dragoon] uniform."[11]

D'Eon argued that getting rid of his uniform would be like admitting he had done something wrong. Just as the Transaction placed no blame on d'Eon, it should not result in punitive actions toward him. Indeed, he explained to Beaumarchais, for "a maiden" such as d'Eon to participate with honor in military and in political life, she must have unusual degrees of "virtue" and "chastity." Allowing d'Eon to keep the uniform would be an acknowledgment of his "extraordinary" character; forcing him to give it up would malign that character.

Beaumarchais's impetuous behavior had propelled d'Eon to articulate a more radical vision of his future, in which he would continue his political and military career as a woman. While Querelle des Femmes authors may have dreamed of such heroic Amazons, a female Dragoon officer would certainly have been something unique in eighteenth-century France. If d'Eon sometimes saw becoming a woman as an escape from political life, now he seemed to view his gender transformation as the means that would provide him with the necessary moral regeneration to fully renew his career.

Whatever his motivation, d'Eon's negotiation with Beaumarchais had escalated from the question of which sex d'Eon would assume to what kind of woman d'Eon would become. Vergennes, Beaumarchais, and Louis XVI expected d'Eon to retire passively, preferably to a convent, where he could learn the qualities of "modesty, virtue, and chastity." D'Eon, however, now hoped that his life as a woman would be as active as the one he had led as a man. As if to acknowledge this change from the beginning of 1776, Vergennes, Beaumarchais, and others began to refer to d'Eon simply as "the Amazon" in their correspondence with one another.[12]

Beaumarchais "To Mlle Genev. L. Deon de Beaumont"

LONDON, 18 JANUARY 1776[1]

You have seen me, Mademoiselle, moved by your misfortune in England, listen sensitively to your secrets and your tears, promise you my feeble intervention on your behalf in France, and keep my word to you in all sincerity before ever knowing that I would have a mission from the King that had anything to do with you. The efficacy of my services and my generosity have shown you, since that time, that you did not place your trust in me in vain. . . .

I give you a week to calm down . . . and repent of your error; but once that time has elapsed, I say this with pain, I will be compelled to leave and break off all relations with you. My only sorrow will be to go back to France carrying the cruel conviction that your enemies knew you better than your friends. Alas! What sadness for me if I cannot achieve any other success for myself than to have unmasked an extravagant maiden in the disguise of a man of bad faith, just as your enemies have always claimed to see in you. . . .

You now pretend to believe that the criticism concerned the revelation of your sex! Would I have repeated to you (using the terms of your letter) that you had been unfaithful to your word of honor in the Transaction, *if it had been a question of your sex,* when one of the articles of the Transaction is precisely to terminate a cross-dressing that has become so scandalous because of the publicity it has received, and all the foolishness that has been written about it and what it has done to others and perhaps to you yourself?

I noted that your announcement in the newspapers, whose goal, according to you, was to discourage bets on your sex, was so strangely worded as to seem written solely to stimulate such speculation and thus so contrary to the ostentatious disinterestedness that you affect. . . .

If I sent this miserable letter to France, it would only upset your friends; all your adversaries would be justly vindicated. That's her, they would say, just as we have always maintained; it is no longer against her so-called enemies that she now carries out her crazy and detestable ruses, it is against her only friend, he whom she has called her support, her liberator, and her father; that's her.

Forced myself to accuse you along with them, who would dare pity you and excuse you? You would forever lose your honor and be covered with shame, and it would be all over for you.

Repent, I beg you, repent. If you ignore this salutary and final advice, I regret to say this to you, I will . . . acknowledge, however awkwardly, at the feet of His Majesty that I was terribly blind, when I guaranteed the good sense, honor, and loyalty of the Demoiselle d'Eon. . . .

This is what will be the course that you have forced me to follow against you, if you don't promptly redeem yourself. And as to your person, may the scorn, the tacit proscription, and France's short memory concerning you be your only punishment; and above all may your honest and unfortunate family not suffer for your personal wrongs! This is the most ardent wish in my heart.

I implore you, Mademoiselle, reflect most seriously on all of this, and be well persuaded that it is with the most painful sorrow that I would force myself to change titles from your defender to your most implacable prosecutor. . . .

D'Eon to Beaumarchais

STAUNTON-HERALD, 30 JANUARY 1776[1]

I will not respond, neither to the reproaches nor to the uncalled-for abuse that you heap upon me in your lively and masculine anger. I regard all that as the first consequence of the deranged mood of the cleverest and most agreeable monkey that I have ever encountered in my life, who is forever and ever the same,[2] *and who loses his temper only when he must stop short and admit his defeat....*

I grant you permission to do as you threaten; to go throw yourself at the feet of all the kings and ministers on earth, in order to depict me, following your words, as an "extravagant maiden," and at the same time the shrewdest maiden in Europe. You can therefore tell them, with all the eloquence, dynamism, and apish antics of which you are capable, everything bad about me that you wish. Say white, say black, I am and will be, *as the refrain of your favorite song goes, forever and ever the same; and though I would be fine to be one up on* all the barbers of Seville, *I will only respond with the simplicity and truthfulness that is appropriate for a well-born maiden....*

Your reproach concerning the incomplete transmission of the papers is unfounded, Monsieur, first, because neither you, nor any of the past, present, and future ministers, nor My Lord the Prince de Conti, nor even M. the Comte de Broglie, can know everything that passed in secret in 1755 and 1756 between the deceased King, the Empress Elizabeth, and the Chancellor of Russia, Count Woronzow. M. Tercier, the Chevalier Douglas, and I were the only ones who participated in this important secret negotiation, of which even M. Rouillé, Foreign Minister, knew nothing. It was only in 1757 that the Comte de Broglie was let in on part of this secret, and that he, by order of the King, brought me in on and made me aware of his other secret correspondence.

Eventually, when all the ministers and functionaries in Versailles were against me, how could they guess whether I had given over all or part of the papers of my secret correspondence in Russia, Germany, France, and England? How could they guess what they were totally unaware of, if I chose not to tell them or give it to them?

It is an act that depends totally upon my good will and my free will. I will make up my mind depending on whether they execute the articles of the Transaction, and depending on the good or bad that is done to me, according to the degree of justice that is given me. Is there a single power on this earth that can break into my fortified camp on my island, which belongs to me as it does to any Englishman? Since I pay taxes and obey the laws of this land, and do not violate any, I should therefore enjoy the rights of a free citizen in England. . . .

Since I saw those whom I believed to be my most faithful patrons dupe me; since I saw the most honest of my protectors, Louis XV, he who sent me on a mission to England, speak well of me in public only to support me feebly in private; since I saw this august protector tremble at the first sign of the storm, leaving me alone to bear the full brunt of the furor; since I saw him obsessed by the double-dealing trickery and lies of his courtiers; since I saw unavoidable death bury him in this pitiful state and leave me to the vagaries of my sad destiny; I said to myself: Poor d'Eon, don't despair. Henceforth you will find your salvation only in the force of your courage, of justice, and of your innocence. I thus thought that the bravest of my emissaries would be myself, that my best friend was my money, and my most faithful protector my own prudence while awaiting the day when I might expose to the justice of the young King my innocence and the double-dealing of my former prosecutors. . . .

Why, during your last trip to London, did you contract a venereal disease, which was probably given to everyone in Paris; while, in order to amuse yourself certainly at my expense, or to make me look ridiculous, you let it be known in circles of your elegant women that you were supposed to marry me after I spent several months in the Abbaye des Dames de Sainte-Antoine?

I admit, Monsieur, that a woman sometimes finds herself in awkward situations in which necessity forces her . . . but she accepts it because she understands the fundamental purpose. The more adept and sensitive is the man who wants to do her a favor, the greater the danger is for her. But these reflections remind me of considerable torment! This only tells me that, through a blind trust in you and in your promises, I have found in you the master of my sex; that through gratitude, I gave you my portrait; and that through esteem you promised me yours. There were never any other commitments between us. Everything that you have promoted beyond that, according to what has been sent to me from Paris, can only be understood by me to be some sort of mockery on your part. If you have taken more seriously this token of remembrance and gratitude, your conduct is as pitiful as is your disease. *This is truly scornful and an infidelity that a woman of Paris, as tamed as she seems to be, in accordance with the current mores of married men, could not forgive, even more so a maiden whose virtue is as stringent as is mine, and whose spirit is so high-minded when her good faith and sensitivity are wounded.*

Why did I not remember at that moment that men are only good in this life to deceive girls and women? Alas, there are injustices that are so wounding and outrageous when they come to us from those to whom we are the most sincerely attached that it forces even the most prudent person to lose control. Do we need experience to recognize the control that the mere appearances of virtue necessarily have over the heart? I thought only of acknowledging your merit and of admiring your talents and your generosity. There's no doubt that I loved you! But I was so naive about this situation. I was very far from believing that love could be born in the midst of trouble and heartache. Never could a virtuous soul become open to love if love did not employ virtue even if only in order to touch it.

Monsieur, you must stop taking advantage of my condition and wanting to profit from my misfortune to make me look as ridiculous as you: you, whom I had so esteemed, whom I regarded as the most virtuous of men; you, who had persuaded me that you had some respect for my extraordinary position. It's you who covers me with shame and who is digging an abyss beneath my footsteps all the more dangerous for me in that you hide its depths from my eyes. How did you choose me as the unfortunate victim of the delirium of your mind and your mores? Oh, I doubtlessly more than deserved the scorn you have for me since I allowed you to know the weakness of my condition, which I should have kept hidden even from myself. And I am well punished for it! But was it your responsibility to punish me? Although it may not be according to your opinion nor mine that the public judges us, if you had wanted to preserve my reputation, you would have been more careful of this public, which cannot know by itself what the truth is and which can only judge according to appearances. Already they suspect my virtue because I am a maiden and a Dragoon captain. But what is the profession practiced by women which is not exposed to the public's malice?

The travesty behind which I have lived for more than forty-five years, without my having it made known to men, is the most definite proof of my circumspection. . . .

How can I, dressed as a maiden, serve the King? Dressed as a man, by contrast, I can serve him in war and in peace, as I have always had the courage and the good fortune to do for twenty-two years. If, however, the King and his ministers still insist upon the execution of our agreement, I will fulfill it in obedience; but I hold you on your side to execute the fourth article and to ensure that I receive the just demands contained in my last letter dated on the 7th. Then I will faithfully return the papers. Give me my trousseau, pay my dowry and the expenses of the loan, and then harmony will be restored between us. Then, no matter how ill I may be, I will return to London to embrace you. . . .

D'Eon Sues Morande

THESE LETTERS ONLY RAISED the level of acrimony between Beaumarchais and d'Eon until finally Beaumarchais became so frustrated with his adversary that he delegated responsibility for the negotiations to his assistant, Charles Morande. Meanwhile, Beaumarchais spent most of his time in London facilitating secret French support for the American Revolution.[1]

On 11 April 1776, Morande dined at d'Eon's London apartment along with three of d'Eon's friends. Morande admitted that the previous November he and Beaumarchais had indeed exploited their knowledge of the secret Transaction by placing huge bets on d'Eon's sex, but neither he nor Beaumarchais could understand why this upset d'Eon. To the contrary, they hoped he would reconsider his position on the matter, as such enormous sums were about to be made that there was money enough for everyone. Then Morande offered to give d'Eon thousands of British pounds in cash from the bets if he would drop his opposition.[2]

Angered by this latest insult to his character, but armed with political ammunition, d'Eon cut off all negotiations with Morande and Beaumarchais, and wrote directly to Vergennes. He meticulously recounted Beaumarchais's sordid activities in London, highlighting his relationship with Morande. After all, how could Vergennes expect d'Eon to negotiate in good faith with rogues who were placing bets on his sex behind his back? D'Eon also complained about the disrespectful way Beaumarchais behaved toward women. Insulting d'Eon by treating him like a child was no aberration—d'Eon saw it as part of a pattern. The only women Beaumarchais seemed to get along with, so d'Eon informed Vergennes, were the "many groups of girls on the streets," who danced for him in the nude "during their filthy and exotic orgies." Vergennes should never have allowed someone like Beaumarchais, with his dim view of women, to negotiate with a "virtuous maiden" like d'Eon.[3]

Vergennes defended Beaumarchais and counseled d'Eon not to worry: as long as d'Eon continued to cooperate with Beaumarchais, everything would soon be resolved.[4] But by this time d'Eon despised Beaumarchais, and couldn't bring himself to talk with Morande. The situation reached a boiling point in early August when Morande threatened to publish a long article about the d'Eon affair.[5] D'Eon was so upset by the piece that he immediately stormed over to Morande's home and challenged him to a duel. Morande refused on the pretext that he could not possibly fight with a woman. "Mr. de Morande," reported one newspaper, "very politely replied, that it was impossible for him to meet d'Eon anywhere but in a bed."[6] A few days later d'Eon's brother-in-law, Thomas O'Gorman, challenged Morande on behalf of d'Eon. Since I am a man, O'Gorman told Morande, "I hope that you will make no objection to my sex and will not allege that I am neither husband nor father, since it is as husband and father that I wish to avenge the honor of my family." But Morande refused anyway, and sought refuge in the courts. Since dueling was technically illegal, he secured an injunction from the King's Bench, presided over by Chief Justice Lord Mansfield, that forbade anyone to duel with d'Eon.[7]

D'Eon now fought fire with fire. If Morande was going to use the English courts to defend himself, so would he. Immediately d'Eon launched a suit with Lord Mansfield against Morande for libel. Considering Morande's reputation as a professional libeler, the suit seemed promising. But the trial did not go well for d'Eon. When evidence was produced that d'Eon had made disparaging remarks in public about Morande, Mansfield dismissed the suit on the grounds that at the very least, both parties had libeled each another.[8]

How much money Morande and Beaumarchais made wagering over d'Eon is not clear—it is not even known whether they ever collected on their own bets. Their venture into the gambling market, however, does seem to have reversed public opinion regarding d'Eon's gender. As word of the November 1775 Transaction spread beyond London, most people concluded that d'Eon was indeed a woman. For instance, around February 1776, Louis XVI's declaration that d'Eon was permitted a safe return to France was published in London and Paris. Not everyone was yet convinced that d'Eon was a woman, but skeptics now seemed to be in a minority. The question Londoners asked was not whether d'Eon was a woman, but when he would finally admit it and return to France.

Of course, crucial to molding public opinion was the treatment of the story in the press. The *Morning Post* reported that "Monsieur d'Eon de Beaumont, of whom there has been so much talk, and who is at present the subject of universal conversation, has actually received the King's grace, with a pension of 12,000 livres, and a perpetual assurance of safety in his return to France. The doubts with regard to the sex of Mons. d'Eon, which have prevailed these some years past, appear to be destroyed, as it is absolutely decided that she is a woman, and intends very soon to take the habit of her gender."[9]

In February 1776, the *Public Ledger* ran a story titled "The Discovery of Sex," in which the editors self-consciously proclaimed the veracity of the article: "Notwithstanding the preceding article appears in a newspaper, the public may rest assured of the authenticity of the relation. D'Eon is called on to deny the particulars if she can; Count de Guines [French ambassador to England] is at liberty to refute them—if he dare."[10]

The article opened by announcing that an extensive correspondence between d'Eon and Louis XV had been discovered among the dead king's papers. These letters were quite recent, from the 1760s and 1770s, when d'Eon was supposedly outlawed from France. Louis XV, the article posited, had been playing a double game with those around them, including his ministers. "To all appearance his Majesty was desirous to have the Chevalier apprehended. Frequently he would censure his ministers for their tardiness in the business. . . . No sooner was the King apprised of this, than he communicated the particulars to d'Eon, with salutary cautions to guard against those very stratagems his ministers had laid for the detection of the Chevalier." The only reason, the story went on, that Louis would have engaged in such duplicity is that he knew d'Eon was a woman, and was himself aware of the origins of d'Eon's transvestism: "pecuniary motives induced her parents to educate her as a boy, to preserve an estate in the family, which would otherwise have lapsed to another branch for want of an heir-male."

The article claimed that when Louis XVI's agents confronted d'Eon with this correspondence, d'Eon confessed that he was indeed a woman, and that is what prompted the arrangements leading up to the signing of the Transaction, the highlights of which the paper reprinted. Finally, the story claimed that d'Eon would soon retire to a convent in France, "until she hath accustomed herself to the habit of a female."

This article (and perhaps others) was most likely given to the press by Morande or Beaumarchais, because while it offers a fascinating cocktail of truth and falsehood, it also portrays the truth as the French government saw it in the spring of 1776. They had just become aware of the role d'Eon had played as a secret agent for Louis XV; they firmly believed that d'Eon was a woman, raised by her parents to be a man; and finally, while it was not spelled out in the Transaction, they hoped d'Eon would spend several months in a convent after his return to France. Just as Morande and Beaumarchais were still in the dark about the extent of the King's Secret, including its plans for an invasion of England, so those dark secrets were not exposed at this time. Only d'Eon's role after 1766, as a special correspondent with Broglie and Louis XV, was brought to light.

Regardless of its source, this version of d'Eon's life story—"pecuniary motives induced her parents to educate her as a boy"—now became the way the European public understood the origins of his gender confusion. "She was born a girl," one lawyer announced to a French court of law in 1779. "She was baptized and nursed as a girl, but raised as a boy."[11] About this time, the story spread throughout Europe that the Prince de Conti and Louis XV had both sent d'Eon to Russia in the 1750s aware that he was a woman, and had ordered him to dress as one in order to become an aide to the Empress Elizabeth. D'Eon's successful efforts to invent a patriotic cover for himself turned out to be an important factor in his public rehabilitation.[12]

But this new image for d'Eon cut two ways. There were many among the English who now felt double-crossed. Before 1776, d'Eon had become a kind of hero for Londoners, an exile from the despotic French who could live safely in free England. Besides, his well-known friendship with John Wilkes had endeared him to Wilkes's supporters, some of whom watched out for d'Eon by protecting his home and roughing up his critics. Even when the rumors about his gender started circulating, Londoners stuck by him. But the stories regarding d'Eon's secret correspondence with Louis XV changed all that. Apparently, d'Eon was not a male French exile, but a woman who spied for Louis XV. Some Londoners reacted to this news like insulted hosts.

This new perception of d'Eon was first apparent during the summer of 1776, at the time of the Morande suits. In challenging Morande to a duel, d'Eon was engaging in the most aggressive social act, obviously reserved only for men. But since d'Eon had refused to verify anything about his sex beforehand, and since he was now perceived to be a woman (as Morande's refusal made clear), d'Eon's virile challenge was interpreted as shameless Amazonian audacity. Indeed, the crowds that had protected d'Eon some years earlier now turned on him, throwing rocks through his windows.[13]

For many, d'Eon was now nothing but a rogue and a trickster, not unlike Morande and other French exiles who used London as a base from which to exploit British freedom and defame both countries. Indeed, d'Eon was worse than Morande precisely because he was a woman. Having convinced themselves of d'Eon's female identity, the London papers now started to attack him in the most misogynist language. "The little, tricking, disingenuous artifices, peculiar to your sex, shall not save you!" warned the editor of the *Public Ledger*. After d'Eon's lawyer had referred to him in court as one of the truly great French noblemen of the age, the *Morning Post* warned that the attorney "will be much disappointed when the farce is over, to find that his *protectress! this princess! this great woman,* greater (as he says and thinks) than Sully, Colbert, or Bolingbroke, turns out a poor kind of man, a wrongheaded, Burgundy *bourgeoise.*"[14]

But the most viciously misogynist campaign was waged by the lesser-known *Westminster Gazette,* which admitted that its coverage of d'Eon dramatically increased its sales. "What is the *gallant Chevalier* about?" it asked rhetorically in early September 1776. "As a man she hath been excelled to the skies. As she is a woman it is a pity that we are compelled to despise her." D'Eon angered the paper because even as a woman he had continued to act with "noisy turbulence," dressing in his military uniform and challenging foes to duels when he ought to have recognized the consequences of his own womanhood. "The qualities of her sex," the *Gazette* explained, "are discretion, modesty, amity, etc.," so far unknown to the impetuous Chevalier.[15]

The growing consensus regarding d'Eon's status as a woman meant that financiers who had wagered a great deal of money on the side of d'Eon's womanhood demanded payment. Meanwhile, of course, those who had bet that d'Eon was a man, however convinced they were to the contrary, refused to pay unless irrefutable evidence was put before them. Consequently the search for proof intensified. D'Eon was constantly offered money, at one point as much as £30,000, to disrobe in the presence of a physician acting as an independent arbiter. Of course d'Eon repeatedly refused such offers, and spent as much time as possible with his friend Lord Ferrers in the country.[16]

Some bettors went to almost desperate lengths to find compelling evidence, as the following newspaper announcement illustrates:

The printer of this paper is authorized to assure the public, that an eminent banker has in his hands £10,000, which have been deposited on purpose to enable him to make the following proposal:

This gentleman declares d'Eon (alias the Chevalier d'Eon) a WOMAN, in the clearest sense of the word; this declaration he supports with a bet of any such sum of money from one to five thousand guineas, or he proposes to any one, who will deposit five thousand guineas in the hand of his banker, to pay ten thousand pounds if d'Eon proves herself either a MAN, an HERMAPHRO-DITE, or any other animal than a WOMAN.[17]

Lord Mansfield's Court

BY THE SUMMER OF 1777, the chances of producing irrefutable proof of d'Eon's sex were quickly fading because, as the press reported, the Chevalier was about to leave England for France. Some gamblers, who had had enormous sums of money tied up since 1771, were getting nervous, and began filing civil suits against one another for payment. The most famous of these was heard by Chief Justice Mansfield at the Court of King's Bench on 2 July 1777—the eve of d'Eon's departure.

That such a high court would hear the case is indicative of how important the bets over d'Eon had become. Mansfield was perhaps Britain's most distinguished judge, having served as chief justice since 1756. Many considered him the greatest British intellect of his day.[1] He was particularly familiar with the d'Eon case. As a judge, he had heard the disputes between d'Eon and Guerchy in the 1760s, and he had also presided over d'Eon's more recent libel case against Morande. Over the years, Mansfield had developed an intense dislike for d'Eon, but he kept it to himself until after d'Eon had left for France.[2]

For this trial, Mansfield secured a "special jury," meaning a jury of merchants and gentlemen, and the trial was held not in the open and disorderly Westminster Hall, but in the more staid Guildhall, located in the financial district, where every hearing took place in a private room.

This suit concerned a surgeon, Mr. Hayes, who had purchased a life insurance policy on d'Eon for £100 in 1771 from the insurance broker Mr. Jacques. The policy stipulated that Mr. Jacques return £700 to Mr. Hayes if d'Eon was discovered to be a woman. Now Hayes was attempting to recover his money. Although d'Eon did not attend the trial, it was nonetheless a dramatic spectacle. So many people tried to crowd into the public galleries that in d'Eon's own words, "half the world" seemed to be there.[3]

Mr. Hayes's attorney opened the trial by promising to "call our witnesses to prove that *he* is a *woman*." The first witness was a fellow surgeon and male midwife named La Goux. "I have been acquainted with the Chevalier four or five years; I know it is a woman," he declared. Under questioning by Lord Mansfield, La Goux explained that some years earlier d'Eon had sought his care after becoming ill with what was apparently a female disorder. D'Eon supposedly confessed to La Goux that he was a woman, and when the surgeon examined him, he "found *it* to be a woman." D'Eon ordered La Goux not to mention a word of his sex to anyone. Although many people had earlier offered La Goux money if he would testify, he had always refused. He had appeared today, he told Mansfield, only because he had been subpoenaed.[4]

Hayes's next witness was none other than Charles Morande. Cross-examined by the defendant's attorney, Morande declared under oath that on 3 July 1774, d'Eon had provided Morande with intimate proof: "She one day showed me her woman's clothes, earrings, and showed me her breasts. Some time after, I was one morning (being myself a married man) introduced into her bed-chamber; she was in bed, and with great freedom bid me satisfy myself of what we had so often been jocular about, for she had often used to say I was to be godfather. I put my hand into bed, and was fully convinced she was a woman."

Amazingly, the defense did not challenge Morande's perjurious testimony, nor that of the other witnesses. Indeed, the defense did not dispute that d'Eon was a woman, and rested its case on two main arguments: First, the plaintiff's case depended on admitting indecent testimony into the court, dishonoring the entire institution of justice. The courts were no place for the discussion of a woman's private parts; consequently, the testimony of Morande and the two physicians ought to be dismissed on the grounds of obscenity. Second, the defense claimed that the bet should be considered fraudulent since Mr. Hayes clearly had information regarding d'Eon's sex that was unavailable to Mr. Jacques.

Since these two arguments did not question d'Eon's sex, but constituted more technical challenges to the legality of the trial, they were resolved by Lord Mansfield. He agreed with the defense that the lurid testimony of Morande and others was beneath the dignity of the court. He told the court that he found the whole business of betting over someone's sex outrageous and wished that he could find a way to make both parties lose. But he could not. Under English law, he explained, what had happened between Mr. Hayes and Mr. Jacques was perfectly legal, and their dispute had to be heard, however ignoble. The insurance policy under question was indeed a legal contract under British law. Nor did Mansfield have any sympathy for the defendant's second objection. Noting that the Chevalier d'Eon had refused to cooperate with any party, Hayes did not possess the kind of inside information that would have rendered the bet fraudulent. Consequently, Mansfield told the jury to ignore both objections.[5]

Given the weight of the evidence presented, "the jury, without going out of court, after consulting about two minutes, gave a verdict for the Plaintiff of £700." The jury's decision served as a kind of legal declaration of d'Eon's womanhood. Immediately many gamblers who had bet that d'Eon was a man now paid off their opponents rather than be dragged into an expensive civil suit. Thousands of pounds changed hands, and those who still refused to pay were brought to court.[6]

D'Eon did not attend any of these trials and could only have felt enormously ambivalent about them. On the one hand, the trials culminated a six-year effort to present himself as a woman before the English and European public. Insofar as England now regarded him legally as a woman, he could have taken solace. Instead, however, he viewed the trial as a kind of tragedy: "I took to bed in my depression and isolation, begging the heavens for relief from my anxiety and confusion."[7]

What upset d'Eon so much was, of course, the manner in which his body could be discussed in a public forum without his consent. The trial seemed to affirm the right to turn the body of a nobleman into a commodity. Moreover, d'Eon was deeply hurt that Mansfield had allowed such rogues as Morande to pollute the court with what were obviously lies and slander. D'Eon wanted to be known as a woman, but he would not have people who hardly knew him discussing his body so brazenly in public. This is why d'Eon told the papers that he still refused to divulge his true sex and warned all gamblers against paying off their debts. In one letter to a newspaper, he reminded readers of his threat that if the betting did not stop, he would flee the country. Now, d'Eon announced, given the results of this trial, he had no choice but to return to France immediately.[8]

D'Eon stuck to his word. Six weeks after the verdict, he was on a boat to France. But the timing of the Mansfield verdict and d'Eon's departure from England were, in fact, coincidental. It was Vergennes and Louis XVI, not Mansfield or the English, who had kept d'Eon in England. Although since November 1775 he had been welcome to return to France under the terms of the Transaction, d'Eon spent the next eighteen months quibbling with Beaumarchais, Vergennes, and even Louis XVI himself over various details regarding the Transaction's terms, testing its limits. Specifically, he wanted to make certain that all his debts were paid before he left England. As he explained to Vergennes, he had managed to acquire a library of over 6,000 volumes, a collection so large that it had to remain in England. If he left debts unpaid, he was afraid that creditors could attach liens to his beloved library, and even sell some of it off. By the summer of 1777, however, enough of his debts had been paid that he finally felt ready for the grand voyage. Nonetheless, he still felt he had to keep his departure date absolutely secret, lest he be kidnapped. It seems that only Ferrers and one other friend knew the date. Finally, on 14 August 1777, d'Eon left London virtually unnoticed. His exit was only made public in the newspapers a few days later.[9]

In the six years since rumors about his sex had first surfaced, d'Eon had achieved a remarkable transformation. He had been relieved of his seemingly insurmountable debt problems; his political rehabilitation by Louis XVI was made all the more convincing by the public view that his years in London had not been an exile after all, but had been spent in the secret service of Louis XV; finally, without ever dressing as a woman, he had managed to convince everyone, including his closest friends, that he was an anatomical female who had been raised as a male.

Even after d'Eon left for France, Lord Mansfield continued to hear civil suits resulting from insurance policies bought on d'Eon's sex. The judge grew increasingly angry about such wagers, and sought to develop a legal principle by which he could disqualify all of them. In December 1777, Mansfield heard the case of Joshua Mendes Da Costa vs. Jenkin Jones, identical in virtually every way to Hayes vs. Jacques, even to the point of calling many of the same witnesses, including the crucial testimony of Morande. Mansfield acted no differently in his handling of the case, and like its predecessor, this jury found in favor of the plaintiff. But during his closing remarks after the jury had delivered its verdict, Mansfield let it be known that he would welcome a motion by the defense to arrest the judgment of the court. That would allow the Chief Justice to consider in more depth not the question of d'Eon's sex, but whether such an insurance policy was indeed permissible under British law.

Sure enough, the defense made the requisite motion, and a month later attorneys were back in Mansfield's Court of King's Bench to debate the legality of the wagers. After dutifully hearing the arguments, Mansfield ruled in favor of the defendant, Jenkin Jones, overturning his previous judgment, and effectively rendering all wagers on d'Eon unenforceable. Mansfield made it clear that his judgment did not concern d'Eon's sex— at least three juries had decided d'Eon was a woman—nor was Mansfield assaulting the right of Englishmen to make bets that would be recognized in court as enforceable contracts. Rather, Mansfield's decision invalidated wagers that were made between two indifferent persons upon the sex of another for two principal reasons: first, because such bets tended to require the admission of indecent evidence for no compelling reason; and second, because such bets invariably violated the security and reputation of the innocent third party.[10]

Thus the question of d'Eon's gender not only became a favorite topic of conversation in the British press and at London soirées, but it led England's most distinguished legal mind to define new principles of the law. From now on, Englishmen would be prevented from legally contracting with each other over someone's gender, a principle d'Eon had been advocating for years. Indeed, now d'Eon had achieved two victories: He had transformed the public's view of him from male to female, and he had prevented anyone in England from making money off his gender.

Part V

D'EON'S CHRISTIAN FEMINISM

Clothes are but a symbol of something hid deep beneath. It was a change in Orlando herself that dictated her choice of a woman's dress and of a woman's sex. And perhaps in this she was only expressing rather more openly than usual—openness indeed was the soul of her nature—something that happens to most people without being thus plainly expressed. For here again, we come to a dilemma. Different though the sexes are, they intermix. In every human being a vacillation from one sex to the other takes place, and often it is only the clothes that keep the male or female likeness, while underneath the sex is the very opposite of what it is above. Of the complications and confusions which thus result everyone has had experience; but here we leave the general question and note only the odd effect it had in the particular case of Orlando herself.

—*Virginia Woolf,* Orlando

Considering Convents

D'EON RETURNED TO FRANCE one of the century's most famous and remarkable women. Everywhere he went, every-one—from ordinary servants to the King and Queen—wanted to have a look at him. The papers regularly ran stories about him and fans continued to send him admiring mail. Pierre-Joseph Boudier de Villemart featured d'Eon in his 1779 book on Europe's most famous women, as did a woman author in an early feminist tract.[1] A short time later, in 1780, one of France's few well-known female sculptors, Marie-Anne Collot, the daughter-in-law of the great Falconnet, made a bust of d'Eon that attracted notice in the press, and for which Blin de Sainmore wrote the following poem:[2]

> Ce marbre, où de d'Eon le bust est retracé,
> A deux femmes assure une gloire immortelle
> Et par elles vainçu, l'autre sexe est forcé
> D'envier à la fois l'artiste et le modèle
>
> [This marble out of which d'Eon's bust is drawn
> assures immortal glory to two women
> And defeated by these two, the other sex is forced
> To envy both the artist and the model]

During the next three decades that d'Eon lived as a woman, no one publicly challenged his identity: everyone accepted him as a chevalière—this despite the fact that when a person met d'Eon for the first time, d'Eon behaved in an unabashedly masculine fashion. "I adapted to my condition," d'Eon later recalled, "without changing my appearance or speech, as others may have wished."[3] Despite his having assumed women's clothes and identity, he continued to act chivalrously toward other ladies, performing as always small polite masculine duties, such as pouring coffee when he found a lady's cup empty. When one gentleman remarked to d'Eon that as a man he had shown a very handsome leg, d'Eon is said to have lifted his petticoats and announced, "If you are curious, voilà!" Likewise, he enjoyed putting on fencing demonstrations at these soirées. Such extraordinary behavior caused at least one magazine to note that d'Eon "still seems more like a man than a woman."[4]

Whereas Frenchmen were intrigued by d'Eon's behavior, many Englishmen found it offensive and outrageous, among them James Boswell, who talked with d'Eon at a party one evening in 1786. "I was shocked to think of her a kind of monster by metamorphosis. She appeared to me a man in woman's clothes." Horace Walpole "found her loud, noisy and vulgar—in truth I believe she had dined a little *en dragon*. The night was hot, she had no muff or gloves, and her hands and arms seem not to have participated of the change of sexes, but are fitter to carry a chair than a fan."[5]

What is amazing about the reactions of Boswell and Walpole is that they did not follow their instincts and declare that d'Eon was actually a man dressed as a woman. Rather, despite what they perceived, they identified d'Eon as an Amazon, a thoroughly masculinized woman. They assumed female in what they could *not* see; they perceived male in what they could see. To them, d'Eon was anatomically female, but socially a man: this is what came across so appallingly to these conservative Englishmen.

Convincing a European public that he was a woman who had posed as a man was no longer the central problem of d'Eon's life; rather, he now had to face the even more difficult challenge of carrying on a public career as a woman. Despite Vergennes's instructions, d'Eon did not intend to retire from politics. He had come to regard his gender transformation as a means to regenerate a stalled political career. He wanted somehow to continue to take on diplomatic posts, serve as a military officer, and write books that kept his name before the public—but now self-consciously as a woman. His struggle with the government over the right to wear the uniform of a Dragoon officer was simply the opening shot in his battle to enter the ranks of Old Regime statesmen as a woman. While some women, such as Mme de Pompadour and the salonnières associated with the Enlightenment philosophers, may have wielded enormous political power, they had achieved their influence through unofficial channels. Political and military posts were the monopoly of men. It was this bastion of gender exclusivity that d'Eon sought to crash after his return to France. He wanted to open up the most traditional political and military offices to women—and increasingly during the years after 1777, he came to see his struggle as not merely personal, but undertaken on behalf of all women.

Unfortunately for d'Eon, his crusade to increase opportunities for elite women in public life went sharply against prevailing cultural trends. Public roles for women were beginning to narrow instead of widen. D'Eon associated the new attitude toward women not with Rousseau, but more personally with Beaumarchais. Once both d'Eon and Beaumarchais were back in Paris, the latter continued spinning his devious tales about d'Eon's interest in marrying him. Such stories threatened to turn d'Eon into the laughingstock of Paris. People would not see in him a patriotic heroine, but simply a sexually frustrated spinster, out to snag a husband and retire from political life. Already Beaumarchais's stories were having an effect: At many salons, women began to masquerade as d'Eon, telling risqué stories and flirting with male guests.[6]

D'Eon complained bitterly to Vergennes about the slander and defended himself against Beaumarchais in pamphlets that appeared in the spring of 1778. Not only were Beaumarchais's stories completely false, d'Eon declared, their obscene nature revealed a truly depraved character. D'Eon reiterated his earlier charges that Beaumarchais had exploited his position as an agent for Louis XVI to place bets on d'Eon's sex, and, given his inside information, to make a lot of money. So great was Beaumarchais's fortune that d'Eon suggested he should be known as "Bon Marché" (good deal).[7]

D'Eon argued that by slandering him, Beaumarchais was, in reality, slandering all women. In a special "Appel à mes contemporaines" (A Call to My Fellow Women), written on the Feast of the Purification, d'Eon "denounced" Beaumarchais "in the name of all the women of my epoch." D'Eon contended that by placing a bet on the sex of a woman, Beaumarchais had acted like a pimp, trying to use d'Eon's body for money. For d'Eon, Beaumarchais's exploitation of his body constituted an act of the vilest misogyny.[8]

D'Eon's hatred for Beaumarchais became increasingly obsessive. In him d'Eon saw the upstart, the parvenu, who had wormed his way into the aristocracy only to destroy it from the inside. In the coming years, d'Eon would slowly gather materials for a projected four-volume biography of Beaumarchais. His own negotiations with Beaumarchais would be carefully detailed in the third volume. Eventually, d'Eon lost interest in the project, and it was never completed.[9]

Nonetheless, d'Eon felt a jubilant sense of victory over Beaumarchais when in February 1778 news reached him of Lord Mansfield's decision to outlaw gambling on his sex. In a letter to the judge, d'Eon forgave the British for harassing him with various lawsuits, comparing himself with Joan of Arc, who, 300 years earlier, had also been maligned by the English legal system. And yet, like hers, "the entire life of the Chevalière d'Eon is full of acts of courage, wisdom, bravery, and loyalty," d'Eon wrote.[10]

In a short article titled "Seconde lettre aux femmes," d'Eon announced that Mansfield's judgment was not simply a personal victory for him but a victory for women everywhere. If men could make wagers about women's bodies without their permission, no woman would be protected from such shame. But now, with this decree, men could not slander women and get away with it. "Your honor is triumphant," d'Eon told his women readers.[11]

For a very different reason, February 1778 marked another turning point in d'Eon's adaptation to womanhood: France joined the American War of Independence against Britain. Now there could be no question of d'Eon's retirement from the military. Despite his adopted sex, d'Eon was first and foremost a soldier and patriot; if his country was at war, that is where he belonged. This was never more true than now: Here was the war d'Eon had longed for to avenge the defeat of 1763. This new war represented France's chance to recover her national honor.

D'Eon petitioned government officials, asking them to rescind the decree requiring him to wear women's clothes. He explained that he despised female attire, and begged to be allowed to resume his military uniform. Once he was granted permission to return to the dress of a Dragoon captain, he could then apply for special duty in America.[12]

The government, of course, would hear of no such thing. Far from having any intention of allowing d'Eon to enter the war, it wanted him out of Paris, removed from the public spotlight. The government did everything it could to pressure d'Eon to enter a convent and become a nun. The women of the court, such as Mme de Maurepas, wife of the interior minister, told d'Eon that there was simply no way any unmarried woman could have political influence. She advised d'Eon either to marry and exercise influence through her husband, or to enter a convent.[13]

The idea of getting married was, of course, out of the question. But d'Eon gave the idea of becoming a nun serious consideration. After all, what was a fifty-year-old spinster to do? Indeed, d'Eon's good friends thought entering a convent a good idea.[14]

Most of our notions of eighteenth-century French convents come from the Enlightenment *philosophes* who despised them. In Denis Diderot's short novel *La Religieuse* (The Nun), for example, convents were portrayed as tiny dictatorships, where hypocrisy and deception led to lesbianism. Cut off from the world, isolated from the enlightened atmosphere of the city, nuns drowned in a sea of superstition and sexual depravity. Full of spoiled girls who didn't want to be there, Diderot's convents seemed large dungeons, where reason and virtue were unwelcome if not unknown.[15]

This picture of the cloistered life was probably drawn for polemical purposes; it had little to do with reality. Convents in eighteenth-century France were not dungeons of ignorance isolated from the real world. In fact, they were centers of genuine learning and piety that provided important intellectual opportunities for young women.

More often than not, convents were finishing schools for the upper classes. Most girls from the bourgeoisie and aristocracy, and even many from the lower classes who were subsidized by scholarships, went to convent boarding schools for a year or two during their adolescence. There they learned how to read and write, and while their education was not as rigorous as a boy's, we should not make light of it. With young women moving in and out of convents, the institutions were neither isolated nor provincial. Like good colleges located outside big cities today, convents maintained large endowments and close relations with the leading families of the country.[16]

At the best convents, nuns could read, write, and converse in a community made comfortable by a sumptuous refectory and splendid library. Indeed, well-run convents were perhaps the only places in eighteenth-century France where women could participate in intellectual and religious endeavors relatively independent from men. Run by and for women, convents offered women positions of leadership and responsibility unattainable in the secular realm. In short, convents attracted not only women who were already committed Christians, but women of various religious moods who wanted to pursue their interests among other women.

It is not surprising, then, that such a community would appeal to d'Eon. Even in Protestant countries, aristocratic women came to idealize convents as retreats where strong feminine characteristics could flourish without inhibition. In the Querelle des Femmes literature, such communal spinsterhood was sometimes seen as a positive alternative to marriage.[17] Drawn to womanhood out of an admiration for the virtuous female character, d'Eon naturally considered convents as an authentic feminine community that might, at least among the best of them, institutionalize virtue. "I am humiliated and depraved among men," d'Eon confessed in the autobiographical fragments. "I am elevated and exalted among women."[18]

At least two of the best convents in France invited d'Eon for an extended visit in the hope he would choose to live there. In September 1778 d'Eon first visited the Abbaye Royale des Dames at Fontevrault, in the Loire valley. Famous as one of the oldest religious institutions in France, the convent was originally founded as a mixed-sex abbey at the end of the eleventh century. Its founder, the preacher Robert d'Arbrissel, took the unusual step of appointing a woman to direct both the nunnery and monastery. During the medieval and early modern period, many royal families sent their daughters to this convent, and by the eighteenth century it had an exalted national reputation.[19]

About the same time, d'Eon also visited the even more impressive convent of Saint-Cyr, located just outside Versailles. Founded much later than Fontevarault, by Louis XIV, Saint-Cyr was especially favored by the Bourbon kings and their relatives. A girl usually had to prove four degrees of nobility to be admitted. Aristocratic girls who did not intend to become nuns could live in the convent between the ages of seven and twenty. The nunnery was especially known for its lavish grounds. If d'Eon would be happy at any convent, this seemed to be it. And the nuns wanted d'Eon, too. After his first visit, one nun wrote him that he had won the admiration of all the sisters; she hoped he would return soon and stay for as long as he liked.[20]

D'Eon didn't pretend to be a different kind of woman for the nuns, but continued to project his own virile Amazonian image of womanhood. After one successful visit, he sent them a copy of a popular print, sold in London bookstalls since 1773, of d'Eon as the goddess Pallas (page 206), exiting her military tent to prepare her troops for battle. The nuns were appreciative of this gift, and returned the favor by sending him this original poem:[21]

De l'antique Pallas, d'Eon a tous les traits
Elle en a la sagesse et le masle courage
Je me trompe: d'Eon, par d'héroïques Faits
Cent fois plus que Pallas merite notre homage.
Qu'etoit ce que Pallas? un Estre fabuleux
Un brillant avorton du cerveau des Poëtes.
La Brave d'Eon vit, et cent mille gazettes
Vantent par l'univers ses exploits glorieux

[D'Eon has all the traits of ancient Pallas
She has her wisdom and her virile courage
I am mistaken: d'Eon, by virtue of heroic acts
Merits our homage a hundred times more than Pallas.
What was Pallas? a being of fable
a brilliant puny offspring of the mind of poets.

The valorous d'Eon lives, and 100,000 gazettes
Declaim throughout the universe her glorious exploits]

D'Eon appreciated his visits to both convents, and seriously contemplated joining one of these two as well as others. At one point, he even drew up a list of a dozen convents that he thought appropriate for serious consideration.[22] He saw in the cloistered life a "temple of purity where God disseminates his laws in the hearts" of the nuns.[23] D'Eon was especially drawn to the piety he found in these communities; the sisters' virtue did not disappoint him, and he believed that he would have much to learn from their moral courage.

But in the end d'Eon could not go through with it. A nun, he believed, had to demonstrate modesty and humility in order to live for God alone. She had to follow "the doctrine of Saint Augustine," which directed religious men and women to ignore their own will and live only by "the grace of God." But d'Eon had to admit that he could not, or would not, suppress his own ego. Despite admitted ambivalence and confusion, he knew that his change of gender had not stifled his worldly ambitions.[24]

Put differently, despite his deep and sincere admiration for the virtue and integrity of the nuns he encountered, convent life bored him. Living in a convent meant retiring to a community where nothing happened, where each day was the same, where d'Eon could become nothing more because he had ceased to live—in short, entering a nunnery meant, in his own words, "dying in this world in order to live for God," something he was not yet prepared to do. Besides, he rationalized, if an egocentric statesman such as himself joined a convent, he might unwittingly corrupt the modesty of the other girls, and that would be especially sinful. Even Jesus had once said, d'Eon recalled, that a person who sways another away from the path of salvation is himself worthy of death.[25]

"The spirit of my inborn valor, being held back and repressed in my dress at the convent," d'Eon explained in his memoirs, "closely resembled the wine of my native land, Tonnerre. If you put it in a new cask that has been poorly washed, scoured, and tied, in only a few months all of the body of the wine evaporates; there remains nothing but the death-head of the wine, that is, the dregs." In the same way, d'Eon argued that he needed time on the outside to test his moral character, that he was simply not ready for the purely contemplative life of a nun—but someday he hoped he would be.[26]

By the end of 1778, d'Eon had resolved that he could not enter a convent but must, by hook or by crook, get to America and fight with France for the colonies' independence. He embarked on a writing campaign, sending letters not just to several of the King's ministers but also to their wives and to "the great ladies of the court." He explained that for over a year he had tried to live in a domesticated fashion, outside of public view, and it just hadn't worked. "The sedentary lifestyle has totally ruined my muscle tone and my spirit. For fifty years I have always been ready for an active life," but now "the repose is killing me." Please, d'Eon begged, convince the King to approve "my continued military service for the duration of this war."[27]

When d'Eon received no reply, he went even further, sending forty copies of a letter originally written to Interior Minister Maurepas, to the Princes of the Blood and other well-placed persons. He also wrote directly to an admiral at Brest, the Comte d'Orvilliers, asking for permission to cross the Atlantic on one of his ships. D'Orvilliers replied that only Maurepas could approve such an assignment, but as far as he was personally concerned, he would be happy to transport d'Eon to America. D'Eon then lobbied several Maréchals of France to ask "M. the Comte de Maurepas to allow me to return to war."[28]

D'Eon knew that his behavior would seem audacious to the King and his ministers. But he argued that what he was asking for was really not that strange. He cited the wives of the ancient Gauls, who routinely accompanied their husbands into battle. They made an important contribution, stimulating the courage and virility of the soldiers. As an Amazonian warrior, d'Eon, too, would stimulate the prowess of the troops with his exemplary behavior.

Vergennes and Louis XVI were outraged by d'Eon's behavior and agreed that he must be stopped once and for all. On 2 March 1779 the King gave d'Eon just three days to retire to Tonnerre, where he was ordered to remain until further notice. Furthermore, the King insisted that d'Eon remain in woman's clothes at all times, forbidding him to wear his Dragoon's uniform. D'Eon complained that the royal decree was not fair and went against the 1775 Transaction; under pressure, however, he agreed to submit to the King's will.[29]

But d'Eon did not move fast enough for King Louis. A month later, he was still living at Versailles, complaining of a sickness brought about by his lethargic life. This time Louis would tolerate no insubordination from d'Eon. In the middle of the night the police stormed the home of the Duc and Duchesse de Montmorency-Bouteville, where d'Eon had been staying, and despite d'Eon's vigorous resistance, carried him off a hundred miles east to the dungeon beneath the Château of Dijon. D'Eon was informed that he had been jailed because of his "blind passion to want to return to his miserable occupation in the war." Still, d'Eon refused to believe that the King would actually incarcerate him for simply requesting a military post, and he blamed his misfortunes on the machinations of Beaumarchais.[30]

D'Eon later compared his imprisonment to the time when Joan of Arc was held captive at Chinon for wearing a military uniform. Where, wondered d'Eon, does the Criminal Code state that it is illegal for a woman to dress in a military uniform to defend her country against enemies? "I am a former Captain of Dragoons; I have a right to wear the uniform that I earned . . . through spilling my own blood three times on the field of battle."[31]

D'Eon begged his friends the Duchesse de Montmorency-Bouteville and the Comtesse de Maurepas to get him out. They would only do so, however, if he agreed to abandon his military ambitions. "Was it not crazy," Montmorency-Bouteville asked, for d'Eon "to believe that after having been officially recognized before the entire court as a maiden, they would all approve you going off to war?" Reluctantly, d'Eon agreed that if freed he would immediately go to Tonnerre, where he would retire on his estate. After he had spent nineteen days in jail, his friends secured his release, and by May he was back in Tonnerre with his mother.[32]

Reborn Again

FOR THE NEXT SIX YEARS, from 1779 to 1785, d'Eon spent
most of his time with his mother at the family's home in Tonnerre.
Sometimes he was able to take vacations with friends in other parts
of France, but during the first years, at least, he had to secure special permission to leave. For example, in April 1780 d'Eon's friend Bertier de
Sauvigny, the Intendant of Paris, granted his request to visit the capital,
but for only two weeks, and with the stipulation that d'Eon would remain
in women's clothes for the duration of the visit. Once d'Eon was in Paris,
the government assigned a spy to follow him and report on his every
move.[1] Thus despite d'Eon's attempts to squirm back into public life, the
government successfully shut down his career and forced him into a reluctant retirement.

One consequence of this retirement is that d'Eon's days finally became
placid and boring. Thinking about his vineyards and planting trees on his
estate were his primary occupations. Except for a few relatively brief
moments, after 1779 the melodrama of his previous career was lacking. To
be sure, he continued to lead an active social life, especially after he moved
back to England in 1785.[2] He was sought after for parties and dinners,
and was frequently the topic of light gossip and after-dinner talk. But
such chatter now focused on his past. Although d'Eon would live another
thirty years, he would never again fight in a war, hold political office, or
publish any books. His public career was virtually finished.

However uneventful d'Eon's life was on the outside, a transformation
was taking place in his heart that would come to affect the way he

thought about everything else, particularly women and gender. Simply put, d'Eon became a Christian. His faith in Christ, his devotion to the Gospels, and to Saint Paul especially, colored everything he did and thought. "The doctrine of the Gospel is totally divine," d'Eon wrote to the Duchesse de Montmorency-Bouteville as early as May 1778. "The Apostles are only its trustees and spokesmen. God alone is its source and Jesus Christ the Doctor and the great Master. It is neither the invention of the human mind, nor the fruit of philosophical study; but a gift of God from Jesus Christ."[3]

In one sense, of course, d'Eon had always been a Christian. A few days after he was born, his parents provided him with a proper Catholic baptism, and he never wavered in his identity as a French Catholic. As a young man he seems to have taken confession at least occasionally.[4] Likewise, d'Eon's schooling made him quite familiar with the Bible and standard Christian commentaries. He knew Greek, Latin, and even Hebrew well enough to make his way through sacred texts in their original languages. Throughout his life as a man, his religious identity was always important to him, even if it was not a guiding force behind his career. For example, in his revealing 1766 letter to Rousseau (see chapter 28), d'Eon confessed that Christianity was the only major area that separated the two thinkers: "I am always naturally taken to support the demonstration of your systems, except certain points on religion." D'Eon disagreed with Rousseau's efforts to subordinate all matters of faith to reason; he self-consciously maintained a more orthodox position: "It is therefore more advantageous to believe in the words of Jesus Christ who cannot deceive us," he wrote to Rousseau.

On the other hand, d'Eon's interests at that point were certainly eclectic, and it is difficult to find indications of fervent Catholic attitudes before 1777. The Rousseau letter is very rare for even raising the issue of religion. In his voluminous correspondence before returning to France as a woman, he rarely mentions going to Mass, taking communion or confession, or any discussions with priests. Meanwhile, he seemed quite comfortable reading the work of Rousseau's more irreligious colleagues. His own book purchases included the works of Enlightenment *philosophes* such as Hume, Montesquieu, and Voltaire, as well as their classical counterparts, such as Horace. Indeed, it was an epigram of Voltaire's that graced the title page of d'Eon's most famous published work, the *Lettres, mémoires, et négociations* of 1764. Further, d'Eon discussed radical anti-religious ideas with his friends, and welcomed the opportunity to read the works of atheists. For example, in 1770, through a friend of Diderot's, d'Eon procured a copy of Baron Paul-Henri-Dietrich d'Holbach's *Système de la nature,* a work infamous for its atheism and impiety.[5]

After his return to France, d'Eon's reading habits changed. The many book notes included in a diary covering some of the time he stayed at Tonnerre leave little doubt that the majority of d'Eon's reading focused on works of Christian piety. For instance, he jotted down sympathetic words about Dechoyaumont's *Réflexions morales sur l'ancien et le nouveau Testament* and about an etiquette book titled *Manières morale d'un philosophe Chrétien.*[6]

While the evidence is not conclusive, a record of what d'Eon read and wrote indicates that his intense religiosity developed after he had become a woman. His spiritual transformation was the result and not the cause of his gender transformation. D'Eon, then, experienced two consecutive rebirths: first as a woman, and then as a Christian.

Sometime between 1777 and 1779, shortly after his return to France, perhaps as a result of the ladies around him at Versailles, he discovered that merely living as a woman was not enough: he had to be a Christian woman as well. After all, his model, Joan of Arc, wasn't simply a militant Amazon; she was also a pious Christian. D'Eon increasingly came to see that if he was to pursue a complete moral purification, he would need to become a full Christian. If at first such an attitude was a rather artificial process of self-fashioning, it soon became an intense personal conviction. In this sense, his visits to convents were not in vain. Although d'Eon ultimately decided not to join one, certainly what he experienced at Saint-Cyr and Fontevarault led him to feel the necessity of becoming a Christian.

In his memoirs, d'Eon gives much of the credit for his conversion to several interviews he apparently had had with the dean of French Catholicism, Christophe de Beaumont, Archbishop of Paris and a distant relative of d'Eon's. In 1777 the Archbishop was an old and frail man near the end of his life. He had weathered innumerable religious controversies in France and, like d'Eon, had been exiled and rehabilitated by Louis XV. The two men discussed the central theological tenets of Christianity, certainly a well-worn topic for a thinker like d'Eon. However, at this time they seemed to have a new attraction. Whatever Beaumont said had an enormous impact on d'Eon. "Louis XV was my protector; Louis XVI is my liberator; and Christophe de Beaumont is the grand pastor of my soul," he wrote.[7]

The best evidence, however, for arguing that d'Eon's religious rebirth occurred at the end of the 1770s comes from the the diary now preserved in the Archives Nationales. It shows that d'Eon read with unusual devotion the leading Jansenist newspaper, the *Nouvelles ecclésiastiques,* scribbling down notes from its many book reviews of pious and theological Jansenist tracts.[8]

Jansenism was the most significant heretical movement to affect French Catholicism since the era of the Reformation. Begun by a seventeenth-century priest, Cornelius Jansen, the movement was not unlike Lutheran and Calvinist sects in its more fundamentalist approach to questions of sin and grace. In contrast to the more established teachings of the Church, Jansenists believed that no ritual or human activity could mollify a person's sinful nature.

Early in the eighteenth century, Jansenists were persecuted as heretics by both the Catholic Church and the French state, who together saw Jansenism as a threat to order and stability. It was forced underground, and publishing the *Nouvelles ecclésiastiques* became technically illegal. Excluded from Versailles, Jansenists tended to become critics of French absolutism, influencing the often oppositional parlements and developing radical views that contributed to ideas that became popular during the French Revolution.[9]

During the late 1770s, just as d'Eon was returning to France, there was a revival of Christian activity in the capital and elsewhere. Although not Jansenist per se, the movement certainly exhibited a good deal of Christian fundamentalism, and some Jansenists may have reconciled their differences with Christophe de Beaumont. At the same time, d'Eon may have been affected by the religiosity of Tonnerre, which was an intense breeding ground of Jansenist activity throughout the last third of the century.[10]

D'Eon's exposure to these Jansenist ideas made him question the value of Enlightenment thought. He now saw the great philosophers such as Voltaire less as an opposition to the Old Regime and more a reflection of its decadence. "The modern *philosophes* have excluded God from the earth, the king from his throne, and justice from its seat." For d'Eon, the philosophers may have begun with pure intentions, but they had been co-opted and absorbed into Old Regime politics. "How could they resist the corruption of an age that has gorged and devoured all virtue?" he asked himself.[11]

Thus within a year of his return to France, d'Eon's gender transformation was supplemented by a religious one. He had not simply moved from manhood to womanhood, but, equally important in his mind, had moved from a lukewarm Catholicism toward a passionate fundamentalist Christianity. His "new birth"[12] was partly intellectual (the result of conversation and reading), and partly the result of experience. Stuffed away among his autobiographical materials at the University of Leeds is a short, undated essay declaring his new faith that seems to be from 1777 or 1778. Titled "Important Document in my Present State," and beginning with an epigram from Paul's Epistle to the Romans ("Happy are they whose sins are buried away"), it is an attempt to make clear to himself why he needed to become a reborn Christian.[13] Its first page demonstrates d'Eon's sincerity and intensity:

> Given the demands of the critical circumstances under which I live, my most pressing duty is to conduct myself as I do in the eyes of God, the King, the law, and men of faith.
>
> In my present situation, I receive daily practical instruction in all of the duties of a Christian maiden. The grace of the Lord will take care of everything else with time, patience, and obedience to the commandments of God. One is always content with God, and one praises Him in all matters, when one looks only to do his will.

Like his transformation to womanhood, d'Eon's newfound Christianity was the result of his profound alienation from political life. In another rough manuscript, d'Eon describes the religious change as part of a crisis over patronage. He wrote that during his adult life he had had four great patrons: Louis XV, Louis XVI, the Prince de Conti, and the Comte de Broglie. Each in his own way had disappointed d'Eon. If men like these were not worthy of d'Eon's loyalty, who could be? Put this way, the answer is rather obvious: God alone is worthy of our allegiance. He is the only legitimate patron, and we must all strive to be worthy clients. "Only God sees straight into my heart; only He can render justice to me."[14]

D'Eon's conversion gave him a way to cope with the new psychological demands of being an aristocratic lady during the sunset years of the Old Regime. In part, his new faith also gave him a way to deal with the extraordinary anger he felt toward statesmen who continued to exclude him from political power and influence. Instead of interpreting Old Regime politics in purely secular terms as a clash of rival factions, d'Eon used his newfound Christianity to draft criticism that was far more severe: "The impurity of the high and mighty is much more dangerous than in the poor. This kind of vice is most contagious. . . . It is to the soul what the plague is to the body."[15]

And yet his new faith was not simply an ideology for retirement. It became a source of inspiration that led to an enormous output of writing, which, while never published, is evidence of an imaginative and even brilliant mind. "The glory of our Chevalière in the eyes of posterity will be attached to the purity of his morals and to the wise writings from his pen," d'Eon wrote about himself.[16] Indeed, these religious writings from the final decades of his life are more profound than anything he published earlier during his political career.

Return to England

D'EON HAD NEVER WANTED to live in Tonnerre. For his
entire adult life, he had made his home in the capitals of
Europe—Paris, London, even Saint Petersburg. He was made for
city life, with its busy social calendar and political gossip. D'Eon may have
become a woman and a Christian, but much of his personality still
remained as before. After a year or two at Tonnerre managing the family
vineyards, he became restless in the sleepy Burgundian town, and did
everything he could to leave. As far as d'Eon was concerned, the only
valuable thing about Tonnerre was its wine, and that could be enjoyed
anywhere.

When d'Eon's efforts to move to Paris were blocked by the government, he requested permission from Vergennes to return to London. At
first, he explained that his reasons were completely financial: In 1778
Lord Ferrers had died, leaving his estate to a younger brother. D'Eon had
left a large sum of money with Ferrers, who had used it to pay d'Eon's
British expenses, such as the rent and upkeep of the London flat that
housed his book collection. The new Lord Ferrers evidently believed that
his older brother had been too kind to d'Eon; he now acted as if d'Eon's
money was his own, and refused to pay d'Eon's bills.[1]

Vergennes refused d'Eon permission to go to England on the legitimate grounds that the two countries were at war. D'Eon would thus have
to wait to return until the American War of Independence ended in 1783.
But even then, the government was extremely reluctant to see d'Eon leave
the country. Only after d'Eon convinced ministers that his English financial problems were becoming critical, and creditors were about to sell off

his library and papers to raise money, did he receive permission to go. In September 1785, d'Eon left Tonnerre and France for England, where he would remain for the rest of his life.[2]

Of course, his reason for going to England was not purely to resolve financial matters. His decision also represents a distinct preference for one kind of political system over another. In France he had become a political victim of the country's last absolute monarch, living under a kind of house arrest in his hometown. In England, he would be free to reside in the capital and go wherever he pleased. D'Eon projected his own situation onto the very constitutions of the two countries. England was "a country more free than Holland and well worthy of being visited by a man of thought and lover of liberty . . . a liberty established upon a *social contract* between the king and his subjects, or rather, the subjects and the king. . . . Such almost as my friend Jean-Jacques [Rousseau] might wish it, supposing no faults in the king and the subjects, which is impossible on both sides." Echoing a conviction articulated by many French intellectuals since Voltaire had published his *Letters on England* some fifty years earlier, d'Eon maintained that England was the freest and richest country in the world. Indeed, d'Eon understood that England was rich precisely because she was free. "The English regard politics as a function of commerce, and their foreign policy is directed accordingly, while our French leaders, who don't know anything about commerce, regard politics as a great and serious affair." England might not be a perfect state, but it was as good a state as the eighteenth century could produce—at least until the French Revolution.[3]

When the Revolution began in 1789, d'Eon, like so many European observers, believed that France would now become more like England. Consequently, at first no one was more optimistic about the Revolution's potential to transform French political life than d'Eon. Even though he was an aristocrat with old-fashioned values, his own political career had showed him the corrupt and despotic nature of France's absolute monarchy. He knew firsthand that it needed major reforms. He realized that England had created a better, more modern political system which— despite the American rebellion—had shown its superiority to that of France. If France was to regain her honor and lead Europe into the nineteenth century, d'Eon believed, major changes were necessary. And in 1789, the Revolution promised just that: not to topple the monarchy, but to regenerate and purify it. D'Eon called the Abbé Sieyès, architect of the Declaration of the Rights of Man, the "divine French Plato."[4]

D'Eon began to socialize with Londoners and Frenchmen who actively supported the Revolution, seeing in its embrace of constitutional restraints a reincarnation of what the British had achieved a hundred years earlier in their own Glorious Revolution. On the first anniversary of the storming of the Bastille, d'Eon gave British statesman Lord Stanhope a stone from the infamous prison, a precious gift that symbolized freedom. Before 600 celebrants, Stanhope read a statement by d'Eon, praising France's "glorious revolution" for liberating "24 millions of individuals" by recognizing "their inalienable rights as citizens."[5]

A bit later, d'Eon could be found at a dinner party hosted by London radicals in honor of himself and that perennial revolutionary, Thomas Paine. After a few rounds of drinks, one of the most famous of these radicals, the linguist and political activist John Horne Tooke rose to offer a toast in honor of Paine and d'Eon: "I am now in the most extraordinary situation in which ever man was placed. On the left of me sits a gentleman, who, brought up in obscurity, has proved himself the greatest political writer in the world, and has made more noise in it, and excited more attention and obtained more fame, than any man ever did. On the right of me sits a lady, who has been employed in public situations at different courts; who had high rank in the army, was greatly skilled in horsemanship, who has fought several duels, and at the small sword had no equal; who for fifty years past, all Europe has recognized in the character and dress of a gentleman."[6]

Like Paine, who wrote on behalf of the French Revolution and even served in its National Assembly, d'Eon wanted to participate in the rebirth of his beloved country. But now in his sixties, what could the old Chevalière possibly do?[7]

D'Eon saw his chance to participate in the Revolution immediately after France declared war on Austria in April 1792. As had been the case since the 1750s, d'Eon thought of himself as first and foremost a military officer, and despite his advanced years, if his country was at war he wanted to help her. He addressed a letter to the National Assembly, asking for permission to be reinstated into the army, commissioned again as a infantry officer, and given a regiment of Amazonian women that would lead France in glorious battles. On 12 June 1792, his petition was read aloud at an official session of the National Assembly:

"I have passed successively from the state of a girl to that of a boy; from the state of a man to that of a woman. I have experienced all the odd vicissitudes of human life. Soon, I hope, with weapons in my hands, I shall fly on the wings of Liberty and Victory to fight and die for the Nation, the Law, and the King."

The letter was interrupted several times by applause and laughter. It was referred to the Military Committee and ordered to be honorably mentioned in the minutes.[8]

On behalf of the Assembly's Military Committee, Anacharsis Cloots, himself famous for his radical political views, welcomed d'Eon's offer, urging him to return to his country as soon as possible, where the old soldier would fight for France as a new "Joan of Arc, helping us deliver the world from the infernal fire of tyrants." Cloots invited d'Eon to appear before the National Assembly, where "your presence will excite a general enthusiasm and you will attain your request by acclamation." Then Cloots imagined that d'Eon would raise a "phalanx of Amazons who will cut down all oppressors of humanity. Come, and victory will be ours!"[9]

At least one other member of the Military Committee, Lazare Carnot, soon to be known as the "Organizer of the Victory," also encouraged d'Eon's return to military life: "Perhaps you are destined to save your country as another Joan of Arc." The revolutionary Carnot, ever cognizant of social differences, could not help finding an ironic comparison between the two Amazons, however: "Joan of Arc was born a simple shepherdess and was raised to the rank of chevalier, while as for you, Chevalière, the constitution has placed you at the rank of shepherdess, and your misfortunes might have made you regret that you were not born there."[10]

Today scholars emphasize the degree to which the French Revolutionaries tried to exclude women from participation in the new political life of the country. For the Jacobins, a regenerated France was a male France. The historian Dorinda Outram has described the French Revolution as a "contestation between male and female" that tended "to validate the political participation of men and culpabilize that of women."[11] But while women certainly lost ground during the Revolution, Outram's characterization seems exaggerated. Especially during the early years of the Revolution, the possibilities for women in public life seemed hopeful. In this respect, the reactions of Carnot and Cloots were not extraordinary. During the spring and summer of 1792, women armed themselves throughout France, and many, like d'Eon, asked to join the army. For example, the activist Pauline Léon submitted a petition signed by 300 women requesting that women be given the right to bear arms. Professor Susan P. Conner documented more than fifty cases of women who legally enlisted in the French army between 1792 and 1794. One way or another, many women managed to reach the front.[12]

Even after England declared war on France in January 1793, it appears that the French government had been anticipating d'Eon's return warmly enough that they forged a British passport to make his exit from England easier.[13] What prevented d'Eon from returning, then, was not politics but money: he simply could not afford it. Ever since the Revolution began in 1789, d'Eon's annual pension had been suspended. Theoretically, because his pension was for services rendered to the state (as opposed to an honorific noble office), he was entitled to receive it until August 1792, when the monarchy itself was finally abolished. But long before that, d'Eon had stopped receiving any money from the King. The Revolution, after all, had begun as a financial crisis in which the government was bankrupt and could no longer pay its creditors, among whom was d'Eon.[14]

D'Eon, who never saved a cent no matter his income, was not prepared for this catastrophe. By 1791, he had become so poor that when a French friend visited him for one night, she paid him rent for the stay![15] Finally, his creditors became impatient enough that he was forced to put his huge library up for sale. The collection was so large and so valuable that the auctioneer, Christie, published a catalogue "on sale at various London Bookstores for 1 shilling" that included a twenty-page preface about d'Eon's life. A notice of the sale and review of its catalogue appeared in most London papers and even in the Paris *Moniteur*.[16]

But even the sale of his books did not yield enough to cover his debts. From time to time, d'Eon made money by entering fencing tournaments. Even before the Revolution, he had fought in public duels both as a way to make money and to spread his reputation as a gallant Amazon. Evidently there was great interest in these tournaments, and d'Eon became known as the world's best swordswoman. He even fought a famous tournament viewed by the Prince of Wales.[17]

By the mid-1790s, however, d'Eon was approaching seventy, too old to enjoy these tournaments anymore. Still, his need for money sometimes propelled him into the spotlight. In 1796, at a tournament in Southhampton, he was wounded seriously enough to force him to retire from fencing altogether.[18] Indeed, although he would live fourteen years more, he never fully recovered from this injury. Shortly after his last tournament, he moved in with Mrs. Cole, whose husband, a British admiral, had died years earlier. Increasingly, d'Eon's health prevented him from accepting dinner invitations, and besides, he was now too poor to afford a decent wardrobe.

Nonetheless, perhaps d'Eon was lucky that he had not gone to France in 1793. After Louis XVI was put to death, the Revolution became much more radical. During its most intense phase, the year of the Terror (1793–1794), officers like d'Eon with aristocratic blood were routinely purged from the army and often sent to the guillotine. Someone with d'Eon's flair for the dramatic would have had difficulty maintaining a low profile.

Naturally, watching these developments from England caused d'Eon to change his view of the Revolution. Where he had initially respected

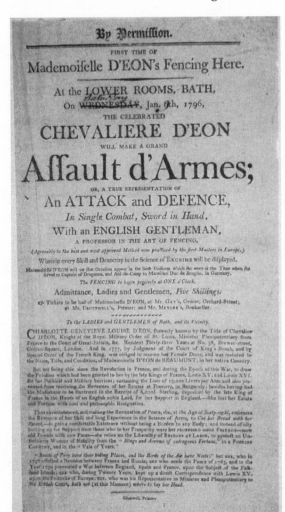

Poster announcing a fencing match featuring d'Eon.
(Courtesy of the Brotherton Collection, University of Leeds Library)

Sieyès and Lafayette, he now had nothing but contempt for the so-called democratic leaders, calling them "the frenzied immoral tyrants like the Marats, the Robespierres, the Dantons, and the other earthly monsters." In d'Eon's view, they had brought no glory to France, only the most senseless violence and killing. Like so many of his day, d'Eon came to see the Revolution in apocalyptic terms:

"If we consider, in a religious as well as a moral view, the events which have taken place in my dear native land and in the rest of the world, it is clear that we are not contemplating a mere political revolution, but the accomplishment of the preordained end of the world, which approaches total destruction, and feels all the visitations of the almighty's wrath. We must consider the wisdom of our great modern *philosophes* as mere madness, worthy of the tenants of Bedlam alone."[19]

Given his poor health, his age, and his worsening poverty, d'Eon spent roughly the last decade of his life inside his apartment, on cold days rarely even leaving his bed. "Today I am 72 years old," d'Eon wrote in 1800. "I am sick, with wounds suffered in war and in peace, subject to exhaustion, from work and other tribulations, and oppressed by the climate of this island, which is neither good for my body nor my soul. For four and one-half years I have not left my bed. From one day to the next I think I am going to die of weakness and misery."

But d'Eon didn't die. He lived for ten more years. And although they were years of misery, they remained exceptionally productive. He had neither money nor a social life, but his intellect was completely intact, so the Chevalière d'Eon spent most of his day writing reflections about his long life. For years, he had been preparing his memoirs, but in his last decade of life they took on a more formal structure. As early as 1778, d'Eon began writing essays about his earlier life for his friend and confidante the Duchesse de Montmorency-Bouteville. There is evidence that in 1786 d'Eon was considering hiring Charles Morande to edit his memoirs into a publishable manuscript.[20] Perhaps this edition was rendered obsolete by the 1793 publication of Louis XV's secret correspondence, which showed d'Eon less a victim of Old Regime cabals and more a participant in the King's Secret.[21]

In 1799, d'Eon seemed almost ready to publish another version of these memoirs.[22] Finally, in 1805, he signed a contract for an autobiography that would be titled *La Pucelle de Tonnerre: Les vicissitudes du chevalier et de la chevalière d'Eon,* to be published in ten volumes by the Richardson brothers of London, nephews of the famous publisher and novelist Samuel Richardson. D'Eon received a £500 advance, which allowed him to live just above poverty. A translator and editor was also hired, Thomas Plummer, who would assist d'Eon and produce an English version. Unlike previous efforts, this was to be a formal autobiography filled with d'Eon's reflections on his own life, clearly modeled after both Augustine and Rousseau's autobiographies.[23]

Despite the contract, the autobiography was never published. Both Plummer and the Richardsons wanted to print the material, but were blocked by d'Eon's stalling. Although only a small portion of his autobiographical writings were in a polished form before his death, this would have constituted at least one important volume. As a Christian, d'Eon might have worried that publishing reflections on his own life was too egotistical, unbecoming for the kind of woman he tried to be. He had criticized Rousseau's *Confessions* because it tended to glorify its author at the expense of God. The only worthy model for an autobiographer was Augustine, who wrote his *Confessions* in the form of a prayer. D'Eon knew he was no Augustine, "a Christian who became the greatest genius of his century and of the church."[24]

A more likely reason that d'Eon prevented publication of his autobiography is that he realized he had not gotten it right. While his writings reveal an honest history of his heart, they portray him as an anatomical female who lived the first half of life as a man, when, obviously, the exact opposite was the truth. D'Eon was writing as a Christian, as a Jansenist disciple of Augustine. Lies to oneself there would and must be. But self-conscious deceit built into the book's very core could have no place in d'Eon's pious outlook.

Consequently, when d'Eon died in 1810 he hadn't published a word of these autobiographical writings. For over a hundred years they remained in private hands, virtually ignored by scholars and biographers. Even after they were sold to the University of Leeds Library during the 1930s, they remained largely forgotten. Nonetheless, these manuscripts reveal a self-consciousness about women and gender that is remarkable for its originality and insight.

Gendered Theology

A T HIS DEATH, d'Eon left behind more than 2,000 pages of manuscripts. Most were drafts of the unfinished autobiography. But some, such as a history of women religious figures who dressed as men, were book-length manuscripts, albeit with obvious autobiographical significance.[1] In these voluminous writings it is often difficult to distinguish between correspondence, essay, fiction, and autobiography, since d'Eon mixed the genres. Some are in a polished shape, while others are simply scraps of paper filled with notes.

It is difficult to generalize about such a disparate group of writings, produced at different times, in different moods, perhaps for different purposes. Nonetheless, some striking patterns can be found throughout the texts. Rhetorically most of these manuscripts roughly imitate the style Saint Augustine used in his own autobiography, the *Confessions*. Many are written in the form of a prayer or epistle as one finds in the Gospels, filled with quotes, references, and allusions to biblical stories. Clearly, d'Eon identified his own life with Augustine's. Born at the end of the Roman Empire, Augustine became a worldly intellectual who searched in vain for the truth until he discovered Christianity relatively late in life. With the help of his mother, Monica, and Ambrose, Bishop of Milan, he went on to become, in d'Eon's words, "one of the greatest minds of the Church."[2] For d'Eon, Augustine's story represented the classic tale of a spiritual journey from sin to virtue.

Just as Augustine lived in the decline and fall of his civilization, so d'Eon lived during the collapse of the Old Regime. And just as Augustine became a prominent university student and intellectual, so d'Eon began his life as a man of letters before moving on to political life. Where Augustine attributed his conversion to the influence of Ambrose and Monica, d'Eon cast Christophe de Beaumont, Archbishop of Paris, in a role similar to Ambrose's, identifying his own mother with Monica. "Follow me," d'Eon reports his mother as saying. "I am planning, like Saint Monica planned with her son Augustine, to convert you to the Christian religion."[3]

D'Eon's use of Augustine was more than literary. His reading of the New Testament was thoroughly Augustinian, or in terms of eighteenth-century France, Jansenist. This meant, first and foremost, seeing human will as depraved and sinful. It also meant believing that since the fall of mankind, all men and women have been tainted with original sin; no one can escape that fundamental fact, at least not without God's help. The Christian certainly cannot shed sin, no matter how righteous his or her behavior on this earth, in this view; the starting point for a Christian is to recognize the fact of his own depravity, and to hope for God's salvation from it. In this sense, "the present life is only a demonstration" of the one to come, d'Eon thought. "The inhabitants of the City of God form an Elite of voluntary soldiers, of an army for Jesus Christ, where they are deservingly called the Elect."[4]

A Christian had to recognize the weakness of his will in order to appreciate his total dependence on God for salvation, d'Eon believed; nothing people do on their own could direct their behavior away from sin. And yet sometimes people don't behave sinfully, d'Eon admitted; sometimes good acts are performed. Therefore, d'Eon interpreted Augustine, good acts were never the achievement of any particular person's will, but rather a manifestation of grace—of God's loving kindness acting in the world.

"All that I know is only by the grace of God," d'Eon wrote. "I am what I am and only His grace guides me not in vain. That which made me what I am has a right to require of me whatever I can be for Him. I have achieved much more than ordinary men and extraordinary women: not that I achieved any of it, but it was the grace of God within me."[5]

Therefore, since anything good that happens is the result of grace, it is incumbent upon Christians to do everything they can to foster the grace of God. D'Eon believed that the whole business of a Christian in this life must be to prepare oneself for receiving God's grace, and having the ability to recognize it when it comes. Such an effort was by no means easy, he thought, because the will was constantly tricking the mind into mistaking it for the true grace of God, but the rewards of everlasting life among "the elect of God" were there for those who could achieve such a pure moral and religious state.[6]

D'Eon followed Augustine, but he was even more a disciple of Saint Paul, whom he quotes far more than any other source. "I have closely followed the teachings of the Gospel and the advice of Saint Paul and Saint Augustine."[7] Many of his manuscript writings can be considered an extended commentary on Paul's letters; indeed, several of d'Eon's religious writings are themselves called "epistles" and take the form of long letters to friends and relatives. Like Augustine, d'Eon identified with the life and thought of Paul, who had also been converted to Christianity rather late in his life. D'Eon was especially influenced by Paul's first letter to the Corinthians, in which the apostle explained his own conversion:

> In the end he appeared even to me. It was like an abnormal birth; I had persecuted the church of God and am therefore inferior to all other apostles—indeed not fit to be called an apostle. However, by God's grace I am what I am, nor has his grace been given to me in vain; on the contrary, in my labors I have outdone them all—not I, indeed, but the grace of God working with me.[8]

Directly after citing this passage, d'Eon wrote about his own life in similar terms:

> In the eyes of men, I am like an aborted fetus. But by the grace of God, I am what I am and the grace given to me has not been in vain. God gives everyone a body as He sees fit. It is engulfed in corruption; it will be reborn incorruptible. It is engulfed in weakness; it will be reborn in strength. It is engulfed in horror; it will be reborn in glory.[9]

While no person is free enough from sin to deserve God's blessing after his death, d'Eon believed, through his grace God bestows love on a few souls, whom he saves from purgatory and damnation. These souls d'Eon called "the congregation of the Elect." Reflecting the Jansenist influences around him, d'Eon's own belief in predestination was unambiguous: "Predestination is an eternal decree of God, who preestablished his predilection for all eternity."[10]

The hope of every Christian, then, is to gain admittance to this congregation. When God makes that decision, the only criteria he uses are a person's faith and moral character. "All differences in a person's condition will disappear at the last Judgment."[11] Whether that person lived as a man or as a woman is of no importance. "Sexual difference is irrelevant for salvation. Thus it is written, 'God has no regard whatsoever for the appearance of persons.'"[12] D'Eon demonstrated this claim with several references to the Bible.[13]

In an "epistle" written to the Duchesse de Montmorency-Bouteville in the style of Paul, d'Eon again insists that "God has no regard for the external appearance of persons," but now supports it with stronger evidence: *"Are we not all children of God by faith in Christ Jesus?"* he asked, paraphrasing Gal. 3:26 and himself underlining the passage for emphasis.[14] Elsewhere d'Eon reiterated what was for him an issue of profound importance: "There is no sexuality whatsoever in the Kingdom of God. Men will not take wives there, nor women husbands. We will serve one another like the angels."[15] At the end of a preface to an 1806 version of his memoirs, he added this important line from Gal. 3:28: "There is no such thing as Jew and Greek, slave and freeman, male and female; for you are all one person in Christ Jesus."[16]

Among religious scholars today, Gal. 3:26–28 remains a subject of intense controversy, especially since Paul seems to make contrary statements about women in other letters. Some scholars believe Paul was merely quoting a baptismal formula, while others claim that the apostle was articulating his own egalitarian convictions. Although our purpose here is not to determine the validity of d'Eon's reading of Paul, it is certainly noteworthy that his analysis seems to anticipate many of the claims made recently by feminist theologians.[17]

Obviously d'Eon interpreted this passage in a literal way, drawing from it a striking view of Paul's egalitarianism. From an understanding of the minimal role that sexual difference will play in God's judgment, d'Eon reached the following conclusion about how gender functions on earth:

> Let us then live the life of children of God, and let us stop simply usurping that name. God makes clear whenever he pleases that he is the master of the heart. He alone can change us; he alone must be glorified for our change; for allowing us to overcome prejudices from birth and habit. Since the [Original] sin, nature is a servant who only engenders infant bodies and sinners. Nature has its strict rules; but God chooses his time for works of grace. Christian liberty consists in renouncing everything that is independent to his true will.[18]

Gal. 3:26–28 gave d'Eon a unique vantage point from which to view the relationship between gender, nature, and God. On the one hand, d'Eon seems to see nature as the opposite of God. The Lord stands outside of nature, which at least since the time of the Fall has been a cruel facilitator of sin. God's grace is a force that corrects the limitations of nature. Likewise, d'Eon places gender squarely within the natural realm. Sexual differentiation may have meaning in the natural world, but it has no importance whatsoever for God. And just as God's grace can deliver us from nature, so for the true Christian, in d'Eon's view, God's grace can and will liberate us from the natural limitations that gender imposes. For d'Eon, the heavenly city does not recognize sexual differentiation.[19]

Gender is given an even lesser role than one would think, because the status of "nature" is also degraded here. When d'Eon tells us that since the Fall, nature has engendered sin, he comes very close to interpreting gender as something merely historical and therefore transitory; that is, he is close to saying that before the Fall, there was no engendering, hence, no sexual differentiation. Such an idea in itself was not new. In Rabbinic commentaries on Genesis, for example, Rabbi Jeremiah ben Leazar believed that Adam was originally created as a hermaphrodite, without any particular gender, and it was only with the creation of Eve and the Fall that humanity was engendered. Such an idea, popular among medieval Jews, seems to be what d'Eon had in mind.[20]

D'Eon was quite familiar with these Jewish sources. In his library were not only Hebrew-language Old Testaments, but various Rabbinic commentaries and texts. D'Eon confessed to the Archbishop of Paris that he had learned enough Hebrew "to be damned with the Jews."[21] And damned he certainly thought they would be. Running throughout the d'Eon manuscripts is a passionate anti-Judaism. D'Eon's studies of Jewish religious texts had firmly convinced him that Jews were the least prepared people to receive the grace of God; consequently, they would be the last people saved. While Christ's message was universal and no one was beyond redemption, the Jews were certainly closest to being hopeless, he thought.

For d'Eon, the central problem with Judaism was that it celebrated the human body. This is best seen in d'Eon's discussion of circumcision, which he firmly opposed for two fundamental reasons: First, it celebrated the marking of human flesh, transforming a bodily operation into a religious ritual, a sign of God's covenant. Jews were thereby denying the sinful nature of flesh, and giving the body rather than the soul entirely too much importance. Second, by marking male flesh alone (that is, signifying male flesh as male), Jews were making sexual differentiation religiously significant, when d'Eon wanted to do precisely the opposite.[22]

On his side, d'Eon drew on Paul's Letter to the Romans, 3:28: "The true Jew is not he who is such in externals, neither is the true circumcision the external mark in the flesh. The true Jew is he who is such inwardly, and the true circumcision is of the heart, directed not by written precepts but by the Spirit; such a man receives his commendation not from men but from God."[23]

Nothing about a person's body could ever be important to a "true Jew," or Christian because, d'Eon steadfastly believed, God has no regard for the outward appearance of a person. God cares only about inward appearance; that is, he is concerned only about the quality of a person's faith. Again, d'Eon quoted from Romans: "Do you suppose God is the God of the Jews alone? Is he not the God of Gentiles also? Certainly, of Gentiles also, if it be true that God is one. And he will therefore justify both the circumcised in virtue of their faith, and the uncircumcised through their faith."[24]

The Jews had once walked with God, but by ignoring their own sins of the flesh, they had wrecked their opportunity to remain God's chosen people. "Grace be rendered to Jesus Christ," d'Eon wrote in another manuscript, "who has delivered us from the servitude of Jewish law, so that we can give all of our care and attention toward purifying our hearts, and to consecrating our heart to God."[25]

Ultimately what so offended d'Eon about Judaism was its refusal to accept a fundamental distinction between the body and the soul. Such a dualism lay at the heart of d'Eon's theology. During the early modern period, the old metaphysical distinction between mind and matter became more rigid and sophisticated, especially after Descartes's writings became part of mainstream European thinking. For Descartes, the mind or soul constituted an independent agency from the body, such that Cartesians tended to believe that animals were organic machines without souls. Descartes's thought had significance for the feminist writers of the Querelle des Femmes. Given the dualism between mind and body, early modern feminists such as Poulain de la Barre claimed that "the mind has no sex," and that, consequently, women and men ought to be regarded as intellectual equals. They therefore contended that all cultural institutions, from schools and colleges to academies and theaters, ought to be open to women.[26]

D'Eon, who owned several books by followers of Poulain de la Barre, was of course very familiar with this kind of Cartesian feminism. He gave it a distinctively religious emphasis, applying the notion that "the mind has no sex" to the Christian problem of salvation. Since the soul had no sex, since God himself knew no sex, d'Eon believed that Christians who were preparing themselves for the next life ought to respect the same kind of androgynous perspective in the life they led.

D'Eon's ideas came dangerously close to the Manichean idea that the body itself was inherently evil and could not have been created by an all-loving and merciful God. But d'Eon remained squarely within orthodox Catholic thinking on this point, never straying from the notion that God had created bodies just as he had created souls.

Thus the question arose, If God created bodies, why did he create different sexes? What purpose could he have had in creating men and women if it wasn't to distinguish them in meaningful ways? D'Eon directly addressed this point:

> But as for my own view, I believe that the intention of the Lord Creator in creating this multiplicity and this diversity of men and women on this earth has been to render them all equal in the eyes of God and his law, in order to glorify him all together, and in order to live as brothers and as sisters, all members of one family, with God himself as the chief of that family, preparing our reward in the heavens that will bring unending happiness.[27]

God made a diverse world, but his intention was always for men and women to live as equals, without regard for sexual differentiation, readying themselves for that time when they would not have to concern themselves with bodies at all. At the very least, this constitutes a remarkable vision that undermines the significance of gender distinctions altogether.

D'Eon did not leave the issue there. Although "the intention of the Lord" was that men and women live as equals on earth as in heaven, men did not live as God intended. They used their physical strength to dominate and exploit women, developing patriarchal institutions that systematically excluded women from positions of status and authority.

"Men," d'Eon argued, "who by their strength and their gallantry seem like lions and tigers, have seized authority, all political positions, all honors, all worldly riches, leaving women only the pain brought by having babies."[28]

Men were not simply sexist, then, they used women to indulge in worldly things. Acquiring political power, military authority, material wealth, honors of one kind or another—this is what virility was all about. "The love of vainglory" lay at the heart of d'Eon's critique of manhood.[29] Consequently, for a Christian a man's sexism was only one manifestation of his turning away from God, indulging in pleasures of the flesh.

In other words, d'Eon believed that the superiority of male strength turned out to be a great moral pitfall for men, insofar as a culture of virility encouraged men to celebrate earthly pleasures gained from their own flesh. While God really wanted both men and women to be equally devoted to his service, men were more likely to turn away from God toward their own selfish pursuits. On a small scrap of paper left behind by d'Eon titled *l'homme*, he reflected on this exceptionally rich and original idea: "God created [woman and man], the one for doing good, the other for doing bad. So long as a man is a man, the earth is his; so long as a woman is a woman, virtue is hers. There is no man without sin; for *every man is a liar, says Scripture.* It is God alone who is naturally perfect. Grace alone makes the virgin perfect."[30]

This statement cannot be construed as a finished philosophical product; it was jotted down as a private note, perhaps representing nothing more than a momentary idea. Nonetheless, when taken together with other parts of the manuscripts, it shows that d'Eon believed men were less virtuous and therefore morally inferior to women. Men were less prepared for God's grace.[31]

In an important sense, d'Eon believed that men were much like Jews. In his view, the central problem regarding the salvation of Jews was their insistence on celebrating the flesh, their refusal to acknowledge that the body was tainted with sin. D'Eon discovered that men are in exactly the same moral position: Politics, warfare, statecraft, honors, and the martial arts are like circumcision in that they make one turn away from God and toward glorifying the physical characteristics of one's own body.

By contrast, the physical weakness of women liberated them from earthly power, allowing them to devote more of their energies toward the promise of salvation. To be sure, d'Eon did not think women were without sin. But he thought them far more ready to acknowledge their moral weaknesses honestly and sincerely, and assume the obligations of a Christian. The relationship between women and men, then, d'Eon saw as much like the relationship between Christians and Jews: Both groups are God's children, loved equally by him, but one group ignores God, turning away from his loving Son, indulging in pleasures of the earth, celebrating the body; so long as men continue to behave virilely, they will never be able to prepare themselves for Christ's redemption. Perhaps this is what d'Eon meant when he confessed to a priest that "my own particular theology is to believe that men will be saved by the grace of God and that women will be saved by the mercy of Our Lord; for having Himself been surrounded by weakness during His mortal life, He was tested like us, with all sorts of temptations, but He was without sin. . . . He was moved by a just compassion for women who sin from ignorance and error."[32]

At first glance, this perplexing remark makes no sense, since a Christian like d'Eon should believe that salvation can come only through Christ, as indeed he proclaims elsewhere. Because he was a virgin who experienced life on earth as a victim of authority, abused by (patriarchal) power, d'Eon thought that Jesus is especially attuned to the condition and experience of women. Men, on the other hand, like Jews, while in desperate need of salvation, are not worthy of a close relationship with Christ and are therefore left to cultivate the more difficult and distant relationship with God, d'Eon theorized.

D'Eon imaginatively confused sacred history with his own biography. Just as the history of the world went from the Old Testament of the Jews to the New Testament of the Christians, so d'Eon's own life was marked by his great transformation from a "bad boy to a good girl."[33] As a boy, he had been raised to enter the army, whose values were those he associated with the Old Testament—a people who conquered a promised land; a wrathful and jealous God who at times stood distant from his people. But as a woman, visiting life in a convent, d'Eon came to know a new sense of religiosity. God was no longer associated with the martial arts but, through Christ, with love. "I marched in fear of God," d'Eon wrote of his former military life. "At present as I wear my dress, I march in the love of Our Lord, and so I have nothing more to fear."[34]

"I have often wondered to myself," d'Eon wrote to the Duchesse de Montmorency-Bouteville, "whether women were aware of their immense advantages and . . . superiority."[35] While originally created equal, and intended to be equal in the next life, d'Eon believed that women thus turn out to be morally superior in the sense that they are closer to Christ than men and better equipped to receive his grace. In short, he claimed that women make better Christians than men. "The character of a Christian girl is the cross."[36] Ironically, it is the physical weakness of women that places them in this elevated position. "Despite their weakness, women are stronger in faith than men, and God loves each one more than all men put together."[37]

D'Eon believed that women were better able to develop emotional bonds and, that unlike men, women do not fight with other women. "I have had no disputes, nor quarrels, nor duels with any woman," he noted. Unlike men, who are always out for themselves and never seem to get beyond their own egos in their relationships, d'Eon believed, solidarity is at the essence of female sociability; women engage in meaningful friendships with one another, such as the one between d'Eon and the Duchesse de Montmorency-Bouteville. "Their state is a mutual reciprocity of parallel things in the end different only by form." Women, in other words, recognize the value of mutuality, friendship, and interdependence, while men are burdened with a solitary and lonely existence; consequently, while men play at politics and fight wars, pious women actually do some good in the world through acts of charity, he believed.[38]

Just as Christians were morally superior to Jews, and women were morally superior to men, so among women there was also a moral hierarchy in imitation of Jesus, in d'Eon's view. Closest to Christ were women who had maintained their virginity, which d'Eon venerated as being closer to godliness than any other human virtue. "The more I reflect upon it," d'Eon mused, "the more I feel that virginity is the greatest gift of virtue from God. For virgins are flowers that ornament the ground of the Church, and the delicious fruits that embellish the garden of heaven. They are the most illustrious part of the army of Jesus Christ, and the company of Mary, Mother of purity itself. O Saint Virginity! Only Paradise deserves to be your Homeland." Virginity is a dignity so grand, so noble, and so perfect that "the son of God would only be born from a virgin, chose a perfect virgin to be his precursor and an apostle virgin to be his oldest disciple, and consecrated virginity in his very being by himself always remaining a virgin."[39]

Virginity, a human's most perfect state, was usually associated with women but could, as Jesus' own example demonstrated, be achieved by a man. Virginity signified the full renunciation of the flesh, the very opposite of circumcision. Instead of marking through circumcision that part of the body that would eventually, by Jewish law, defeat virginity, d'Eon hoped that the body would be left completely unmarked and untouched. Virginity represented the first step toward transcending the body, toward liberating the soul from the constraints of physical needs and desires. Virginity, then, signified a way that people could finally reach beyond gender even before their death.

There is no doubt that d'Eon's ideas here border on Catharism, the medieval heresy that was particularly strong in southern France, Italy, and Spain.[40] Cathars exaggerated the dualism between body and soul, believing that even death was good insofar as it freed a soul from a sinful body. Cathars therefore prayed for a day when they—and all people—would stop reproducing so that all souls could be liberated from bodies and return to heaven. Although d'Eon never went this far, he certainly did make disparaging remarks about marriage. In response to a question from an English friend, Lady Robinson, d'Eon claimed that his mother repeatedly told him that "marriage is an invention of Satan for conserving the race of Rascals on earth."[41]

D'Eon's theology of gender was not intended as an original theological system, but rather, sheds light on his own life, on the reasons he passed across the gender barrier.[42] These ideas, in other words, were theology serving autobiography. To his contemporary readers, d'Eon wanted to explain why a woman who was raised as a man, and lived as a man, would want to change back into a woman. To posterity, d'Eon was sincerely trying to explain why a man might want to live as a woman. No doubt there is also a good bit of self-therapy in these writings: he is trying to explain his own life to himself.

At the heart of the relationship between d'Eon's life and his theological ideas lay his own virginal state. Repeatedly throughout his memoirs, d'Eon reminds his reader that he has always been a virgin. "I am still such as nature made me without consulting me, and by the grace of God I am still that what I am and thanks to me it has not been in vain. It is not because of certain acts that I was found a virgin, but by the circumstances set by the grace of God, who protected it among the Dragoons."[43]

D'Eon emphasized his virginity with such intensity and even pride that although there is no proof, it seems very probable that he was indeed a virgin. If this was the case, then to some extent his autobiography, if not his life itself, can be explained partly as a way of coping with his earlier and unspoken renunciation of sexual behavior. Perhaps it was a reaction to his childhood urinary disorder discussed in chapter 9.

Whatever the case regarding d'Eon's virginity, there can be no doubt that he saw his gender transformation as a religious experience. Becoming a woman offered d'Eon a way to get closer to Jesus, a means of renouncing or at least controlling his virile behavior, and preparing himself for life after death. "My transformation is a miracle due not to the will of men, but to the will of God."[44]

D'Eon repeatedly referred to his own change as being a "conversion from a bad boy into a good girl." As a young man, d'Eon knew that he had extraordinary talents and much good fortune. But where had these led him? "The hopes of a good patriot" had been in vain. As a Christian woman, however, d'Eon could refashion himself according to a model that seemed more pure and just: "The Gospel is the humiliation of men of letters and the elevation and consolation of women with faith in Jesus Christ."[45]

Christian Feminist

WAS D'EON CORRECT in thinking that his approach to Christianity would improve opportunities for women? Or was his image of womanhood itself patriarchal and, as it seemed to celebrate female weakness, potentially misogynist? The question of whether Augustinian Christianity is inherently anti-female is, of course, among the most controversial issues facing feminist theologians today. Professor Rosemary Radford Ruether, who has carefully explored the ways virginity has been venerated in the history of Christianity, has noted that several early Church thinkers, such as Gregory of Nyssa, interpreted Gal. 3:28 in much the same way as d'Eon, as implying a God that was sexless and androgyny as a Christian ideal. But Ruether also notes that these monastic thinkers associated womanhood with weakness, passivity, and intellectual inferiority. Consequently, she argues that however much these early religious thinkers believed they were honoring women through their celebration of virginity, their ideologies were actually "anti-female." Misogyny and the praise of virgins constituted "two sides of a dualistic psychology that stand together."[1]

Other contemporary feminist scholars sharply disagree with Ruether and offer an analysis of early Christian attitudes toward gender that closely parallels d'Eon's own perspective. They show how early Church Fathers such as Gregory Nazianzen, Basil of Caesarea, and Gregory of Nyssa all stressed the genderless quality of God, Christ, and the human soul. According to Verna E. F. Harrison, these early Christian thinkers viewed Jesus' maleness as insignificant and interpreted sexual differentiation as only a biological fact that had the most narrow procreative purpose; the heavenly world was genderless. Like d'Eon, early Christians praised male and female virginity as a way of overcoming the limitations created by gender: "The manliness of the virgin woman," Jo Ann McNamara writes, "was a transcendence of the sexual nature itself." Thus many feminist thinkers today believe that Catholicism's traditional stress on virginity and asceticism may have once served women well as an alternative to more virulent strains of patriarchalism.[2]

D'Eon was very much aware that women constituted one of the most vital aspects of seventeenth- and eighteenth-century French Catholicism. Religious women wrote popular books of piety, ran hospitals and schools, led convents, and organized large works of charity. This was especially true of Jansenist women, who argued that girls should receive an education no less rigorous than boys'. Nor did these religious women isolate themselves. Rather, many lived in the cities and maintained close ties with the ladies of the court and salons. Indeed, the religious communities of early modern France offered women a rare opportunity for cultural freedom and independence from men.[3]

More important, d'Eon's theological ideas about women need to be seen in association with his strong positive feeling toward the concept of Amazonian women. As he perceived them, Christian virgins were in no way distinct from Amazons; he saw them as part of an integrated ideal: "The perfection of a *femme forte* consists in the good use of reason and religion."[4] Again, Joan of Arc represented the embodiment of this ideal. She brought together the pious virgin whose Christian virtue was severely tested in the company of rough men, and the Amazon, the *femme forte*, who put on a soldier's uniform and defended France for her king.

In fact, just as d'Eon hoped that his own "conversion from a bad boy to a good girl" would not be an end to his political career, but merely a way to regenerate and rehabilitate it, so he hoped that in Europe's future more Joans might come forward to take roles of political and military leadership.

Mixed in with his religious thoughts, d'Eon's writings contain observations about women of other cultures, gleaned no doubt from travel literature. These women seemed to have more authority than their European counterparts. For example, he noted approvingly that the Native Americans in Florida educated their girls and boys together, giving them the same tests "on the race track, on the hunt . . . in the lake, in war." The result was that "women there are exceptionally agile." Likewise, d'Eon was very impressed with the Huron women of French Canada, who had so much political power that all deliberations included their full participation. From Gauthier Schouten's seventeenth-century travel account of the East Indies, d'Eon learned that the Emperor of Mataram was protected by a regiment of 6,000 female soldiers. All of these examples provided d'Eon with concrete evidence that his ideas regarding female political behavior, no doubt originally inspired by Querelle des Femmes literature, were not so far-fetched.[5]

D'Eon identified his own life closely with Jean-Jacques Rousseau's, but in fact d'Eon's gender politics are virtually at the opposite pole from his better-known contemporary's. Where Rousseau criticized Augustinian Christianity for developing effeminacy and refinement in men, d'Eon embraced it for similar reasons; where Rousseau was repulsed by masculine women, d'Eon tried to become one.[6]

D'Eon's vision was, then, a feminist one, because he wanted to improve conditions for European women, opening up opportunities for at least those women lucky enough to belong to the upper classes. D'Eon was no democrat, but surely he advocated a special kind of liberation for women. His dreams placed elite women in the highest positions of the Church, government, and the military. Nor was d'Eon a hypocrite or "armchair philosopher" in this respect. By becoming a Christian woman, and by repeatedly attempting to reenter the public sphere, d'Eon himself tried to live out his own imaginative ideas. Indeed, far more than Condorcet, the famous champion of women's rights during the French Revolution, d'Eon deserves to be considered perhaps the most pronounced male feminist in early modern history.

Yet at the same time we admire d'Eon for these creative notions, we must again qualify such praise by recalling that nowhere does he present his feminism in a systematic or polished format. He was forever articulating his religious beliefs and ideas about womanhood as a means of explaining his own behavior. But that behavior inevitably went beyond even d'Eon's understanding. Consequently, his feminist theology as a system is limited by the great strains upon it, such as the tension between the militant Amazon (*femme forte*) and the pious virgin; or between the woman who participates in the public sphere in order to change the world and the woman who enters a convent in order to leave it. No idealizing of Joan of Arc could gloss over these intellectual fault lines. That d'Eon never published his autobiography is itself evidence that he was not satisfied with what he had written. Ultimately, then, what is most significant about d'Eon's autobiographical manuscripts is not the feminist theology, but rather, the way he kept revising them in order to develop a coherent explanation for himself about why he had done something that no other political figure in European history had done before or since.

Notes

ABBREVIATIONS FOR NOTES

ULBC   Papers of d'Eon, Brotherton Collection, University of Leeds Library: 14 boxes of autobiographical material. The material in the first seven boxes is divided into folders; after that the arrangement is much looser. Unless otherwise noted, numbers refer to file and page number; or in the case of Boxes 7–14, box and page numbers.

ULBC-EI   Special Extra-Illustrated Edition of Ernest Alfred Vizetelly, *The True Story of the Chevalier d'Eon*, collected and arranged by A. M. Broadley and Godefroy Mayer, 7 folio vols., 1904, Brotherton Collection, University of Leeds Library

AAE   Archives de Ministère des Affaires Etrangères (Paris), Correspondance politique, Angleterre

AN   Papiers de d'Eon, Archives Nationales (Paris), 277 AP/1, divided into six dossiers, correspondence, and notebooks

BMT   Papiers de d'Eon, Bibliothèque municipale de Tonnerre: 2,184 pieces organized into 19 folders, including family documents, correspondence, and manuscripts of published works.

BL   British Library, Additional Manuscripts
           11339: Letters and account books of d'Eon
           11340 English newspaper accounts of d'Eon
           11341 D'Eon papers and documents
           30877 John Wilkes correspondence

KS   Broglie, Duc de, Albert, *The King's Secret: Being the Correspondence of Louis XV with His Diplomatic Agents from 1752 to 1774*, 2 vols., 2nd ed. (London, n.d.)

CSI   *Correspondance secrète inédite de Louis XV, sur la politique étrangère*, ed. Edgar Boutaric, 2 vols. (Paris, 1866).

CS   *Correspondance secrète du comte de Broglie avec Louis XV, 1756–1774*, ed. Didier Ozanam and Michel Antoine, 2 vols. (Paris, 1959 and 1961).

PROLOGUE: THE DISCOVERY

1. The following account is based on [Thomas Plummer,] *A Short Sketch of Some Remarkable Occurances During the Residence of the Late Chevalier d'Eon in England* (London, 1810), especially 4–5. Plummer worked with d'Eon near the end of his life as a translator and editor of his still unpublished memoirs (see ULBC 30, unpaged note dated 11 May 1805). Evidence for what d'Eon ate during his last years is found in random grocery bills preserved in ULBC-EI. "Livre journal, ULBC Box 10," makes clear on p. 1 that d'Eon and Cole began sharing a home in 1796; but ULBC 38:52 seems to suggest December 1798.

2. "Livre journal."

3. Untitled newspaper obituary, 23 May 1810, in "Collection of Portraits, Views, and Newspaper Clippings (Partly Mounted) on the Chevalier D'Eon," Houghton Library, Harvard University, *fFC7 E0563 ZZX.

INTRODUCTION

1. Geneviève Reynes, *L'Abbé de Choisy ou l'ingénu libertin* (Paris, 1983); Oscar Paul Gilbert, *Men in Women's Guise. Some Historical Instances of Female Impersonation*, trans. Robert B. Douglass (London, 1926); F. Thompson, *Men Who Dress As Women and Women Who Dress As Men* (New York, 1993); Peter Ackroyd, *Dressing Up; Transvestism and Drag: The History of an Obsession* (New York, 1979). Until recently historians thought that the colonial American governor Edward Hyde, Viscount Cornbury, was among the more famous members of this group; but see Patricia U. Bonomi, "Lord Cornbury Redressed: The Governor and the Problem of Portrait," *William and Mary Quarterly*, 3rd Series, 51 (January 1994): 106–18, who shows this case to be a fable.

2. For three examples see Rudolf M. Dekker and Lotte C. Van de Pol, *The Tradition of Female Transvestism in Early Modern Europe* (New York, 1989); John Anson, "The Female Transvestite in Early Monasticism," *Viator* 5 (1974): 1–32; and *Sexual Practices of the Medieval Church*, ed. Vern Bullough and James Brundage (Buffalo, N.Y., 1982), 43.

3. *The Memoirs of Jacques Casanova de Seingalt,* trans. Arthur Machen, 6 vols. (New York, 1959), 2:159.

4. This discussion relies on Arnold I. Davidson, "Sex and the Emergence of Sexuality," *Critical Inquiry* 14 (1987): 16–48; David M. Halperin, "Is There a History of Sexuality?," *History and Theory* 28 (1989): 257–74; and especially on the various later writings of Michel Foucault—in addition to his *History of Sexuality, Volume I,* see especially his introduction to *Herculine Barbin, Being the Recently Discovered Memoirs of a Nineteenth-Century Hermaphrodite,* trans. Richard McDougall (New York, 1980).

5. Alphonse Le Roy, *Recherches sur les habillemens des femmes et des enfans; ou Examen de la manière dont il faut vêtir l'un et l'autre sexe* (Paris, 1772), 233. (D'Eon owned a "handsome edition" of this book; see chapter 33.)

6. In addition to the works mentioned above, see Jeffrey Weeks, *Sexuality and Its Discontents: Meanings, Myths, and Modern Sexualities* (London, 1985), and idem, *Against Nature: Essays on History, Sexuality, and Identity* (London, 1991); David A. Coward, "Attitudes Toward Homosexuality in Eighteenth-Century France," *Journal of European Studies* 10 (1980): 231–55. Randolph Trumbach argues that homosexual identity emerges in eighteenth-century England. See his "Sodomitical Subcultures, Sodomitical Roles and the Gender Revolutions of the Eighteenth Century: The Recent Historiography," in *'Tis Nature's Fault: Unauthorized Sexuality During the Enlightenment,* ed. Robert Purks Maccubbin (Cambridge, 1987), 109–21; and idem, "The Birth of the Queen: Sodomy and the Emergence of Gender Equality in Modern Culture, 1660–1750," in *Hidden from History: Reclaiming the Gay and Lesbian Past,* ed. Martin Bauml Duberman et al. (New York, 1989), 129–34.

7. Joan Kelly, "Early Feminist Theory and the *Querelle des Femmes,* 1400–1789," in *Women, History, and Theory* (Chicago, 1984), 65–109; Pierre-Jean-Georges Cabanis, *On the Relations Between the Physical and Moral Aspects of Man,* trans. Margaret Duggan Saidi, 2 vols. (Baltimore, 1981), 1:219–22.

8. Cynthia Eagle Russett, *Sexual Science: The Victorian Construction of Womanhood* (Cambridge, Mass., 1989).

9. For an introduction to the political opportunities open to elite women during the early modern period, see Natalie Zemon Davis, "Women in Politics," in *A History of Women in the West: III. Renaissance and Enlightenment Paradoxes,* ed. Natalie Zemon Davis and Arlette Farge (Cambridge, Mass., 1993), 167–84. On the reduction of such opportunities after 1789, see Barbara Corrado Pope, "Revolution and Retreat: Upper-Class French Women After 1789," in *Women, War, and Revolution,*

ed. Carol R. Berkin and Clara M. Lovett (New York, 1980), 215–36.

10. Joan B. Landes, *Women and the Public Sphere in the Age of the French Revolution* (Ithaca, N.Y., 1988); Dena Goodman, *The Republic of Letters: A Cultural History of the French Enlightenment* (Ithaca, N.Y., 1994); Jeannette Geffriaud Rosso, *Etudes sur la féminité aux xviie et xviiie siècles* (Pisa, 1984). Montesquieu believed that women had more personal liberty in European monarchies than in any other type of government; see *Spirit of the Laws,* trans. Anne Cohler et al. (1748; Cambridge, reprint 1989), 104.

11. Landes, *Women,* 66–89; Joel Schwartz, *The Sexual Politics of Jean Jacques Rousseau* (Chicago, 1975); and Penny A. Weiss, *Gendered Community: Rousseau, Sex, and Politics* (New York, 1993).

12. Barbara Corrado Pope, "The Influence of Rousseau's Ideology of Domesticity," in *Connecting Spheres: Women in the Western World, 1500 to the Present,* ed. Marilyn J. Boxer and Jean H. Quataert (New York, 1987), 136–45; and Ruth Graham, "Rousseau's Sexism Revolutionized," in *Women in the Eighteenth Century and Other Essays,* ed. Paul Fritz and Richard Morton (Toronto, 1976), 127–39. For one fascinating example of a woman reader who had serious misgivings about Rousseau's portrayal of women, see Mary Trouille, "The Failings of Rousseau's Ideals of Domesticity and Sensibility," *Eighteenth-Century Studies* 24 (1991): 451–83.

13. Landes, *Women,* 169–200; Madelyn Gutwirth, *The Twilight of the Goddesses: Women and Representation in the French Revolutionary Era* (New Brunswick, N.J., 1992); Christine Fauré, *Democracy Without Women: Feminism and the Rise of Liberal Individualism in France,* trans. Claudia Goodman and John Berks (Bloomington, Ind., 1991); Geneviève Fraisse, *Reason's Muse: Sexual Difference and the Birth of Democracy,* trans. Jane Marie Todd (Chicago, 1994); and Erica Rand, "Depoliticizing Women: Female Agency, the French Revolution, and the Art of Boucher and David," *Genders* 7 (1990): 47–68.

14. Lynn Hunt, *The Family Romance of the French Revolution* (Berkeley, Calif., 1992).

15. [Mme Bernier,] *Discours qui a remparté le prix à la société des sciences et des arts du Département du Lot, séante à Montauban le 30 Prairial an XI sur cette question: quel est pour les femmes le genre d'éducation le plus propre à faire le bonheur des hommes en société,* 2nd ed. (Paris, An XII [1804]), 3, 4, 15. Attitudes toward manhood became more restrictive as well. Note what the British agronomist Arthur Young jotted down on a trip to France in 1797 (quoted in Leonore Davidoff and Catherine Hall, *Family Fortunes: Men and Women of the English Middle Class, 1780–1850* [Chicago, 1987], 411): "What is a man good for after his silk breeches and stockings are on, his hat under his arm, and his head well powdered?

Can he botanize in a watered meadow? Can he clamber the rocks to min-
eralize? Can he farm with the peasant and the ploughman? He is in order
for the conversation of ladies which is to be sure . . . an excellent employment; but it is an employment that never relishes better than after a day
spent in active toil and animated pursuit."

16. Montesquieu, *Spirit of the Laws*, 316; Paul Bowles, "John Millar,
the Four Stages Theory, and Women's Position in Society," *History of
Political Economy* 16 (1984): 619–38; Adam Smith, *The Theory of Moral
Sentiments* (1759; Indianapolis, Ind., reprint 1982), 28; and Chris Nyland,
"Adam Smith, Stage Theory, and the Status of Women," *History of Politi-
cal Economy* 25 (1993): 617–40.

17. Colman quoted in Kristina Straub, "The Guilty Pleasures of
Female Theatrical Cross-Dressing and the Autobiography of Charlotte
Charke," in *Body Guards: The Cultural Politics of Gender Ambiguity*, ed.
Julia Epstein and Kristina Straub (New York, 1991), 153; Montesquieu,
Oeuvres complètes, ed. Roger Caillois, 2 vols. (Paris, 1949 and 1951),
2:1234. On his ambivalent attitudes toward female power, see Jeannette
Geffriaud Rosso, *Montesquieu et la féminité* (Pisa, 1977). For a more theo-
retical discussion, see Daniel Gordon, "Philosophy, Sociology, and Gen-
der in the Enlightenment Conception of Public Opinion," and Sarah
Maza's response, in *French Historical Studies* 17 (1992): 889–911 and
935–53; and Lawrence Klein, "Gender, Conversation, and the Public
Sphere in Early Eighteenth-Century England," in *Textualities and Sexualities*, ed. Judith Still and Michael Worton (New York, 1993), 100–15.

18. This, of course, despite what d'Eon himself wrote in "Epître de
Généviève," 1545 (ULBC Box 7): "I arrived either too early or too late for
this world."

19. Havelock Ellis, "Eonism," in *Studies in the Psychology of Sex*, vol. 2
(New York, 1936), 78, 100, 110.

20. Anne Bolin, *In Search of Eve: Transsexual Rites of Passage* (South
Hadley, Mass., 1988); Vern L. Bullough, "Transsexualism in History,"
Archives of Sexual Behavior 4 (1975): 561–71. For challenges to notions of
transsexualism, see Janice G. Raymond, *The Transsexual Empire: The
Making of the She-Male* (Boston, 1979); and Judith Shapiro, "Transsexualism: Reflections on the Persistence of Gender and the Mutability of Sex,"
in *Body Guards*, 248–79. For a transsexual's own criticism of these arguments (and mine), see Sandy Stone, "The *Empire* Strikes Back: A Post-
transsexual Manifesto," also in *Body Guards*, 248–304. For the impact of
Ellis's ideas on later sexology, see Janice Irvine, *Disorders of Desire: Sex and
Gender in Modern American Sexology* (Philadelphia, 1990); and for a sharp
critique of Ellis, see Margaret Jackson, " 'Facts of Life' or the Eroticization

of Women's Heterosexuality," in *The Cultural Construction of Sexuality*, ed. Pat Caplan (London, 1987), 52–81.

21. Jan Morris, *Conundrum* (New York, 1974), 151.

22. Note, for example, John Money and Patricia Tucker's comments about d'Eon in *Sexual Signatures: On Being a Man or a Woman* (Boston, 1975), 29: "He simply could not bring himself to renounce irrevocably either his male or female personality. His history indicates that his male personality, dominant until middle age, gradually gave way to his female personality, but neither could completely eliminate the other. . . . a sort of Dr. Jekyll and Miss Hyde alternation, each with its own name and personality." For a more theoretical statement of Money's influential view, see "Gender: History, Theory and Usage of the Term in Sexology and Its Relationship to Nature/Nurture," *Journal of Sex and Marital Therapy* 11 (1985): 71–79. For d'Eon biographies written from this viewpoint, see especially André Frank, *D'Eon: Chevalier et Chevalière: Sa confession inédite* (Paris, 1953); and Eugène Boysède, *Considerations sur la bisexualité, les infirmités sexuelles, les changements de sexe et le Chevalier-Chevalière d'Eon* (Paris, 1959).

23. The American Psychiatric Association (*DSM-III* [Washington, D.C., 1980], 269) defines transvestism as "the recurrent and persistent cross-dressing by a heterosexual male that during at least the initial phase of the illness is for the purpose of sexual excitement."

24. *Gender Dysphoria: Development, Research, Management*, ed. Betty W. Steiner (New York, 1985).

25. If d'Eon's views resemble those of any of today's gender theorists, they perhaps come closest to Carolyn Heilbrun's views on androgyny: "I believe that our future salvation lies in a movement away from sexual polarization, and the prison of gender, toward a world in which individual roles and the modes of personal behavior can be freely chosen." *Toward a Recognition of Androgyny* (New York, 1973), cx.

CHAPTER 1: MAIDEN VOYAGE

1. D'Eon to Lautern, 14 Aug. 1777, BL 11339:225. The weather is described on the frontispiece to *Gentleman's Magazine,* July 1778.

2. *Annales politiques, civiles, et littéraires du dix-huitième siècle* 1, no. 7 (1777):383.

3. *Annual Register* (London, 1781), "Characters," p. 29.

4. These events are described in closer detail in part IV.

5. ULBC 7:56.

6. ULBC 4:1521.

7. Paul Hoffmann, *La femme dans la pensée des Lumières* (Paris, 1977);

see also Denise Riley, *"Am I That Name?": Feminism and the Category of "Women" in History* (Minneapolis, 1988).

CHAPTER 2: FOREIGN MINISTER VERGENNES

1. Letters from "WRT" to Vergennes, AAE Supplement 17:38–42.
2. "Histoire des femmes-hommes . . . ," 16, ULBC Box 8. On Mme Louise, see Michel Antoine, *Louis XV* (Paris, 1989), 889–91. D'Eon described Mme Louise in these terms: "If I was once an evil Captain of Dragoons, Mme Louise of France is the model of purity and saintliness" (ULBC Box 7, 1653).
3. The account of this incident that follows is based on ULBC 1, chap. 3, 5–13. See also 28:233. A slightly different version appeared in Paul Fromageot, "La Chevalière d'Eon à Versailles," *Carnet historique et littéraire* (1901): 259–64.
4. Horace Walpole, *Correspondence,* ed. W. S. Lewis, 48 vols. (New Haven, Conn., 1932–83), 6:474.
5. Baron Friedrich Melchior von Grimm, *Correspondance littéraire* 12 (October 1777) :6. See also A. J. B. A. d'Origny, *Annales du Théâtre italien depuis son origine jusqu'à ce jour,* 3 vols. (Paris, 1788), 2:115.
6. See especially Guy Chaussinand-Nogaret, *The Nobility of Eighteenth-Century France,* trans. William Doyle (Cambridge, 1985).
7. Simon Schama, *Citizens: A Chronicle of the French Revolution* (New York, 1989), 184–94.
8. On Vergennes see Orville T. Murphy, *Charles Gravier, Comte de Vergennes: French Diplomacy in the Age of Revolution 1719–1787* (Albany, N.Y., 1982).
9. ULBC 19:10
10. ULBC 1, chap. 3, p. 15; copy of the King's 27 Aug. 1777 order in AAE Supplement 17:45.
11. "Extraits pour la vie de Mlle D'Eon en 1777 et 1778. Son retour en France," ULBC 2, p. 111; and ULBC 46:1659.
12. ULBC 1, chap. 3, p. 16.
13. Ibid., pp. 16–17.

CHAPTER 3: TONNERRE

1. *Correspondance secrète sur Louis XVI, Marie-Antoinette, la cour et la ville de 1777 à 1792,* ed. M. de Lescure, 2 vols. (Paris, 1866), 1:94–95.
2. "Préface général de l'éditeur de Paris, qui en 1798 . . . ," ULBC, Box 7, p. 59.
3. D'Eon to Vergennes, 29 Aug. 1777 (copy), AAE Supplement 17:49–50.

4. ULBC 1, chap. 4.

5. D'Eon's characterization of his mother reminds one of the orthodox heroines during the reign of Louis XIV noted for their religious piety. Their memoirs were popular during d'Eon's era. For one example, owned by d'Eon, see *Lettres de la Madame la Duchesse de la Vallière, morte religieuse carmelite . . .* (Liège and Paris, 1767).

6. ULBC 21:808 (original in English).

7. For one analysis of how a similar parade reflected this fluid social structure, see Robert Darnton, "A Bourgeois Puts His House in Order," *The Great Cat Massacre and Other Episodes in French Cultural History* (New York, 1984), 107–43.

8. This section is based on ULBC 1, chap. 5.

9. ULBC 21:809.

10. ULBC 1, chap. 4, pp. 4–8.

11. Bertier to d'Eon, 12 Oct. 1777 (copy), AAE Supplement 17:51.

CHAPTER 4: D'EON'S PATRONS

1. Sharon Kettering, *Patrons, Brokers, and Clients in Seventeenth-Century France* (Oxford, Eng., 1986); Kristen B. Neuschel, *Word of Honor: Interpreting Noble Culture in Sixteenth-Century France* (Ithaca, N.Y., 1989).

2. Quoted in Gordon S. Wood, *The Radicalism of the American Revolution* (New York, 1993), 175–76.

3. ULBC 1, chap. 6, p. 3.

4. Ibid.

5. ULBC 1, chap. 4, p. 7 (extract in d'Eon's hand).

6. ULBC 40:12.

7. ULBC 1, chap. 1; 5:17.

8. The visit is described in ULBC 1, chap. 6, pp. 5–6.

9. D'Eon to Maurepas, 19 Oct. 1777 (copy), ULBC 1, chap. 6, p. 6.

CHAPTER 5: ROSE BERTIN

1. Pierre de Nouvion and Emile Liez, *Un ministre des modes sous Louis XVI: Mademoiselle Bertin, Marchande des modes de la Reine, 1747–1813* (Paris, 1891), 43–48; see also random bills in ULBC-EL.

2. Emile Langlade, *Rose Bertin, The Creator of Fashion at the Court of Marie Antoinette*, trans. Angelo S. Rappoport (New York, 1913).

3. AAE Supplement 17:49–55.

4. ULBC 1, chap. 7, pp. 1–3.

5. This section is based on ULBC 1, chap. 8, pp. 1–12.

6. ULBC 1, chap. 9, p. 1.

7. ULBC 1, chap. 7, p. 7.

8. ULBC 6:23.

9. Quoted by d'Eon in ULBC 2:113.

10. ULBC 7:61; and 6:202, where d'Eon says: "It was in the house of Mesdames and Mademoiselles Genet that I learned to respect the decency of a woman at court," an opinion he himself reverses in ULBC 1, chap. 1. See also Rough Notes II, ULBC Box 8, 618–24.

11. Rough Notes II, ULBC Box 8, 833.

12. ULBC 18:263–64; 42:1222.

13. Rough Notes II, ULBC Box 8, 850–53.

14. D'Eon to Mme Montmorency-Bouteville, 18 Nov. 1777 (copy), ULBC 46:1656–60.

CHAPTER 6: MARIE-ANTOINETTE

1. *L'Espion anglais* vol. 8 (London, 1784), 23, says the meeting took place on 23 Nov., but Letter 48 in *Correspondance secrète sur Louis XVI, Marie-Antoinette, la cour et la ville de 1777 à 1792,* ed. M. de Lescure, 2 vols. (Paris, 1866), 1:115 indicates that it happened before 17 Nov.

2. This conversation was recorded by d'Eon in ULBC 26:52–57.

3. On the common tendency for eighteenth-century aristocratic men to cry, see Anne Vincent-Buffault, *A History of Tears: Sensibility and Sentimentality in France,* trans. Teresa Bridgeman (New York, 1991), 15–46.

CHAPTER 7: FRANKLIN AND VOLTAIRE

1. For one example, see d'Eon's letter to the well-known lawyer Falconnet in the Folger Shakespeare Library, Washington, D.C.

2. David Schoenbrun, *Triumph in Paris: The Exploits of Benjamin Franklin* (New York, 1976), 95. See also Anne-Claude Lopez, *Mon Cher Papa: Franklin and the Ladies of Paris* (New Haven, Conn., 1966).

3. D'Eon to Franklin, 24 Jan. 1778, in *The Papers of Benjamin Franklin, Vol. 25, October 1, 1777, through February 28, 1778,* ed. William B. Willcox (New Haven, Conn., 1986), 515. On d'Eon's interest in the American revolution, see also AN 1:3.

4. [Delauney,] *Histoire d'un pou françois, ou l'espion d'une nouvelle espèce, tant en France, qu'en Angleterre . . .* , 4th ed. (n.p., n.d.), translated as *History of a French Louse; or The Spy of a New Species in France and England . . .* (n.p., n.d.). The quotes cited in this section come from pp. 13–14 and 20.

5. Voltaire to d'Argental, 5 March 1777, in *The Complete Works of Voltaire,* ed. Theodore Besterman, 135 vols. (Oxford, 1970–77), 128:199; on Amazons see Abbey Wettan Kleinbaum, *The War Against the Amazons* (New York, 1983).

6. George Keate to Voltaire, 15 Aug. 1777, *Complete Works,* 128:339–41.

7. Voltaire to D'Eon, 16 Sept. 1777, *Complete Works,* 129:24.

8. Louis Petit de Bachaumont, quoted in Edna Nixon, *Royal Spy: The Strange Case of the Chevalier d'Eon* (New York, 1965), 205; see also ULBC 1, chap. 3, p. 7, and chap. 7, p. 1.

CHAPTER 8: PUBLIC PERCEPTIONS

1. "Sur La Chevalière d'Eon," *L'Espion anglais,* 4 Jan. 1778, reprinted in *L'Espion anglais* vol. 8 (London, 1783), 26.

2. Ibid., 23–24.

3. Penny Storm, *Functions of Dress: Tool of Culture and the Individual* (Englewood Cliffs, N. J., 1987), 44.

4. ULBC 2:13 (original written in English).

5. *British Martial: Or an Anthology of English Epigrams* (London, 1806), 90.

6. ULBC, file without number titled "Important d'Eon Papers."

7. "Chanson sur le Chevalier D'Eon," *L'Espion anglais,* vol. 8 (London, 1783), 28–30. Here I cite three of the seven verses.

CHAPTER 9: D'EON ON D'EON

1. Mme du Deffand to the Duchesse de Choiseul, 3 Dec. 1777, in *Correspondance complète de Mme du Deffand avec la Duchesse de Choiseul...,* ed. M. le Mis. de Sainte-Aulaire, 3 vols. (Paris, 1877), 3:311.

2. For examples of such requests, see the Duchesse de Montmorency-Bouteville to d'Eon April 1779 (copy), in ULBC 45:486–88, and d'Eon's response to Lady Robinson in ULBC 36:23ff.

3. La Fortelle, *La Vie militaire, politique, et privée de Mademoiselle d'Eon* (Paris, 1779). At least two editions exist. An abbreviated Italian translation, *La vita militare, politica, e privata della Signora d'Eon ... scoperto femmina l'anno 1770,* was published in Venice during the same year. The Library of Congress has a very rare copy of a 1787 Russian translation.

4. On the importance of self-fashioning for early modern aristocrats, see Stephen Jay Greenblatt, *Renaissance Self-Fashioning: From More to Shakespeare* (Chicago, 1980); and more specifically applied to gender issues, idem, "Fiction and Friction," in *Shakespearean Negotiations* (Berkeley, Calif., 1988), 66–93.

5. D'Eon's account of his father and childhood is found in ULBC 1, chap. 1, pp. 1–10, 2:2–11, 21–24. See also La Fortelle, *La Vie militaire,* 9–10.

6. Marguerite (1724–1788) remained close to her mother and to

d'Eon throughout her life, although, according to d'Eon (ULBC 2:16–18), she resented d'Eon's accomplishments, especially his military career. In 1757 she married the Irish nobleman Thomas O'Gorman. They had two sons. D'Eon notes (ULBC 2:6) that his brother was baptized on 4 Feb. 1727, as Théodore-Andre-Thimothée-Louis-César d'Eon de Beaumont. He died on 6 Aug.

7. ULBC 2:6.

8. ULBC 2:8; ULBC 1:1.

9. ULBC 1:2.

10. ULBC 2:22. *Fourreau,* defined in *The Concise Oxford French Dictionary* as a "tight-fitting dress or underdress," is a curious word here; it is not clear precisely what it means. Antoine Furetière's seventeenth-century dictionary, *Le dictionnaire universel* (Paris, [1690] 1978), defines it as "ce qui sert à couvrir, à envelopper, à conserver quelque chose . . . en fait d'habits, des *fourreaux* de manches, des *fourreaux* d'enfans, pour empêcher qu'ils ne gastent leurs habits." This story about a urinary illness is found only in this one version, and is omitted in the more polished version found in ULBC 1.

11. ULBC 4:2–3.

CHAPTER 10: THE HOPES OF A GOOD PATRIOT

1. The first bit of direct evidence of d'Eon claiming that his parents gave birth to a biological girl and raised her as a boy comes from an attorney who made this claim on d'Eon's behalf in a court of law in August 1779. On the case see the *Gazette des tribunaux* 8, no. 38 (1779): 180–83.

2. Rudolf M. Dekker and Lotte C. Van de Pol, *The Tradition of Female Transvestism in Early Modern Europe* (New York, 1989), 1–2.

3. ULBC 20:4.

4. Ross Hutchinson, *Locke in France, 1688–1734* (Oxford, 1991).

5. ULBC 1, chap. 1, p. 2.

6. ULBC 48:117. See also Joel Schwartz, *The Sexual Politics of Jean-Jacques Rousseau* (Chicago, 1975).

7. D'Eon's baptismal record, describing him as the "son of noble Louis d'Eon de Beaumont," is fully reproduced in Pierre Pinsseau, *L'Etrange Destinée du chevalier d'Eon, 1728–1810,* 2nd ed. (Paris, 1945), 18n; for a photograph of it, see Michel de Decker, *Madame le chevalier d'Eon* (Paris, 1987), 94–95.

8. Letters from Turquet de Mayenne to d'Eon, 23 Sept. 1755 and 17 Jan. 1756, BMT C4 and C5.

9. BMT E3.

10. *Essai historique sur les différentes situations de la France, par rapport*

aux finances sous le regne de Louis XIV et la régence du duc d'Orléans (Amsterdam, 1753). "There is a young man called Déon," Elie Fréron, editor of the influential journal *L'Année littéraire,* wrote to a friend in 1753, "who is working on a book about finances. Ballard is printing it. This young man is handsome enough. He is thin and is about twenty-four or twenty-five years old." Cited in *Le dussier Fréron: Correspondances et documents,* ed. Jean Balcou (Paris, 1975).

11. "Les Espérances d'un bon patriote," *L'Année littéraire* 6 (1759): 55–67; this quote from p. 57. D'Eon's ideas fit what Keith Michael Baker has identified as an "administrative" model for reforming France. See "French Political Thought at the Accession of Louis XVI," *Journal of Modern History* 50 (1978): 302.

CHAPTER 11: LOUIS XV'S DIPLOMACY

1. Broglie, "Mémoires sur la politique étrangère" (1773), in CSI 1:455.

2. Montesquieu, *Spirit of the Laws,* trans. Anne Cohler et al. (Cambridge, 1989), 132; Frederick the Great, "Considerations sur l'état present du corps politique de l'Europe," *Oeuvres* (Berlin, 1846–56), 8:15.

3. M. S. Anderson, "Eighteenth-Century Theories of the Balance of Power," in *Studies in Diplomatic History* (New York, 1970), 183–99; Jeremy Black, "The Theory of the Balance of Power in the First Half of the Eighteenth Century: A Note on the Sources," *Review of International Studies* 9 (1983): 55–61.

4. Jeremy Black, *The Collapse of the Anglo-French Alliance 1727–1731* (New York, 1987); idem, *Natural and Necessary Enemies: Anglo-French Relations in the Eighteenth Century* (London, 1986).

5. Thomas Carlyle, *The French Revolution: A History,* ed. K. J. Fielding and David Sorenson (1837; reprint Oxford, 1989), 25.

6. *Les Fastes de Louis XV* (Villefranche, 1782), part 1, 98.

7. Stéphanie Felicité de Genlis, *Memoirs of the Countesse de Genlis* (New York, 1825), 164–66.

8. G. Capon and R. Yve-plessis, *Vie privée de la Prince de Conty, Louis-François de Bourbon (1717–1776)* (Paris, 1907).

9. Cited in Norman Davies, *God's Playground: A History of Poland,* 2 vols. (Oxford, 1981), 1:347.

10. In 1725 Louis XV had married Marie Leszczynski, the daughter of yet another candidate to the Polish throne. And in 1732 France had gone to war with Russia and Saxony to preserve Poland for her father, Stanislas Leszczynski. The result was a defeat in which Stanislas

Leszczynski had to abdicate the throne and was given the Duchy of Lorraine in compensation. France quickly abandoned any pretensions of landing Leszczynski on the throne, and began to influence Polish events through the Saxon dynasty instead of against them. In 1747 the daughter of the Saxon king married the Dauphin. See H. M. Scott, "France and the Polish Throne," *Slavonic and East European Revue* 53 (1975): 370–88.

11. These well-known details are covered in KS and in Gilles Perrault, *Le Secret du Roi. Tome I. La passion polonaise* (Paris, 1992).

CHAPTER 12: THE KING'S SECRET

1. *Politique de tous les cabinets de l'Europe, pendant les règnes de Louis XV et de Louis XVI; contenant des pièces authentiques sur la correspondance secrète de comte de Broglie . . .* , 3 vols. (Paris, 1793).

2. Cited in KS 1:29–30 from CSI 1:195.

3. Quoted in KS 1:59.

4. A similar conclusion about the Secret, based on other material, is made by Rohan Butler, "Paradiplomacy," in *Studies in Diplomatic History and Historiography,* ed. A. O. Sarkissian (London, 1961), 12–25.

CHAPTER 13: CONTI AND RUSSIA

1. H. M. Scott, "Russia as a European Great Power," in *Russia in the Age of Enlightenment,* ed. Roger Bartlett (New York, 1990), 7–39; Michel Antoine and Didier Ozanam, "Le Secret du roi et la Russie jusqu'à la mort de la czarine Elisabeth en 1762," *Annuaire-Bulletin de la Société de l'histoire de France,* 1954–55, 69–93.

2. D'Eon describes Douglas in ULBC 5:3–4.

3. CSI 1:203–207.

4. For one example, see "Memoirs of the Life of Mademoiselle La Chevelière d'Eon," *European Magazine and London Review* 19 (March 1791): 163–66, which d'Eon clipped and saved, in ULBC Box 12, large leather notebook, 49.

5. The following account is drawn from "Mémoires historiques et secrètes contenant le récit abrégé de mes trois voyages à la cour de russie," ULBC 5:1–19 and 1169–71. For other versions, see ULBC 1, chap. 1, p. 13, and 20:18ff.

6. ULBC 5:8.

7. ULBC 5:10.

8. This account is based on ULBC 5:1–19.

9. See ULBC 6:39 for a slightly different version.

10. Here I shift to ULBC 5:1169–71.

11. ULBC 6:50.

12. ULBC 6:47.
13. ULBC 6:56–57.
14. ULBC 6:66–68.

CHAPTER 14: THE RUSSIAN MYTH REEXAMINED

1. Marsha Keith Schuchard, "Blake's 'Mr. Femality': Freemasonry, Espionage, and the Double-Sexed," in *Studies in Eighteenth-Century Culture*, vol. 22, ed. Patricia B. Craddock and Carla H. Hay (East Lansing, Mich., 1992), 55. For other biographers' belief in his story, see, for example, Michel de Decker, *Madame le Chevalier d'Eon* (Paris, 1987), 43–53; Edna Nixon, *Royal Spy: The Strange Case of the Chevalier D'Eon* (New York, 1965), 39–52; and Pierre Pinsseau, *L'Etrange Destinée du chevalier d'Eon 1728–1810*, 2nd ed. (Paris, 1945), 25–29.

2. See chapter 44 for an extended discussion of this interpretation. During earlier secret reminiscences of the Russian trip, probably written in the 1760s, d'Eon never mentions cross-dressing or the story about becoming the Empress's tutor. See AAE Supplement 16 and 17, and BMT O2.

3. See chapter 47 on d'Eon's efforts to join the French army in America.

4. *The Memoirs of Jacques Casanova de Seingalt*, trans. Arthur Machen, 6 vols. (New York, 1959), 2:159; and the memoir heard "from Mademoiselle d'Eon herself," in the Abbé Georgel, *Mémoires pour servir à l'histoire des événemens de la fin du dix-huitième siècle . . .*, 6 vols., 2nd ed. (Paris, 1820), 1:290.

5. Tercier to d'Eon, 2 July 1756, in BMT D2.

6. D'Eon to Tercier, 24 July–13 Aug. 1756, Bibliothèque Nationale, NAF 23975, pp. 66–68.

7. R. Nisbet Bain, *The Daughter of Peter the Great* (New York, [1899] 1970), 139.

8. J. T. Alexander, "Favoritism and Female Rule in Russia, 1725–1796," in *Russia in the Age of Enlightenment . . .*, ed. Roger Bartlett and Janet Hartley (New York, 1990), 106–24.

9. *The Memoirs of Catherine the Great*, ed. Dominique Maroger, trans. Moura Budberg (London, 1955), 78–79, 185–86.

10. Ibid., 358–59.

CHAPTER 15: DIPLOMACY IN RUSSIA

1. Michel de Decker, *Madame le chevalier d'Eon* (Paris, 1987), 67–68.

2. Michel Antoine, *Louis XV* (Paris, 1989), 684–85.

3. John Woodbridge, *Revolt in Prerevolutionary France: The Prince de Conti's Conspiracy Against Louis XV, 1755–1757* (Baltimore, 1995). See

also Louis XV to Tercier, 21 Sept. 1757, quoted in L. Jay Oliva, *Misalliance: A Study of French Policy in Russia during the Seven Years' War* (New York, 1964) 52–53; and CSI 1:212–13, 224.

4. Woodbridge, *Revolt.*

5. L'Hôpital to Bernis, 18 Nov. 1757, quoted in Oliva, *Misalliance,* 99; 101.

6. Broglie to Louis XV, 2 Dec. 1757, in CS 1:43–44; quoted in Oliva, *Misalliance,* 102.

7. ULBC 6:30, 196.

8. Louis XV to Broglie, 3 March 1758, in CSI 1:237: "I don't believe like you that the Duc de Choiseul has any knowledge of the Secret."

9. Didier Ozanam, "La Disgrâce d'un premier commis: Tercier et l'affaire *de l'esprit* (1758–1759)," *Bibliothèque de l'Ecole des Chartres,* 113 (1955):140–70.

10. D'Eon to Vergennes, 28 May 1776, BMT R23 (copy), in CSI 1:232–33n. The *Gazette d'Utrecht,* 27 May 1757, p. 3, reported that Elizabeth gave d'Eon a gift of 500 ducats.

11. Broglie to Louis XV, 1 Feb. 1762, in CS 1:138.

12. "Epître de Mademoiselle d'Eon . . . 1 juin 1805," 50, ULBC Box 8.

13. Woodbridge, *Revolt.*

14. *The Chinese Spy,* 2:20.

CHAPTER 16: DRAGOON CAPTAIN

1. Pierre Pinsseau, *L'Etrange destinée du chevalier d'Eon, 1728–1810,* 2nd ed. (Paris, 1945), 44–50. Established by Louis XIV, the Dragoons were designed to attack or defend a post with precision and speed, usually going ahead of the infantry on dangerous assignments. They needed to be lighter, quicker, and smarter than either their own forces behind them or the enemy in their midst. See Lucien Mouillard, *Les régiments sous Louis XV . . .* (Paris, 1882), 81–85.

2. Richard Waddington, *La Guerre de Sept Ans,* 5 vols. (Paris, 1899–1915), 5:120ff.

3. Broglie to Louis XV, 18 Sept. 1761, in CS 1:128–32.

4. Waddington, *La Guerre,* 5:147.

5. Quoted in Pinsseau, *L'Etrange destinée,* 50.

6. Louis XV to Tercier, 19 June 1762, in CSI 1:275.

7. James C. Riley, *The Seven Years' War and the Old Regime in France: The Economic and Financial Toll* (Princeton, N.J., 1986).

8. CS 1:141n; and Louis XV to Tercier, 31 Aug. 1762, in CSI 1:278.

9. Louis XV to Breteuil, 10 Sept. 1762, in CSI 1:283.

CHAPTER 17: MAKING PEACE

1. Zenab Esmat Rashed, *The Peace of Paris, 1763* (Liverpool, 1951), 189.

2. Ibid., 194.

3. Emile Blampignon, *Le duc de Nivernais* . . . (Paris, 1888); Lucien Perry, *La fin du xviiie siècle: Le duc de Nivernais*, 2nd ed. (Paris, 1891).

4. D'Eon, *Lettres, mémoires, et négociations* (London, 1764), three parts in one volume, 1:101. This translation from KS 2:94.

5. Nivernais to the Duc de Choiseul, 2 Oct. 1762, quoted in d'Eon, *Lettres, mémoires* 2:2; Nivernais to Mme d'Eon, 31 March 1763 (copy), in ULBC Box 7, 1385.

6. *London Chronicle*, 24–26 Feb. 1763, 193.

7. Nivernais to Praslin, 7 March 1763, in AAE 450:39–41 and 235. On d'Eon's appointment, see also Nivernais to Praslin, 11 April 1763, and d'Eon to Praslin, 24 April 1763, both in AAE 450:235 and 308; and BMT G167.

8. Mme d'Eon to Nivernais, 24 March 1763 (copy), in ULBC Box 7, 1379.

9. Choiseul quoted in Rashed, *Peace of Paris*, 186. Louis XV to Tercier, 26 Feb. 1763, in CSI 1:288–89. Pompadour to Nivernais, 22 Oct. 1762, in Blampignon, *Nivernais*, 133.

10. Lord Shelborne quoted in Rashed, *Peace of Paris*, 204. Many in the French government blamed the defeat at least partially on France's new alliance with Austria. "Europe became accustomed to regard France as a secondary power in international relations," the Comte de Broglie wrote in 1773. "In short, as a body who took its orders from Austria." See his "Mémoires sur la politique étrangère," in CSI 1:450.

11. "Letter from a French Gentleman on the Late Peace," *London Chronicle*, 10–13 Sept. 1763, 252.

CHAPTER 18: THE SECRET IN ENGLAND

1. Broglie to the diplomat François-Michel Durand, 19 Feb. 1763, AAE, Mémoires et Documents, 538:186. Broglie to d'Eon, 8 Feb. 1763, in AAE Supplement 16:19.

2. Broglie to Durand, 19 Feb. 1763, cited in AAE, Mémoires et Documents, Angleterre, 59.

3. Ibid.

4. Louis XV to Durand, 26 June 1763, CSI 1:295–96.

5. Louis XV to Broglie, 7 April 1763, CSI 1:291. See also Louis XV to La Rozière, 7 April 1763, CS 1:152–53n. Durand was one of d'Eon's closest colleagues in the Secret. A career diplomat since 1748, he had

served ambassadors in various courts, including Poland from 1755 to 1760, where he had been brought into the Secret and worked for Broglie. In 1762 he too was appointed to Nivernais's negotiating team. When he returned to France he worked in the Foreign Ministry until 1772, although he returned to England as Plenipotentiary Minister twice during the 1760s.

6. Praslin to Nivernais, 26 March 1763, and Nivernais to Praslin, 31 March 1763, AAE 450:140 and 171. Despite the promotion in rank, for the next few years the correspondence between the King and members of the Secret still referred to "Sieur d'Eon."

7. D'Eon to Praslin, 21 and 28 April 1763, AAE 450:280 and 318; *Gazette d'Utrecht*, 31 May 1763.

8. Broglie to d'Eon, 17 May 1763, in Jacques de Broglie, *Le Vainqueur de Bergen et le Secret du Roi* (Paris, 1957), 201–2. See also Broglie to d'Eon, 19 March 1763, extracted in AAE, Mémoires et Documents, Angleterre, 59ff.

9. Broglie to d'Eon, 3 June 1763, AAE Supplement 16:58; Louis XV to d'Eon, 3 June 1763, CSI 1:293–94; for slightly different versions see AAE Supplement 16:60 and Mémoires et Documents, 538:195.

CHAPTER 19: REVERSAL OF FORTUNE

1. On the prisoner issue, see Pierre Coquelle, "Le comte de Guerchy, ambassadeur de France à Londres (1763–1767)," *Revue des études historiques* 74 (1908): 437–38.

2. AAE Supplement 16:64; Roger Soltau, "Le Chevalier d'Eon et les relations diplomatiques de la France et de l'Angleterre au lendemain du traité de Paris (1763)," in *Mélanges d'histoires offerts à Charles Bémont* (Paris, 1913), 658–60.

3. AAE 451:34–47. Modern diplomatic historians as well have been impressed by d'Eon's analysis of British politics; see Soltau, "Le Chevalier d'Eon," 660–64.

4. Pierre Coquelle, "Le Chevalier d'Eon, ministre à London," *Bulletin historique et philosophique* (1908): 217; "Mémoire pour servir d'instruction au Sieur comte de Guerchy . . . 3 October 1763," in *Recueil des instructions aux ambassadeurs et ministres de France. XXV-2. Angleterre. Tome 3 (1698–1791)*, ed. Paul Vaucher (Paris, 1965), 416.

5. Horace Walpole, *Correspondence*, ed. W. S. Lewis, 48 vols. (New Haven, Conn., 1932–83), 10:70.

6. D'Eon de Mouloize to his father, 24 June 1763, AN 6:17.

7. ULBC 2:12. Indeed, even in d'Eon's own lifetime his own name and Tonnereois wine became linked. "Tonnerre is an ancient town of

France in the Department of Yonne and late province of Burgundy," reads one geographical dictionary from 1795 (Richard Brookes, *The General Gazetteer; or Compendiums Geographical Dictionary* . . . , 9th ed. [London, 1795], clipped by d'Eon himself in ULBC 20:3). "It is the birthplace of the celebrated Mademoiselle d'Eon. . . . Tonnerre is famous for its good wines."

8. Thomas Walpole to d'Eon, 3 Nov. 1762, in BMT F14.

9. D'Eon to Grenville, 19 Sept. 1763, in *The Grenville Papers,* ed. William James Smith, 4 vols. (London, 1852–53), 2:124–25; Grenville to d'Eon, 20 Sept. 1763, in BMT G216. D'Eon's successor, the Comte de Guerchy (also a Burgundian), ran into the same kind of trouble with Grenville over wine. See Coquelle, "Le comte de Guerchy," 434–35.

10. BL 11339, 48–51; see also BMT F14.

11. Broglie to Louis XV, 24 July 1763, CS 1:168–69.

12. During this period a French diplomat would often pay expenses out of his own pocket and then request reimbursement. Often that reimbursement came in the form of a pension or annuity from the King that went far beyond the value of the so-called debt. Thus diplomatic service constituted a sort of financial investment or gamble on the part of the diplomat. In June 1763, for example, d'Eon personally took out a loan from a financier, Buraglo, to cover his expensive habits. See BMT G153.

13. Saint-Foy to d'Eon, 14 Aug. 1763, extract in d'Eon, *Lettres, mémoires, et négociations* (London, 1764), 1:16–17. For one modern estimate of d'Eon's spending habits, see Coquelle, "Le Chevalier d'Eon," 217–46.

14. Quoted in KS 2:111.

15. Nivernais to d'Eon, 17 Sept. 1763, in d'Eon, *Lettres, mémoires* 1:27.

16. Ibid.

17. Tercier to d'Eon, 5 Sept. 1763 (copy), AAE Supplement 16: 82–84; this translation amended from KS 2:114–15. See also Tercier to d'Eon, 6 Oct. 1763 (copy), AAE Supplement 16:92–94, for a reiteration of these same ideas.

18. Saint-Foy to d'Eon, 18 Sept. 1763, in d'Eon, *Lettres, mémoires* 1:61–62.

19. D'Eon to Saint-Foy and d'Eon to Moreau, both 25 Sept. 1763, in d'Eon, *Lettres, mémoires* 1:62–73.

20. D'Eon to Broglie, 25 Sept. 1763, extract in AAE Supplement 16:88–90. Not all the letters were so insolent. Between 2 August and 11 October, for example, d'Eon wrote at least twenty-five letters to Praslin, most of which were routine, informative, and harmless. See AAE 451, passim.

21. Broglie to d'Eon, 7 Oct. 1763, KS 2:115–17. I have amended the translation slightly. The French version is in [Albert] Le duc de Broglie, *Le secret du roi . . .* , 2 vols. (Paris, 1878), 2:132–33.

CHAPTER 20: RECALLED

1. Praslin to d'Eon, 4 Oct. 1763, in d'Eon, *Lettres, mémoires, et négociations* (London, 1764), three parts in one volume, 1:101. This translation of the recall and Tercier's remarks are taken from KS 2:124.

2. Tercier to Louis XV, 7 Oct. 1763, cited in AAE, Mémoires et Documents, Angleterre, 59; Louis XV to Tercier, 11 and 12 Oct. 1763, CSI 1:299.

3. D'Eon to Guerchy, 27 Sept. 1763, AAE 451:279.

4. Praslin to d'Eon, 19 and 29 Oct. 1763, AAE 451:426, 532.

5. Hertford to Walpole, 25 Nov. 1763, in Walpole, *Correspondence*, ed. W. S. Lewis, 48 vols. (New Haven, Conn., 1932–83), 38:242–44.

6. See Broglie to Durand, 8 Dec. 1763, extracted in AAE, Mémoires et Documents, FD Angleterre: "He [La Rozière] assures me that d'Eon is not any more crazy than he."

7. "Declaration de M. d'Eon," 11 July 1775, ULBC 9:9.

8. Quoted in KS 2:100.

9. D'Eon to Broglie, 19 Oct. 1763 (copy), in "Pièces pour servir à la mémoire de la Chevalière d'Eon," p. 1686, ULBC Box 7. On Pompadour as "the source of my troubles," see also d'Eon's memoir of the Guerchy affair dated 14 July 1775 in AAE 511:115–20.

10. This is one reason Broglie was lionized when his secret correspondence was first discovered during the French Revolution. See the introduction to the first volume of *Politique de tous les cabinets de l'Europe, pendant les règnes de Louis XV et de Louis XVI . . .* , 3 vols. (Paris, 1793).

11. D'Eon de Mouloize to his father, 28 Nov. 1763, AN 6:23.

12. Louis XV to Tercier and Louis XV to Guerchy, 4 Oct. 1763, CSI 1:302–3.

13. Louis XV to d'Eon, 4 Nov. 1763, CSI 1:303–4.

14. Earl of Halifax to the Advocate and Solicitor General, 21 Nov. 1763, in *Calendar of Home Office Papers of the Reign of George III, 1760–1765*, ed. Joseph Redington (London, 1878), 328; *London Gazette*, 3–6 Dec. 1763.

15. See, for example, CS 1:238n.

16. D'Eon, *A Letter Sent to His Excellency Claude-Louis-François Regnier, Count de Guerchy* (London, 1763).

CHAPTER 21: D'EON TO LOUIS XV AND BROGLIE

1. AAE Supplement 13:118–31, reprinted in Fréderic Gaillardet, *Mémoires sur la Chevalière d'Eon* (Paris, 1866), 138–45. A partial copy exists in d'Eon's hand in AAE Supplement 16:96–99.

2. In his memoirs, d'Eon adds that he was vomiting blood and was given medicine by a physician (ULBC Box 7:1618).

CHAPTER 22: BROGLIE TO LOUIS XV

1. AAE, Mémoires et Documents, France, 539:153–58; reprinted in CS 1:186–96.

2. This must be the letter of Louis XV to d'Eon of 4 Nov. 1763, ordering him to go along with Praslin's Order of Recall. The letter was attached to one addressed to Guerchy. Both letters are reproduced in CSI 1:303–4.

CHAPTER 23: SCAPEGOAT

1. In the full text of the letter, Broglie mentions other issues to display his sympathy for d'Eon. Like d'Eon, Broglie sees Guerchy as essentially a pawn of Praslin's, meant uniquely to harass d'Eon. Like d'Eon, Broglie is angered by Guerchy's use of men such as Vergy. Indeed, Broglie is particularly upset by the behavior of Nicolas Monin, who had apparently changed sides. Until the fall of 1763 Monin had been in the Conti circle (he was Conti's personal secretary from 1754 to 1756). With the Broglies exiled and Conti long gone, Monin knew which way the wind was blowing, and gracefully switched sides. What is surprising is not that he incurred Broglie's wrath for such disloyalty—that would be expected—but that Broglie would be so open with the King about his feelings toward Monin. After all, Monin knew nothing about the 3 June 1763 instructions; he was merely trying to goad d'Eon into returning all the papers from his brief tenure as Plenipotentiary Minister.

2. Louis XV to Tercier, 30 Dec. 1763, CSI 1:310–11.

3. Ibid.

4. CS 1:198–299.

5. [Pierre-Henri Treyssac de Vergy,] *Lettre à M. de la M*xxx, *Ecuyer* . . . (London, 1763); d'Eon, *Note remise à son excellence Monsieur le comte de Guerchy* (London, 1763); [Ange Goudar,] *Contre-Note ou Lettre à M. le marquis de L . . .* (Paris [sic: London], 1763).

6. Louis XV to Tercier, 30 Dec. 1763, CSI 1:310–11.

7. *Mémoires secrets* 1 (21 Dec. 1763): 313.

8. Horace Walpole to d'Eon, 25 Feb. 1764, BMT F22.

9. Broglie to Louis XV, 29 Feb. 1764, CS 1:211.
10. D'Eon to Tercier, 23 March 1764, AAE Supplement 13:156–57.

CHAPTER 24: THE *LETTRES,*
MÉMOIRES, ET NÉGOCIATIONS

1. Guerchy to Nivernais, 23 March 1764; Nivernais to Guerchy, 31 March 1764, both in Emile Blampignon, *Le duc de Nivernais . . .* (Paris, 1888), 221–28. See also Guerchy to Praslin, 30 March 1764, AAE 450:160–62. Unlike the small *A Letter Sent to . . . Guerchy* that d'Eon had published somewhat hastily in November, the *Lettres* was a handsome folio edition. A receipt dated 13 March 1764 in ULBC-EI 7 indicates that d'Eon paid John Dixwell £310 to print a thousand copies and distribute them.

2. Diary entry for 28 March 1764, in *The Grenville Papers . . . ,* ed. William James Smith, 4 vols. (London, 1852–53), 2:501; Praslin to Guerchy, 7 April 1764, AAE 450:181; *Mémoires secrets* 5 (9 and 14 April 1764): 42–45.

3. Letter of 23 July 1764, *Lettres de Geneviève de Malboissière à Adélaide Méliand (1761–1766),* ed. Le Comte de Luppé (Paris, 1925), 126–28.

4. *Mémoires secrets,* 1 (14 April 64): 45; Walpole, *Correspondence,* ed. W. S. Lewis, 48 vols. (New Haven, Conn., 1932–83), 38:356; Wilkes to Churchill, 10 April 1764, in *The Correspondence of John Wilkes and Charles Churchill,* ed. Edward H. Weatherly (New York, 1954), 82.

5. Roger Chartier, "Book Markets and Reading in France at the End of the Old Regime," in *Publishing and Readership in Revolutionary France and America,* ed. Carol Armbruster (Westport, Conn., 1993), 125.

6. Keith Michael Baker, "Politics and Public Opinion Under the Old Regime: Some Reflections," in *Press and Politics in Pre-Revolutionary France,* ed. Jack R. Censer and Jeremy D. Popkin (Berkeley, Calif., 1987), 210–11.

7. The best book on Wilkes is still George Rudé, *Wilkes and Liberty: A Social Study of 1763 to 1774* (Oxford, 1962).

8. *North Briton* no. 28, December 1762, and no. 31, January 1763, quoted in George Nobbe, *The North Briton: A Study in Political Propaganda* (1939; reprint New York, 1966), 118, 148.

9. Quoted in Raymond Postgate, *That Devil Wilkes* (New York, 1929), 59.

10. Wilkes to Humphrey Cotes, 5 Dec. 1764, in *The Correspondance of the Late John Wilkes . . . ,* ed. John Almon, 5 vols. (London, 1805), 2:93–94; for d'Eon's comment, see his marginalia in his clipped copy of

the *Gazette d'Utrecht,* 7 Dec. 1764, in ULBC. Even before the publication of d'Eon's book, his colleagues were comparing him to Wilkes; see Saint-Foy to d'Eon, 14 Aug. 1763, and d'Eon to Saint-Foy, 19 Aug. 1763, both in d'Eon, *Lettres, mémoires, et négociations* (London, 1764), three parts in one volume, 1:16–17.

11. Guerchy to Praslin, 6 April 1764, AAE 450:202.

12. John Brewer, *Party Ideology and Popular Politics at the Accession of George III* (Cambridge, 1976), 163–218; Baker, "Politics and Public Opinion," 214–21.

13. Jack R. Censer, *The French Press in the Age of Enlightenment* (London, 1994), 176–83.

14. Wilkes to Humphrey Cotes, 5 Dec. 1764.

15. See d'Eon to Broglie, 8 June 1764 (copy), AAE Supplement 16:155–66; Broglie to Louis XV, 25 June 1764, CS 2:249.

16. D'Eon to Broglie, 8 June 1764 (copy), 165–66: "The people love me, and drink publicly to my health and to that of Wilkes." *Mémoires secrets* 2 (7 July 1764): 71–72.

17. *London Chronicle,* 14–17 July 1764, 52.

CHAPTER 25: LIBEL

1. D'Eon to Broglie and Louis XV, 20 April 1764 (copy), AAE Supplement 13:168.

2. Guerchy to Praslin, 30 March and 6 April 1764, AAE 450:160–62, 202; *The Grenville Papers . . .* , ed. William James Smith, 4 vols. (London, 1852–53), 2:501, 280–89; 3:10, 48; Horace Walpole to Lord Hertford, 27 March 1764, in Walpole, *Correspondence,* ed. W. S. Lewis, 48 vols. (New Haven, Conn., 1932–83), 38:356–57.

3. Broglie to Louis XV, 27 June 1764, CS 2:251. A year later France gave Hume a taste of his own medicine in its handling of the case of William Chepmel, a ten-year-old English boy who had come to the Normandy city of Caen for a year of study. When William's parents got word that the boy had converted to Catholicism, was living in a monastery, and would never return home, they sought the assistance of Hume, who wrote Foreign Minister Praslin, soberly arguing that no child of ten could make such a difficult decision rationally, and therefore, such a conversion, performed without the knowledge or approval of the parents, must be considered against his will. Hume insisted that any civilized country, no matter its religious persuasion, ought to recognize the universal notion that children belong to their parents and cannot act without their approval. Praslin responded that according to French law, seven was the minimum age at which a child could convert and leave his parents. Therefore,

Praslin told Hume, the situation was analogous to that of the Chevalier d'Eon in England: Since the boy had broken no French laws, the French had no grounds to extradite him. See *New Letters of David Hume*, ed. Raymond Klibansky and Ernest C. Mossner (New York, 1983), 128n and 224–25.

4. Louis XV to Tercier, 10 April and 1 May 1764, CSI 1:320, 322; and CS 2:238n.

5. Broglie to Louis XV, 30 April and 3 June 1764, CS 1:225, 242–43.

6. Guerchy to d'Eon de Mouloize, 8 May 1764, and d'Eon de Mouloize to his parents, 24 Sept. 1764, AN 6:24, 27.

7. Charles Jenkinson to J. S. Mackenzie, 4 July 1764, in *The Jenkinson Papers 1760–1766*, ed. Ninetta S. Jucker (London, 1949), 310.

8. *Nouvelles lettres du Chevalier d'Eon . . .* (London, 1764). See also the newspaper clipping attached to the copy of this pamphlet in the Houghton Library, Harvard University.

9. Jenkinson to Grenville, 5 July 1764, in *The Grenville Papers* 2:382–83; *Mémoires secrets* 5 (17 July 1764): 75; *Gentleman's Magazine* 34 (November 1764): 544.

10. Broglie to Louis XV, 21 Jan. 1765, CS 1:306. On Wilkes's cross-dressing, see the *London Chronicle*, 11–13 Aug. 1763, 146: Wilkes "made his escape disguised in women's clothes; and the delicacy of his figure, the softness of his deportment, but above all, the inexpressible beauty of his face, deceives the nicest observers."

11. [Pierre-Henri Treyssac de Vergy,] "Seconde lettre à Monseigneur le duc de Choiseul," in *Suite des pièces relative aux lettres, mémoires et négociations particulières du Chevalier d'Eon* (London, 1764), 19–61. In December 1763, Vergy was thrown into debtor's prison, where he sat for the next nine months. Perhaps it was anger over Guerchy's refusal to pay his debts that prompted him to offer aid to d'Eon.

12. Ibid., 37.

13. Walpole to Hertford, 25 Nov. 1764, in Walpole, *Correspondence*, 38:467.

14. D'Eon to Broglie, 2 Nov. 1764 (copies), AAE Supplement 13:186 and 16:173; also in CSI 1:332. A similar copy of a letter to the Maréchal de Broglie is in AAE Supplement 13:187.

15. Louis XV to Tercier, 1 Dec. 1764, CSI 1:333; Broglie to Louis XV, 12 Jan. 1765, CS 1:288 (see also 372). Nort and others had been shuttling between d'Eon and the Secret throughout the fall of 1764. See, for example, *London Chronicle*, 4–6 Oct. 1764, 334; CS 1:272–88; and d'Eon to Broglie and Tercier, 8 Dec. 1764 (copy), AAE Supplement 16:185.

16. CS 1:286n.

CHAPTER 26: INDICTMENT

1. D'Eon to Comtesse de Massol, 14 Jan. 1765, AN 6:31 and 31 bis. See also d'Eon to Tercier, 16 Jan. 1765, AAE Supplement 16:190; d'Eon to Lautern, his wine merchant and landlord, 2 Feb. 1765, BL 11339:172. For background, see Jean-Claude David, "La querelle de l'inoculation en 1763: trois lettres inédites de Suard et du Chevalier d'Eon," *Dix-huitième siècle* 17 (1985): 271–84.

2. Cited in Pierre Pinsseau, *L'Etrange destinée du chevalier d'Eon, 1728–1810,* 2nd ed. (Paris, 1945), 119–20.

3. Broglie to Louis XV, 22 March 1765, CS 1:336. Of course, Hume was offering a highly idealized, if classic, view of British law. For how it actually operated during the period, see J. M. Beattie, *Crime and the Courts in England 1660–1800* (Princeton, N. J., 1986).

4. D'Eon to Broglie, 20 March 1765 (copy), AAE Supplement 16:258–65. See also Grenville to Duke of Bedford, 3 March 1765, in *Additional Grenville Papers 1763–1765,* ed. John R. G. Tomlinson (Manchester, 1962), 248; Captain J. Buchan Telfer, *The Strange Career of the Chevalier D'Eon de Beaumont* (London, 1885), 181–82.

5. John Brewer, *Party Ideology and Popular Politics at the Accession of George III* (Cambridge, 1976), 240.

6. D'Eon to Broglie, 14 Dec. 1765 (copy), AAE Supplement 16:220.

7. Broglie to Louis XV, 29 June 1765, CS 1:368.

8. Meanwhile, Guerchy had lost any effectiveness as an ambassador. After an extended vacation in France, he finally resigned, and was temporarily replaced by François-Michel Durand, a man not only known and liked by d'Eon, but himself a veteran spy for the Secret. It was Durand who completed the negotiations with d'Eon. Thus d'Eon was the clear victor in the feud with Guerchy. As for Vergy, in 1767, shortly before Guerchy's death at the age of forty-two, he threatened the ex-ambassador with the publication of a truly libelous pamphlet titled "La Guerchiade," and in an all-too-common eighteenth-century practice, tried to sell the manuscript to Guerchy to prevent publication. Evidently the extortion scheme worked, because Vergy, who lived on until 1774, never published the diatribe. See Vergy to Guerchy, 12 and 19 Aug. 1767, and "La Guerchiade," AAE 474:286–91 and 325–26.

CHAPTER 27: ROYAL DECREE OF 1 APRIL 1766

1. This chapter is reproduced from AAE Supplement 16:234; ULBC 4:36a; CSI 1:349–50. It was perhaps first made public in *Pièces rélatives aux démêlés entre Mademoiselle d'Eon . . . et le Sieur Caron dit de Beaumarchais* (n.p., 1778), 22, and was reprinted the next year in La Fortelle, *La*

Vie militaire, politique, et privée de Mademoiselle d'Eon, 2nd ed. (Paris, 1779).

CHAPTER 28: D'EON TO JEAN-JACQUES ROUSSEAU

1. *Correspondance complète de Jean-Jacques Rousseau,* ed. R. A. Leigh, 46 vols. (Oxford, 1965–87), 28:313–18; original in BMT.

2. Rousseau's masterpiece of political theory, *The Social Contract,* had been published four years earlier, in 1762.

3. Although *Emile* was first published in Amsterdam in 1762, Rousseau's hometown of Geneva censored the book and exiled its author soon after its publication.

4. In book IV of *Emile,* Rousseau used "The Creed of a Savoyard Vicar" to attack notions of miracles and revelation in religion. Primarily for this reason, *Emile* was condemned by the Catholic Church.

CHAPTER 29: ROUSSEAU'S DISCIPLE

1. See AAE 484.

2. AAE Supplement 17:23; ULBC 18:264 and Box 8, Rough Notes II, 679 and 681.

3. D'Eon to Mme d'Eon de Mouloize, 6 Feb. 1766, AN 6:41.

4. D'Eon to Mme d'Eon de Mouloize, 12 June 1765, AN 6:33.

5. ULBC 6:194.

6. D'Eon *Lettres, mémoires, et négociations* (London, 1764), three parts in one volume 1:131.

7. Jean Le Rond d'Alembert, *Preliminary Discourse to the Encyclopedia,* trans. Richard N. Schwab (Indianapolis, 1963), 103–4. See also Samuel S. B. Taylor, "Rousseau's Contemporary Reputation in France," *Studies on Voltaire and the Eighteenth Century* 27 (1963): 1545–74.

8. Jean Starobinski, *Jean-Jacques Rousseau: Transparency and Obstruction,* trans. Arthur Goldhammer (Chicago, 1988), esp. chap. 2 and 7.

9. D'Eon to Mme d'Eon, 30 Dec. 1763, in d'Eon, *Lettres, mémoires,* 125. "In fact," writes Rousseau, "the real source of all those differences is that the savage lives within himself, whereas social man, constantly outside himself, knows only how to live in the opinion of others; and it is, if I may say so, merely from their judgment of him that he derives the consciousness of his own existence" (Jean-Jacques Rousseau, *The Social Contract and the Discourse on the Origin of Inequality,* trans. Lester G. Crocker [New York, 1967], 245).

CHAPTER 30: D'EON'S LIBRARY

1. Bill of 20 Dec. 1764 from J. Dixwell, ULBC-EI 7; d'Eon to Vergennes, 18 July 1777, AAE Supplement 17:31–32.

2. *Catalogue of the Scarce Books and Valuable Manuscripts of the Cheval-ière d'Eon* ... (London, 1791); *A Catalogue of the Historical, Biblical, and Other Curious Mss. and Library of Printed Books of the Chev. d'Eon* ... (London, 1813).

3. On the Horace collection see *Boswell: The Applause of the Jury, 1782–1785*, ed. Irma S. Lustig and Frederick A. Pottle (New York, 1981), 214n. He refers "my friend Horace" in ULBC 46:1661. D'Eon bought the collection from Dr. James Douglass, an obstetrician to Queen Caroline, who had gained particular fame for investigating the case of a woman who claimed to have given birth to rabbits. See Lisa Cody, "'The Doctor's in Labour; or a New Whim Wham From Guildford,'" *Gender and History* 4 (1992): 175–96.

4. *Catalogue* (1791) 6:141.

5. For example, see *Catalogue des livres de la bibliothèque de Turgot d'après le catalogue manuscrit conservé dans la Bibliothèque Nationale*, ed. T. Tsuda (Paris and Tokyo, 1974); and *Catalogue de la bibliothèque de Montesquieu*, ed. Louis Desgraves (Geneva, 1954).

6. The library also included an extensive collection of engravings of women. See Pierre Coquelle, "Le Chevalier d'Eon, ministre à London," *Bulletin historique et philosophique* (1909): 217.

7. Compare with Dominique Varry, "Grandes collections et bibliothèques des élites," in *Histoire des bibliothèques françaises: Les bibliothèques sous l'Ancien Régime 1530–1789*, ed. Claude Jolly (Paris, 1988).

8. Pierre Le Moyne, *Gallery of Heroick Women*, 2 vols. (London, 1652), 2:25.

9. Claude Charles Guyonne de Vertron, *La Nouvelle pandore, ou Les Femmes illustres du siècle de Louis le Grand*, 2nd ed., 2 vols. (Paris, 1703). On this theme see Faith E. Beasley, *Revising Memory: Women's Fiction and Memoirs in Seventeenth-Century France* (New Brunswick, N. J., 1990); and Joan DeJean, "Amazons and Literary Women: Female Culture During the Reign of the Sun King," in *Sun King: The Ascendancy of French Culture During the Reign of Louis XIV*, ed. David Lee Rubin (Washington, D.C., 1992), 115–28.

10. Vertron, *La Nouvelle pandore*, 4–8.

11. *Biographium Faeminem. The Female Worthies; or Memoirs of the Most Illustrious Ladies of All Ages and Nations Who Have Been Eminently Distinguished for Their Magnanimity, Learning, Genius, Virtue, Piety, and Other Excellent Endowments*, 2 vols. in 1 (London, 1766) iii, vii.

12. Jean-Zorobabel Aublet de Maubuy, *Les vies des femmes illustres de la France*, 6 vols. (Paris, 1762–68), 1: vii.

13. Joan Kelly, "Early Feminist Theory and the Querelle des Femmes, 1480–1789," *Signs* 8 (1982): 4–28, in Kelly's *Women, History, and Theory* (Chicago, 1984), 65–109.

14. "Les Pieuses Métamorphoses . . . ," ULBC Box 7, 47–48. On Le Franc, see Constance Jordan, *Renaissance Feminism: Literary Texts and Political Models* (Ithaca, N.Y., 1990), 92.

15. Kelly, "Early Feminist Theory and the Querelle des Femmes"; Jacques Du Bosc, *L'Honneste femme* (Paris, 1647); François Poulain de la Barre, *The Equality of the Sexes,* trans. Desmond M. Clarke (Manchester, [1673] 1990); Carolyn Lougee, *La Paradis des femmes: Women, Salons, and Social Stratification in Seventeenth-Century France* (Princeton, N. J., 1980); Ian Maclean, *Women Triumphant: Feminism in French Literature 1610–1652* (Oxford, 1977); Erica Harth, *Cartesian Women: Versions and Subversions of Rational Discourse in the Old Regime* (Ithaca, N.Y., 1992); and Joan DeJean, *Tender Geographies: Women and the Origins of the Novel in France* (New York, 1991).

16. Mary Astell, *Some Reflections Upon Marriage,* 4th ed. (London, 1730 [reprint ed.: New York, 1970]), 99. See also Ruth Perry, *The Celebrated Mary Astell: An Early English Feminist* (Chicago, 1982). For the wider context see Hilda Smith, *Reason's Disciples: Seventeenth-Century English Feminists* (Urbana, Ill., 1982); and Jerome Nadelhaft, "The Englishwomen's Sexual Civil War: Feminist Attitudes Towards Men, Women, and Marriage 1650–1740," *Journal of the History of Ideas* 43 (1982): 555–79.

17. [Judith Drake,] *An Essay in Defense of the Female Sex,* 2nd ed. (London, 1696), 21–22.

18. Ibid., 22–23.

19. Ibid., 16.

20. William Walsh, *A Dialogue Concerning Women, Being a Defense of the Sex, Written to Eugenia* (London, 1691). D'Eon owned the 1768 French translation of this work, *Discours sur les femmes, adressé à Eugénie.*

21. Joseph Warder, *The True Amazons: or, The Monarchy of Bees: Being a New Discovery and Improvement of Those Wonderful Creatures . . . ,* 4th ed. (London, 1720), 44–46. See also Jeffrey Merrick, "Royal Bees: The Gender Politics of the Beehive in Early Modern Europe," *Studies in Eighteenth-Century Culture* 18 (1988): 7–37.

22. One scholar who is attentive to the eighteenth century is Marc Angenot, *Les Champions des femmes: examens du discours sur la superiorité des femmes 1400–1800* (Quebec, 1977).

23. Herodotus, *The Histories,* trans. Aubrey de Sélincourt (Baltimore, 1954), 277–79.

24. Abbey Wettan Kleinbaum, *The War Against the Amazons* (New York, 1983).

25. Claude-Marie, Abbé Guyon, *Histoire des amazones anciennes et modernes,* 2 vols. (Paris, 1740), 1:clxiv.

26. Ibid., 1:5–13, clxiv, 46–47.

27. Ibid., 1:lvi
28. DeJean, *Tender Geographies*, 42.
29. *Female Rights Vindicated* (London, 1758), 59, 74, 90–92.

CHAPTER 31: POMPADOUR AND LA PUCELLE

1. The best biography of Joan is Marina Warner, *Joan of Arc: The Image of Female Heroism* (New York, 1981); on Pompadour, see Pierre de Nolhac, *Madame de Pompadour et la politique* (Paris, 1928). See also Jeffrey Merrick, "Sexual Politics and Public Orders in the *Mémoires secrets* and *Correspondance secrète*," *Journal of the History of Sexuality* 1 (1990): 68–84; idem, *The Desacralization of the French Monarchy in the Eighteenth Century* (Baton Rouge, La., 1990); and Thomas E. Kaiser, "Madame de Pompadour and the Theaters of Power," *French Historical Studies* (forthcoming, 1995 or 1996).

2. Nicolas Lenglet Dufresnoy, *Histoire de Jeanne d'Arc dite la Pucelle d'Orléans*, 3 vols. (Amsterdam, 1775), 1:ix. On Joan's reputation during this period, see Jeroom Vercruysse, "Jeanne d'Arc au siècle des Lumières," *Studies on Voltaire and the Eighteenth Century* 90 (1972): 1659–1729.

3. *Pucelle* is often translated as "maid," implying a very young woman, around the age of menarche, who is still not fully developed, and is certainly a virgin.

4. D'Eon, "Notice sur l'Abbé Lenglet-Dufresnoy," *L'Année littéraire*, 1 (1754): 219; Pierre Le Moyne, *Gallery of Heroick Women*, 2 vols. (London, 1652) 2:129; see also Jean-Zorobabel Aublet de Maubuy, *Les Vies des femmes, illustres de la France*, 6 vols. (Paris, 1762–68), 1:2–3.

5. Claude-Marie, Abbé Guyon, *Histoire des Amazones anciennes et modernes*, 2 vols. (Paris, 1740), 1:clxvii; Le Moyne, 2:112–38. [Philippe-Joseph Caffiaux,] *Défense du beau sexe, ou Mémoires historiques, philosophiques, et critiques, pour servir d'apologie aux femmes*, 4 vols. (Amsterdam, 1753), 1:176, 184, 226–32; *Female Rights Vindicated* (London, 1758), preface; William Walsh, *A Dialogue Concerning Women, Being a Defense of the Sex, Written to Eugenia* (London, 1691), 124–25. Joan is called a "beautiful Amazon" in a poem by Malesherbes inserted between parts I and II of Lenglet's book about her cited in note 2.

6. Jacques Soyer, "Projet par Pigalle d'un monument à élever à Orléans en l'honneur de Jeanne d'Arc (1761)," *Bulletin de la société archéologique et historique de l'Orléanais* 15 (1908–10): 51–54.

7. Michel Antoine, *Louis XV* (Paris, 1989), especially 493–510.

8. Marianne-Agnès Pillement de Fauques, *The Life of the Marchioness de Pompadour*, 4th ed. (London, n.d.) 1:6–7.

9. Ibid., 7–8. (This charge is essentially reconfirmed by Antoine, *Louis XV*, 493.)

10. Ibid., 25.

11. Ibid., 2:3.

12. Ibid., 2:94–95. Fauques's potent image of Pompadour is perhaps most skillfully reflected in one of the century's most popular and misogynist novels, Pierre Choderlos de Laclos's *Les Liaisons dangereuses* (1782). Note how French scholar Aram Vartanian's description of Laclos's diabolical protagonist, Mme de Merteuil, resembles Fauques's image of Pompadour: "She personifies the possibility of an equivalence, or confusion, of the sexes; that is, she is an embodiment of the thought, both perversely fascinating and obsessively disturbing, that the distinction of the sexes might not, after all, be real or necessary; that it is possible to be simultaneously a man and a woman, or more precisely—since the fantasied transgression of the sex barrier is apprehended here from the male standpoint of the author—she represents the danger that a woman might usurp, and add to her role already given, that of a man." ("The Marquise de Merteuil: A Case of Mistaken Identity," *L'Esprit créateur* 3 [1963]: 176).

13. [Charles Théveneau de Morande,] *Le Gazetier cuirassé; ou Anecdotes scandaleuses de la cour de France* ([London,] 1771); [Mathieu-François Pidansat de Mairobert,] *Anecdotes sur M.* [sic] *la comtesse du Barri* (London, 1775); idem, *L'Espion anglais; ou Correspondance secrète entre Milord All'ege et Milord All'er;* [Mouffle d'Angerville,] *La Vie privée de Louis XV; ou Principaux événemens, particularités, et anecdotes de son regne* (London, 1781), cited by d'Eon in AN 5:1.

14. Robert Darnton, *The Literary Underground of the Old Regime* (Cambridge, Mass., 1982), and most recently, *Edition et sédition. L'Univers de la littérature clandestine au xviiie siècle* (Paris, 1991). See also Merrick, *Desacralization of the French Monarchy;* Jeremy Popkin, "The Prerevolutionary Origins of Political Journalism," in *The French Revolution and the Creation of Modern Political Culture. Vol I. The Political Culture of the Old Regime,* ed. Keith Michael Baker (Oxford, 1987), 203–23. Similar attacks on the morals of Marie-Antoinette have their root in earlier slanders during the reign of Louis XV. See Lynn Hunt, *The Family Romance of the French Revolution* (Berkeley, Calif., 1992), 17–52 and 89–123.

15. Fauques, *Pompadour,* 3:5n; Voltaire, *La Pucelle,* ed. Jérôme Vercruysse (Paris, [1755] 1970).

16. AAE 511:115–20, ULBC 19:42.

17. The full title was to be *La Pucelle de Tonnerre ou Les Vicissitudes du chevalier et chevalière d'Eon.* For other references to d'Eon as La Pucelle de Tonnerre, see ULBC 19:23, 22:90, and Box 8, Rough Notes II, 1026.

CHAPTER 32: CONTRA ROUSSEAU

1. See Joan Landes, *Women and the Public Sphere in the Age of the French Revolution* (Ithaca, N.Y., 1988), 66–89.

2. Jean-Jacques Rousseau, *Politics and the Arts: The Letter to d'Alembert on the Theater,* trans. Allan Bloom (Ithaca, N.Y., 1968), 82–83, 100–101.

3. Domna C. Stanton, *The Aristocrat as Art: A Study of the Honnête Homme and the Dandy in Seventeenth- and Nineteenth-Century French Literature* (New York, 1980).

4. Rousseau, *Emile, or Education,* trans. Allan Bloom (New York, 1979), 365.

5. Ruth Graham, "Rousseau's Sexism Revolutionised," in *Women in the Eighteenth Century,* ed. Paul Fritz and Richard Morton (Toronto, 1976), 127–39.

6. Samuel S. B. Taylor, "Rousseau's Contemporary Reputation in France," *Studies on Voltaire and the Eighteenth Century* 27 (1963): 1545–74.

7. Jean-Zorobabel Aublet de Maubuy, *Les Vies des femmes illustres de la France,* 6 vols. (Paris, 1762–68), 1:viii; [Riballier and Mlle Cosson,] *De l'éducation morale et physique des femmes, avec une notice alphabétique de celles qui se sont distinguées dans les différentes carrières* (Brussels, 1779), 25–36, 217–19.

8. Rousseau, *Emile,* 357. A similar reading of Rousseau has recently led Penny A. Weiss to conclude that Rousseau rejected androgyny because he believed it undermined community, not because he believed natural or biological differences rendered the female sex inferior or fundamentally different. See her *Gendered Community: Rousseau, Sex, and Politics* (New York, 1993), 121.

9. Unpublished fragment titled by editor "Sur les femmes [c1743]," *Oeuvres de Rousseau,* ed. Bernard Gagnebin and Marcel Raymond, 4 vols. (Paris, 1964), 2:1254–55.

10. "Observations du préjugé sur la différence des sexes . . . ," in the Rousseau/Dupin Collection, Harry Ransom Humanities Research Center, University of Texas at Austin. My thanks to Linda Ashton, assistant curator at the HRHRC, for guiding me through these papers. For the circumstances surrounding these manuscripts, see Anicet Sénéchal, "Jean-Jacques Rousseau, Secrétaire de Madame Dupin, d'après des documents inédits avec un inventaire des papiers Dupin dispersés en 1957 et 1958," *Annales de la Société de Jean-Jacques Rousseau* 36 (1963–65): 178–290.

11. Pierre-Joseph Boudier de Villemart, *Le Nouvel ami des femmes; ou, La philosophie du sexe* (Paris, 1779), 241.

12. Ibid., 29.

13. David Williams, "The Fate of French Feminism: Boudier de Ville-mart's *Ami des femmes*," *Eighteenth-Century Studies* 14 (1980–81): 44.

14. Patrick Delany, *Reflections Upon Polygamy, and the Encouragement Given to That Practice in the Scriptures of the Old Testament* (London, 1737), 32–33.

15. D'Eon owned a 1770 edition of *Les souvenirs de Madame de Caylus.*

16. Historians are finally noting the importance of these religious women. See F. Ellen Weaver, "Women and Religion in Early Modern France: A Bibliographic Essay on the State of the Question," *Catholic Historical Review* 67 (1981): 50–59.

CHAPTER 33: CONTEXTS

1. BMT I59 and J1. A bill in ULBC-EI 7 shows that d'Eon purchased a print of Garrick on 2 July 1763.

2. The lines quoted here and below were first printed in the *London Chronicle,* 3–5 Feb. 1763, 128–31, and reprinted in *The Plays of Frances Sheridan* (Wilmington, Del., 1984), 41–102. The play ran in February 1763 and was revived by Garrick in 1776, 1779, and 1780.

3. Felicity Nussbaum, *The Brink of All We Hate: English Satires on Women* (Lexington, Ky., 1984).

4. Dianne Dugaw, *Warrior Women and Popular Balladry, 1650–1850* (Cambridge, 1989), 177. See also Kristina Straub, *Sexual Subjects: Eighteenth-Century Players and Sexual Ideology* (Princeton, N.J., 1992). On Gay's opera see Peter Ackroyd, *Dressing Up: Transvestism and Drag: The History of an Obsession* (New York, 1979), 98.

5. Henry Fielding, *The Female Husband and Other Writings,* ed. Claude E. Jones (Liverpool, 1960), 29–51.

6. Madeleine Kahn, *Narrative Transvestism: Rhetoric and Gender in the Eighteenth-Century Novel* (Ithaca, N.Y., 1991); Tassie Gwilliam, *Samuel Richardson's Fictions of Gender* (Stanford, Calif., 1993), 15–49; Nancy K. Miller, "'I's' in Drag: The Sex of Recollection," *Eighteenth Century* 22 (1981): 47–57; James Carson, "Narrative Cross Dressing and the Critique of Authorship in the Novels of Richardson," in *Writing the Female Voice: Essays on Epistolary Literature,* ed. Elizabeth C. Goldsmith (Boston, 1989), 95–114.

7. See Kahn and Gwilliam cited in note 6.

8. Sylvia Harcstark Myers, *The Bluestocking Circle: Women, Friend-ship, and the Life of the Mind in Eighteenth-Century England* (Oxford, 1990), 140; Tom Keymer, *Richardson's Clarissa and the Eighteenth-Century Reader* (Cambridge, 1992).

9. John Brown, *An Estimate of the Manners and Principles of the Times* (London, 1757), 51.

10. [Portia,] *The Polite Lady; or A Course of Female Education,* 2nd ed. (London, 1769), 102–3. Of course, etiquette books were written for upper-class women and men. What of their working-class counterparts? Even here, as Anna Kirsten Clark's recent study "Womanhood and Manhood in the Transition from a Plebeian to Working-Class Culture" (Ph. D. diss., Rutgers University, 1987) makes clear, gender confusion was as apparent at the bottom of the social ladder as at the top. Clark argues that the gender segregation that marked Victorian popular culture was generally not in place during the eighteenth century. Men and women did not work and play in separate spheres. Even working-class men, Clark claims, were much more feminine before 1790; only after that was there a renewed and intense concern with virility.

11. Dugaw, *Warrior Women;* on fencing see Kathleen Vivienne Crawford, "The Transvestite Heroine in Seventeenth-Century Popular Literature" (Ph.D. diss., Harvard University, 1984), 193–94.

12. Quoted in Anne Buck, *Dress in Eighteenth-Century England* (New York, 1979), 20.

13. In July 1773 the *Lady's Magazine* offered the following definition: "A *Macaroni* is a thing that has some resemblance to a man, as it is in appearance like a man. The difference between the two is precisely this. A man applied himself to the serious in life; the Macaroni to that which is trifling. The man is grave, the latter studies to adorn his body; as for instance he strives to appear disengaged, holds his head up, wears his hair powdered and curled, and never goes out till he has formed his countenance according to the rules of the latest fashions. His pace is slow, he has a fine leg, and a very pretty foot. He walks with a noise to excite attention. He has likewise a very handsome watch, set with precious stones, a snuff-box of the highest taste, and some other glittering trifles. . . . He pretends to be in love and sighs according to fashion. He has a peculiar jargon of his own; his expressions are concise and so concise that they have seldom any meaning." Quoted in Aileen Ribeiro, *The Dress Worn at Masquerades in England 1730–1790, and Its Relation to Fancy Dress in Portraiture* (New York, 1984), 331.

14. Brown, *Estimate,* 34. See also *The Pretty Gentleman* (London, 1747); and John Barrell, "The Dangerous Goddess: Masculinity, Prestige, and the Aesthetic in Early Eighteenth-Century Britain," *Cultural Critique* 12 (Spring 1989): 101–31; Ellen Moers, *The Dandy: Brummell to Beerbohm* (London, 1960), 11–12. That the Macaronis evolved into dandies is clear from an 1818 article that identified "a new race of men who wear stays. . . . Their gender is not yet ascertained, but as their prin-

cipal ambition seems to be to look as pretty as women, it would be most uncharitable to call them men" (quoted in Clark, "Womanhood," 182).

15. Abbé Georgel, *Mémoires pour servir à l'histoire des événemens de la fin du dix-huitième siècle . . .*, 6 vols., 2nd ed. (Paris, 1820), 1:170–71.

16. Both quotes in Terry Castle, "The Culture of Travesty: Sexuality and Masquerade in Eighteenth-Century England," in *Sexual Underworlds of the Enlightenment*, ed. G. S. Rousseau and Roy Porter (Manchester, 1987), 169. See also Castle's *Masquerade and Civilization: The Carnalvalesque in Eighteenth-Century English Culture and Fiction* (Stanford, Calif., 1986). Castle argues, mistakenly I believe, that masquerade reaffirms conventional patriarchal notions of gender.

17. On this influential term, see Gayle Rubin, "The Traffic in Women: Notes on the 'Political Economy' of Sex," in *Towards an Anthropology of Women*, ed. Rayna R. Reiter (New York, 1975), 157–210.

18. *Elizabeth Montagu: The Queen of the Bluestockings. Her Correspondence from 1720–1761*, 2 vols., ed. Emily J. Climenson (New York, 1906), 2:280–81.

19. Joseph La Porte, *Histoire littéraire des femmes françaises*, 5 vols. (Paris, 1769), 1:vi–vii. See also Faith E. Beasley, *Revising Memory: Women's Fiction and Memoirs in Seventeenth-Century France* (New Brunswick, N.J., 1990); Joan DeJean, *Tender Geographies: Women and the Origins of the Novel in France* (New York, 1991); Dena Goodman, "Enlightenment Salons: The Convergence of Female and Philosophic Ambitions," *Eighteenth-Century Studies* 22 (Spring 1989): 329–67.

20. Marie-Anne de Roumier Robert, *Voyages de Milord Céton . . .* (Paris, 1765). On Robert see Erica Harth, *Cartesian Women: Versions and Subversions of Rational Discourse in the Old Regime* (Ithaca, N.Y., 1992), 150–67.

21. William Alexander, *The History of Women from the Earliest Antiquity to the Present Time*, 2 vols. (London, 1779), 2:3. A few years later Mary Wollstonecraft celebrated the extent to which (upper-class) French men and women related on a relatively even plane. See *A Vindication of the Rights of Women*, ed. Carol Postan (1792; reprint New York, 1975), 3.

22. Hannah More, *Percy: A Tragedy* (London, 1784), Prologue; see also Thomas Davies, *Memoires of the Life of David Garrick*, 2 vols. (London, 1780), 2:333–34.

CHAPTER 34: RUMORS

1. "Memoirs of Mademoiselle d'Eon de Beaumont . . . ," *London Magazine*, September 1777, 445. Louis XV to General Monet, 28 Oct. 1770, CSI 1:411–12.

2. CS 2:187n.

3. Horace Walpole, *Correspondence*, ed. W. S. Lewis, 48 vols. (New Haven, Conn., 1932–83), 4:493–94.

4. D'Epinay to Galiani, 13 Jan. 1771, in *La Signora d'Epinay e l'abae Galiani: Lettere inedite (1769–1772)*, ed. Fausto Nicolini (Bari, 1929), 136–37.

5. *Public Advertiser*, 12 March 1771; *Gazetteer and New Daily Advertiser*, 11 March 1771; *London Evening Post*, 9–12 March 1771.

6. *Gazetteer and New Daily Advertiser*, 11, 13, and 16 March 1771.

7. *London Evening Post*, 11–14 May 1771. For one example of an insurance policy used in this affair (dated 24 April 1771), see ULBC Box 12:356–57 (copy in d'Eon's hand). For one recent discussion of the relationship between stock investing and gambling, see H. V. Bowen, "The Pests of Human Society: Stockbrokers, Jobbers, and Speculators in Mid–Eighteenth Century England," *History* 78 (1993): 38–53.

8. *Oxford Magazine; or University Museum*, August 1771; *Morning Chronicle, and London Advertiser*, 28 March 1771. For one example of d'Eon's denials, see d'Eon to Broglie, 7 May 1771, AAE 498:27–28.

9. D'Eon to Mme d'Eon, 1 March 1771, ULBC-EI 4:between 232–33.

10. D'Eon to Broglie, 25 March 1771, AAE 498:18–21.

11. *London Evening Post*, 23 to 26 March 1771, 3; *Gazetteer and New Daily Advertiser*, 26 March 1771; *Morning Chronicle, and London Advertiser*, 28 March 1771.

12. *Lloyd's Evening Post and British Chronicle*, 8–10 May 1771.

13. *London Packet or New Evening Post*, 24–27 May 1771; *Public Advertiser*, 17 April 1771. For evidence of d'Eon's relationship with Wilkes during this period, see AAE 484: 123–32.

14. *Gazetteer and New Daily Advertiser*, 28 and 30 May 1771. In general, the belief in the existence of hermaphrodites had largely disappeared by d'Eon's era. Although we can find echoes in popular culture, most educated people, and especially those in the medical community, warned against any such belief. See especially J. A. Paris and J. S. M. Fonblanque, *Medical Jurisprudence*, 2 vols. (London, 1823), 1:228–29, where a physician who had examined d'Eon's body upon his death comments on the legal ramifications of classifying him a hermaphrodite. On the debate over hermaphrodites, see Lynne Friedli, " 'Passing Women': A Study of Gender Boundaries in the Eighteenth Century," in *Sexual Underworlds of the Enlightenment*, ed. G. S. Rousseau and Roy Porter (Manchester, 1987), 234–60.

15. For example, one policy, dated 24 April 1791, states that the

money would be paid only "in case the Chevalier d'Eon should hereafter prove to be a female." See ULBC Box 12:357.

16. *London Evening Post,* 9–11 May 1771, 4. On Cotes and d'Eon see BL 11339:11.

17. *St. James's Chronicle or British Evening-Post,* 18–21 May 1771; *London Evening Post,* 14–16 May and 4–6 June 1771, 4; *Gazetteer and New Daily Advertiser,* 13 May 1771; *Public Advertiser,* 15 May 1771; *Lloyd's Evening Post and British Chronicle,* 20–22 and 22–24 May 1771; *Newcastle Journal,* 25 May 1771.

18. *London Packet or New Evening Post,* 20-22 May 1771.

19. ULBC Box 10 (first volume of newspaper clippings), 335.

20. *London Evening Post,* 20–21 June 1771, 3; *Gazetteer and New Daily Advertiser,* 25 June 1771; *Gazette d'Utrecht* 53 (25 June 1771).

21. D'Eon to Broglie, 7 May and 5 July 1771, AAE 498: 27–35. Broglie wrote d'Eon's mother to tell her to ignore the reports about d'Eon's disappearance. See Broglie to Mme d'Eon, 25 June 1771 (copy), ULBC Box 9 (Hodgekin folder).

22. *Gazetteer and New Daily Advertiser,* 5 July 1771.

23. *Public Advertiser,* 1 July 1771. See also *Gazette d'Utrecht,* 9 July 1771; *Morning Chronicle, and London Advertiser,* 1 July 1771; *Gazetteer and New Daily Advertiser,* 2 July 1771.

24. For one example, see BMT Y1.

CHAPTER 35: DROUET'S VISIT

1. See the article on Ferrers in John Charnock *Biographia Navalis or Memoirs of Officers of the Navy of Great Britain,* 6 vols. (London, 1794–98).

2. "Réponses aux questions du substitut et de l'avocat général," 16 June 1772, AAE 498:266–77.

3. *Public Ledger,* 16 June 1772. This same issue also reported that d'Eon had been assaulted: "A few days since another attack was made upon the Chevalier d'Eon, in order to discover the sex of that *he-she* thing. An adventurer in the Alley, who has rescued a large sum upon the policies lately opened, meeting the Chevalier in the narrow passage which leads from Spring Gardens to Forest's Coffee House, attempted to seize both the arms of the Chevalier and to thrust his hand into the bosom of that hero; the Chevalier, with great alertness, disengaged himself, and . . . drew a sword."

4. *London Evening Post,* 5–7 March 1772.

5. D'Eon to Broglie, 2 Dec. 1771 and 13 March 1772, AAE 498:148–50 and 191–92. D'Eon must be referring to the controversy over

the passage of the Royal Marriage Act, a bill drafted by Lord Mansfield. See John Brooke, *King George III* (Frogmore, Eng., 1974), 438.

6. Broglie to Louis XV, 9 April 1772, CS 2:338–39.

7. Broglie to Louis XV, 28 June, 8 July, and 12 July 1772, CS 2:356–60.

8. *Mémoires secrets* 5 (September 1771): 322.

9. *London Packet*, 22–25 March 1771; *General Advertiser*, 31 May 1786. See also "Epître de Généviève," 1473, ULBC Box 7.

10. Broglie to Louis XV, 12 July 1772, CS 2:360.

11. Princess E. D. Daskova, *Memoirs*, ed. K. Fitzlyon (London, 1958).

12. ULBC-EI 5:between 272–73; BMT J152; AAE 498 passim.

13. For one readable introduction to the Maupeou years, see Durand Echeverria, *The Maupeou Revolution: A Study in the History of Libertarianism. France, 1770–1774* (Baton Rouge, La., 1985).

14. CS 1:xc–xci.

15. D'Eon to Drouet, 25 April 1777 (copy), in ULBC 3:254.

CHAPTER 36: MACAULAY, D'EPINAY, AND THE *FEMME SAVANTE*

1. For example, see *Public Advertiser*, 6 June 1771. On Macaulay see Bridget Hill, *The Republican Virago: The Life and Times of Catherine Macaulay, Historian* (Oxford, 1992). For Hume's reaction to Macaulay's *History*, see *The New Letters of David Hume*, ed. Raymond Klibansky and Ernest C. Mossner (New York, 1983), 80–82.

2. *Gazetteer and New Daily Advertiser*, 26 March 1771.

3. *Public Advertiser*, 6 April 1771.

4. Macaulay to d'Eon, 10 March 1768, in BMT H131. Later, Macaulay defended the right of all women not only to write history, but to make history as well. "When we compliment the appearance of a more than ordinary energy in the female mind," she wrote in her *Letters on Education* ([London, 1790], 204), "we call it masculine; and hence it is, that [the poet Alexander] Pope has elegantly said *a perfect woman's but a softer man.* And if we take in the consideration, that there can be but one rule of moral excellence for beings made of the same materials, organized after the same manner, and subjected to similar laws of Nature, we must either agree with Mr. Pope, or we must reverse the proposition, and say, that a *perfect man is a woman formed after a coarser mold.*"

5. For example, of the 756 known subscribers to the important newspaper *Mercure de France* in 1756, at least 117 were women. See Jack R. Censer, *The French Press in the Age of Enlightenment* (London, 1994), 186. For an analysis of women intellectuals in the Enlightenment, see Dena

Goodman, *The Republic of Letters: A Cultural History of the French Enlightenment* (Ithaca, N.Y., 1994).

6. *Les conversations d'Emilie*, 2 vols. (Paris, 1774). On d'Epinay, see Elisabeth Badinter, *Emilie, Emilie. L'Ambition féminine au xviiie siècle* (Paris, 1983).

7. D'Epinay to Galiani, 4 Jan. 1771, cited in Francis Steegmuller, *A Woman, A Man, and Two Kingdoms: The Story of Madame d'Epinay and the Abbé Galiani* (New York, 1991), 153–54.

8. Galiani, "Dialogue sur les femmes," in *Correspondance*, ed. Lucien Perey and Gaston Maugras, 2 vols. (Paris, 1890), 2:50–62.

9. Antoine-Léonard Thomas, *Essai sur le caractère, les moeurs, et l'esprit des femmes dans les différens siècles*, ed. Colette Michael (Paris, [1772] 1987), 52–56. D'Eon calls Thomas his "old friend" in ULBC Box 7:1645.

10. D'Epinay to Galiani, 14 March 1772, in *Qu'est-ce qu'une femme?*, ed. Elisabeth Badinter (Paris, 1989), 193.

11. Denis Diderot, "On Women," *Dialogues of Diderot*, trans. Francis Birrell (London, 1927), 185–96.

12. Ibid., 194–95.

13. Ibid., 195.

14. Diderot, "Supplement to Bougainville's Voyage," in *Rameau's Nephew and Other Works*, ed. and trans. Jacques Barzun and Ralph Bowen (Indianapolis, 1964), 194.

15. Mary Wollstonecraft, *A Vindication of the Rights of Women*, ed. Carol Postan (1792; reprint New York, 1975), note at the end of chap. 4; and Mary Robinson, *A Letter to the Women of England on the Injustice of Mental Subordination* (London, 1799), 71n.

CHAPTER 37: HANNAH SNELL AND THE AMAZONS

1. *The Female Soldier; Or, The Surprising Life and Adventures of Hannah Snell* (London, 1750). See also the important introduction by Dianne Dugaw in a 1989 facsimile edition published by the Augustan Reprint Society of UCLA's William Andrews Clark Library.

2. Ibid., 41.

3. Ibid., 2.

4. Ibid., 7–8.

5. Rudolf M. Dekker and Lotte C. Van de Pol, *The Tradition of Female Transvestism in Early Modern Europe* (New York, 1989), 1–2. See also Barton Hacker, "Women and Military Institutions in Early Modern Europe: A Reconnaissance," *Signs* 6 (1981): 643–71; and John A. Lynn, "The Strange Case of the Maiden Soldier of Picardy," *MHQ: The Quarterly Journal of Military History* 2 (1990): 54–56.

6. Quoted in Dianne Dugaw, *Warrior Women and Popular Balladry, 1650–1850* (Cambridge, 1989), 140. Less helpful than Dugaw's masterly study but important for later decades is Julie Wheelwright, *Amazons and Military Maids: Women Who Dressed As Men in the Pursuit of Life, Liberty, and Happiness* (London, 1989).

7. Sheridan, *The Camp*, in *Plays*, ed. Cecil Price (London, 1975), 301–30. Sheridan (son of playwright Frances Sheridan), John Wilkes, and d'Eon often dined together; see Henry Angelo, *Reminiscences*, 2 vols. (London, 1904), 1:41.

8. "Female Warriors," in *The Miscellaneous Works of Oliver Goldsmith* (London, 1893), 309–11. Scholars today doubt the attribution. For a similar kind of transvestite satire, though one dealing with family life and not warfare, see Henry Fielding, *The Female Husband and Other Writings*, ed. Claude E. Jones (Liverpool, 1960).

9. On the origins of Amazons, see William Blake Tyrrell, *Amazons: A Study in Athenian Mythmaking* (Baltimore, 1984).

10. W. J. Chetwode Crawley, "The Chevalier d'Eon: J. W. of Lodge No. 376, Grand Lodge of England," *Ars Quatuor Coronatorum* 16 (1908): 231–51.

11. AAE Supplement 16:404 (in English) contains a notice that accompanied some versions of the print. For a general study of how Minerva was often portrayed, see Francis H. Dowley, "French Portraits of Ladies as Minerva," *Gazette des beaux arts* 45 (May–June 1955): 262–86. This Amazonian tradition harked back to the seventeenth century, when aristocratic women associated with the Fronde were especially celebrated for their virility. See Faith E. Beasley, *Revising Memory: Women's Fiction and Memoirs in Seventeenth-Century France* (New Brunswick, N.J., 1990), especially 74, 127–28.

12. ULBC Box 12, large leather book, 32.

13. AAE Supplement 16:404 (in English).

14. Simon Linguet, "Gagure sur le sexe du Chevalier d'Eon," *Annales politiques, civiles, et littéraires du dix-huitième siècle* 1, no. 7 (1777): 383–97.

15. ULBC Box 12, large leather book, 204; see also 32 and 181 for two other examples: "Jeanne d'Arc eut besoin d'un siècle encore gotique/ pour s'acquérir un nom;/ Mais ce siècle philosophique/ rend un double hommage à d'Eon" [Joan of Arc needed a century that was still Gothic/ in order to make a name for herself/But this philosophical century/pays double homage to d'Eon]; and "Jeanne cette fiere Pucelle/Jadis affronta le Trepaix/D'Eon tout aussi brave qu'elle/fut vierge et ne se vanta pas" [Joan that proud maiden/Long ago confronted death/D'Eon just as brave as she/was a virgin but not proud of it].

16. Ann Harker's speech is reproduced in James Armstrong Neal, *An Essay on the Education and Genius of the Female Sex* (Philadelphia, 1795), 15–20; this quote is from p. 17; d'Eon to Henri Grégoire, 25 Jan. 1803 (copy), ULBC 39:1078.

17. ULBC Box 12, large leather book, 142.

CHAPTER 38: MORANDE

1. D'Eon to Broglie, 3 Jan. 1773, AAE 501:4. See also d'Eon to d'Aiguillon, 17 July 1771, AAE 497:93; d'Eon to Vrillière, 2 Oct. 1773, in the Huntington Library, Manuscript 20608; d'Eon to Maupeou, 1 Oct. 1773, AAE 503:12–13.

2. For one example, see *The Diary of Sylas Neville, 1767–1788*, ed. Basil Cozens-Hardy (London, 1950), 32–33.

3. For example, see Broglie to d'Eon, 26 Aug. 1773 (extract), AAE 504:307–8; and d'Eon to Broglie, 22 Sept. 73, AAE 502:386.

4. D'Eon to Broglie, 13 and 15 July 1773, AAE 502:177–79 and 181–83; also in CSI 2:356–58. The title of Morande's book was to be *Mémoires secrets d'une femme publique ou recherches sur les aventures de Mme la comtesse du B**** depuis son berceau jusqu'au lit d'honneur.*

5. Joan Haslip, *Madame du Barry: The Wages of Beauty* (New York, 1992).

6. Paul Robiquet, *Théveneau de Morande* (Paris, 1882), is the standard biography; it should be supplemented with Robert Darnton's colorful description in *The Literary Underground of the Old Regime* (Cambridge, Mass., 1982), 30–35.

7. Robert Darnton, *Edition et sédition: l'univers de la littérature clandestine au xviiie siècle* (Paris, 1991), 169.

8. D'Eon to Broglie, 12 Dec. 1773, AAE 503:256.

9. D'Eon to Broglie, 29 Sept. 1773, AAE 502:416; Morande to d'Eon (copies with notes by d'Eon), 4 and 8 Jan. 1774, AAE 504:20–31.

10. Morande to d'Eon, 21 Dec. 1773, AAE 503:308–10.

11. For the progress of the negotiations, see Morande to Lord Ferrers, 17 Nov. 1773 (extract), AAE 503:170; Broglie to Louis XV, 18 Nov. 1773, CS 2:464–66.

12. D'Eon to Broglie, 18 April 1774 (extract), AAE 505:168.

13. "Acte de vente entre Morande et Mr. Van Neck," 24 April 1773, AAE 504:197–200. See also d'Eon to Broglie, 18 April 1774 (extract), AAE 505:168. For Beaumarchais's 1774 mission to England, see especially Gunnar and Mavis Von Proschwitz, *Beaumarchais et le Courrier de l'Europe*, 2 vols. (Oxford, 1990), 1:7–8 and 221–23. Curiously, the story of Morande's manuscript is described in a contemporary libel of du Barry

that *was* published during this period by another French exile living in London. See [M. F. Pidansat de Mairobert,] *Anecdotes sur . . . la comtesse du Barri* (London, 1775), 314–16.

14. Haslip, *du Barry,* 49; Broglie to Louis XV, 22 Oct. 1773, CS 2:454–56.

15. D'Eon to Broglie, 1 April 1774, AAE 505:110.

16. Morande to d'Eon, undated, AN 1:109.

Chapter 39: Louis XVI

1. Jeffrey Merrick, "Politics in the Pulpit: Ecclesiastical Discourse on the Death of Louis XV," *History of European Ideas* 7 (1986): 149–60.

2. Broglie to Louis XVI, 13 May 1774, CSI 2:387–92.

3. Broglie to Louis XVI, 30 May 1774, CSI 1:393–94.

4. CS 1:cvii–cix.

5. Broglie to d'Eon, 7 July 1774, AAE 506:30; "De Par le Roy sa Majesté," 29 Aug. 1774, AAE Supplement 16:390–95; "Liste des pensions accordées par Louis XVI aux agents de la correspondance secrète," 10 Sept. 1774, and Broglie to d'Eon, 10 Sept. 1774, CSI 2:437–42.

6. Broglie to d'Eon, 1 Sept. 1774, at the Musée de la Poste, Paris (my thanks to Professor Dena Goodman for acquiring a copy of this letter); and 10 Sept. 1774, CSI 2:437–38.

7. *Correspondance littéraire secrète* 27 (1 July 1775); Pierre Pinsseau, *L'Etrange Destinée du Chevalier d'Eon (1728–1810),* 2nd ed. (Paris, 1945), 163–67.

8. Vergennes to Louis XVI, 26 Jan. 1775, CSI 2:444.

9. Louis XVI to Vergennes, 26 Jan. 1775, CSI 2:445. It should be noted that the King's use of a male pronoun does not indicate he believed d'Eon to be male. In Old Regime parlance, the pronoun technically referred to the person's title, not so much to his body. Thus in this case the pronoun referred to the "Chevalier d'Eon," or the "Sieur d'Eon," both male titles.

10. Broglie to d'Eon, 18 Jan. 1775, CSI 2:442–43.

11. On Beaumarchais's reputation see Sarah Maza, *Private Lives and Public Affairs: The Causes Célèbres of Prerevolutionary France* (Berkeley, Calif., 1994), 131–40.

12. Beaumarchais to Sartine, 17 Nov. 1774, quoted in Gudin de la Brenellerie, *Histoire de Beaumarchais,* ed. Maurice Tourneux (Paris, 1888), 170.

13. On such phenomena, see Robert Darnton, *The Literary Underground of the Old Regime* (Cambridge, Mass., 1982), 41–70.

14. CS 2:40.

15. See the contract signed by Vignoles on 3 April 1775 in AN 2 (no file number). Vignoles was to get £210 for his editorial work.

16. Beaumarchais to Louis XVI, 27 April 1775, quoted in Gudin, *Beaumarchais*, 166–69. Gudin was Beaumarchais's personal secretary who accompanied him on this trip to England, and who himself was equally convinced of d'Eon's womanhood. See also the three undated letters from Morande to d'Eon in AN 1:184–85.

17. AAE 511:113–20; BMT R5 (documents justifying d'Eon's financial claims dated 14 July 1775).

18. See the "Transaction" (discussed below) in BMT R7: "the disguise of his condition and sex, of which his parents alone are guilty."

19. D'Eon to Tercier, 18 and 20 Jan. 1764, AAE Supplement 16:119–36. See also Duc de Broglie, *The King's Secret*, 2 vols. (London, n.d.), 2:115n, where Broglie shows that d'Eon faked similar letters. The story about Pompadour's jealousy is repeated in ULBC 4:33–34: "The Sieur was in the most intimate confidence of the King his master. She [Pompadour] discovered further that the Chevalier d'Eon is a girl disguised as a man and the protégée of the Prince de Conti whom she feared as much as she detested." See also the discussion in Octave Homberg and Fernand Jousselin, *Un aventurier au xviiie siècle, Le Chevalier d'Eon, 1728–1810* (Paris, 1904), 61.

20. Vergennes to Beaumarchais, 21 June 1775, in Gunnar and Mavis Von Proschwitz, *Beaumarchais et le Courrier de l'Europe*, 2 vols. (Oxford, 1990), 1:227–29.

CHAPTER 40: THE LETTER TO POISSONIER

1. In AAE, Mémoires et documents, 538:302ff, the artist or lawyer Falconnet claims that M. Lesecq, former curé of a church in Tonnerre, said d'Eon was male.

2. D'Eon discusses his relationship with Poissonier in a letter to Broglie, 3 Aug. 1773, AAE 504:254. See also ULBC Box 8, 109; and Albert Vandal, *Louis XV et Elisabeth de Russie* (Paris, 1882), 331.

3. AN 4:235–38. This is actually a draft of the letter in d'Eon's hand. It was donated to the Archives Nationales in 1960.

CHAPTER 41: THE TRANSACTION

1. "Permission . . . de rentrer dans le Royaume de France avec sauf-conduit . . . ," AAE Supplement 16:395–97; "Copie de l'ordre et commission du Roi, au Sr. Caron de Beaumarchais, de retirer des papiers de

correspondance secrète . . . ," AAE Supplement 16:443 and BMT R7. Both these documents are countersigned by Vergennes and Louis XVI. Both are dated 25 Aug. 1775, but they were probably decided on orally on this date, written some weeks later, and backdated. See Pierre Pinsseau, *L'Etrange Destinée du Chevalier d'Eon 1728–1810,* 2nd ed. (Paris, 1945), 177–80. There is also a third document often cited along with these two: a statement supposedly signed by the King and countersigned by Vergennes, again dated 25 Aug. 1775, ordering d'Eon to dress as a woman. But since only one copy exists of this document (AAE Supplement 16:398–99), a copy in d'Eon's hand, it is probably a forgery, or at least a document that has been altered by d'Eon. For example, directly after ordering d'Eon to wear women's clothes is the phrase "as he had done previously in the service of the late King." For an intelligent discussion see Pinsseau, *L'Etrange Destinée,* 178–79.

2. *Correspondance littéraire secrète* 43 (21 Oct. 1775); Beaumarchais to d'Eon, 5 Sept. 1775, ULBC 31:139.

3. I am following the copy of the Transaction not in d'Eon's hand in AAE Supplement 16:436–42; see an additional copy in BMT R7; reprinted in Pinsseau, *L'Etrange Destinée* 184–90. For related documents that shed light on the Transaction, see also AAE Supplement 16:444; BMT R8; ULBC 31:138, 144.

4. Vignoles to d'Eon, 4 Nov. 1775, AN 2:40. In ULBC 29:2, d'Eon refers to "my two births."

5. D'Eon to Broglie, 5 Dec. 1775 (copy), BMT R10.

CHAPTER 42: BEAUMARCHAIS BETS

1. "Campagnes du sieur Caron de Beaumarchais en Angleterre," BMT R22.

2. Cited in Louis de Loménie, *Beaumarchais and His Times,* trans. Henry S. Edwards, 4 vols. (London, 1856), 2:208. See also Gudin de la Brenellerie, *Histoire de Beaumarchais,* ed. Maurice Tourneux (Paris, 1888), 181.

3. *Correspondance littéraire* 11 (November 1775): 162; *Morning Post and Daily Advertiser,* 10 Nov. 1775.

4. *Morning Post and Daily Advertiser,* 11 Nov. 1775.

5. The total figure comes from d'Harvelay to Vergennes, 14 Nov. 1775, AAE Supplement 16:446.

6. *Morning Post and Daily Advertiser,* 13 (in French) and 14 (in English) Nov. 1775.

7. D'Eon to Beaumarchais, 7 Jan. 1776 (extract), AAE 514:24–33;

also in Fréderic Gaillardet, *Mémoires sur la Chevalière d'Eon* (Paris, 1866), 403–10.

8. *Correspondance littéraire*, 11 (November 1775): 162: "For several days the gossip has spread that the Chevalier d'Eon will return to this country; they say that M. de Beaumarchais will marry him. This news is too crazy not to seem factual." See also Mme de Courcelles to d'Eon, 1 Jan. 1776, BMT Autog. 166; d'Eon to Vergennes, 27 May 1776, BMT R20.

9. Beaumarchais to d'Eon, 9 Jan. 1776, ULBC 31:139–42; a copy exists in BMT R13.

10. D'Eon to Beaumarchais, 7 Jan. 1776 (extract), AAE 514:24–33; reprinted in Gaillardet, *Chevalière d'Eon*, 403–10.

11. Ibid.

12. For example, Vergennes to Beaumarchais, 10 Feb. 1776, in Loménie, *Beaumarchais*, 2:203; Morande to Beaumarchais, 2 June [1776], in Gunnar von Proschwitz and Mavis Von Proschwitz, *Beaumarchais et le Courrier de l'Europe*, 2 vols. (Oxford, 1990), 1:289.

CHAPTER 43: BEAUMARCHAIS "TO MLLE GENEV. L. DEON DE BEAUMONT"

1. ULBC 31:146–53; a copy is in BMT R16[bis].

CHAPTER 44: D'EON TO BEAUMARCHAIS

1. BMT R17[bis] (copy). D'Eon's footnotes demonstrate that this copy was intended for publication, probably to be included in *Pièces rélatives aux démêlés entre Mademoiselle d'Eon . . . et le Sieur Caron dit de Beaumarchais* (n.p., 1778). However, it does not appear in that volume, nor in any other contemporary publication.

2. From Beaumarchais's poem "Robin," in *Oeuvres complètes de Beaumarchais*, ed. Marc Saint-Mark Girardin (Paris, 1865), 733.

CHAPTER 45: D'EON SUES MORANDE

1. Beaumarchais to Vergennes, 3 May 1776, in Gunnar Von Proschwitz and Mavis Von Proschwitz, *Beaumarchais et le Courrier de l'Europe*, 2 vols. (Oxford, 1990), 1:276–78.

2. "Déclaration qui preuve que les Sieurs de Morande et Beaumarchais . . . ," signed by James Dupré, Jean-Joseph de Vignoles, de la Chêvre, and d'Eon, London, 8 May 1776, BMT R18[bis].

3. "Campagnes du Sieur Caron de Beaumarchais en Angleterre, pendant les années 1774–1775–1776 . . . ," 27 May 1776, published in La Fortelle, *La Vie militaire, politique, et privée de Mademoiselle d'Eon*, 2nd ed.

(Paris, 1779), 137–65; d'Eon to Vergennes, 28 May 1776, in BMT R23. See also Ferrers to Vergennes, 24 May 1776, in BMT R19; Thomas O'Gorman (d'Eon's brother-in-law, who had just arrived in London and spent the next several months working on d'Eon's behalf) to Vergennes, 20 May 1776, AAE Supplement 17:6 ; Morande to Beaumarchais, 2 June [1776], in Von Proschwitz, *Beaumarchais* 1:289–93; and Morande to d'Eon, 4 June 1776, AN 1:258.

4. Vergennes to Ferrers, 15 July 1776, BMT R24.

5. This manuscript has been lost. For d'Eon's reaction see AAE Supplement 17:7–12.

6. *Westminster Gazette,* 6–10 Aug. 1776.

7. O'Gorman to Morande, 12 Aug. 1776 (copy), AAE Supplement 17:14.

8. The trial can be followed in the *Public Advertiser;* see issues for 22, 27, 28, 30, and 31 Aug., 2, 3, 5, 6, 9, 11, 16 Sept., and 28 Nov. 1776.

9. *Morning Post and Daily Advertiser,* 9 Dec. 1776.

10. *Public Ledger,* 23 Feb. 1776. On its importance, see also Vignoles to d'Eon, 24 Feb. 1776, AN 2:38–39.

11. *Gazette des tribunaux* 8 (1779):180.

12. The spread of the Russia myth can be seen in *L'Espion anglais* 8 (1778):6n; *The Memoirs of Jacques Casanova de Seingalt,* trans. Arthur Machen, 6 vols. (New York, 1959), 2:159; Abbé Georgel, *Mémoires pour servir à l'histoire des événemens de la fin du dix-huitième siècle . . . ,* 6 vols., 2nd ed. (Paris, 1820), 1:289–90; Marquis de Bombelles, *Journal, Volume I: 1780–1784,* ed. Jean Grassion and Frans Durif (Geneva, 1977), 135–36; [Louis Dutens,] *Memoirs of a Traveller Now in Retirement,* 5 vols. (London, 1806), 3:138–41; *Journal inédit du Duc de Croÿ 1718–1784,* ed. Vte Grouchy and Paul Cottin, 4 vols. (Paris, 1907), 4:58–62; Mme Campan, *Mémoires sur la vie privée de Marie-Antoinette,* 2 vols. (London, 1823), 1:190–92.

13. *Public Advertiser,* 31 Aug. 1776.

14. *Public Ledger,* 27 Aug. 1776, *Morning Post,* 27 Aug. 1776. Sully and Colbert were seventeenth-century French statesmen; Bolingbroke served as a British minister early in the eighteenth century.

15. *Westminster Gazette,* 31 Aug.–7 Sept. 1776.

16. See, for example, *Morning Chronicle,* 15 July 1777. The £30,000 figure comes from *Scots Magazine* 39 (August 1777): 453.

17. *Westminster Gazette,* 7–10 Sept. 1776.

CHAPTER 46: LORD MANSFIELD'S COURT

1. See, for example, James Boswell, *The Journal of a Tour to the Hebrides with Samuel Johnson, LL.D.*, ed. R. W. Chapman (Oxford, [1785] 1924), 220.

2. On Mansfield see the introduction to James Oldham, *The Mansfield Manuscripts and the Growth of English Law in the Eighteenth Century*, 2 vols. (Chapel Hill, N.C., 1992); Edmund Heward, *Lord Mansfield* (Chicester and London, 1979); ULBC 1, chap. 4, 7.

3. ULBC 45:460.

4. Quotes from the trial come from *Gazetteer and New Daily Advertiser*, 2 July 1777, and *Morning Chronicle*, 2 July 1777. See also *Scots Magazine* 39 (August 1777): 451–56.

5. As to the second objection, Mansfield told the following story to serve as an analogy: "I remember a dispute which once happened between two persons, relative to the dimensions of a statue of the Venus de Medici. A wager was proposed by one of the parties. The other replied, 'I will not lay anything; it would be unfair, for I have measured the statue.' The other answered, 'Why, do you think I would be such a fool as to propose a bet unless I had measured it also!'" *Scots Magazine* 39 (August 1777): 453.

6. Oldham, *Mansfield Manuscripts*, 1: 534–40.

7. ULBC 45:462; see 484–85 for a slightly different version.

8. See d'Eon's letter dated 10 Aug. 1777 in the *St. James Chronicle or British Evening Post*, 14–16 Aug. 1777. In his memoirs, d'Eon reveals his feelings during these weeks by citing letters between family members and himself. See Mme d'Eon (his mother) to d'Eon, 18 July 1777, and d'Eon's reply, ULBC 30:1757–59 and 19:6; Mme O'Gorman (d'Eon's sister) to d'Eon, 28 July 1777, ULBC 30:1737.

9. D'Eon to Vergennes, 1 and 18 July 1777, AAE Supplement 17:29–32; D'Eon to Louis XVI, 28 May 1777 (copy) , ULBC 3:268–85 and AAE Supplement 17:23–28.

10. Henry Cowper, *Reports of Cases Adjudged in the Court of King's Bench . . .* , 2 vols., 2nd ed. (London, 1800), 2:734–36. A slightly different version is in a newspaper article clipped by d'Eon in ULBC Box 12, large leather book, 202.

CHAPTER 47: CONSIDERING CONVENTS

1. Pierre-Joseph Boudier de Villemart, *Le Nouvel ami des femmes, ou la Philosophie du sexe* (Paris, 1779), 241; [Riballier and Mlle Cosson,] *De l'éducation morale et physique des femmes . . .* (Brussels and Paris, 1779), 217–19.

2. *Journal de Paris,* 24 Oct. 1780. Collot's sculpture of d'Eon has disappeared. See Louis Réau, "Une femme-sculpteur française au xviiie, Marie-Anne Collot (1748–1821)," *Bulletin de l'histoire de l'art français* (1924): 227: D'Eon was even mentioned in books that had nothing whatsoever to do with him. For instance, when a French translation of a Swedish book about Ireland appeared in 1781, the translator could not resist inserting into the notes, rather awkwardly, a short poem about d'Eon: "Belles, que vos amours embellissent l'histoire/Le beau sexe en d'Eon s'embellit par la gloire" (Uno Von Troil, *Lettres sur l'islande* [Paris, 1781], 239n).

3. "Epître de Généviève," 1547, ULBC Box 7.

4. *L'Espion anglais* 8 (1778): 23–24; anecdotes from *Scots Magazine* 9 (June 1778): 286–87. On his fencing exhibitions, see *Secret Memoirs of Princess Lambelle,* ed. Catherine Hyde (Akron, Ohio, 1901), 111.

5. Journal entry of 5 March 1786, in *Boswell: The English Experiment, 1785–1789,* ed. Irma S. Lustig and Frederick A. Pottle (London, 1986), 48. Walpole to Lady Ossory, 27 Jan. 1786, in Walpole, *Correspondence,* ed. W. S. Lewis, 48 vols. (New Haven, Conn., 1932–83), 33:510.

6. *Réponse de Mademoiselle d'Eon à Monsieur de Beaumarchais* (Rome, [1778]); d'Eon to Vergennes, 20 Jan. 1778, AAE Supplement 17:71–83, reprinted in La Fortelle, *La Vie militaire, politique, et privée de Mademoiselle d'Eon,* 2nd ed. (Paris, 1779), 175–211. See also *Mémoires secrètes,* 16 and 25 Feb. 1778; and *L'Espion anglais* 9 (1778): 1–19.

7. D'Eon to Vergennes, 10 Jan. 1778, AAE Supplement 17:76.

8. "Appel à mes contemporaines," 2 Feb. 1778. Two manuscript copies in d'Eon's hand exist in BMT R30 and AAE Supplement 17:97–98; published in *Réponse de Mademoiselle d'Eon à Monsieur de Beaumarchais,* 11–14, and in *Pièces rélatives aux démêlés entre Mademoiselle d'Eon . . . et le Sieur Caron dit de Beaumarchais* (n.p., 1778), 39–41. For a recent assessment of Beaumarchais's attitudes toward women, see Jack Undank, "Beaumarchais: A Woman's Place . . . ," in *Eighteenth-Century Women and the Arts,* ed. Frederick M. Keener and Susan Lorsch (New York, 1988), 37–43. For further evidence that d'Eon was genuinely concerned about male exploitation of women during this period, see the "Lettre écrite de Caen, aux auteurs de ce journal, par Mme D * * *, sur une question intéressante pour le beau sexe," *Journal encyclopédique ou universel* 5 (1780): 144–46, which d'Eon clipped and saved in ULBC Box 12.

9. For d'Eon's notes, see BL 11341:212–17.

10. D'Eon to Mansfield, 8 Feb. 1778, BL 11341:127–30.

11. "Seconde lettre aux femmes," 10 Feb. 1778, published in *Réponse*

and in *Pièces rélatives,* 47–49. Two manuscript copies in d'Eon's hand are in BMT R37 and AAE Supplement 17:110–11.

12. D'Eon to Antoine de Sartine, 27 June 1778, BMT R34; and various petitions by d'Eon, AAE Supplement 17:117–31.

13. ULBC 37:1210.

14. See, for example, William Seward to Lady Ferrers, quoted in ULBC 19:19.

15. Diderot, *The Nun,* trans. Leonard Tannock (1796; reprint Hammondsworth, 1974).

16. Martine Sartine, *L'Education des filles au temps des Lumières* (Paris, 1987); Geneviève Reynes, *Couvents de femmes: La vie des religieuses contemplatives dans la France des xvii⁴ et xviii⁴ siècles* (Paris, 1987); Albert Luppé, *Les jeunes filles à la fin du xviii⁴ siècle* (Paris, 1925).

17. Bridget Hill, "A Refuge from Men: The Idea of a Protestant Nunnery," *Past and Present* 117 (1987): 107–30. See also ULBC 46: 1644–47, where d'Eon has transcribed English proposals for the reestablishment of convents around 1800.

18. ULBC 43:1147.

19. D'Eon describes the convent in a letter to his mother, 17 Sept. 1778, cited in ULBC 6:15.

20. "Epître de d'Eon de Beaumont pour servir d'introduction à son ouvrage adressé aux douze tribes . . . ," ULBC 1406. See also the correspondence between d'Eon and Sister Marie-Agnès-Marguerite de Durfort in the Bibliothèque municipale de Versailles, manuscript brochure 7. (I am most grateful to Professor Carolyn Lougee for providing me with information regarding this correspondence.)

21. D'Eon to Durfort, 12 Sept. 1778, and Durfort to d'Eon, 20 Oct. 1778, ibid.

22. Unpaginated sheet titled "couvent à choisir," AN 5:1.

23. D'Eon to the Comtesse de Maurepas, 16 Sept. 1778, cited in ULBC 2:121.

24. D'Eon to Mme d'Eon, 17 Sept. 1778 (copy), ULBC 6:15–21. This letter supposedly was written from the Abbaye Royale at Fontevarault. See also the letter supposedly written on the same day to Archbishop Christophe de Beaumont in ULBC 2:58–62.

25. D'Eon cites Mark 9:41, Matt. 18:6, and Luke 17:2 in ibid.

26. ULBC 30:1689; 6:16; 19:18. Throughout the Leeds memoirs, d'Eon mentions visiting a third convent, the "Filles de Sainte Marie." This is probably the Filles de la Visitation Sainte-Marie located in Bourbilly (Burgundy), not far from Tonnerre. See Paul and Marie-Louise

Biver, *Abbayes, monastères, couvents de femmes à Paris des origines à la fin du xviiie siècle* (Paris, 1975), 148–56.

27. D'Eon to Vergennes, 16 Jan. 1779, d'Eon to Maurepas, 8 Feb. 1779, and d'Eon to the Prince de Montbarey, February 1779, AAE Supplement 17:140–41, 146–47, and 156–57; and "d'Eon aux Plusieurs Grandes Dames de la Cour," *Correspondance littéraire* 12: 215.

28. D'Eon to Maurepas, 8 Feb. 1779 (copy), in the Bibliothèque municipale de Dijon; Admiral d'Orvilliers to d'Eon, 3 March 1779, cited in ULBC 19:22, and d'Eon's remarks in a newspaper article pasted in ULBC-EI 5, front cover.

29. AAE Supplement 17:160–68; ULBC 19:22.

30. Montmorency-Bouteville to d'Eon, 2 April 1779, cited in ULBC 46:1664–65; d'Eon to Vergennes, 13 April 1779, AAE Supplement 17:179; Robinet to d'Eon, 20 April 1779, cited in ULBC 19:22; d'Eon mentions putting up resistance in ULBC 22:63; he blames Beaumarchais in ULBC Box 8, Rough Notes II, 631.

31. ULBC 40:1847.

32. Montmorency-Bouteville to d'Eon, 2 April 1779, cited in ULBC 46:1664–69 and 45:486; d'Eon to the Comtesse de Maurepas, 1 June 1779, cited in ULBC 11:4; see also ULBC 2:36.

CHAPTER 48: REBORN AGAIN

1. Bertier to Amelot, 7 April 1780, Bertier to d'Eon, 11 April 1780, and "Extrait du journal de la conduite qu'à tenue à Paris . . . ," all in AAE Supplement 17:227–39.

2. See, for example, his diary/calendar for June–October 1787, preserved in AN 7.

3. "Extrait de l'Epître de la Chevalière d'Eon à Madame la Duchesse de Montmorency-Bouteville à Versailles Mai 1778," 11, ULBC Box 8.

4. D'Eon to Tanley, 10 July 1755, in BMT C29.

5. Mlle Jodin to d'Eon, 3 July 1770, in Denis Diderot, *Correspondance,* ed. Georges Roth and Jean Varloot, 16 vols. (Paris, 1955–70), 10:83–84. A bill in ULBC-EI 7 shows that d'Eon bought twenty volumes of Voltaire on 2 July 1763.

6. AN 5:1.

7. ULBC Box 8, Rough Notes II, 1013, and 124:30–33. "Versailles is my Nazareth," d'Eon writes in ULBC 45:1668.

8. AN 5. On the significance of the journal, see Bernard Plongeron, "Une image de l'Eglise après les *Nouvelles ecclésiastiques,*" *Revue d'histoire de l'Eglise de France* 16 (1967):241–68.

9. Dale Van Kley, *The Jansenists and the Expulsion of the Jesuits from France, 1757–1765* (New Haven, Conn., 1975); idem, *The Damiens Affair and the Unraveling of the Old Regime, 1750–1770* (Princeton, N.J., 1984).

10. On the revival in Paris, see François Bluche, *La Vie quotidienne au temps de Louis XVI* (Paris, 1980), 166; [M. F. Pidansat de Mairobert,] *L'Espion anglais*, 10 vols. (London, 1785), 3:101–11; for Tonnerre, see Suzanne Desan, *Reclaiming the Sacred: Lay Religion and Popular Politics in Revolutionary France* (Ithaca, N.Y., 1990), 39.

11. ULBC 18:14; "Grand Requête," ULBC Box 8, 1690. Another reason for identifying d'Eon as a Jansenist is his rather Protestant attitude toward clerical marriage; see ULBC 124:34.

12. ULBC Box 8, 36.

13. ULBC, Box 8, 34–41. Rom. 4:7 reads " 'Happy are they,' he [David] says, 'whose sins are buried away; happy is the man whose sins the Lord does not count against him.' " All biblical quotes hereafter are from *The New English Bible with the Apocrypha, Oxford Study Edition*, ed. Samuel Sandmel, 2nd ed. (Oxford, 1976).

14. "Epître de Génévière," ULBC Box 7, 1458.

15. ULBC Box 8, 10.

16. ULBC 19:52.

CHAPTER 49: RETURN TO ENGLAND

1. "Affaires de Mlle d'Eon . . . Ferrers" and "Mémoire adressée à M. Le Comte de Montmorin . . . ," ULBC Box 8. "Epître de Génévière," ULBC Box 7, 1544–45. Here d'Eon says that in 1763, when he moved to his flat in London's Golden Square, he signed a forty-year lease. He subletted it from 1777 until he returned in 1785.

2. For these years, see the relevant correspondence in AAE Supplement 17:260–324.

3. Houghton Library, Harvard University, *fFC7. EO563. ZZX (Collection of d'Eon Papers); ULBC Box 12, diamond notebook, p. 23. However, in a "Note sur l'Angleterre," ULBC Box 8, Rough Notes II, 863, d'Eon complained that despite its free political system, England was filled with too many lawyers, who were always ready to litigate one another under the smallest pretext.

4. On d'Eon's early reactions to the Revolution, see ULBC 45: 466; the remark about Sièyes is found in 47:1041.

5. D'Eon to Stanhope, 14 July 1790. A copy of this letter is pasted in William Seward's copy of d'Eon's *Lettres, mémoires, et négociations* in the British Library.

6. Cited in Thomas Rickman, *Life of Thomas Paine* (London, 1819), 102–3; the invitation for this dinner can be found in ULBC-EI 5:322–23.

7. When d'Eon wrote the government requesting to take a loyalty oath to the new regime, a somewhat perplexed minister explained to him that only the legislature, and not a minister, could enable women to participate in the swearing of loyalty oaths. See "Copie du serment civique de Mlle d'Eon," 5 Jan. 1791, and Montmarin to d'Eon, 20 Jan. 1791, AAE Supplement 17:355.

8. *Moniteur,* 13 June 1792; this English translation is adapted from *Gentlemen's Magazine,* July 1792, 658.

9. Cloots to d'Eon, 12 May and 14 July 1792, AAE Supplement 17:356–58.

10. Carnot to d'Eon, 18 July 1792, AAE Supplement 17:357.

11. Dorinda Outram, *The Body and the French Revolution: Sex, Class, and Political Culture* (New Haven, Conn., 1989), 156.

12. Susan P. Conner, "Les Femmes Militaires: Women in the French Army, 1792–1815," *The Proceedings of the Consortium on Revolutionary Europe 1750–1850* 12 (1982): 290–302; Darlene G. Levy and Harriet B. Applewhite, "Women, Radicalization, and the Fall of the French Monarchy," in *Women in the Age of Democratic Revolution* (Ann Arbor, Mich., 1990), 81–110; F. Gerbaux, "Les Femmes soldats pendant la Révolution," *La Révolution française* 47 (1904): 47–61.

13. AAE Supplement 17:362.

14. Ibid., 346.

15. "Livre de dépense," ULBC Box 9.

16. *Moniteur,* 29 April 1791; *Catalogue des livres rares et manuscrits précieux du cabinet de la Chevalière d'Eon* ... (London, 1791); *European Magazine and London Review,* March 1791, 162–66.

17. Newspaper clippings about these tournaments are in ULBC-EI 5:322–23.

18. ULBC 7:1; BL 29994:48.

19. ULBC 7:13.

20. Morande to d'Eon, 15 and 17 Aug. and 3 Dec. 1786, AN 1:297–300.

21. *Politique de tous les cabinets de l'Europe, pendant les règnes de Louis XV et de Louis XVI; contenant des pièces authentiques sur la correspondance secrète du comte de Broglie* ... *Manuscrits trouvées dans le cabinet de Louis XVI,* 3 vols. (Paris, 1793). See ULBC Box 7, 1664–68, for evidence that d'Eon had prepared his own commentary on these volumes.

22. See the printed proposals announcing a subscription for the memoirs, dated 20 April 1799, in ULBC 52.

23. Thomas Plummer to d'Eon, 14 Dec. 1806, ULBC Box 7:197–204; 20:4.

24. ULBC 18:217 and the file titled "Grand Requête," 1688–95.

CHAPTER 50: GENDERED THEOLOGY

1. "Les Pieuses métamorphoses ou Histoire des femmes qui ont déguisé leur sexe pour se consacrer Dieu et professer la vie monastique et qui ont été reconnue Saintes par l'Eglise Grecque et Latine, par Mademoiselle La Chevalière d'Eon," ULBC Box 7.

2. ULBC 48:203. On Augustine, see Peter Brown, *Augustine of Hippo: A Biography* (Berkeley, Calif., 1967).

3. ULBC 43:1191. Sometimes d'Eon also identified the Augustinian motif with Milton: "Elle regarde sa vie passée parmi les Dragons comme *le Paradis perdu de Milton,* et elle considere sa vie passée parmi les filles de Ste. Marie comme *le Paradis rétrouvé de Milton*" (ULBC 19:19).

4. ULBC 124:56, 119.

5. "Epître de Mademoiselle d'Eon pour servir à la conclusion de l'abregé historique de sa vie militaire et diplomatique, London, 1 Juin 1805," ULBC Box 8, 80.

6. ULBC 37:1283.

7. ULBC 51:601.

8. 1 Cor. 15:8–10, cited by d'Eon in ULBC Box 7, 1639, and 43:1176, where it was used as an epigram on the title page of an essay.

9. ULBC Box 7, 1639.

10. ULBC 37:1273.

11. "Epître de Mademoiselle d'Eon," 54.

12. ULBC 19:14.

13. D'Eon quotes the following passages: Deut. 10:17, "He is no respecter of persons"; Acts 10:34, "God has no favorites"; Rom. 2:11, "For God has no favorites"; Eph. 6:9, "He has no favorites"; Gal. 2:6, "God does not recognize these personal distinctions"; Col. 3:25, "He had no favorites"; 1 Pet. 1:17, "the One who judges every man impartially."

14. "Extrait de l'Epître de la Chev. d'Eon à Madame la Duchesse de Montmorency-Bouteville à Versailles mai 1778," ULBC Box 8, p. 8. Gal. 3:26 reads: "For through faith you are all sons of God in union with Christ Jesus." D'Eon changed "sons" to "children" and "you" to "we."

15. ULBC 25:10.

16. ULBC 24:1144 and 39:1080.

17. Robin Scroggs, "Paul and the Eschatological Woman," *Journal of*

the American Academy of Religion 40 (1972): 283–303; William O. Walker, Jr., "The 'Theology of Woman's Place' and the 'Paulinist' Tradition," *Semeia: An Experimental Journal for Biblical Criticism* 28 (1983): 101–12; idem, "1 Corinthians 11:2–16 and Paul's Views Regarding Women," *Journal of Biblical Literature* 94 (March 1975): 94–110; Denis Ronald Macdonald, *There Is No Male and Female* (Philadelphia, 1987).

18. "Extrait de l'Epître de la Chev. d'Eon," 8.

19. Whether consciously or not, d'Eon's ideas resemble second-century Gnostic interpretations of Paul. For example, the Marcionites prohibited all sexual activity and practiced an extreme form of sexual equality, while the Nassenes preached castration in order to transcend the confines of sexuality. See Elaine Pagels, "Paul and Women: A Response to Recent Discussion," *Journal of the American Academy of Religion* 42 (1974): 541.

20. Macdonald, *There Is No Male and Female*, 38n; David Biale, *Eros and the Jews: From Biblical Israel to Contemporary America* (New York, 1992), 41; and Howard Eilberg-Schwartz, *God's Phallus and Other Problems for Men and Monotheism* (Boston, 1994), 202–8.

21. ULBC 124:30–33.

22. My reading of d'Eon on Paul and circumcision has been informed by Daniel Boyarin, "'This We Know to Be the Carnal Israel': Circumcision and the Erotic Life of God and Israel," *Critical Inquiry* 18 (1992): 474–505; idem, *Carnal Israel: Reading Sex in Talmudic Culture* (Berkeley, Calif., 1993); and Elliot R. Wolfson, "Circumcision, Vision of God, and Textual Interpretation: From Midrashic Trope to Mystical Symbol," *History of Religions* 27 (1987): 189–215; and *People of the Body: Jews and Judaism from an Embodied Perspective*, edited by Howard Eilberg-Schwartz (Albany, N.Y., 1992). Unfortunately, Daniel Boyarin's important book, *A Radical Jew: Paul and the Politics of Identity* (Berkeley, Calif., 1994) arrived too late for me to use.

23. Discussed by d'Eon in ULBC 39:1081.

24. Rom. 3:29, discussed by d'Eon in ibid.

25. "Chapitre," unpaginated [fourth page], ULBC Box 8.

26. Erica Harth, *Cartesian Women: Versions and Subversions of Rational Discourse in the Old Regime* (Ithaca, N.Y. 1992), especially chap. 1; Londa Schiebinger, *The Mind Has No Sex? Women in the Origins of Modern Science* (Cambridge, Mass., 1989). Interestingly, Erica Harth notes that scholars have traced the notion of "the mind has no sex" back to Augustine.

27. ULBC 20:120–21 or 22:120, quoting from a letter d'Eon supposedly wrote to his mother in December 1778.

28. "Epître de Mademoiselle d'Eon," 55–57. Another version appears in ULBC 48:412: "If I must deplore the condition of manhood that I left, I must bemoan the sort of woman that I have become; for men have taken everything for themselves and have allowed nothing for women except the pain of having babies."

29. ULBC 52:1199.

30. ULBC 48:408.

31. Perhaps d'Eon found this idea in the Querelle des Femmes literature. See, for example, Claude-Charles Guyonne de Vertron, *La Nouvelle Pandore, ou, Les femmes illustres du siècle de Louis le Grand,* 2 vols. (Paris, 1698), 1:4–8: "the virtue of women reestablishes what the vice of men have corrupted."

32. ULBC 37:1061.

33. "Extrait de l'Epître," 26 and 38.

34. "Epître," 880–81, ULBC Box 8.

35. ULBC 46:1665.

36. ULBC 48:454; 124:57.

37. ULBC 37:1648; 19:14: "The weakest becomes the strongest when fortified and animated by grace."

38. "Epître de Génévieve," ULBC Box 7, 1552–56; "Epître de Mademoiselle d'Eon," 75. For a strikingly modern parallel, see Carol Gilligan, *In a Different Voice: Psychological Theory and Woman's Development* (Cambridge, Mass., 1982).

39. ULBC 43:1125–26. "Virgins are the angels of the earth, as angels are the virgins of the heavens" (Box 8, 823); "The devotion of the Saintly Virgin, says Saint Bernard, is a mark of predestination. The best worship that one can practice in this regard, and the one most recommended by the Saints, is to imitate her excellent virtues, particularly her love for purity, humility, and heroic patience in the great afflictions that happened to her" (1606).

40. For one readable case study, see Emmanuel Le Roy Ladurie, *Montaillou: The Promised Land of Error* (New York, 1978).

41. ULBC 36:24. See, "Chapitre," eighth unpaginated page, and 36:58, where in general, his attitudes seem similar to late-seventeenth-century feminists, such as Mary Astell, whose *Some Reflections Upon Marriage* was part of d'Eon's library. In another book, *A Serious Proposal* (London, 1694), Astell advocated the establishment of "religious retirements," where upper-class married women could temporarily withdraw among themselves. See Ruth Perry, *The Celebrated Mary Astell: An Early English Feminist* (Chicago, 1986), chap. 5.

42. As theology, d'Eon ignores Paul and Augustine's more negative view of women. On Augustine, see Kari Elisabeth Borresen, *Subordination and Equivalence: The Nature and Rôle of Woman in Augustine and Thomas Aquinas*, trans. Charles H. Talbot (Washington, D.C., 1981), part 1; for Paul, see Walker, "The 'Theology of Woman's Place.'"

43. ULBC 36:24.

44. ULBC 48:400.

45. "Epître," 861.

CHAPTER 51: CHRISTIAN FEMINIST

1. Rosemary Radford Ruether, "Misogynism and Virginal Feminism in the Fathers of the Church," in *Religion and Sexism: Images of Woman in the Jewish and Christian Traditions*, ed. idem (New York, 1974), 150, 165. When Ruether turns from ideology to history, she tones down her position; see her "Mothers of the Church: Ascetic Women in the Late Patristic Age," in *Women of Spirit: Female Leaders in the Jewish and Christian Traditions*, ed. idem and Eleanor McLaughlin (New York, 1979), 72–98.

2. Verna E. F. Harrison, "Male and Female in Cappodocian Theology," *Journal of Theological Studies* 41 (1990): 441–71; Jo Ann McNamara, "Sexual Equality and the Cult of Virginity in Early Christian Thought," *Feminist Studies* 3 (1976): 145–58. See also Elizabeth Castelli, "Virginity and Its Meaning for Women's Sexuality in Early Christianity," *Journal of Feminist Studies in Religion* 2 (1986): 61–88; Elizabeth Clark, "Ascetic Renunciation and Feminine Advancement: A Paradox of Late Ancient Christianity," in her *Ascetic Piety and Women's Faith: Essays in Late Ancient Christianity* (New York, 1986), 175–208; and Peter Brown, "The Notion of Virginity in the Early Church," in *Christian Spirituality: Origins to the Twelfth Century*, ed. Bernard McGinn and John Meyendorff (New York, 1985), 427–43.

3. F. Ellen Weaver, "Cloister and Salon in Seventeenth-Century Paris: Introduction to a Study in Women's History," in *Beyond Androcentrism: New Essays on Women and Religion*, ed. Rita M. Gross (Missoula, Mont., 1977), 159–80; Weaver, "Erudition, Spirituality, and Women: The Jansenist Contribution," in *Women in Reformation and Counter-Reformation Europe*, ed. Sherrin Marshall (Bloomington, Ind., 1989), 189–206. For a more general introduction to female spirituality during the early modern era, see Elisja Schulte van Kessel, "Virgins and Mothers Between Heaven and Earth," in *A History of Women in the West. III. Renaissance and Enlightenment Paradoxes* (Cambridge, Mass., 1993), 132–66.

4. ULBC Box 7, 1653.

5. ULBC 40:1852 (Florida); Box 7, 1667 (Hurons); and 1467 (Mataram), where d'Eon cites Gauthier Schouten, *Voyage aux indes orientales,* 2 vols. (Rouen, 1725).

6. Rousseau, *Lettres écrites de la montagne* (1764), in *Oeuvres complètes. III. Du contrat social. Ecrits politiques,* ed. Bernard Gagnebin and Marcel Raymond (Paris, 1964), 705.

Bibliography of Works
By and About d'Eon

PUBLISHED WORKS BY D'EON
IN ORDER OF PUBLICATION

Essai historique sur les differentes situations de la France par rapport aux finances sous le regne de Louis XIV et la regence du duc d'Orléans. Amsterdam, 1753.

"Eloge du comte d'Ons-en-Bray, Président de l'Académie des Sciences." *L'Année littéraire* (1753).

"Eloge au panégyrique de Marie-Thérèse d'Este, duchesse de Penthièvre." *L'Année littéraire* (1754): 112–17.

"Notice sur l'abbé Lenglet-Dufresnoy." *L'Année littéraire* (1755).

Mémoires pour servir à l'histoire générale des finances, 2 vols. (London, 1758); 2nd ed. (Amsterdam, 1760); 3rd ed. (London, 1764) under the title *Considerations historiques et politiques sur les impôts des Egyptiens, des Babyloniens, des Perses, des Grecs, des romains, et sur les differérentes situations de la France. . . .*

"Les Espérances d'un bon patriote." *L'Année littéraire* (1759): 55–67; published separately in pamphlet form in 1760.

Note remise à son excellence Claude-Louis-François Regnier, comte de Guerchy. . . . London, 1763. English translation (*A Letter Sent to His Excellency, Claude . . .*) published simultaneously.

Lettres, mémoires, et négociations particulières . . . . Three parts in one volume. London, 1764.

Nouvelles lettres du chevalier d'Eon .... London, 1764. [Brief letters written in June 1764 to Mansfield, Bute, Temple, and Pitt.]

Dernière lettre du chevalier d'Eon de Beaumont à M. le comte de Guerchy, en date du 5 août 1767 .... London, 1767.

Les Loisirs du chevalier d'Eon de Beaumont ... , 13 vols. Amsterdam, 1774; reprinted in a 7-vol. ed. in 1775.

Pièces rélatives aux démêlés entre Mademoiselle d'Eon de Beaumont ... et le Sieur Caron, dit de Beaumarchais .... Paris, 1778.

Très-humble réponse à ... Beaumarchais. London, 1778.

Réponse de Mademoiselle d'Eon à Monsieur de Beaumarchais. Rome, 1778.

Epître aux Anglais dans leurs tristes circontances présentes. London, 1788.

"Mémoire en faveur des Protestants de France, rédigé par M. Dutens en 1775 et addressé par la chevalière d'Eon au Baron de Breteuil. 1787." *Bulletin de la Société de l'Histoire du Protestantisme Français* 9 (1860): 253–58.

WORKS ABOUT D'EON PUBLISHED
DURING HIS LIFETIME

A Catalogue of the Historical, Biblical, and Other Curious Mss. and Library of Printed Books of the Chev. D'Eon. London, 1813.

Catalogue of the Scarce Books and Manuscripts of the Library of the Chevalière D'Eon ... London, 1791; French translation: *Catalogue des livres rare et manuscrits précieux du cabinet de la chevalière d'Eon* ... published simultaneously.

[Delauney.] *History of a French Louse or The Spy of a New Species* ... London, n.d. French edition: *Histoire d'un pou françois; ou l'espion d'une nouvelle espèce* .... Paris, n.d.

Examen des Lettres, mémoires, et négociations particulières, du chevalier d'Eon. London, 1764.

[Goudar, Ange.] *Contre-note ou Lettre à M. le marquis L* .... London, 1763.

La Fortelle. *La Vie militaire, politique, et privée de madmemoiselle d'Eon.* Paris, 1779; 2nd expanded edition 1779; translated into Italian (1779) and Russian (1787).

Lovejoy, Lutretia [pseud]. *An Elegy on the Lamented Death of the Electrical Eel* ... *at the Expense of the Countess of H—, and the Chevalier-Madame d'Eon.* London, 1777.

Matrimonial Overtures, From an Enamour'd Lady to Lord G. ... London, 1778.

Musgrave, James. *Dr. Musgrave's Reply to a Letter Published in the Newspapers by the Chevalier d'Eon.* London, 1769.

Pièces authentiques pour servir au procès criminel intente au tribunal du roi d'angleterre par . . . d'Eon . . . contre . . . Guerchy. London, 1765.

[Plummer, Thomas.] *A Short Sketch of Some Remarkable Occurances During the Residence of the Late Chevalier D'Eon in England.* London, 1810.

[Vergy, Pierre-Henri Treyssac de.] *Suite des pièces rélatives aux lettres, mémoires, et négociations particulières. . . .* London, 1764; reprinted 1765.

————. *Lettre à Monseigneur le duc de Choiseul.* Liège, 1764.

————. *Lettre à M. de la M***, ecuyer, et de la Société Royale d'agriculture . . . en réponse à une lettre à Monsieur le duc de Nivernais.* London, 1763.

NONFICTION BOOKS AND ARTICLES ABOUT D'EON

D'Avout, Le Vicomte A. *Court étude sur le chevalier d'Eon.* Dijon, 1906.

Boysède, Eugène. *Considerations sur la bixsexualité, les infirmités sexuelles, les changements de sexe et le chevalier-chevalière d'Eon.* Paris, 1959.

Cabanis, Docteur. "Quel était le sexe du chevalier d'Eon?" in *Les énigmes de l'Histoire*, pp. 151–200. Paris, 1930.

Cadéac, M. *Le Chevalier d'Eon et son problème psychosexuel.* Paris, 1966.

Charmain, Armand. *La Vie étrange de la chevalière d'Eon.* Paris, 1929.

Coqvelle, M. P. "Le Chevalier d'Eon ministre à London." *Bulletin historique et philologique* (1908): 217–46.

Coryn, Marjorie. *The Chevalier d'Eon 1728–1810.* London, 1932.

Cox, Cynthia. *The Enigma of the Age: The Strange Story of the Chevalier d'Eon.* London, 1966.

Crawley, W. J. Chetwode. "The Chevalier d'Eon: J. W. of Lodge No. 376, Grand Lodge of England." *Ars Quatuor Coronatorum* 16 (1908): 231–51.

Dascotte-Mailliet. *L'Etrange demoiselle de Beaumont.* Paris, 1917.

David, Jean Claude. "La Querelle de l'inoculation en 1763: Trois lettres inédites de Suard et du chevalier d'Eon." *Dix-huitième* 17 (1985): 271–84.

Decker, Michel de. "Le Chevalier d'Eon apprivoise l'ours russe." *Historia* 511 (1989): 12–20.

————. *Madame le chevalier d'Eon.* Paris, 1987.

Ellis, Havelock. "Eonism." *Studies in the Psychology of Sex. Volume II, Part II*, pp. 1–110. New York, 1936.

Frank, André. *D'Eon: chevalier et chevalière.* Paris, 1953.

Fromageot, Paul. "La Chevalière d'Eon à Versailles en 1777." *Carnet historique et littéraire* (1901): 254–72.

Gaillardet, Fréderic. *Mémoires du Chevalier d'Eon...*, 2 vols. Paris, 1836 (other editions: Brussels, 1837; Paris, 1967).

———. *The Memoirs of Chevalier D'Eon.* [1836 edition] translated by Antonio White. London, 1970. Paperback ed.: London, 1972.

———. *Mémoires sur la chevalière d'Eon.* Paris, 1866.

Giardini, Cesare. *Lo Strano caso del cavaliere d'Eon.* Milano, 1935; 2nd ed., Verona, 1949.

Gilbert, Oscar Paul. *Men in Women's Guise: Some Historical Instances of Female Impersonations,* pp. 105–227 on d'Eon. London, 1926.

Great Britain. Royal Commission on Historical Manuscripts. *The Manuscripts of J. Eliot Hodgkin, esq., F. S. A. of Richmond, Surrey.* London, 1897.

Homberg, Octave. *La Carrière militaire du chevalier d'Eon.* Paris, 1900.

Homberg, Octave, and Jousselin, Fernand. *Un aventurier au XVIII* siècle, le chevalier d'Eon, 1728–1810.* Paris, 1904.

———. *D'Eon de Beaumont: His Life and Times.* Translated by Alfred Richelieu. London, 1911.

Jacquillat-Despréaux. "Notice sur la vie du chevalier Deon, extraite de ses papiers." *L'Annuaire statistique de l'Yonne* (1839).

Larcher, Albert. *Le Chevalier d'Eon, le mal connu.* Tonnerre, 1985.

Le Maistre. "Le Chevalier d'Eon." *Bulletin de la société des sciences historiques et naturelles de l'Yonne* 8 (1854): 171–95.

Letainturier-Fradin. *La Chevalière D'Eon.* Paris, 1901.

Mazé, Jules. "Le Chevalier d'Eon." *Visages d'autrefois,* pp. 156–206. Paris, 1951.

Moiset, Charles. "Le Chevalier Eon de Beaumont." *Bulletin de la société des sciences historiques et naturelles de l'Yonne* (1892): 1–98.

Moura, Jean, et Paul Louvet. *Le Mystère du chevalière d'Eon.* Paris, 1929.

Nixon, Edna. *Royal Spy: The Strange Case of the Chevalier D'Eon.* New York, 1965.

Pinsseau, Pierre. *L'Etrange Destineé du chevalier d'Eon 1728–1810.* 2nd ed. Paris, 1945.

Pryts, W. *Hombre o mujer? (un caso historico de hermafrodismo).* Barcelona, 1932.

Schuchard, Marsha Keith. "Blake's Mr. Femality: Freemasonry, Espionage, and the Double-Sexed." *Studies in Eighteenth-Century Culture* 22 (1992): 51–71.

Soltau, Roger. "Le Chevalier d'Eon et les relations diplomatiques de la France et de l'Angleterre au lendemain du traité de Paris (1763)." *Mélanges d'histoires offerts à Charles Bémont.* Paris, 1913.

Telfer, Captain J. Buchan. *Chevalier D'Eon de Beaumont: A Treatise.* London, 1896.

———. *The Strange Career of the Chevalier D'Eon de Beaumont.* London, 1885.

Thompson, C. J. S. *Ladies or Gentlemen?* New York, 1993.

Vizetelly, Ernest Alfred. *The True Story of the Chevalier d'Eon.* London, 1895.

Wallace, Irving. "Was Beaumont a Man or a Woman." *Facts* (1945): 77–81.

FICTIONAL WORKS ABOUT D'EON

Bayard and Dumanoir. *Le Chevalier D'Eon, Comedie en trois Actes, mêlee de chant.* Paris, 1837.

Beamish, Noel de Vic. *For the Honour of a Queen.* London, 1967.

Brousson, Jean-Jacques. *La Chevalière d'Eon ou Le Dragon en denteues.* Paris, 1934.

Depeuty, Charles Désiré. *La Chevalière d'Eon, comédie.* Paris, 1837.

D'Eon, Leonard. *The Cavalier.* New York, 1987.

Mélinand, Gabrielle. *D'Eon l'indomptable; roman historique.* Paris, 1961.

Moreau, Charles-François-Jean-Baptiste. *La Chevalière d'Eon, ou Les Parieurs anglais, comédie en un acte. . . .* Paris, 1812.

Moreau de Balasy, François. *J'Etais le chevalier d'Eon.* Paris, 1972.

Pikoul, Valentin. *Le Chevalier d'Eon et la Guerre de Sept Ans.* Translated by Max Heilbronn. Paris, 1983.

Royer, Jean Michel. *Le Double je: mémoires du chevalier d'Eon.* Paris, 1986.

York, Alison. *The Scented Sword.* London, 1980.

Acknowledgments

HISTORIANS ARE SO DEPENDENT on archivists and librarians that they deserve our first thanks. This book could not have been written without the full cooperation of Christopher Sheppard, Sub-Librarian of the University of Leeds Library. Archivists at the Bibliothèque municipale de Tonnerre and the Archives du Ministère des Affaires Etrangères also went out of their way to help me.

At home, where the Trinity University Maddux Library is the jewel of the campus, all of the library staff has been extremely helpful both in securing rare works found elsewhere and in encouraging further lines of research. I appreciate their help. Likewise, I am blessed with wonderful colleagues in the History Department, who have provided me with an exciting environment in which to work, and who have pushed me to move beyond traditional modes of historiography. I especially want to thank Linda Salvucci, Char Miller, and my Europeanist colleague John Martin for reading various drafts of the work, and seemingly never growing tired of talking with me about d'Eon. I also must acknowledge the debt I owe to Bill Walker, Trinity's Dean of Humanities and Arts, for tutoring me through the letters of Saint Paul and early Christian thought.

Many scholars helped me greatly by sending me juicy nuggets from their own research. For their labors on my behalf, as well as for their open spirit in sharing what was often unpublished material, I thank Susan Boettcher, Jack Censer, Suzanne Desan, Dena Goodman, Carroll Joynes, Tom Kaiser, Carolyn Chappell Lougee, Claude-Anne Lopez, Laura Mason, Karen Offen, Mary Sheriff, Don Spinelli, Dale Van Kley, and John Woodbridge.

Much of the material found in part I was first published in *Body*

Guards: The Cultural Politics of Gender Ambiguity edited by Julia Epstein and Kristina Straub (New York, 1991); Epstein and Straub helped me greatly to sort out difficult issues involved in gender history. Chapters that make up part II were first written under the auspices of a 1991 NEH Summer Seminar, "Gender and Narrative in Early Modern France," held at the Bunting Institute, Radcliffe College. The members of that superb seminar, and especially its director, Professor Erica Harth, opened my stiff mind to gender theory and literary criticism.

Professors of French Nina Ekstein and Roland Champagne devoted many hours to helping me translate difficult passages from primary sources. Despite their work well beyond what any friend has a right to expect, I did not show them all of the translated passages in the book, and thus, the responsibility for any error lies squarely with me. Jeffrey Merrick and Hedy Rutman read the entire manuscript, and provided me with many helpful suggestions.

Judi Lipsett and Marcy Kates both gave too much time neither could afford to editing the manuscript. One a sister by birth, the other almost a sister by choice—each made an enormous difference to the book's outcome. I will never be able to repay Judi, but perhaps Marcy can claim a right to share equally in the book's dedication page.

—*San Antonio, Texas*
15 February 1995

Index